D1271016

ARNOLD SCHWARZENEGGER
CONVERSATIONS

ARNOLD SCHWARZENEGGER
CONVERSATIONS
THE AMERICAN DREAM

BY FIAZ RAFIQ

First published in hardback in December 2011

All photographs and front cover photograph courtesy of
Corbis. About the Author photographs courtesy of the author.

ISBN: 978-0-9562586-5-6

Designer: Martin Jennings
Written, Compiled & Edited by: Fiaz Rafiq
Published by: HNL Publishing Ltd
A division of HNL Media Group
Suite 185, 6 Wilmslow Road, Manchester, M14 5TP,
United Kingdom

Distributed by:

USA
Midpoint Trade Books
27 West 20th Street, Suite 1102,
NEW YORK NY 10011

UK
PGUK 8 The Arena,
Mollison Avenue, Enfield,
LONDON EN3 7NJ

ACKNOWLEDGMENTS

I would like to thank the staff at *M.A.I.* and *Impact* magazines: Moira, Martin, Neal, John, Roy and my good friend and editor Bob Sykes. I would also like to thank the professional personalities I've interviewed for this book and my other books and also for the magazines; from Hollywood actors, directors and producers, friends and colleagues of Bruce Lee, Muhammad Ali and Arnold Schwarzenegger, professional boxers, martial artists, athletes, bodybuilders and UFC fighters. Also, thanks to some of the behind-the-scenes people who have been instrumental. Also, I would like to thank the various national and international magazines I've written for. Thank you to long-time friend Diana Lee Inosanto from Los Angeles for her friendship and support over the years, and her family. Thanks to Royce Gracie for his friendship and support - obrigado, hombre! Also, thanks to my friend Joe Egan.

Being a private person, I never really mention my personal friends and family when it comes to acknowledgments. This does not mean I've forgotten them or don't appreciate them. Work, for me, is a passion and a profession, as much as I made it an obsession in my life, family and close friends are the heart and soul, so is my religion - nothing is worth living for if these three integral elements are absent.

In life we strive to elevate ourselves and reach higher plain. Some of us take our passion to the extreme and become totally consumed by it. Of course, to succeed and realize our dreams we must endeavor to pursue our passion wholeheartedly and be dedicated. Achievements and accolades and acclaim are all great, of course, but sooner or later we may, or should, realize that the core happiness and meaning of life lies not in merely fulfilling our ambitions and achievements, but by cherishing those who are close to us and appreciate the simple things in life and be content.

CONTENTS

CHAPTER FOUR: POLITICAL FRATERNITY

FOREWORD

In an age where the word "superstar" is seemingly tossed around lightly, its true meaning has become all but lost. Arnold Schwarzenegger, a global celebrity, the greatest bodybuilder in history, an icon of machismo and Hollywood action heroism and former politician, built one of the greatest success stories of all time; he epitomizes superstar status. He is to many the embodiment of the American Dream. The life and career of this modern-day celebrity has been one of inexorable rise. He exudes a self-confidence that is derived from unprecedented success in diverse fields, and he fills the criteria of a classic rags-to-riches tale.

Known for his ferocious work ethic born out of a tough childhood and impoverished youth in his native Austria, he spent indulging and dreaming of a better life. In his quest for fulfilling his boyhood aspirations, he embarked on an ambitious endeavor and came looking for providence in the land of opportunity, and rose to stardom from middle-class obscurity and conquered Hollywood.

I have always been enamored by legendary and iconic figures - particularly in the sporting and entertainment fields - whose potent effect and indelible influence on pop culture continues to endure. After completing my magnum opus biographical books on two of the greatest icons of the century (Bruce Lee and Muhammad Ali), I began to mull over the possibilities of paying homage to an adulated celebrity with global star appeal, beyond ephemeral appeal. In a sense, Arnold Schwarzenegger has always been to bodybuilding what Bruce Lee is to martial arts. Lee, whose legendary exploits guaranteed a frisson and paroxysms of excitement and exultation, achieved worldwide fame coming to America, just as Arnold had to emigrate to gain notoriety and global presence in his sport, then parlayed unprecedented success as a bodybuilder into a new career in the movies.

While Arnold may not be perceived as being on the same pedestal as Lee and Ali, nevertheless, he somewhat makes up for it in what he was able to achieve - global fame and superstar status - to the magnitude which very few manage to attain. Not only is he acknowledged for being the greatest bodybuilder of all time, but he became Hollywood's biggest superstar, and, furthermore, a man of serious political ambitions, he leapt into the political arena. This axiomatically defines him as a man with broader social and political factors.

Personally, I have always tried to refrain from embellishing my subjects for the sake of sensationalizing them, for whatever reason, which many biographers seemingly incline toward. I've never really aspired to being a muckraking hack, nor do I feel this sensationalist route is a necessity for a compelling read. In fact, brimming with hero-worship I forthrightly avouch to culminating on, for most part, the positive, yet balanced, approach to my subjects which is rather palatable, as opposed to the diatribe often favored by most biographers. Of course, at the same time, as a biographer, not deviating by overlooking integral events surrounding the subject which would be devoid of painting a complete portrait. This would be nebulous and lacking true essence of the work and wouldn't do justice to the work.

As may be expected from Hollywood celebrities embroiled in scandals, which merely reflects the complexities of real life, controversies surrounded when he stood for governor. The action hero's derogatory past was dragged out pertaining to his personal life and anti-Semitism claims. He had to contend with his personal life, which had long been a subject of public interest, being dissected in the tabloid press, irrespective of circumspection and prudence. In spite of one's sentiments toward Arnold's personal life, or how they perceive his political views, his optimism and a tendency to expect the best possible outcome in pursuit of achieving excellence, his is a success story which is intriguing and one which can inspire mere mortals. I personally think he should be adulated and not judged because of the events surrounding his personal life. Nor should he have been vilified because of his father's past.

As with my previous biographical works, I continue to utilize the colloquial approach; a most unique method to tell someone's life story. For the first time ever, this biographical book on Arnold Schwarzenegger is based on exclusive interviews with his personal and close friends, fellow bodybuilding colleagues and training partners, Hollywood co-stars, directors, executive producers and journalists, and political personalities and journalists, who offer first-hand accounts. Prominent personalities are given a voice reflecting Arnold's life and career, with added commentary for optimal balance.

You will discover Arnold's meteoric rise to fame, from pursuing his goal of becoming the greatest bodybuilder in the world, using the sport he loves as a platform and stepping stone to fulfil his ambitions in Hollywood. After reaching the pinnacle of his professions, his career trajectory further took another turn when he became the governor of California. Arnold's political goals did not stop there; the movie-star-turned-politician seriously contemplated running for president, but the US Constitution prevents foreign citizens from holding the nation's top job.

Arnold is an ambitious, intelligent, humorous and a profoundly driven individual, a beacon of what monomaniacal drive, doggedness and tenaciousness can accomplish. For me, one of the most striking aspects of this most enthusiastic proponents of success is his resolute optimism, drive, ambition, business savvy and insatiable desire to venture beyond the limits. The veracity of the matter is that Arnold is the personification of the American Dream.

As always, it gives me unquantifiable enjoyment, once again, to meticulously create a portrait of a rather complex career-focused celebrity. Most importantly, you discover that this man has had a successful multifaceted career. You get a glimpse into the opulent life of a top celebrity. Whether you're a fan of the sport, movies, the man, or the life of a Hollywood superstar or politician evokes your interest, you will find Arnold Schwarzenegger an intriguing figure to be adulated whose ubiquitous influence is felt. Who would have thought the once scrawny son of a European village cop, with an unpronounceable name and an inexplicable accent, willed himself to first become the world's greatest bodybuilder and then the biggest movie star in Hollywood and subsequently a politician.

INTRODUCTION

Born Arnold Alois Schwarzenegger on July 30, 1947, in a small village called Thal in Austria, to Aurelia and Gustav, the young boy developed immense ambition and restless energy which left him perpetually hungry for new challenges, which most people may have perceived an aberrant fantasy. Gustav was a local police chief and had served in the Army. Gustav and Aurelia also had a son called Meinhardt, who was a year older than Arnold. Gustav was a stern man who favored his elder son. Arnold was brought up by his father's martinet methods, who was a strict disciplinarian, despite Arnold's defiance.

After taking up bodybuilding in his early teens, without the imprimatur of his parents, the young teenager focused on becoming the best bodybuilder in a sport which was often frowned upon. His father told him not to cherish this stupid notion and to pursue a "real" career. Arnold indulged his grandiose adolescent dreams fuelling his nascent imagination through an obsession with bodybuilding and beyond. Inspired by the legendary bodybuilder Reg Park, he began to read about and follow his idol's methods to build up his body. Park, who starred in the Hercules movies at the time, became the teenager's hero. When Arnold started to compete, soon a mentor-protégé relationship cultivated, which lasted until Park's demise. After winning several bodybuilding championships in Europe, the desire to take things further on a more global stage were apparent.

Decades later, Arnold recalled, "The hunger and the desire, this burning desire inside that I want to be somebody, I want to make it and I want to be the best, I think that came from growing up in a little village. I wanted to go out of there and I wanting to be part of something big. And for me, America symbolized that." As a potential route to escape from his secluded village in his native Austria, comfortable of stultifying prospects, and in his quest for fulfilling his grand ambitions, he left for America in 1968. Ever since he was a ten-year old boy, he had dreamt about moving to America one day. Arnold was invited by the bodybuilding magnet Joe Weider and decamped in America - Southern California, the Mecca of bodybuilding and the motion picture industry.

Keen to embrace American individuality and culture, it didn't take long for Arnold, who aptly was named the "Austrian Oak", to weave himself right into the fabric of the land of opportunity. Continuing in his pursuit of bodybuilding fame, he planted the seeds to his career unparalleled in its success. When the young Austrian arrived, it was a turbulent year of civil unrest and assassinations in America. The twenty-one-year old ambitious youth arrived with absolutely nothing, other than a gym bag, $20 and a grand dream. Hardly able to speak a word of English, Weider immediately took his future star under his wing.

Unparalleled success in bodybuilding followed, which culminated in Arnold winning the Mr. Olympia title - the most prestigious bodybuilding title - seven times. After appearing in Pumping Iron in 1977, which helped disparate certain myths which apparently surrounded the sport and its competitors, soon he was on the cutting edge of American physical culture. Later, when he broke into Hollywood, his contribution to bringing the sport of bodybuilding into mainstream acceptance was unparalleled. Arnold has done more than anyone to popularize bodybuilding. With Hollywood right down the freeway, his next course of action was almost predestined.

"I wanted to be the best at whatever I did. I had a lot of motivation and energy and had a very clear vision of what my goals were, and I was going to achieve them. And I went after my dream," stated Arnold unequivocally. "I've always thought if you achieve your goals and become the best, then you will achieve notoriety and fame, anyway. It follows naturally. It is wrong to seek the fame before the substance, in my view." To a certain extent, he was driven to success by a rabid neediness engendered by childhood neglect from his parents.

After various appearances in several movies in the 1970s, it wasn't until 1982 with the release of his fist major picture, Conan the Barbarian, when his big break came; a film which was the perfect vehicle to catapult him into stardom. In 1984, he made the first of three appearances as the eponymous character, and what some would say was the signature role in his acting career, in Terminator, which propelled him to superstardom and his reputation as a box office draw was sealed. Box office success alone induced the critics to acknowledge him as an actor of merit. Famed for his high-octane action roles, a string of action movies later Arnold became the king of the multiplex and the highest paid actor in the world. Despite his enormous success, Arnold remained a prominent face in the bodybuilding world, because of his love for the sport, which he believes was the vehicle which brought him to making movies. He also invested in real estate and would go on to become an astute businessman.

The 1980s and 1990s were the decades which encapsulated testosterone-fuelled action movies. With Sylvester Stallone, Steven Seagal, Bruce Willis, Jean Claude Van Damme, Dolph Lundgren and Arnold dominating the action genre. Despite the ambivalence which surrounded his acting skills, this brawny, laconic action man's undeniable star presence and gleaming muscles made him an instant hit. His popularity peaked and in 1993 a poll conducted divulged Arnold was the man most Americans would want to spend time talking to on a long-distance flight. Oprah Winfrey was the only person to outscore him in the poll. The public is enamored by Arnold's celebrity appeal and can resonate with this quintessential action movie star who played the action hero, and in some cases the villain.

To Arnold, unprecedented success in the motion picture industry was not enough. He married into American royalty when he tied the knot with Maria Shriver, the niece of President John F. Kennedy. As a result of this, he was catapulted into America's elite. To many, they became America's most incongruous celebrity couple. Not content on having made history by becoming the greatest bodybuilder in history and becoming the highest paid and number-one movie star in the world, he reached even further heights when he prevailed in American politics. "I had a great experience with acting and doing movies," Arnold said. "It was always a big dream of mine when I was a kid. I used bodybuilding as a means to get into movies, just like my hero Reg Park, who did the Hercules movies. All of a sudden I realized that, you know, I've done this; I've gotten to the top. The highest paid actor that there ever was in history. Done all of these different things. So I said to myself, I'm tired of the same things, jumping over car hoods three in the morning and then going up to someone and saying, 'I'm back', and blow him away. All of this is great, but eventually it gets old."

In 2003, he became the governor of California; his term ended in early 2011. Arnold, a staunch Republican, had an interest in politics well before he came to America. And he admired President Ronald Reagan, who himself went from a movie star to venturing out into politics and becoming the president. An element which is apparently noteworthy about Arnold is that he's a complex character who reached the pinnacle of his success in several different fields. It's open to conjecture whether the boy from a small village in a European country was precarious whether he would achieve the level of success he ultimately did. Moreover, it's transparent the drive, ambition, which were all visible, and his win-at-all-costs attitude embedded in his mind that he knew he was going to triumph; he was able to delineate his future cultivating the psychological framework for the drive that led to his ultimate success.

Arnold's life has been a celebration of self. Many may perceive him as a man with an inflated ego, which, by the way, if utilized in the right manner can be a great asset to have, which can be an integral factor in contributing to achieving an unprecedented level of success and push you to achieve goals. Other's perception is of a man instilled with a work ethic and a burning desire for supremacy. Some perceive the former governor of being domineering, others confident, intelligent individual and a businessman who refuses to settle for second best. These characteristics are deeply rooted in him.

Arnold is a man defined by unbridled ambition, for years as the governor of California reshaping the political landscape, critics and the press were ambivalent about his success as a politician, more often than not focusing on the negative end of the scale. Hollywood is a town of mystery, glitz and glamor, thousands every week move to Tinseltown to seek the American Dream and fame and fortune where most actors are unemployed. Arnold Schwarzenegger cultivated a worldwide persona that brought him countless riches and everlasting fame. He is one of the most famous Hollywood celebrities in the world; this is something no one can deny him.

CHAPTER ONE

BODYBUILDING FRATERNITY

FRANCO COLUMBU

Franco Columbu, a two-time Mr. Olympia winner and a legend in the bodybuilding world, has been Arnold's best friend since the 1960s. When he first arrived in America, he was one of the strongest men in the world. Both Arnold and Columbu were training partners.

When did you first meet Arnold, was it in Germany in the 1960s?
Franco Columbu: In 1965, October 30, we met in Stuttgart in a competition. I competed in a powerlifting competition and I won. I won first place. And Arnold competed in the Junior Mr. Europe, he was only eighteen at that time, and he won first place too. So, we met on the stage and we received the winner's trophies.

Did you then pursue to converse with him?
Franco Columbu: The conversation was very simple. I knew all the bodybuilders in Germany, and I said to him, "I know all the people here. I've never seen you before. Who are you?" He said, "Oh, I'm not from Germany; I'm from Austria. I'm from Graz." And he said, "I've never heard of you, either." I said, "I'm from Italy. I just moved to Munich." And then we went to a restaurant and talked, we had dinner and beer. I was training in Munich at the time. Then he told me, "I want to come to Munich and train with you." I really didn't believe much because many people, even in Italy, had said to me, "I'm going to come to Germany. I'm going to come to Munich. I'm going to train with you." I forgot about it when he left. Then a couple of months later, he shows up at the gym, and the owner of the gym in Munich made him an instructor. He became a gym instructor. And then we started to train together.

In 1966, Arnold moved to Munich in Germany and started to manage the Putzingger Gym, which he bought a year later. He started to hang out with people at night, which included entertainers, hookers and bar owners. He told OUI magazine in a 1977 interview that he had a girlfriend who was a stripper. Arnold was an innocent young man from a farm town growing up rapidly in a big city. He started working as a trainer and manager at the gym, which was owned by Albert Busek, who would become a lifelong friend. In the beginning, he lived in a small room, which was in the vicinity of the gym. Later, he was able to get his own apartment. The young teenager from a small village settled in rapidly in a big city. In those days, weight training was not in vogue; bodybuilders, powerflifters, boxers and wrestlers were the main people who trained with weights. Arnold befriended a wrestler named Harold Sakuta, who had a role in the James Bond film Goldfinger.

Often struggling to make ends meet, Arnold avoided telling his parents about the problems he was inundated with, their understanding was their son was earning decent money working and was happy. Had he told his parents about the harsh reality of survival in a city, they would have admonished him to come back home. In 1967, Arnold competed in a stone-lifting contest in Munich. The stone - weighing 508 German pounds (254 KG/560 pounds) - is lifted between the legs while standing on two foot rests. Arnold won the competition and broke the existing record. By now Arnold was on his way to becoming a star, often being interviewed and photographed by the members of the media. As a result of this, he let this go to his head, Arnold admitted later when he was at the peak of his bodybuilding career.

Would I be right in saying you introduced Arnold to powerlifting?
Franco Columbu: Powerlifting at that time was pretty big in Europe, you know, in Prague, in France, in Germany. I told him, "Look, you know, you're the strongest." But he said, "I want to be Mr. Olympia, Mr. Universe." I said, "Let's do both." Then we did training, like, for bodybuilding parts we always did three main exercises, (including) squats and bench press to get stronger. And that really was the principle then. We discovered that by lifting heavy weights it developed bodybuilding too. It was really, really a good thing that powerlifting helped bodybuilding.

Can we talk about when you both came to America and stayed together in California in the early days?
Franco Columbu: When Arnold competed in 1968 in London in the NABBA Mr. Universe, he won and then he was invited to America to compete. He wanted to come to America. Then Joe Weider invited him to come to the United States. And he came to America, around November1968. Then we kept in contact, and then in June 1969, which was six months later, I sold my car and bought a plane ticket and I went to California. Then we started training, again, here together and lived together for two, three years in a small apartment. At the time, we would wake up at seven o' clock, have a protein drink and go to the gym for three hours. We trained really heavy. Then at ten o' clock we would go

have breakfast, and then we would work part-time in construction.

I got a bricklaying license, and we did that and we made some money. Because at that time, we didn't receive much money (from bodybuilding), we only got paid $80 from Joe Weider for taking pictures and writing articles. It was not enough money - $80 each. So we went to work and we made few hundred bucks working. Then we were able to buy more food and everything, and that really made us become good friends. And the success really started right there. Because then we really started working in construction, and we trained a lot and we started winning like crazy - every competition.

Columbu had suggested to his Austrian friend they should get into the construction business. Columbu would lay the bricks and Arnold would mix the cement, and they would make some money, which would help them to make ends meet. Columbu went downtown to apply for a license - a temporary license. The duo placed adverts in a newspaper advertising European Brickworks. Columbu recalled there came a time when they were inundated with phone calls that they didn't have enough time to do the actual work, because they had to answer the phone so much. Owing to the pair's marketing savvy and an onset of high demand following the 1971 Los Angeles earthquake, the business flourished. Soon the duo had a force of sixteen people working for them. The profits Arnold generated from this venture would later be utilized to finance a mail order business pertaining to bodybuilding products. Later, the profits accumulated from this venture, along with his bodybuilding competition earnings, would be invested in real estate.

What are your recollections of training with Arnold at Venice Beach?
Franco Columbu: We trained at Gold's Gym, in the original Gold's Gym in Santa Monica. Then also sometimes we went to Venice to do a second workout in the afternoon, training in the sun and all that stuff. The sessions were, like, things like, we liked to train in the public. I remember one time I was doing squats with 500-600 pounds, I could only do three or four reps. And Arnold says, "There are people in the gym from Italy behind you and they're watching you. You cannot do just four reps; you should do eight." When I heard that I did another six, then went up to ten reps. And that shows you how the mind controls the body in doing what you want. That was in Venice. When we trained at Venice, with thousands of people watching, we really, really trained hard, heavy and screamed like.... So motivation was there and the body responded well, we got in shape and it was incredible.

What was Arnold's inclination as far as bodybuilding and training principles are concerned?

Franco Columbu: We trained heavy: do your bench press, get strong in the bench press, deadlift for powerlifting, but let's do the rest and train the entire body, let's train four hours. And the key was to getting strong in every part of the body, the arms...everything. Strength in brutal training.

Arnold developed a philosophical approach to bodybuilding. "You can actually create a vision of what your body will look like. Then you mold your body closer and closer to that vision, and actually you would turn that vision to reality," explains Arnold. "The experience of being much stronger than everybody else, I think that's an unbelievable experience. You feel richer, you feel that sooner or later you can do anything." He would often take his mind-power to an elevated level when training, and he would visualize his goals and has glowingly expressed innumerable times of the benefits of such practice. He wrote in Joe Weider's magazine Muscle Builder/Power, "Whenever I go into the gym for a workout, it is like a boxer at the height of his fury to deliver a knockout blow. My mind is focused on bombing that workout with ferocious power and with all the mental and physical energy I am capable of generating."

RICKY WAYNE

Ricky Wayne won numerous professional bodybuilding titles, including Mr. Universe. He was a prominent bodybuilding journalist and wrote for Joe Weider's Muscle Builder and FLEX. Wayne's authored several books. Wayne and Arnold became good friends and often trained together.

When did you meet Arnold and under what circumstances, was it in the 1960s?
Ricky Wayne: That's correct. Early '60s or it was in the mid-'60s. He had come to compete in the Amateur Mr. Universe. I was already competing and winning in the States. And I got a message from somebody, a mutual friend, a German friend, who asked me to come at the theater because Arnold wanted to meet me. I went and that's how we met the first time. Shortly after that, the people he was working with in Munich, Arnold called them to bring me over to do a guest posing exhibition in, I think it was either Munich or Dusseldorf. We became very good friends right after that.

You worked as a bodybuilding journalist writing for the prominent magazines. Did you interview Arnold when he competed in the Amateur Mr. Universe, and what was your impression as far as his body development?
Ricky Wayne: He was big, but that was about all. He wasn't even tanned. He went up against a guy called Chet Yorton, who was a much experienced American from California. But Arnold made a fantastic impression, because he was young, nineteen and big. He didn't win but he made a very good impression. And he, of course, had all the self-confidence which he is known for - he had it back then. In his book The Education of a Bodybuilder, he mentions that he asked me what I thought his chances were in the several coming months. I said I didn't think they were pretty good yet. And he refers to that in the book. But within a couple of years, Arnold changed totally. If I recall correctly, he won the Mr. Universe the next year.

In 1966, Arnold flew out to the United Kingdom for the first time to compete in the NABBA Mr. Universe contest in London. Although he finished second to an experienced American Chester Yorton, he made an impression on the fans and was swarmed by autograph-seeking fans as he made his way out of the theater. Later, he reminisced he was like a puppy venturing out into the world when he first came to London, and it was the first time he had ever been on a plane. Wag and Dianne Bennett ran two gyms in the East End of London, one beneath their home, which was in Forest Gate, and the other down on Romford Road. Wag Bennett recalled, "I said to him after the show that his calves had stopped him from winning, and Arnold agreed. I said the best thing you can do is to go home and cut the trousers off of the knees, so that you can't hide your weak points. And Arnold went home, cut the trousers off of the knees, worked very hard on his calves and luckily his calves responded and grew."

The Bennetts detected potential in this young ambitious bodybuilder and invited him to stay at their home to live with them. This was the beginning of a nurturing relationship that would endure even when Arnold conquered Hollywood many years later. "When I first came to London, I was only planning to stay a few days or so, but I was just blown away by the hospitality that Wag and Dianne showed me," Arnold recalled. "I remember feeling very comfortable right away, with the children all running around and Wag talking about bodybuilding the whole time. I just ate it all up, you know."

Arnold stayed with Wag and Dianne Bennett, were you living in England at the time?
Ricky Wayne: Was I living there? Sure. Wag Bennett was the guy who ran a gym in East London, Stratford, and I trained there. I was a very close friend of the family. When Wag met Arnold at the first Mr. Universe, he befriended him and Arnold became kind of like a son. So whenever he was in London, more often than not he stayed at Wag's house. That's how we all became good friends.

According to friend Albert Busek, not many people are aware that Arnold had a terrible problem in getting to the1968 NABBA Mr. Universe contest in London. "A few days before the contest, the owner of our gym presented Arnold with an endorsement contract, which Arnold would not sign, because the guy would have owned all sorts of rights for life. The owner owed Arnold 1,000 deutsche marks for a guest appearance he had made at the European Championships I had organized in Munich two weeks earlier," Busek said. "Because Arnold would not sign the contract, the owner refused to pay him the 1,000 deutsche marks. Arnold was counting on that money for his flight to London. In front of the owner, my boss, I gave Arnold 500 deutsche marks for his plane ticket and risked losing my job."

Arnold's experience with the Bennetts made him much more sophisticated. He says at that age you're always looking for approval, attention love and guidance. The Bennett family fulfilled those needs and became cognizant of the fact Arnold needed the care, love and attention. "Especially my need to be the best in the world, to be recognized and to feel unique and special," remembers Arnold.

In London at the 1970 Mr. Universe competition, several prominent bodybuilders, Reg Park, Frank Zane and Dave Draper, competed. Can you recall this event?
Ricky Wayne: Yeah. Arnold won. I wrote something about that somewhere. Reg Park was, of course, Arnold's hero. But by then he was getting old, and I don't know why he chose to compete again as he had won Mr. Universe many times. Why go up against Arnold, who was just really getting into his prime? So, they were talking in the dressing room, where Reg Park was pumping up. And Reg Park turned around and said to Arnold, "Look, I gotta go. I can't keep talking to you; I have a contest to compete and prepare for." Arnold said to him, "What contest?" Meaning that there was no contest. Of course, Reg was very upset about that. But later on, Arnold publicly apologized for that and made the point that he'd always wished him good luck. Besides, he spent a lot of time at Reg Park's house in South Africa.

What about Frank Zane?
Ricky Wayne: Well, yeah. Arnold went to Miami to compete in a contest, I forget what it was called, shortly after the first Mr. Universe. And because, of course, he's huge, Frank is more medium built. When Arnold got there and saw what condition Frank was in - Frank beat him! In fact, that's the one time Arnold said that he would never compete in it again. Because now he was going to start training, and he knows he can beat him this time.

Can you tell me about training with Arnold in London, what was his English like in those early days - was he able to converse quite easily?
Ricky Wayne: We trained at the same gym - Wag Bennett's gym. I also trained with him at Gold's Gym in California. He also trained with Dave Draper, Frank Zane, most of the guys, but I think Franco Columbu was his main training partner. The first year, within a year he was making jokes, all kinds of jokes in English. Arnold was a fast learner - very fast learner. He is one of the most fascinating people I ever know.

In America you worked for the Weider publications. When you interviewed him for the magazines, what do you remember most about interviewing him?

Ricky Wayne: We had all kinds of conversations when I was working for the magazines, whether I was writing in Arnold's name or in my name. We knew each other well. The main thing and the most important thing was Arnold had a great self-confidence, and that's what brought me to his.... We had conversations. You'd always be with him on a positive note regardless of what it was. Whether it was the movies, whether it was bodybuilding, whether it was a contest, he always believed he was going to be number one. And that's what keeps you alive.

Would you say that in those days he was cocky but in a nice way?

Ricky Wayne: I don't know how you can be cocky in a nice way. Cocky is one thing and confidence is another.

Arnold won his second NABBA Mr. Universe title, one of the competitors he was up against was the formidable Dennis Tinerino, who witnessed his opponent brimming with self-confidence. Arnold boasted to the Italian American favorite, "Tenerino, I want to wish you all the best, the best man shall win, and you're looking at him." The following year, his ambition lay in conquering America and he devised a plan which encapsulated capturing three major bodybuilding titles in a year - the major and most prestigious federations.

Joe Weider's ardent propagation of the sport has endured for decades. He was responsible for bringing Arnold over to America. How would you define their relationship?

Ricky Wayne: It was like a father and son relationship. As a matter of fact, the way he got to the States, right after he had competed in the Mr. Universe contest I wrote to Joe Weider, because I used to write for the Weiders in England. And I wrote to Joe and said try to get this guy on a contract very quickly, and that's how the whole thing started. And eventually, Joe called him over. Joe likes to hype a lot in his main investments - Arnold was one of them. His big thing with Joe was over Sergio Oliva, because a lot of people thought there was a lot of racism involved there. But I wrote articles about that. I said if you ask, "Who is the greater bodybuilder?" I might say Sergio. But if you ask, "Who is the greatest champion?" I would say Arnold. And there's a lot between those two things.

Arnold was a fantastic promoter of bodybuilding. He spoke well. He was very much a personality. He would go to seminars, and he was able to talk to the press better. And he had all those things. Sergio, on the other hand, was a Cuban, came over from political strings attached from Cuba and so on. Sergio was not nearly the nice guy Arnold was or supposed to be. Body for body, Sergio probably had the better body, but Arnold certainly was the better champion. Arnold was far more competitive.

He started a mail order business where Weider would give him free adverts in the magazines. Then later, Weider started to send invoices for payment. They had kind of an on-and-off relationship, didn't they?
Ricky Wayne: Yeah. For Arnold it was good, very lucrative. I think he still does it. It was very lucrative for him.

Joe Weider, a Canadian Jew, along with his brother Ben transformed bodybuilding into a hugely successful sport embraced globally, now with over 170 national federations spanning every continent. At age seventeen, he began his bodybuilding and publishing empire with a mere $7. The ambitious young entrepreneur published his first magazine (Your Physique) in 1940. In 2003, his company Weider Publications was sold to American Media for a reported $300 million. In 1975, as Arnold was coming to the end of his competitive career, Arnold told Sports Illustrated, "All of these magazines, Weider's, Hoffman's, Lurie's, I call them comic books, circus books!" He exclaimed they all endeavored to expose each other and said: why wouldn't these get together? "I'll tell you why," he continued. "It is because none of these silly people are really interested in bodybuilding anymore. They are interested only in the money that can be made from it."

He said he asked why Joe printed such junk - all those silly words. Weider told him it sold the magazine. By the early 1980s, thanks to Weider's marketing skills and great effort in promoting the sport of bodybuilding and propagating the benefits of weight training, health and fitness through weight training was ingrained in the public consciousness, creating a fitness boom. Today, going to the gym has become the norm. Arnold recalled in 1997, "I saw the Joe Weider magazines with all these fantasy articles." He had read about how the bodybuilding magnet trained champions, and they were given supplements and sent to the Weider Research Clinic. "I thought the clinic was a huge research center somewhere in America connected to the movie industry, and full of guys wanting to be Hercules," Arnold recalled. There were alternating periods of good and bad fortune and spirits as far as Arnold's relationship with Weider is concerned. Nevertheless, both men had depended on each other to elevate themselves in the past, and, regardless of the past, the friendship endured.

Arnold competed with Sergio Oliva; Arnold lost to him in the 1969 Mr. Olympia. He may have been rather crude at that point. Did he talk to you about this after the defeat, and was he sentimental in any way?
Ricky Wayne: What he said was it won't happen again. I covered most of the Olympias up till 1980.

Arnold was cognizant that the only way he could beat the giant Cuban was to be in the best shape possible. Oliva was so good he could beat you in the dressing room. His shirt would come off and there would be that incredible mass. Arnold recalls the events surrounding his first Mr. Olympia, "When it came time to go onstage for the pose down, Sergio took the long apron off and started walking in front of me down the hall. Then, nonchalantly lifting one of his shoulders, he spread the largest lat muscle I had ever seen. Then he repeated the same movement with the other shoulder. His back muscles were so huge that he seemed to be as wide as the hall itself. As far as I was concerned, I already knew - then and there - I would lose against him." This would be the last and only time Arnold would be defeated by Oliva. The following year, in 1970, when Arnold took the Olympia title for the first time, Oliva says he knew he would not lose against Arnold, because he had no weak spots. But the judges saw it differently, and this was the first of seven Sandows Arnold would bring home.

Sergio Oliva stayed at the Bennett house when competing in England. What was Arnold's and Sergio's relationship like?
Ricky Wayne: Arnold was always friendly with Sergio. When they were not, it was usually Sergio's fault. Sergio had this thing in his head that Weider was favoring Arnold because he was white.

Any social moments you can recall with Arnold?
Ricky Wayne: Very fun guy, made a lot of jokes, but sometimes his jokes got him in trouble. But that was a time when political correctness was not around yet. So, you know, a lot of people quote him saying he said this and he said that, but they forget that at the time political correctness was not around. Like, whatever he might have said about women. The things we could've said about women back then, if we said them now you would get in trouble.

He settled in America, which was the beginning of pursuing the American Dream. Arnold once said, "The Mr. Universe title was my ticket to America, the land of opportunity, where I could become a star and get rich." This may have been a myopic vision, but he did pursue it.

Ricky Wayne: Oh, he loved California. He loved it. California is great for bodybuilding. The weather is fine, there's a lot of competition, there's fun, it's Hollywood. You have a lot of opportunities with the magazines, you can go on TV and so on. You don't have that in England, especially back then.

To Arnold, the blond bodybuilder Dave Draper represented the epitome of California bodybuilders. Draper also had pursued the entertainment industry with roles in Don't Make Waves, which starred Tony Curtis, and various TV shows. This made the ambitious Austrian cognizant of the possibilities of opening doors beyond the confines of the bodybuilding arena. Arnold says his challenge was to compete against the great bodybuilders and defeat them. Ben Weider had met Arnold for the first time in 1967 at a competition in which Arnold was victorious.

The young champion told Weider that he wanted to come to America to compete. Weider responded, "If you come straight the way you are, you're going to lose. You're great as far as the Europeans are concerned, but as far as the Americans are concerned, you won't win." This did not dishearten Arnold by any measure; the very next year Arnold would be invited to America by Ben's brother, and this was the initiation of a long relationship which would benefit both individuals. Joe Weider was a ruthless businessman, and he often took advantage of his new star, which often irritated Arnold. But Arnold gained a plethora of publicity and learned a lot from his mentor. Whether it was about making a business deal or promoting, Weider the Master Blaster was the best!

Monetary rewards were minimum in professional bodybuilding when Arnold was competing. Bodybuilding has changed, would you say this is true?

Ricky Wayne: Ermm, not really. When Arnold won the Olympia, the money was $1,000. It was Arnold who, when he started promoting, started making the money bigger and pushed for that. Where bodybuilders made some bucks was in personal appearances and endorsements for Weider. Later on, they started doing their own courses, their own postal business, Weider gave them ads so on. There wasn't really big money in bodybuilding. Three or four guys at the top made big money, considering the number of people who were champions.

How often did Weider cover Arnold in his magazines?

Ricky Wayne: There was hardly an issue where Arnold wasn't in it. That goes on even now, the other magazines are doing well, because Arnold has always been a seller. He has a lot of bodybuilding fans, movies, and even as a politician, it's a good reason to put him on the cover.

What was his training philosophy?
Ricky Wayne: Very simple philosophy: train hard and often. That's it. Everybody tries to complicate bodybuilding. How far you go in bodybuilding depends on your genes. Some people have it; some people don't have it. And the discipline, how determined you are. And Arnold had all of those work for him. He was very careful of his eating habits as well, extremely.

Can you distinguish between the bodybuilding scene in Europe and America back in the 1960s? There was more exposure in America.
Ricky Wayne: Far more exposure and far more encouragement. That's why a lot of the champions in Europe had to go to the States to be somebody.

What was Arnold's hardest competition?
Ricky Wayne: The first one against Sergio, and the last one in Sydney, Australia. He won and after did the movies. But everybody booed and there was a lot of trouble over there (Sydney).

What was the most fascinating thing you saw in Arnold pertaining to training?
Ricky Wayne: The intensity of his workouts - when he was training he trained!

Arnold filtered into the movie business, Pumping Iron was an integral chain to his success. Did he talk to you about pursuing the movies, when he was still competing and achieving his bodybuilding goals?
Ricky Wayne: He went before that. Shortly after he came to the States, he got a break in a movie called Hercules in New York, which was crap! Yes, that was his main thing (breaking into the movies). Reg Park and Steve Reeves were his idols and both of them had made movies. Arnold wanted to be like them. So movies were always on his mind. He always wanted to get into the movies, whenever the movies came, it's just that they came along at his time.

LARRY SCOTT

The first ever Mr. Olympia (1965 and 1966), Larry Scott personified the sport's beach Adonis image back in the 1960s. He was bodybuilding's top star in the 1960s, and goes down in history as one of the legends of the sport.

Larry, you, of course, won the first two Mr. Olympias in 1965 and 1966. Arnold went on to win seven. First of all, can you tell me how did the Weider brothers start this new contest?

Larry Scott: In 1965, around that time I had just won Mr. America, a year before and Mr. Universe, that was as far as you could go. So Joe Weider, his wife Betty and I were over at a restaurant in California. And Joe says - I can't remember if it was Joe's or Betty's idea, but he said, "We've got to have a contest. We've got to create a contest that will help the bodybuilders to continue, because after they win Mr. Universe they just drop off; they don't do anything. We've got to have something that they continue to get ready for, a contest year after year." And I'm listening, and I say, "That's a good idea." So Betty gave her input and I gave my input. I thought it was a good idea. I thought it would be nice to continue to compete, because you're right: how can you get excited for training if you don't have a contest to compete in? You could always train hard for a contest than you can for everyday fitness.

So, once we agreed that we're going to create a new contest, then Joe said, "What do we call it?" There were a number of options that came up. I'm not sure how we came up with an idea, but anyway, I can't remember what my idea was, but Joe says, "Let's call it Mr. Olympia!" I said, "I don't think that's a good idea, because there's Olympia beer. It's like we're selling beer." He says, "No! No! It's like Mount Olympus, like where all the Greek Gods were on Mount Olympus." Betty argues with him for a while, but we finally agree with Joe's idea. And we thought, OK, we'll call it Mr. Olympia. That's where it came from.

Can you tell me how much of an impact Steve Reeves had in the 1950s and the 1960s era on bodybuilding, and how much of a part he played promoting bodybuilding before Arnold brought it to the public's consciousness?

Larry Scott: I don't think Steve ever worked with the muscle magazine owners. And so the impact he had on bodybuilding was the impact of his own physique and his own charisma. He had probably overall the best package of anyone has ever had. He had the perfect proportions: his neck, his arms and his calves were all the same size. And he was really good-looking. He was just a wonderful representative of bodybuilding, and we all looked up to him. Just to say that you knew Steve was something. He and George Eiferman were good friends. They would chum together and they would do shows together. I first met Steve and George in Salt Lake City. They came out to do a guest posing for the contest promoter. And Bob Delmonteque, the photographer for Weider at the time, happen to see us, and we saw him at a local health club where we were exercising getting ready to trying to shape up. You wanted to feel like you had a pump when you went to a physique contest. I mean, you felt much bigger when you went in.

So I trained hard before I went into that physique contest, in which Steve Reeves was going to guest pose, as well as George Ivan Eiferman. Bob Delmonteque offered to take us up to the motel room where Steve and George were staying. He took us and introduced us. That was the first time we had to really chat to Steve Reeves. It was really an honor and inspiring. I could hardly even think of the questions I wanted to ask. Something came out of my mouth, "How do you get big?" He smiled a little bit, but he gave us a few tips for training. They were just resting waiting for the presentation for the show that night. Anyway, Steve lived in California so he spent a lot of time in Muscle Beach. It had quite an impact on the muscle-building world down in the California area.

Can you tell me when you first met Arnold? Back then you were a major bodybuilding star, and Arnold was a novice just getting into the sport.
Larry Scott: Yes. When I went to Europe to do a guest posing show over at Albert Busek's...what did he call it? Mr. Austria, I think. It was about the year I won the Olympia the second time. So it was in '65 or '66. I was backstage getting ready to go out to do a posing exhibition when Arnold came backstage and asked for an autograph. And I said to him, "Could you wait till I get done posing, because I want to focus on this first?" He told me later that he was put off by me asking him to wait for an autograph, and he said, "Now that I've been in the same position, I can understand." Anyway, we got to know each other a little bit there. We didn't know each other; it was first becoming acquaintances. Then short time after that Arnold came out to California, and he came out to Vince's gym where I was training.

Vince Gironda had a great gym out in the San Fernando Valley, a gym where a lot of the former Mr. Americas were training. We had six training at one time. Arnold came down there to that gym, and he said, "Can you give me some advice on what I should do? Who should I contact?" I said, "Let me tell you something. This is what I would do if I were you. You've got to have three things to be successful. One, you've got to get in the magazines, you've got to have somebody who can help you with your photos and somebody who could help you with nutrition. If you've got three things lined up, then you've got a good chance. You've got a good body already, but you need these three things in order to make progress." And then I told him, "These are the three that I'm working with. And I recommend them highly because they're very good." I said, "When you meet Joe Weider, start getting in his magazines, because people don't know who you are unless they see you in the magazines." So he went over and he met Joe Weider and became friends with him.

I said, "You also have to meet this other guy, because he's the best nutritionist there is for bodybuilders. He's very good. Thirdly, you've got to find a photographer who will take the photos that will go in the magazines." I recommended a couple of them, one of the ones in the areas was Artie Zeller. He was very good too, he did great photography. There were quite a few others I endorsed, but he was the best photographer. So he lined up with those people I mentioned to him. About that time, I had just got married and I had decided that I knew happiness did not consist on being on the stage, but it required a family life. So I told myself when I won the second Olympia: if I win this contest tonight I'm retiring. So, I was fortunate enough to win it the second time, and I announced to the audience this was my last contest.

Going back to your European visit, what was your impression of the young Arnold when you first met? Was he in the audience or guest posing or competing that day?
Larry Scott: He was there to compete. I didn't see him in the audience. I saw him when he came backstage. Arnold has always been very forward, and he puts himself forward wherever he needs to. He came backstage to introduce himself, and he was just getting that feeling of what it was like being backstage and trying to get the "feel of the ropes" as you might say. He knew he would be soon going into that, so he would ask a few questions and so forth. He was very good at asking questions. I shouldn't say "good" as much as "very wise"- going to the people in the know and humbling himself to ask questions. A lot of times people coming up feel a little shy, or don't want to humble themselves to ask questions, but he was smart! He would ask what he needed to and where to get the information and evolve from there.

In America when he came to your gym, did he train occasionally there?

Larry Scott: He wanted to live near down by the beach in the Santa Monica area, which is right on the beach. He wanted to train down there. There was Gold's Gym down there. Gold's Gym was a good gym. Joe Gold created a few gyms. So, Arnold wanted to train down with the beach crowd. I didn't care for the beach crowd; they were a little too wild for me. I wanted to train where I lived down in San Fernando Valley, where there was a gym out there which was owned by Vince Gironda. It was a terrific gym. Vince really knew how to train. He was a great trainer. One of the things Arnold didn't get was a great trainer to guide him. Joe was pretty good - Joe Gold was good. But Vince was the champion of this. He had great ideas in terms of his thoughts were inclined toward aesthetics. When you're onstage, you want to look good aesthetically as well as just big. And that would have done Arnold some good. Of course, you can't discredit him because he did pretty damn good.

What was Arnold's relationship like with Joe Gold?

Larry Scott: They were good friends. Both lived in the same area. He trained in Gold's Gym, and they became good friends and good business partners.

How would you describe Arnold's physique of the 1960s and how did it evolve?

Larry Scott: In the '60s, when I first saw him my first impression was he was big and that he had possibilities. But I didn't suddenly say, "Wow, this guy's going to do everything!" When I saw Sergio Oliva for the first time, I thought, "Man, this man's from a different world! He's not from the same world as us." His (Sergio's) genetics were incredible. Arnold was big and he had good size and everything, but he was on his way up. He was naturally big. He took after his father, but he wouldn't knock your eyes off, he was just starting, you know. He learned, he got better and better. Arnold is very quick-witted, maybe it's the German in him.

He wants to demean you, because it makes him feel bigger and better. Maybe not, maybe that's not the right thing to say. Let me just say that he had a tendency to be a kidder, and he likes to make you a little uneasy. So you have to be quick on the comeback in order to hold your own with him. And Sergio wasn't that kind of a person at all; Sergio was more mild and not so much quick on the comeback. The other thing is that Sergio was so big. Sergio was big that he became so confident, and he became a little bit full of himself. But as far as Arnold and Sergio are concerned, they had completely different personalities.

Arnold was very aggressive and sharp and quick to respond to any kind of question.

Can you differentiate and elaborate on Arnold and Sergio Oliva's personalities back when they competed together?
Larry Scott: Well, I can't give you an example of Sergio's personality, when he first came when I first met Sergio he'd just come over from Cuba. Joe Weider brought him backstage. He didn't speak any English at all. So he was understandably a little shy, because he hadn't been around the top bodybuilders. Even though he was big and well-esteemed from where he came from, Joe hadn't made a niche for him yet over here in America. He was probably a little bit more withdrawn at that point. Certainly later on, as he grew a prosperity and became well known, he had much more confidence in himself, but he was not as articulate as Arnold. Arnold was very articulate from the get-go.

So, you had two different types of personalities completely. When they were together, there wasn't a lot of interchange. In fact, it was Arnold and Franco, there was a lot of interchange between them. Arnold and Frank Zane, there was a lot of interchange - because they were both articulate. And intelligent people can speak well and use this, as you see a lot more interesting conversations and give and take between those types of personalities than you would from someone who is more non-inclined to give and take conversation, or kidding and so forth. That wasn't Sergio's way.

Frank Zane beat Arnold in Miami when Arnold first came to America.
Larry Scott: Frank did beat Arnold once. I think he's a totally different person than Arnold. He's very cerebral, methodical, trains hard, works hard, he's not one to kid around at all. He's very serious, a very good trainer and very knowledgeable with his nutrition and his training - he still is. He is very heavily into that. He's not left the bodybuilding field at all. Whereas Arnold moved into the political arena, whilst Frank has been involved in bodybuilding and doing his books and training concepts and continues to train regularly. I think Arnold had a hard time to find the time getting away from all these responsibilities to train like I'm sure he would like to. But he's not a person you want to consider he's no longer in the program, because he's got a lot of innovation and ability to bounce back to get in great shape if he wanted to.

Can you ruminate on and share with me some anecdotes?
Larry Scott: Arnold and I have always had a relationship where we're always kidding each other. So, we had a lot of those circumstances in which where we're trying to put the other guy down jokingly, looking

for some way to put the other guy down, and we continually do. So, we had a lot of those kinds of things. Arnold and Franco Columbu were living down in Santa Monica. I was selling insurance. I called him and I asked Arnold if he needed insurance. He said, "Yes, I do." I said, "Do you need medical insurance?" He said, "Yes, I do. I need medical insurance." So, he said, "Why don't you come to our place this Saturday and we'll have breakfast together and you can tell us about the insurance?" I said OK. So I went to his place and we had a nice breakfast. And before we ate I said, "Would it be all right if I offer a blessing on the food?" He looked over at Franco, like, this is unusual. He said, "Yeah, go ahead. Say the blessing." So I said the prayer on the food and then we ate.

We talked about insurance, and I forgot all about it. It went completely out of my mind. Some years later, we were at the Mr. Olympia contest. After the show they always have a nice dinner, and they have tables and they cord it off so the fans can't get in there, so the competitors get the chance to eat in peace and relax. I was at my table and Arnold came over, and he said, "I have a story to tell you about Larry!" So he starts telling that story when I came over to their place for breakfast. He told it just the way it happened. Then he said, "As soon as we started to eat, Larry says, 'Can I pray on the food?' So he prays and he prays and prays. And I said, 'Larry, stop praying, the food is getting cold!'" He likes to turn it into humor. I said, "That's not what happened." He says, "Oh, yes, it is." So, he went back to his table. I was thinking about that, oh, I've got a way to get back at him.

So I went to his table and said, "I've got a story you tell you about Arnold!" Arnold said to his table, "Quiet everybody! I said, "Years ago...." I told the same story about how I went to his house to sell insurance, but I changed it a little bit. I said, "When I got done, I asked if I could say a prayer on the food. He said yes. I said a prayer and when I got done Arnold said, 'No, don't stop, Larry, we need more prayers or else you're not leaving....'" That's been typical. Arnold will be at his Arnold Classic, and he's going to have a story just like that. I've got one I've made up already, which I will use for a comeback, because I know it's going to take place. We only see each other once a year, and we always have that joking way with each other.

Did you talk about specific bodybuilding training with Arnold?
Larry Scott: I never talked bodybuilding training, or nutrition at all with Arnold. We never seemed to moved into that direction. With Frank Zane, I always talked bodybuilding. Sergio, well, I don't think so with Sergio, either. Sergio is very weak now, he's not in good health at all. Whereas Arnold is in good health. One of the things that I do is, I really

like bodybuilding, researching better ways to exercise. That's not Arnold's bag; he's more into different things. But that's my bag, and I like to find better ways to train. I like to find better nutrition packages, and I'm always researching like Frank Zane a lot. Sometimes I'll find a really good exercise and I'll tell Arnold about it. He'll listen and he'll say, "That's a great idea." One time he said, "How do you come up with these ideas?" I said to him, "This is where my heart is. Your heart's in moviemaking, my heart is in finding better ways to exercise." Sometime I'll call him and say, "You've got to try this, this is a great exercise which I've just discovered."

Arnold envisaged himself of becoming the best bodybuilder in the world. The absurdity of Joe Weider's subterfuge pertaining to adverts in his magazines didn't necessarily influence the readers, and he made a star out of Arnold.

Larry Scott: I'm not sure if he was interested in himself of promoting himself, but rather to become a better bodybuilder. That's Joe Weider; Joe Weider is the promoter. Joe was always promoting you to train hard and had him in the magazines and on the covers. He'd put you on the cover. He would also try to get bodybuilders motivated to train hard, because he wants the bodybuilders on the covers of his magazines. And as far as Arnold was concerned, he trained because he loves training. Then, I'm sure he'd like to train now but he's busy. But at that time, he wasn't busy and he trained hard because then it helped him in the movies, Conan the Barbarian so forth. So he's got to train and look good for the kind of movies he was doing. Plus the fact he liked to train and enjoyed the training. And it helps to promote the image he was trying to convey and to keep himself in the limelight.

Some people would say the two body parts Arnold lacked were the legs and calves. How would you assess him in comparison to the other bodybuilders of that era?

Larry Scott: I would say that his legs were not his best parts, but they certainly were in proportion with the rest of his body. His upper body was very, very good; one of the best upper bodies you'll see in the physique world. His legs weren't quite as good, but he had great thighs, really good thighs. And his calves, I don't think he put enough effort in his calves like he did with his upper body. It's hard to do both. But he was very proportionate and he would never have lost any points in a physique contest because of his calves or his thighs if they're always proportionate to the rest of his body. But it's hard to look at his calves and thighs when he's got such great arms, deltoids, chest; you can't take your eyes off those body parts. You can look at those other parts that are not even at that level and not as outstanding as the rest of his body.

In the late 1960s and early 1970s, bodybuilders didn't make much money. Did Arnold have to do jobs to support himself? Did he do construction work among other jobs?
Larry Scott: Yes, he did. He got paid from Joe for some of the things he did. I'm not sure of exactly those initial jobs when he first came over. I do recall him having some work. When he first came over, he was just trying to earn a living and he got some jobs. He started to do some real estate work. He started buying real estate and started making money in that area.

Real estate investments became the part of an integral mix for Arnold's investment strategy as far back as the 1970s. "The guys who own the most real estate in Los Angeles are Europeans," explained Arnold back in the days. "There are people coming over from Yugoslavia with hardly any money. A friend of mine came over from Czechoslovakia in '68 and he now owns four apartment buildings. Americans are still sitting on their ass waiting for it. Europeans are hungry because we don't have that much." Arnold had developed a discerning mind and a penchant for enterprise. He quickly realized America was so much money oriented. But he also noted the downside, and he said the psychiatrists know their business is useless if there were no sick people around, and so they make everybody feel guilty. "You know, all New York City is running to a psychiatrist. All America thinks it has sexual hang ups. Everybody's running to shrinks," Arnold told Time Out magazine in 1977.

When Arnold had retired from bodybuilding and was pursuing a movie career, was he accessible to his fellow bodybuilding buddies?
Larry Scott: When he was working in the movies, this is before he started doing political work, he was more accessible - you could reach him. You could get him on the phone, and you could talk to him about everything. But once he became a governor, then he had a crew of people around him that he kept, and if anybody called you had to make it through them in order to talk to Arnold. It was just too much work to try to get through to him. If you didn't have anything important to say to him, you just tried to stay in touch, it was just too hard to. He was inaccessible for most of us to get through to him, because you didn't have a real reason to contact him other than to keep the friendship alive.

Interestingly, you were in a movie in the 1960s. How did you get this part, did you have any conversations with Arnold pertaining to movie

appearances in those early years?
Larry Scott: I never did. That took place way before Arnold came over. I was training in Vince's gym one day, and, I guess it wasn't the director but the person who looks for people for the movie, they were going to do a movie called Muscle Beach Party. So he came to Vince's gym and asked if we would be interested in being in this movie. And there were several of us. I think it was about ten or twelve of us. We said, "Yeah, we'll do it." They sent us over to a casting at 20th Century Fox. We walked in front of the producers and directors, and they looked at us and they picked out the ones they wanted. That would happen quite a bit, because Vince's gym was right next to Universal Studios, which was one of the biggest movie studios in Los Angeles.

They would come over occasionally to that gym and look for people for parts. That's where Clint Eastwood got his start. He was there training with us, and he got his start. He came over occasionally. Clint was a lot of fun to be with. He didn't take himself too seriously. He trained there regularly but didn't train very hard. I remember one time he was doing shoulders, and I said, "Clint, let me tell you something about that exercise, how you can progress with it. I'll show it to you." I showed him how to do it, and he said, "Oh, man, you're making me tired. I'm going home." So he didn't want to do it at all and he left. Most of the people would want to try it, yeah, that'll be right, but he was, like, "Nah, it's too much."

What are your recollections of some of the more light-hearted moments with Arnold?
Larry Scott: I remember one. He did a movie called True Lies. He's hanging on a helicopter and Jamie Lee Curtis is in a car. And as he flew over, he was yelling to her, "The bridge is out! Reach down and grab my hand!" She was down in a convertible on the freeway, and he's on a helicopter trying to reach her hand. Anyway, several of us were driving to a physique contest, everyone always like to impersonate Arnold because he's easier to do. So, all through the way when we were driving, we were all saying, "The bridge is out! The bridge is out!" It was just silly what we were doing.

When we got to the Mr. Olympia contest, we were in a group, all gathered together before the show. We had been saying that phrase for so long that when Arnold came behind me and tapped me on the shoulder, he said " Larry, how are you doing?" I turned around and the first thing that came out of my mouth - I didn't even think about it - it just came out (impersonating Arnold's accent), "The bridge is out!" He didn't know what to make of it. There was no comeback or anything. He thought I was putting him down because of it. He says, "Where's your lolly, Larry?" In other words, he meant he made a lot of money out of it, whereas the money I didn't make. So, those are the kinds of things that generally take place when we see each other. I'm sure it's going to happen when we see each other again.

Arnold has been an influential figure in the sport of bodybuilding; he has truly left his mark on the sport. How do you perceive his place in bodybuilding history?

Larry Scott: I don't think there's any way you can ever take anything away from Arnold, he's certainly the most well-known bodybuilder in the whole world by far. The virtues of the fact the exposure that he gets, he's a very, very good promoter - the promoter for Arnold - he's very good. The producers want Arnold to do their movies, because he worked so hard to promote the movies. So, he is not afraid of work. It's tough to work with him, because he works so hard and you get exhausted. He has this incredible stamina and endurance. He's an amazing guy. He's not just a make-believe character; he's really real. He's very dedicated. I saw him one day when he came backstage at one of the contests, he looked very haggard, very drawn-out. He said, "I just got back from doing the promotion for Twins." The movie he was in. He said, "I did one hundred and seventeen interviews with the press over in France." And he came right after that to do the physique contest.

I watched him, and what they did, because everyone gets an autograph, they've got two photographers backstage. And they stood on one side, and a person walks up to Arnold, takes a shot with him, and maybe 6 feet away there is another photographer with another person all ready. And Arnold walks over to take a photo with him. He went back and forth for about two hours. I watched the expression on his face - that's very fatiguing. You can't just take a picture with the people, you have to make them feel good. He was very gracious, and he put himself out for each one of them. He made them feel welcomed and pleased in what they saw. He knows how to promote, he does. He puts himself out tremendously.

ED CORNEY

Ed Corney, born in Hawaii in 1933, has been acknowledged as being the greatest poser in bodybuilding history. He won countless competitions, including Masters Olympia twice. In the 1970s, Arnold met Corney and both men became close friends and training partners.

You and Arnold became good friends and training partners. When was the first time you met Arnold and sought to train with him?
Ed Corney: In the early '70s, because in '75 I moved down to LA to live with him. I had heard about him, and I suppose he had heard about me. But I met him at one of the local bodybuilding shows in the Bay area called Mr. San Jose. And, of course, we exchanged greetings, that was about it. I continued on pursuing my career. One day I get a call, he says, "This is Arnold!" I said, "Hey, Arnold, how are you?!" He said, "I want you to come and live with me in Santa Monica, we'll train together and we can do the movie Pumping Iron." So I said, "OK! I'll be there tomorrow." San Jose is about four hundred and fifty miles from Los Angeles. So, I went down to Santa Monica, LA, and met with Arnold. It was a tremendous experience. On the first day of training, he says, "Eddie, we have two choices. Either we train or we train.

I wasn't interested in anything else but training and getting better. Then he says, as we progressed in our training, Arnold said, "You're going to South Africa to compete in the Mr. Olympia." I said, "Oh, my goodness. Now I'm going to compete against my idols, Franco Columbu, Frank Zane, Albert Beckles." I couldn't believe that. But I did. I said OK. Of course, they had the under 200-pound class back then. I was in the under 200-pound class and came second to Columbu. Arnold won the over 200-pound class and then won the overall. Short story.

I was still living with Arnold in Santa Monica, his first investment that he bought was an apartment complex. He lived in the first apartment and rented out the other four. Another time, for taking care of the building, he hired a secretary to take care of everything, that way he could concentrate on bodybuilding. I lived with him and we trained every morning like clockwork. We would eat and rest. We trained in Santa Monica at Gold's (gym). He was unbelievable. I mean, he was very well-focused and trained very hard - very strong. I learned a lot from him. Even though I was older, I still learned a lot from Arnold. And still today, I use those things that I learned from him: you don't make any excuses.

How did you spend the time away from the confines of the gym?
Ed Corney: Here's an example: we all went down to Birmingham, Alabama, we did the movie Stay Hungry. Of course, Arnold was the star, the movie stars Sally Fields and Jeff Bridges. Then when we came back to Santa Monica, Sally put on a party for all the movie people. We were invited and we drove to her home in Bel Air, and the socializing didn't begin till late at night. So we left early, because he said, "We go home now because we have to train tomorrow." So, his determination and focus was there, so we went home. And another time he said, "Eddie, we don't train today. Let's have a glass of wine and rest," and we did. The next day we were super strong. So, his training was very focused and very determined. One time we were on Santa Monica Beach, and there were always women around us. One girl says, "Arnold! Arnold!" He looked up and said, "What is it?" She said, "I can't take my eyes off you." So then he answers her, "I don't blame you."

Which other event did you compete in with Arnold other than the 1975 Mr. Olympia and the 1980 Mr. Olympia?
Ed Corney: Those are the only competitions we competed in the same show together. Other than that, there was my career and he had his own career. To make a long story short, I bested Frank Zane and Albert Beckles; Franco Columbu was the only man I had to beat. Of course, I didn't. I came second to him.

Can you recount the ambiance at the time with bodybuilders training at the Santa Monica gym?
Ed Corney: Everyone was there. Frank Zane, Mike Katz, Bill Grant, everybody training hard, really hard. Ken Waller doing inclined with 150-pound dumbbells. Danny Padilla was there. Up on the wall they had a sign, which stated how many days were left to the Mr. Universe contest, how many days for the Mr. Olympia. It was like a countdown. But you couldn't wait to train. Why? Because everyone was training, that was the atmosphere. People couldn't wait to get into that atmosphere. Everyone trained super hard! And they very friendly too. There was no animosity.

One guy would do a pose and the whole gym would look at him. And we would comment on his pausing to encourage him, "That's it, you're getting better. That's it, a little bit more. Now you've got it!" He would be doing his training and I'd be watching. He'd be telling me,

"You've got to go for more! You've got to do more! You've got to challenge yourself." When he did his set, now it's my turn to do the same, "Challenge yourself. Use heavier weights. Increase your effort, get better." You might say it was the unspeakable force between us, we didn't have to say anything; we just knew about each other and what we both wanted. I had the opportunity to train with the best, and in doing so I became one of the best. Unbelievable.

Did you go around with Arnold guest posing? Did you discuss posing with Arnold - you're probably known for being the best poser in bodybuilding?
Ed Corney: We did one guest posing. Because I had a commitment made, to do the San Francisco show as a guest poser. In the meantime, Arnold was in LA doing Pumping Iron. So, the promoter said, "Do you think Arnold will guest pose?" I said, "You'll have to talk to him." In either case, the promoter brought everybody up to guest pose, myself, Ken Waller, Frank Zane, Franco Columbu and Arnold were the main entry to guest pose. We did discuss posing. We also went to ballet. We discussed body movements, how to move the body from one movement to another, movement with your hands and your head. We discussed posing on how to do certain things. One pose in particular with Arnold. Hitting a front pose, then he turns around and everybody is following him, he does a back pose. While they're committed to a back pose, he wants to know how he can get to the front pose really quickly. And we worked it out and that was interesting.

Regarding Frank Zane, was there a competitive edge between him and Arnold?
Ed Corney: Frank Zane was more on the ripped side. He would get totally ripped, not too much muscular. Arnold had both: muscular and ripped. Friendly! They were competitive as far as competing was concerned, like, "Let's get it over with. Let's get onstage and let them pick the best one. Then let's go have dinner." No animosity. Arnold was like me: very happy, very happy-go-lucky. And he had this magnetism about him, when he walked into a room everyone noticed him, looked up to him. That was his way of letting people know he was there, not in a cocky way, but it was his presence. I suppose he got that from his parents. But he was very welcomed.

Did Arnold have any other hobbies, in which he found merriment, besides his passion for bodybuilding?
Ed Corney: Yes. He and Frank Zane would shoot bow and arrow on Sundays. He also loved guns. He would go to pistol range and let off

some steam I suppose. He came up to San Francisco, he and I were guest posing in the same show at the Mr. USA. We both went to the gun range and shot for two rounds, and then we saw the movie Taxi Driver, which starred Robert Deniro. Great movie. People always told him that he couldn't speak English very well, and he had this accent. But Arnold would tell me, "I'll smile all the way to the bank." And he did. Not only as an actor, but as a director as well.

Did you continue to see Arnold when he became a star in the mid-1980s, and how did you keep in touch?
Ed Corney: He came to Fremont to do The Terminator. Of course, the movie people were up all night and I'm asleep. And in the day, I'm working and he's asleep. So we missed each other more or less. I never used his fame to further myself. He called me not long ago, "Eddie, it's Arnold, your training partner, 1975, remember?" I said, "Of course I remember." We chatted back and forth. I always go to his Arnold Classic bodybuilding show. And he comes over to my table, we'll shake hands, and he'll say, "Eddie, what is this? You're still in shape!" Only because I've kept on training. Then he'll hit a couple of pauses, and I tell him, "If I can help you in anything, let me know." As if I could. Arnold put bodybuilding on the map. His charisma, his focus, his everything was bodybuilding then. He did quite a bit for bodybuilding - an awful lot. He made people notice bodybuilding.

In 1972, you went to Baghdad to compete in the Mr. Universe show, did Arnold accompany you?
Ed Corney: Mr. Universe. Arnold didn't make it to that one. Well, there were three thousand people at the show, and another two thousand couldn't get in. Me being from Hawaii and an ethnic group, I looked like an Iraqi. Dark skinned. But, you know, there was no music for the competition; you just had to be prepared. Of course, Mike Katz won the tall class and I won the medium class and a kid from Japan won the short class. Then I won the overall. Of course, when I won the overall everyone thought I was God. "Ed Corney! Ed Corney! Ed Corney!" They all wanted to touch me and shake my hands and take pictures and what not. It was tremendous.

What were Arnold's attributes, his strong points and body parts as a bodybuilder which inspired the observer to look on with goading awe?
Ed Corney: His strong points were: learn how to act with people; he was a people's person. Of course, he was also a businessman. Shrewdness, I guess you might say he knew how to be a businessman. He knew what he had to do. He came over here from Austria, spoke no

English, so what does he do? He takes English-speaking classes. Doesn't know how to act, so what does he do? He takes acting classes. That was Arnold. His strongest body parts were everything. Tying in with the legs with the calves, everything tied in. He had no favorite, but you exercise all of them. Your favorite body parts would be all of them. In other words, he would train his calves just as hard as he would train his back. So he had everything together.

Did you and Arnold do any cardio in those days, and if so what type - running, jogging?
Ed Corney: Cardio by increasing the reps and the time you rest in between the sets. That was our type of cardio. I started later to jog, when I moved back to Santa Monica again living with Danny Padilla. This is interesting, because our diet was, compared to today's standards, it was nothing. We had beef steak, napkin, green vegetables, egg whites, tuna. We were just using ourselves as guinea pigs, finding out what is good to eat to get a better physique. Arnold's favorite food was cheesecake; he introduced the cheesecake to me. Once we were up in San Francisco, before the Olympia was coming up, and we're having dinner. And Joe Weider is there and everyone else. Arnold said, "Eddie, order two cheesecakes." I did. Everybody is looking and they're saying, "Hey, they're eating cheesecakes!" Of course, cheesecakes are very good for you, but on the day it's got calories, which is good for energy.

He phoned me a while back, and we spoke on the phone. Then after that in Sacramento he called me. Some people wanted to do an interview with me. When Arnold and I spoke, we kept the recording machine on. So when the channel called me, they said they wanted to do an interview. I said OK. They came here 6.30 in the morning. I've got pictures on the wall of Arnold and myself. The TV people asked, "Do you know Arnold?!" I said yes. I pressed the recording machine and his voice came on. Meanwhile, my daughter is downstairs watching me on a big TV, watching my interview. I've always supported him. I'll always support Arnold regardless of what people say or do, even when everybody's pointing a finger at him. He can't please everyone, he's his own person - that's what I am. I'm my own man, don't mean to step on other people's toes or anything like that. But Ed Corney is Ed Corney because of Ed Corney, not because of anyone else.

BILL PEARL

Bill Pearl, born October 31, 1930, is one of the greatest bodybuilding legends, who, at his peak in the 1950s and 1960s, won many bodybuilding titles, including the prestige Mr. Universe title five times. Pearl is a well-liked down-to-earth gentleman.

Bill, you were a prominent bodybuilding champion and star before Arnold came on the scene. Can you please tell me when you and Arnold met for the first time?

Bill Pearl: Yes. I met Arnold in Frankfurt, Germany, and I believe he was eighteen years old. I had just entered and competed in the Mr. Universe contest. I don't remember the exact time, it might be 1965. I guess it was. I was giving an exhibition in Frankfurt, and Arnold and Franco Columbu came to watch the exhibition. Well, it wasn't so much the exhibition, it was my impression of Arnold. He could not speak English, but it was obvious that by looking at him that he was very enthusiastic in the bodybuilding world. There's no question that Arnold was going to rise to the top as he did, and it was just obvious that he was a young kid who wanted to get ahead, that's there all was to it. And whatever it took to get there, he was willing to do it.

Arnold has countless times expressed that it was his biggest dream to go over to America and train with the American bodybuilders. California was the Mecca of bodybuilding.

Bill Pearl: I think Arnold was smart, because the magazines - Joe Weider's magazines, Strength & Health magazines so on - if he wanted to ever get in them, it meant more publicity. So whatever he could do in Germany or Austria, he probably had to come over to America to do this, because that's where the sport was more popular. And if he was going to get any type of notoriety at all, it was about coming and competing in the United States and being with the best we had. This was going to take him where he wanted to go.

Did you see Arnold in America when he arrived in the late 1960s virtually penniless?

Bill Pearl: Yes. When Arnold first came to the United States, I remember him very well. I had a health club in Pasadena, California, at the time and Arnold used to drop by. He and Franco Columbu were just like brothers; you could not separate the two. They would come and visit us at the club in Pasadena. I was away from the Santa Monica Beach area; he preferred to train down in Santa Monica and be with the guys that trained there. He did train at our health club, but he was never a member of my health club. But even back then, Arnold was smart enough to surround himself around the hardcore bodybuilders that we had in the United States at the time. But he was also smarter, and he immediately enrolled in college and continued to advance his education, which I think is the smartest thing he could've done. I saw Arnold on Muscle Beach, but I didn't spend a lot of time on Muscle Beach, because it was not what I was interested in back then. I lived in a different part of California than him. I might go down to Muscle Beach as a fun thing to do, but I did not hang around Muscle Beach. I did not do that.

Other than Reg Park, who Arnold wanted to emulate and adulated, which other bodybuilders did he admire?
Bill Pearl: I think Reg Park was his mentor by far, and he spent time with Reg Park in South Africa after he won the Mr. Universe competition. Reg was a very nice guy, and I'm sure that he maybe turned out to be like a father image to Arnold. I don't know for sure, but I assume this was the case. Arnold went to Santa Monica and trained at Gold's Gym and World Gym, and he hung around with the top athletes there who wanted to do exactly what he was attempting to do. He could just go to a health club and say, "If I'm going to get to the top, I'm going to have to beat these guys to have to do that." And that's what he did.

Reg Park had a profound influence on Arnold, both men became close friends. Arnold was humble enough to express the admiration he had for his mentor long after he became the most famous bodybuilder in history. Arnold recalled, "I was fortunate that he became kind of a mentor to me, became an idol, a hero, a motivating force that motivated me to go to the gym every day, four hours a day. And also have a vision of becoming the world champion in bodybuilding, all because what I read in the magazine. Then, of course, I bought all the magazines, every muscle magazine, read everything about Reg. I was not interested in any of the other guys, if it was Steve Reeves or anyone else; it was Reg Park, that was what I was focusing on."

Competing in 1967 at the NABBA Amateur Mr. Universe, did you actually compete with Arnold and do you have any backstage stories?

Bill Pearl: OK. That was the 1967 Mr. Universe contest. I won the professional class and I got all the votes, and Arnold won the amateur class and he got all the votes. He and I walked onstage together, only I was a professional Mr. Universe winner and he was an Amateur Mr. Universe winner. I rather not get into all that stuff, because I want to keep everything.... Arnold was the type of a person, and he's probably still that type of a person, he's going to win something no matter how he does, that's it, period. So Arnold had an attitude, perhaps still has an attitude, that if you're going to beat him you're going to have to take everything you possibly can to put that guy on the ground - that's all there's to it. He was out to win. There were times backstage where he showed this, but he was never in a position where he did this with me, and I don't know whether he would have done. Maybe out of respect, I don't know.

Can you tell me in those days what the fans were like who attended physique shows compared to the fans in the modern era?
Bill Pearl: That's a very good question. Back then everybody who was onstage was a champion. Regardless of if you won the contest or you did not win the contest. If you are on the stage with the caliber of physiques of Arnold Schwarzenegger or Franco Columbu or Frank Zane or Reg Park, whoever it was, if you were onstage competing you, too, were equally a champion. You may not have been a top champion, but you were a champion. Once, for example, I was talking to Larry Scott on the telephone and he had gone to the Mr. Olympia contest in Las Vegas, and I asked Larry Scott, "Larry, other than J. Cutler, can you tell me of the name of one person who was in the contest other than J. Cutler?" Larry Scott said, "No. I cannot." So, the comment I'm making is: where are all the champions? Who's taking all the champions? Who out there now is taking the champions' places? There's nobody, period!

Arnold mainly trained at Gold's Gym, didn't he?
Bill Pearl: He trained at Gold's Gym, and he also trained at Vince Gironda's gym. Joe Gold, again, definitely became a father figure to Arnold. He felt very comfortable there. The group that was there was a very close, tight-knit family, nobody could just walk in there and get into that family. You had to be invited into that family. Of course, Arnold was there because of his physique, but also because of his demeanor.

Arnold had a great sense of humor and joked around a lot, didn't he? Is there anything you would like to share with me?
Bill Pearl: Nothing I would like to share with you. Arnold could be very, very funny, but he could also be very cruel. When we're talking

about anecdotes and so on, Arnold could be extremely funny at times, but he could also be very funny at other people's expense. I'm not doing anything in the world to demean him in any respect, way, shape or form. If you're talking about Arnold as a person, he joked sometimes at other people's expense, which I did not like.

Did you socialize with Arnold often?
Bill Pearl: I socialized with Arnold, but it wasn't on a business basis and not on a friend basis. I could never consider Arnold a close friend, and I don't think he could consider me a close friend. We were people in the industry who had respect for one another, but we did not run in the same circles. We never had conversations about business. I never talked to him about my weight training, he never talked to me about his weight training. It was obvious what he was doing was good for him, and it was obvious what I was doing was good for me. There were certain things we did, but there was no sense in discussing them, because I wasn't going to change his attitude and he wasn't going to change mine.

Apart from the 1967 Mr. Universe, did you both compete with each other again?
Bill Pearl: In 1971, when I won my last Mr. Universe contest, Arnold made a challenge to me in Weider's magazine on several occasions, that people such as myself who were former champions, we were afraid. He wanted to compete against people such as myself in his contest. So he gave a challenge for all of us, anybody, you know - he wants to be top draw - that's it. He wanted to knock everybody off - that was it. So he made a challenge for me to compete against him in the 1971 Mr. Universe contest in London, England. I trained for the contest, and a week before the contest Arnold backed down. He claims that, I'm not saying this isn't true, he did not compete in the contest because he had a contract with Weider, and he was so popular in Weider's magazines and there was so much publicity in the magazines that if I had beaten him in that contest it would've destroyed Weider's comments he had on Arnold in his magazines. So Weider would not allow Arnold to do that, because of the monetary factors more than anything.

You have to remember that when we were at the contests and so on, there were tremendous amount of people involved. You laid a lot on the line, you're the world champion, the best that there are out there. And in the contest, these guys take this stuff very, very seriously, because it's their entire reputation. They're standing out there and putting it on the line. There was a whole lot of ethics going on. There was a common ground, because these were those guys whose whole lifetime work was put onstage there. It was all business.

The Weiders controlled bodybuilding in America, they did have a competitor, Bob Hoffman. How did you perceive Arnold and Joe Weider's relationship, it seems as though he felt Arnold was beholden to him?

Bill Pearl: You're talking about two different individuals, but I think in some respects, because Arnold was so powerful, psychologically powerful, that Weider was afraid of him. Hoffman couldn't overcome the Weiders; Hoffman was AAU and Weiders were IFBB. Weider totally controlled bodybuilding in the United States. He totally controlled the sport and Arnold was his top man. Arnold was able to get publicity when probably no other physique star at the time could get publicity. And getting in the movies, Pumping Iron and so on, it brought bodybuilding to the mainstream and Arnold Schwarzenegger's name became a household word. So, every time you thought about a bodybuilder, or talked about anybody who was onstage, Arnold Schwarzenegger's name is still in the United States a household name. So, Arnold brought the sport up. Probably from all the bodybuilders combined, Arnold's probably the most responsible for the publicity it got from the late '70s and early '90s.

You were inducted into the Pioneers of Fitness Hall of Fame in 1988, Arnold often was present at such events.

Bill Pearl: There probably aren't many Hall of Fames in the bodybuilding world which I've not been inducted into at one time or another. It's always nice to know that you are remembered, and giving interviews to such as yourself, who is willing to take the time to talk to me, this, too, is much a compliment as getting any achievement where I am. If I could still get people like you ask me questions and so on, that's the biggest compliment as any lifetime achievement award I've ever received. I'm laughing, because every Lifetime Achievement I've ever received, it was given to me by Arnold Schwarzenegger. I've always received it from him. Arnold was always the one passing on the trophy to me.

Did you bump into Arnold at the height of his movie career?

Bill Pearl: We did. One time he was doing a movie up in Oregon. I was living in the state of Oregon, just above California. He was shooting here, and he was kind enough to invite me to come on the set. But you had to be there on a Saturday, and he told me on a Friday, it was impossible for me to make a trip on short notice. I respect Arnold as much for his movies as his political campaign as I do for his bodybuilding field. He's an extremely well-rounded individual. And his entrepreneurship, I'm probably more impressed with that than any of his bodybuilding titles he ever had. He was an extremely good businessman and still is to this day.

49

Bodybuilding era of the 1950s and 1960s, can you differentiate between your generation and the modern-day bodybuilding scene?

Bill Pearl: I think most people in the '50s, '60s and '70s involved in the bodybuilding, they almost took it as if it was a religion, almost as if it was holistic. Today, I think it revolves around drug and money. I think the 1970s and so on, the modern-day bodybuilding as we know it today, Arnold probably brought more crave and notoriety to the sport of bodybuilding than anybody has in the last thirty, forty or fifty years. Even probably more than Joe Weider's magazines, simply because of his demeanor, and, like I say, Arnold Schwarzenegger is a household name, and I can think of very few people than him who have had the impact he has had. So, all the popularity for bodybuilding to this point, Arnold is probably responsible for a great deal of this.

"I don't care who wants to take steroids, because that's a personal choice...that's his life. Now, today everyone has them. I even saw in one of the big magazines that Arnold denies having used them, but Arnold was one of the first to bring steroids over to America. And everybody in the past used them: Zane, Columbu, myself, Arnold, Larry Scott, Harold Poole, Dave Draper and even Steve Reeves. There's no way to deny it," Sergio Oliva told Brian Johnston in an interview. Oliva says it wasn't much compared to what bodybuilders tend to consume today, and he himself used Decca and Dinabol, which was something big at the time.

When Arnold went into politics, do you feel it was an extension of him to reach further heights?

Bill Pearl: Yes, I do. And I think he had that plan even before he came to the United States, to tell you the truth. I think this was something he was talking about when he was a nineteen-year-old kid.

You were scheduled to judge at the 1980 Mr. Olympia in Sydney, and you also did commentary for TV. Arnold was expected to compete, but he then decided he wasn't. But he did compete, even though he had taken a myriad bodybuilding titles and had retired.

Bill Pearl: I can't tell you anything that he has told me, everything I tell you is hearsay. I heard from other people that he had no intention of competing, but when he found out who the judges were - there were several of the judges he personally was in business with - then he made his decision to compete. But he did not tell me this, but I'm telling you what other people have said. I'm reiterating what they said.

Arnold had his reasons for competing at the 1980 Mr. Olympia. When he was delving into politics, he reflected back on the controversial event, "I retired from bodybuilding in 1975, and I signed for a series of Conan movies. Here I was, a big studio behind you, a budget of $20 million, which, of course, in those days was the equivalent of $150 million. I was going to Australia to be a judge at the Mr. Olympia competition. Then all of a sudden, I thought I should compete. I think the competitors felt very disappointed, they felt: why would I do that? Why would I take that trophy away from them when I have everything else in place? So I think there was disappointment. And, you know, I just felt that's something I need to do. I felt very strongly about it, so I competed. So, now you apply that principle, in my political career."

One of the things surrounding the 1980 Mr. Olympia was there was some talk about changing the weight class. Can you tell me if you were present at the meeting, which took place where fifty other people were present?

Bill Pearl: That was Arnold's decision (weight class change), he wanted to have it. I'd say he's a very smart man, believe me, the guy's manipulative. I admire him for his tenacity. But he wanted to make some changes in the rules of the contest. But at that particular meeting, I was there. He actually almost had Mike Mentzer in tears! Just because the comments he had made and so on. Arnold just dominated that meeting, there's no question about it. Arnold was intimidating to the point where he belittled him to the point where Mike was just about ready to start to cry. I think Mike respected Arnold. And he was involved in the meeting. And the comments Arnold made, I can't tell you specifically what they were now, because it makes no difference to me, but to the point he hurt Mike Mentzer's feelings to the point that he nearly broke down.

The tension was unbelievable in that room, believe me. It was unbelievable. Boyer Coe is a tough guy, and he stood up to Arnold's tooth and nail. Boyer wasn't going to have any part of it at all. He's tough. Well, there's a difference between the height class and weight class. Arnold was making sure whatever he decided and what he wanted done was going to be more beneficial to him, let's put it that way. You've got to understand that Mike Mentzer was the editor of the magazine for Joe Weider, and Joe helped him with his posing. And Joe was telling him he was going to win for his...and so on. Mike was a very fragile person psychologically, almost too smart for his own good. He believed all of this pre-release publicity, which he was getting, and when it didn't pan out he was really devastated. He felt his entire bodybuilding career had gone down the tube, because he did not win that particular contest. So, everything he had done prior to that really made no difference to him, because he did not get the jewel and he did not reach that, and that's what broke the guy's heart.

Was Joe Weider present at the meeting, did he intervene to placate the situation?
Bill Pearl: Even though Joe and Ben were there, I don't think Joe probably uttered a word at that meeting at all. Joe was smart enough to keep himself out of that, because if there was going to be something that was going to go off, Joe wanted no part of it. So he was smart enough to keep his mouth shut.

You withdrew from the judging panel, because you had trained one of the competitors Chris Dickerson, is this true?
Bill Pearl: He trained for the contest up at our house here up in Oregon. I didn't feel it was fair for me to judge him. But all these other guys, Frank Zane, Boyer Coe, and all these guys didn't know Arnold was going to compete. But all of these guys are my friends, I didn't want to look bad for Chris, so I stepped off the judging panel because of that.

Onstage, some say Arnold wasn't in the best of shape. Which other bodybuilders were there who were in greater shape? Can you tell me about the strategy Arnold utilized onstage? Arnold would go forward, and as soon as the other competitors came forward, he would go back.
Bill Pearl: If I had placed him in the contest, I would have placed him fifth. Boyer was in really good condition, Chris Dickerson was in very good condition, of course. And all of those guys on the stage, Shamir, were in fabulous condition. Arnold was pushing and shoving on the stage like it was some type of a high school wrestling match - it was ridiculous. To the point where almost the judges lost control, because the guys onstage were pushing each other back and forth like a bunch of little kids. There, again, he was doing everything he possibly could to get attention that he wanted, not only from the judges but the audience as well. But he did that not just walking in front of somebody, but he would shove them and push them to the side like they meant nothing to anybody. I'm not trying to belittle Arnold. Like I mentioned before, he is...and I told him at the end of the contest that he was the most fierce competitor I had ever seen onstage.

Do you think one of the prime reasons for Arnold to come back to compete at the Mr. Olympia was he was going to start filming a Hollywood movie, and it would elevate his profile?

Bill Pearl: I think it was ego. Pure ego. I didn't even know the guy was going to be there, to tell you the truth.

He had told Frank Zane he was coming to Australia to do commentary for NBC. Frank wasn't too happy after the decision. When did Arnold broach that he was going to compete?

Bill Pearl: That was his reason to go over there, he claimed. But I think he decided to enter the contest the day before, when he saw who the judging panel was. And everybody was upset. In fact, when everybody was done we made a ruling where all of us got together. I was the head judge, but Weider and everything, in fact, there was ruling at the time that you had to let them know or announce if you were going to compete in the contest thirty days prior to the contest taking place. And the guy who was the head of the judging, I can't remember his name now, he's from England, he just let him slide into competing because he was Arnold. So he overruled the judging. Those guys trained so hard for the contest and they had so much to put on line, and most of those guys like Frank Zane were making their living from these contests, whereas Arnold wasn't doing this. So their whole reputations were on the line. So it was a very important thing for these guys. Not to have anything going on, that would not make them do what they felt they could possibly do. It's like putting your entire career on the line. That's what all those guys did, Frank, Chris, all of those guys, Boyer in particular - all of them. Arnold came in as a cold turkey almost taking the whole lot, they just couldn't understand it.

When the contest was over, it left a lot of people upset. Some fans were even booing after the contest. Critics may have concluded it was a foul stench permeated Arnold's decision to compete and win when he actually didn't deserve to.

Bill Pearl: They were booing and actually throwing the programs on the stage. I think when Arnold went up to get his trophy, he may have said something, but I can't recall. But he was virtually talking to an empty house, because everybody walked out of there like the contest didn't even take place. Almost all of the competitors that were there were going to boycott the Mr. Olympia contest in 1981. They decided that this was it, there is going to be no more, we're not going to put up with this. A lot of guys who were there at the contest decided there that they were not going to compete in 1981 because of what happened in 1980. After the contest, the following morning, he came up to my table and he made a comment. He said, "I hear you've been saying bad things about me." He came up to me and insulted me. I said, "Arnold, the only thing I've told anybody is you were the most fierce competitor that I've ever seen onstage." And he said, "OK, that's fine." And he walked off and that was it.

How would you sum up the 1980 Mr. Olympia, which has been the most controversial Mr. Olympia contest to date?
Bill Pearl: I can sum it up very simply: it was probably one of the poorest decisions Arnold made in his bodybuilding career to compete that night. He actually gained nothing from the contest at all by winning the contest. He probably had lost more esteem from winning the contest than if he had not competed.

BILL GRANT

Bill Grant, who won Mr. America in 1972 and Mr. World in 1974, became friends with Arnold which went beyond the confines of the gym. He is the president and owner of Grant Nutrition, a company based in New Jersey.

Bill, how and when did you meet Arnold?

Bill Grant: I met Arnold in 1969. I met him in North Hollywood in Vince's gym, which used to be on Ventura Boulevard. Arnold lived not too far from that gym, maybe a couple of blocks. That was all located in North Hollywood. I'll give you the rundown how that worked. Gold's Gym wasn't the top gym; Vince's gym was the big gym back in the days before World's opened up. All the big bodybuilders like Larry Scott, myself and Arnold trained there. All the up-and-coming guys were training at Vince's gym. He was called the "Guru" - he was the guy. Then some guys moved to Gold's Gym some years after, because Vince was a little strange. Vince trained a lot of the movie stars at that gym. I don't think Vince really wanted to deal with a lot of the bodybuilders anymore, so he took some strategically important equipment like the leg equipment, he took that out of the gym. Joe Gold at that time was building Gold's Gym, and everybody started gravitating to Gold's Gym. That's where we ended up going.

I could tell you a good story about Arnold training at Vince's gym in North Hollywood. A good friend of mine, Jerry Brainum - he's also a writer and nutritionist for Iron Man magazine - told me this story. And I told this story as well on Fox News. But I had to really confirm that story with Jerry before I told that story. He and Arnold were walking down a Boulevard one night and they were having a conversation. Arnold said, "Jerry, do you know who Steve Reeves is?" Everybody knew who Steve Reeves was. He says, "Jerry, one day they're going to be talking about me in the same light they talk about Steve Reeves." Jerry was kind of taken back and looked at him, and he says, "Yeah, right. OK." Then Arnold came over with another statement, he said, "Jerry, do you know the most fantastic thing of all? I'm going to be the biggest movie star in Hollywood." This is unbelievable!

Arnold told this story in 1969. I mean, I don't know whether he had a crystal ball in his hands, someone was reading him and telling him what was going to happen and figure out his future. But, anyway, Jerry laughed and said, "Yeah, Arnold, right. With the name Schwarzenegger? You can hardly speak English and you're a bodybuilder. Yeah, right, you're going to be the biggest star in Hollywood!" To this day, Jerry and I still laugh about that story, because as we all know, not only was Arnold the biggest bodybuilder in the world, but he's the biggest actor in the world. He married a Kennedy and he became the governor of California. And he's a billionaire. I mean, how much better can you live the American Dream.

Did you train with Arnold in Vince's gym or later in Santa Monica at Gold's?

Bill Grant: A little bit later on in Venice, that's where Gold's was originally based at. Arnold trained with quite a few guys. We trained a few times together, because we had different programs. Arnold had a different body type. But Arnold would train six days a week, and three of those days would be twice a day. That was pretty common in those days, if your body could handle it. I had such a fantastic metabolism that I really couldn't do it. Arnold would come on those days. On Monday he trained chest and back in the morning, and at night they would come back at late, and that was followed rest of the week. Tuesdays would be shoulders and arms, and Wednesday he would repeat Monday. And on Thursday he would repeat Tuesdays and so on. Arnold really was a very, very competitive person.

I can give you a real anecdote, a real story about what happened one time we were working out together. It's a great story. We were squatting this day. We agreed we'd do twelve reps. And that's the way it worked. I did sets and Arnold does his last set of twelve. And when I'm doing mine Arnold's counting. He says, "Ten, eleven, twelve, thirteen," and I put the bar down at thirteen. Arnold looks at me, and in his heavy accent he says, "Bill, what are you doing? You did thirteen reps!" I said, "Yeah." He said, "But we agreed we'd only do twelve reps." I said, "Yeah, but I did thirteen." I mean, he was pissed and he stormed off upstairs. And he said, "You'll never beat me again." I mean, you're talking about a competitive person! You can't even do one more rep with this guy! That's his whole life: Arnold was totally competitive, not only in bodybuilding but in business and in the movie business. Arnold had a drive that I don't think anyone had. He was a real driving force in the gym, and he had a real positive attitude.

He really didn't like it when people had negative things to say. He'd actually tell you to shut up - I don't want to hear it. But you really had to like Arnold for what he was doing. The guy was motivated. People thought everything was given to Arnold when he came to the United States. They thought Joe Weider gave him everything, that's far from the truth. Joe gave Arnold $100 a week. He paid for the apartment, of course, and a dumpy old Volkswagen to drive around in. That was in 1969. When he first came over, he did not dress well, you know. Arnold went to school at night, he had a job. He had two jobs. He worked with Franco and he was a carpenter. Arnold really did a lot, that's just the way he was, he was determined. I think he saw the advantages of being in America than most Americans did, you know. Sometimes you've got to be outside the store to kind of see how good things are inside. And we're inside looking out, so we don't really realize the opportunities that we have around. But Arnold saw that right away. I think Arnold had that plan when he first came. He seemed like a guy who had a lot of plans and he planned way ahead of time too.

I think he's somewhat of a humanitarian, and he really loves kids. Most people think it was all done for kids with the Special Olympics just to look good, but I can give you a good story about me thinking how genuinely he loves kids. I used to work for United Airlines. I want to make it clear to people: most people thought all of us bodybuilders back in the days didn't have jobs, and that Joe Weider gave us money. No. I had a job. I used to work for United Airlines for ten years. At one point, I took my kids to the gym one day and I had a meeting at United that day. I forgot that I had a meeting, and I bought my kids to the gym. It was time to go to the meeting but I couldn't take my kids. I'm looking around the gym and saying to myself, oh, my God, who's going to watch my small kids while I go to the meeting?

I'm looking around the gym. I'm psyching everybody up and I get to Arnold. I kind of sheepishly walk up to Arnold. I said, "Arnold, I've got a meeting at the airport. I can't take my kids. Do you think you can help me out here and watch my kids for a couple of hours?" There were three boys. Wow, Arnold says, "Don't worry about it. I do it." I'm worried shitless! I'm worried! I'm thinking, oh, my God, what's my wife going to say if he loses my three kids? Anyway, fast forward to a long story short. I get back and I say, "How did everything go, Arnold?" My kids say, "Oh, Dad, it was great! Arnold took us to the beach. He took us to McDonalds. We had hamburgers and ice cream. He was great! We had a lot of fun!"

I thought I was going to faint, man. He did a great job with those kids. That right there told me that Arnold really has some kind of feeling for kids. He really played well with those kids. To me, Arnold is a very rounded person. Of course, he's not perfect like everybody else. He can get angry with people, he can get mad, you know, and all those things. But I think all in all Arnold had a plan. Arnold was very interested in getting ahead, he saw the opportunity here and that's just the way it worked.

Can you relate any anecdotes in the gym?
Bill Grant: I think for Arnold, that was a great time in his life. I mean, it was the biggest thing that could happen to Arnold. Arnold was very good at playing tricks on people. He was a competitor; that's what competitors do. He had a little boyish, prankish thing about him as well. There's another story I can tell you. We were at the gym one night and we were finished training, and Ken Waller was there. Ken Waller was the manager of the gym at the time. So, a guy walks off the street, obviously, he was all whacked out, whatever he was doing. But he stumbled into the gym. He said he wanted to be a bodybuilder, and this was really funny. Arnold was standing and we were standing. Arnold said, "So, you want to be a bodybuilder, huh?" He says to Ken, "Ken, this guy wants to be a bodybuilder. Go get the oil." He says to the guy, "I'm going to teach you to pose now."

Ken Waller comes back with a can of motor oil. Can you imagine? Ken Waller opens it and Arnold says to the guy, "Open your hands," and tells him to wipe it all over his body. I mean, it was harmless, the oil wasn't going to hurt him. But he came in and he wanted to be a bodybuilder. I don't know why because he couldn't be. He put the oil and Arnold had him posing and screaming up and down. I was falling on the floor laughing. Arnold was really a jokester. He was very fun to be around. Again, like most professional athletes, you have fun, you have pranks on each other. He'd do all these things that athletes would do. Arnold loved to play jokes on people, and that was one that I just never forgot. It's like I'm still there looking at it as I tell you the story now.

Can you give me an example of how Arnold treated his friends, did he ever have a mercurial temperament?
Bill Grant: I left LA in about '70 or '71, then I came back for good in '72. So there were three years in between when I didn't see Arnold. We met up again in '72, when we kind of like hung out - that was great. Those were the good times. I was in South Africa in 1975 doing Pumping Iron. As you know, in 1975 there was a lot of apartheid going on in South Africa. Arnold, again, stepped up to the plate. It was really weird. I'll tell you that story and I'll tell you my story about me being there. The bodybuilders got on the bus, and they were told that the black guys could not get on the bus with the white guys. Arnold says, "If these guys don't get on the bus, we don't get on the bus. We're all athletes, we're all friends and competitors together. We all ride on the same bus

or we don't go at all." That's the kind of guy Arnold was, he stuck up for the other guys.

As far as I'm concerned, Reg Park, as you might know, was British, he was Hercules. He lived in Johannesburg. I stayed at his house for a week. As you know, if you were a person of color, there was no such thing as you going into a regular restaurant. I can remember Reg Park calling the restaurant owner and telling him that he was coming into the restaurant, but he had an unusual guest with him. He kind of had to let him know who I was. So, I got to the restaurant and it was really a scary feeling, especially for me. I walked into the restaurant and the place just got quiet. I remember it was '75, apartheid in South Africa and a black man going into a restaurant to eat which was all white. That did not fit well, but the owner graciously said it was OK. The caterers in the restaurant looked and they didn't like it at all. The workers from the kitchen would come out and look at me. People would walk past the window and look at me, because we were sitting near the window, and they looked in wondering, how did this black guy get in to eat when we can't go in there? I mean, that to me was great.

Reg Park didn't put up with that kind of crap. They even told him he couldn't have blacks working in his gym, but he actually told them, "You're full of crap because this is my business. I'll have whoever I want to work in my business and you can't tell me." Reg Park was totally against it. So, for me going to South Africa with all the other guys as an athlete doing the Mr. Olympia, on the hills of Pumping Iron, which everybody thought was going to be a great movie, we didn't know exactly what it was going to do, because it hadn't come out yet. But we knew there was something great about it, something great about Arnold. It was a great experience to go over there with the crew and Arnold and experience what we experienced.

Can you tell me more about the day of the competition?
Bill Grant: The Mr. Olympia thing was absolutely great. Arnold psyched out Louie quite good. It even showed in the movie, where Arnold's telling his father and Louie how he had told his mother that he had won the Mr. Olympia even though it hadn't even taken place. And he asked Louie, "What do you think about that, Louie?" And Louie got very nervous. I think it totally freaked him out right away. Arnold, basically behind the scenes, backstage, was kind of quiet. He kept himself to himself and he pumped up. Arnold was a very focused person, he didn't joke a lot backstage and he was very kind of serious. He did all these things he had to do to get ready. He did like to play the mind game stuff. He always would try to trick people with that kind of stuff. But for some reason or another, I was kind of oblivious to that, but

it worked. But for Arnold, it's whatever it takes. You know, for athletes it's always a psyche-out game.

You're friends. Arnold would say, "Hey, we're friends in the gym and stuff, but when it comes to competition you're my enemy." It's like the same in football and basketball. You're the enemy now and we're fighting against each other. And Arnold would do anything he could to psyche out his opponents, and he was very successful at that. There's another big story most people probably don't know. Arnold was a commentator at one time after he had retired. I remember Frank Zane winning his third Mr. Olympia. As you know, I told you Arnold didn't like to lose. He really hates to lose, like a lot of athletes. He asked a question to Frank Zane, "How do you feel winning your third Mr. Olympia?" And it was really strange what came out of Frank's mouth. He said, "Well, Arnold, guess what, it felt just as good as when I beat you in the Mr. Universe." Wow! You should have seen Arnold's face. His mouth dropped open, like, you can just hear the words coming out of his mouth if he was going to say, "You asshole!" He didn't say it, though, but if it came out of his mouth that's what he would say.

They broke for a commercial and he was pretty upset. You see, most people didn't know, and you probably didn't know, that Frank Zane beat Arnold in Mr. Universe in Florida. When he first came (to America) Arnold wasn't really the greatest bodybuilder. He was smooth, he was bulky and he was big. Even Vince Gironda in all honesty never thought…he used to call him "German Sausage" at Vince's gym. He thought Arnold had no chance in the world as a bodybuilder. Let me tell you, most people had that kind of a view about Arnold. They thought he'd never be a great bodybuilder, let alone be a big actor. But Arnold proved everybody wrong, especially when becoming the governor. You don't have to like Arnold, but you have to respect this guy for what he's done in his life.

Literally, I always tell them, being an American, "He took all of our lunches." I mean, here's a guy who came over from another country, didn't know the law of the land, couldn't speak the language, didn't have a top education and look what he did. It only proves, again, that when you do come here the opportunities are here. Arnold saw them and he took advantage of them. Educational opportunities, the work opportunities, Arnold took the opportunity when it was there. Arnold didn't let any opportunity walk past him. He had some great advice from people. I understand he had a great advisor as far as property is concerned, a guy at the World Gym who was working there helped him out. That was great too. So, the respect is there for me with Arnold. I respect everything he's done. Whether I might disagree with anything else, the respect is there wholeheartedly.

Another bodybuilder who worked out with Arnold was Dave Draper, who was Joe Weider's top star until Arnold came onto the scene. What can you tell me about Arnold's and Dave's relationship?

Bill Grant: That's a good question. Dave Draper is from where I'm from. Draper's from New Jersey, he's from Syracuse. He actually worked for Joe Weider in his warehouse in Union City. That's where I met Joe Weider when I was fifteen. It was on 801 Palisade Avenue in Union City. He worked there with Leroy Colbert and Harold Poole, they worked in the warehouse. Leroy Colbert ran the warehouse and Harold Poole and Dave worked with him. Dave Draper was a great bodybuilder. Like Arnold, he was heavy when he started. Have you ever seen before pictures of Dave when he really got good? I remember Joe Weider, I remember at one point he said he was moving to California, and a couple of years they kept saying they were going. But what he did do was he opened up an extension store on Fifth Street in Santa Monica, which was right up the street from the post office. And he sent Dave Draper out to California to run the store. It was just a small store. I still see that store there. It was like a warehouse store and a regular store to sell the products.

Dave Draper, as you know, they called him the "Blond Bomber". He was the guy Joe was pushing. Joe always had a few guys, he usually had one guy he really promoted and Dave Draper was that guy. I mean, he was a nice-looking guy, very pleasant to talk to and very pleasant to be around. A great personality but very quiet, though. But Dave Draper became a movie star! He was one of the next big movie stars as far as bodybuilders are concerned. He was in Don't Make Waves. He had his own television show. He was in commercials. He was in all the ads Joe had. He was on the cover of all the magazines. He was Mr. America, and, of course, he was Mr. Universe. Then Arnold came.

Dave, I've got to say, was a little bit shy, where Arnold was a little bit more outgoing. I think maybe that was the demise of Dave, why the career went down. Dave wasn't as outgoing, and I don't think Dave really liked all the lights, action and all the publicity you got as a movie star. I think in the beginning he thought it was great, but I think the pressure got to him and it was a little bit too much for him. But Arnold was the exact opposite. Arnold loved the camera. He loved the lights. He loved the attention. And Arnold became the next big star. I mean, he almost, like, took Dave's lunch too. They used to train together as well. But it wasn't anything malicious that Arnold was doing to him, Arnold was just a little bit more hungrier than Dave was and had more insight and foresight of what he wanted to do.

He loved acting. Like I told you, he told that story about how he was going to be the biggest star in Hollywood. That was one of his main focuses. He and Dave trained together, they were very good friends - to this day. I remember when Dave moved from LA, he opened up a couple of World Gyms in Santa Cruz, and Arnold went up to the grand opening. They got on really well. Arnold just became a bigger star. He was a little bit more aggressive maybe. He had a better plan whereas Dave was a little bit more shier. One thing led to another and Dave was out and Arnold was in, let's put it this way. I don't think there was anything malicious from Joe, that Joe would throw him out. If somebody would say that, then that's not the truth. Dave just kind of faded away, and Arnold was becoming a shining star and Arnold was the guy he pushed. I think Arnold is really the one that boosted those magazines. Let's put it this way: they both helped each other along the way. I think Arnold made the magazine and the magazine made Arnold. So, I think it was a nice marriage between Arnold and Joe Weider.

Dave Draper was great, because he actually set a tone for the magazine and started up and kick-started it and made it a great magazine, because he was one of the big players. And other guys came behind. It's like a movie, you have the stars of the movie and you have the cast and characters. Dave was the star and all the other guys surrounded him. It's like Arnold. Arnold was the star and we were the other cast and characters around him throughout the magazine, that's just the way it was. Dave is, to this day, a great guy. I've seen him a couple of years ago. He was down in LA and we all got the Muscle Beach Hall of Fame award. Hopefully, Arnold is going to accept this year. Those two guys really gelled together, they hung out together. There's a lot of pictures of them training together. They would go eat together. So, I would have to say, to this day, they're still good friends, it's just that Arnold became a bigger star than Dave. That doesn't make Dave anything less, but Arnold just got greater and greater.

What would be the most intriguing conversation you ever had with Arnold?

Bill Grant: I had a lot of respect for him and he had for me. But like I said, everybody doesn't agree on everything. Arnold and I had our bouts. We had a couple of disagreements and stuff, you know, it was all about competition. I was very competitive myself, I've got to say. So that maybe made mash heads a little. Sometimes when two people are really working on the same thing, something might mash heads and they might disagree on some things. Arnold and I had a couple of disagreements, and we had a falling out for a little bit. But it's OK. Things happen like that, but I have a lot of respect for Arnold and I think he has a lot for me.

I'm always at the Arnold Classic and they treat me like a star when

I'm there. I'm always talking to Arnold and he always takes the time. To show you the mutual respect we have for each other, at the Arnold Classic Arnold walks in the hall, he has a lot of security and he has certain areas he walks through. There's hundred and fifty thousand people that come to this place, and the place is huge. So, I can remember specifically. I have my own supplements company and we were pushing it at the show. Arnold is walking down the aisles. He wasn't slated to stop at my booth, the one I was at. I had a huge cutout, Fiaz, that you could see all over the hall. Arnold is walking down toward it. And all of a sudden, he walks in the booth I'm in. And the security is looking at him, like, what the hell is he doing? When he jumps in, he says, "This is fantastic. I saw the cutout yesterday and I've been looking for you, and here you are." I felt so great.

He came in and we had a chat and we talked. The security kind of realized, oh, OK, I guess he knows the guy. You know, speaking of the lights, maybe Dave Draper had a thing about that, but the glare of the lights and the cameras were absolutely incredible! The people that push up on you and take pictures. I mean, the place was like a sun had hit me in the face, with all the light bulbs. Arnold said let's go over there where your section is, so I can give you some publicity to promote yourself. Yeah, every time I see Arnold we get along very well. Backstage, he always takes the time to talk to me and we just talk about things going on. He asked me a lot of times how I'm doing and how my company's doing. I get along with Arnold very well. I mean, I can more than likely pick up the phone anytime I want and give him a call.

I think for me, maybe other guys don't think that, I think Arnold has been the prop for bodybuilding for many years. I think if it hadn't been for Arnold, bodybuilding would almost be dead. I'm serious. I think Arnold was the guy that absolutely kept bodybuilding in the mix. That is what I love. I really respect him for that part, because he still loves bodybuilding. You have to understand, when he was the governor they didn't want him to do the show anymore, you might not have heard of this. Because he was the governor of California. He told them no. Like he's always told me, "Bodybuilding is what got me here. This is who I am. I'm a bodybuilder." And he never stopped doing those shows. That, again, I have a lot of respect for him. Maybe a lot of other guys would have bowed down to that pressure if they were in the movie business and the governor. But he didn't listen to one word they said, he continued promoting the Arnold Classic for the whole time he was the governor.

Now that his governorship is over, he'll be promoting it business as usual. So, these are the things you have to respect Arnold for. He never tried to get around who he was; he always let everybody know that he was a bodybuilder first. A lot of guys would never even talk about that if they were doing movies, they would probably want to leave it behind, but not Arnold. That's the reason why he's at where he is today, because of bodybuilding. It's true. I mean, all of us who are doing something have gotten there because of the sport of bodybuilding.

Did he ever talk to you about growing up in Austria, or did he obviate the need for elucidating on this?
Bill Grant: He never really talked too much about that. He just told me that he trained in the gym with a couple of guys. I don't think Arnold talked to many people about his upbringing in Austria. I don't know much about it, only from what I've read. So I can't really interject on anything I don't know. Arnold really didn't talk to any of us about those things. I know he had a brother. I know his father was a police officer, and his mother, he lived in a small town called Graz. Those are the things I know. Other than that, I know Albert Busek. When Arnold moved to Germany, Albert Busek was a big friend and supporter of Arnold back then. Other than that, I really don't know. I wish I did but I don't.

Did you hang out with Arnold and Franco Columbu, who had close fraternal ties, in the 1970s when they were at the peak of their bodybuilding careers?
Bill Grant: Franco was, yes, a good friend of Arnold's. If you don't know, Arnold is the one who helped to get Franco over here. When he got here, he got Franco to come over. I can remember a scene with me, Arnold and Franco together. I remember one day Arnold asked me what I was doing after the workout. Like I said, I worked for United Airlines, but I happened to be off that day. It was on a Tuesday and I was off. I said, "Nothing, Arnold." He said, "Why don't you hang out. I'm going to do a photo shoot." I said, "OK, that's cool." We were doing some photos and Franco and I were sitting on his back. And I can tell you that that's the best thing that ever happened with me. I mean, Arnold said it was going to be a great photo shoot and it was going to be a great article. They've ran one of those photos of me and Franco sitting on his back for the last thirty-five years. The same photo in various magazines. It's been running back and forth.

When Arnold said it was going to be a great article, he wasn't lying. I mean, anything you get involved with Arnold, you know, it always goes in the right direction. It seems like Arnold has a rainbow over his head, man, whatever he touches turns to gold. If he says he's going to do something with you, it always works out well. I also did Friday Night Movie of the Week with Franco. It was called The Hustler of Muscle Beach. It was great, that was a fun time of working together. As you also know, Franco is a chiropractor practitioner at this point of time. Most of the guys would go to him as patients. Of course, as bodybuilders you get injuries so we would go to see Franco. But Franco was a great guy. Franco was a good cook, by the way, when Arnold and him were living together.

Arnold really helped him to get here, they worked together on the jobs. But they also were partners in work. They kind of took care of each other. Arnold took care of Franco and Franco took care of Arnold. They were real great friends. Today, they're still great friends. Those are the kind of stories that I like. Like, the same with me. I have friends from back in the days that I've known for forty-something years, that's what it's all about, this whole sport, making your relationships. Guys came from everywhere; nobody actually lived in California originally, by the way. Dave Draper and all of us guys came from elsewhere. I mean, I'm from Jersey; Ken Waller was from Kentucky; Arnold was from Germany; Danny Gable was from Iowa; Franco was from Sardinia; Dave Draper was from Jersey; Chris Dickerson was from New York.

So, as you can see, all the guys at the Gold's Gym were from somewhere else. If you wanted to be a great bodybuilder, you had to be in California. That's the way it worked at that particular time. In other words, if you wanted to be in the magazine you had to be there. Here's another thing that Arnold did. There's another bodybuilder named Tony Pearson. Now, this is how Arnold wanted to help everybody and make sure everybody got the publicity. Tony Pearson came to the gym, and we introduced Tony to Arnold and told him that he's just come in looking for publicity. You know what Arnold did? He said, "Don't worry about it. You finish the workout, we're going to take you up to Joe and introduce you." He did. He got him publicity in the magazine. Arnold was a better person than what a lot of people think he was. He thought about other people and he loved the sport. As you can see from the last story I told you, about the show with him about not bowing down to the powers who said you shouldn't be doing an event like this bodybuilding when you're the governor.

Arnold did the same: he had a very good feel about bodybuilders and he wanted bodybuilding to grow. And he thought all the guys who worked out hard should deserve some publicity in the magazine. He helped a lot of the guys and it was great. He helped Danny Gable. I remember the parties he had, one of the parties specifically. Because he and I had the most television experience out of the most guys in the beginning. He had a party one time at his house, this was in the '70s, this was when he bought his first house on Twenty-Third Street in Santa Monica. It was an apartment just a couple of blocks around the corner. That was his first investment in property. I was over there several times eating lunch with him. Like I said, we got along real well. For some reason we had the same kind of chemistry.

I was doing something he was doing - especially in the movie business. I was doing Toyota commercials. I was on every television show in Hollywood - Cher Show - it was great. I mean, all those things I did on the Cher Show were good. I also did a pilot with George Burns and Pat Boone. So Arnold and I were on the same kind of level. He would invite me to his house and we'd talk and have lunch together. He was just a genuine and nice person to be around. I liked talking to him. We'd talk about training, careers, where he wanted to go. After I left California, I came over here (New Jersey) some years ago. I own my nutrition company. That's why Arnold stopped by the booth that time to see me. He wanted to know how the nutrition company was going - Bill Grant Nutrition. There's a lot of things that came out of those relationships. I would like to call Arnold and discuss those things with him, it's great. Because he's always asked me what I'm doing, so I'd like to throw those things at him.

Arnold doesn't owe anybody anything, but I'm sure I can pick up the phone and call Arnold and have a conversation with him and get some advice on some of the projects I'm doing. All round I get on very well with Arnold. I don't know about the rest of the people. Arnold's a very motivated guy and he's a no-nonsense guy. I can give you another story. When Arnold tells a person something, say you're in the gym, Fiaz, and you want to know about working out. And Arnold sits down and takes the time and he tells you what you need to do. And if you don't do it and you come back and you ask him again, you know what he tells you? "Get lost." Because he already told you, he doesn't like repeating things over and over again, it just bothers him. And it's, like, once he explained it to you once, but you have to keep coming to him then you're not listening to him. He just walks away from it. I mean, it's, like, he doesn't want to keep repeating things over and over.

He's constantly moving forward. I would say Arnold has a five-year plan. He has a plan what he's going to do, then after that he'll move on to another project. Arnold is pretty methodical about what he does. As he continues his life, he's pretty methodical. He's a guy who's had his own in the movie business for thirty-five years. I can't believe it's that many years that have gone by.

I remember his first movie. You remember his first movie Hercules in New York? Well, I had a friend of mine, God rest his soul, who played in that movie also with Arnold. It was a very, very low-budget movie. If I really get a chance to talk to Arnold, I would love to tell Arnold that he should remix that movie, retool it and put it back out. I think a lot of people would love to see Arnold's first movie. I think maybe, I don't want to speak for him, in his mind he thinks it was such a bad movie and it wasn't that great that he doesn't want to show it. But everyone knows he's improved as an actor and he's much better. People would love to see the first film he was in. I think he will sell millions of dollars worth of that film. That's my opinion. I don't know what everybody else thinks of it, but that's my opinion. I think he'd do very well with that film and a lot of people would love to see it.

I remember doing his campaign, you know, he was having a lot of problems with this groping thing. I got a phone call one time at the gym. It was a guy on the phone, and he said, "Hi." I said, "Who is this?" He said, "I'm Arnold's campaign manager." I said, "What can I do for you?" He said, "Well, you know that groping problem Arnold had, Maria told me to call you. You might know what to do." I said, "I don't know what I could do, but I'll step up for him. I mean, I think Arnold's a great guy." I think they knew I had some contacts with the news media - I did. I was friends with Rita Cosby at Fox News. I immediately called her up and I said I'd like to go on.

She always wanted to put me on the show, but she had to have a hook. And that was the biggest hook that she could have. I said, "I'd really like to go on there and stick up for Arnold for all this crap that's going on with him. I'd like to say a few things about him. Why he's running for governor." I got on the air and I talked about that. I basically just talked about his meager beginnings. I wanted to kind of humanize Arnold a little. Wow. It's been a great ride being a bodybuilder, and meeting Arnold was just another plus in my life I think. I think the guy's doing all the right things, he's really a big backer of bodybuilding and he's never given up on the sport no matter what kind of controversies we have. He's still there. And he's the first one they're going to take a stab at, because he's Arnold and the most visible person.

MIKE KATZ

In the 1970s, Mike Katz was one of Arnold's close friends and training partners. Both men trained and socialized together. Katz also appeared in the Pumping Iron documentary. He competed in many bodybuilding events, including the IFBB Mr. Universe and Mr. Olympia several times.

Can you tell me when you first met Arnold?

Mike Katz: It was either '69 or '70. He had just got to Santa Monica from Austria; Weider brought him in. It's interesting that at that time many Americans, including myself, Dave Draper and Sergio Oliva, were kind of heroes of his, because of the media coverage we got from Joe Weider. So, when he got to this country, he asked Joe if he could get "Big" Mike to come to live in California during the summers, when I wasn't teaching in high school, and train with him. Which I did for four years. I think it was either 1969 or 1970, through making the movie Pumping Iron, which was 1975.

Training with Arnold, how would you describe your experiences training with him?

Mike Katz: I feel two of the reasons why Arnold was just enough better to have won as often as he did, and rarely was ever beaten, was because he had great genetics and he had a great will to win and belief in himself. He also knew how to train with the most up-to-date science that was available at that time, in the '70s. Now, again, things have come quite a bit further, and when you look at the bodies of the '70s compared to maybe, as an example, Cutler, Cutler isn't better; Cutler is bigger. Flex Wheeler would have been better, because he had all the beauty that we had in the '70s but was able to take his genetics a little bit further. Even though he was unfortunate that he never had emotionally what it took to win the Olympia five, six or seven times. His symmetry and genetics were great, he had the science and the nutrition information that somebody in 2000 would have which we didn't have back in the 1970s.

Arnold took his genetics and he took his will and positive approach, as well as training as perfectly as he could. He was like an artist or a musician that could strike the note and paint with the brush in reference to the way he trained. And those are the things I learned from him in the five years that we trained together. No negative attitude, you know, everybody's got genetic flaws, and we use the most appropriate nutritional and training perfection to perfect whatever weaknesses that we have. So, it was a pleasure. It was extremely difficult training as hard as anybody trains today. But very smart training, not just hard training. Not always heavy; sometimes light. Not always with much rest between sets. I think the things we did back in the '70s and late '60s, we were able to be at the forefront of what people are doing today.

And as I say to people today, who continue to make the same mistakes, even in 1970 we didn't rest! I mean, there was no sitting around like a powerlifter resting three minutes between sets. It was high-intensity training. It was cardiovascular necessary to almost be like a marathon runner to be able to get through these workouts. Because of the work load and the resistance that we used and the speed that we went from one exercise to another, we were able to get probably a four-hour workout done in an hour and a half.

What do you remember about the social moments with Arnold and hanging out with him, did he possess a sense of elatedness?
Mike Katz: He was just a great, fun-loving guy, and he still is today. Young boys grow up to be young men, who grow up to be older men, who never lose their boyhood. If they ever have such a time in their life, Arnold knows how to have a good time - he enjoys life. He did when we were kids, and I'm sure as an adult with his own children he has that same type of flair. Every time I go to Columbus and judge the Mr. Olympia during his Arnold weekend in Ohio, he doesn't forget his friends. He's loyal to the people who knew him when he could hardly speak English when he came over. He didn't have any money and was driving around in an old Volkswagen Beatle. And Maria wasn't there; it was just workouts and trying to beat Sergio in Mr. Olympia. And, obviously, becoming a star with Joe Weider in the magazine. So, when we enjoyed ourselves on the beach, in the restaurants that we went to and in the gym and at the contests, he was a real fun guy to be around with. Hopefully, now he doesn't have to worry about being governor or the political office. At present he could even light up a little bit and get back to some of his, as he calls it, "money business" that he enjoyed a lot when he was in private life, as opposed to a sort of public figure being in politics.

Arnold went to school to further his education when arriving in America, and his English was weak. Can you tell me more about him pursuing further education?

Mike Katz: Yeah. When he first came over here, he knew what he lacked. And it was not only convenient, it kind of was interesting how he became friendly with and developed a relationship with a girl named Barbara. She was a very attractive Southern California surfer-looking girl, who happened to be an English teacher. So he was able to, not only with his romantic involvement, and at the time he, obviously, loved her and, again, this was years before Maria came on the scene. I'm sure that Barbara helped him with his business and helped him with his English and some of the American ways - Southern California ways. I really don't know about the college and whatever degrees he got. I know he was studying going to business school, whether it was a college or UCLA in Southern California, I'm not sure. I think he could've done it without anybody. Without going to college, without the involvement with the girlfriend, who happened to be an English teacher. I think Arnold was so motivated and so self-disciplined that he would've learned it himself. But whatever help he could get along the way, it was to get him there quicker.

Barbara wasn't into bodybuilding at all, was she?

Mike Katz: No, no, no. I don't even know how they met. I just knew that at that time, back in the early '70s, that was his girlfriend for a while.

Did you travel with Arnold to guest pose at bodybuilding shows or events?

Mike Katz: Yes, we did a lot of different places. We went pretty much, you know, in the movie Pumping Iron, that exhibition which was in the beginning of the film was in Helio, Massachusetts, which is outside of Springfield, Massachusetts, which isn't far from Connecticut where I live. And the people who made Pumping Iron, Charles Gaines and George Butler, those two fellows did the book. And when Arnold came here, they got that done. They also did a lot of work with still pictures and movie pictures. When they decided to do the film Pumping Iron, they came back to Helio and I guest posed with Lou Ferrigno and Franco and Arnold there. I'm sure there's been other places we've posed together. I competed in Mexico and Arnold gave an exhibition there.

Obviously, in South Africa he was in the Olympia and I was in the Mr. Universe. So, we've been on the stage together. But I was never a pro. He retired for the first time in 1975, at the end of Pumping Iron. I was still an amateur, so I never directly competed against him. But when I won Mr. America, Dave Draper won Mr. World and Arnold won Mr. Olympia in 1970, and that was on the same stage on the same night. It had the World, the America and the Olympia all at the Brooklyn Academy of Music in New York. That was another time we appeared on the same stage.

What's the most intriguing conversation you had with Arnold that's left an enduring impression on you?
Mike Katz: I've mentioned this before, when I've been interviewed before, these are sort of excerpts from my life, my involvement with Arnold. When I had to make a choice to leave my family for a month or two to train with Arnold, it was difficult. Because my kids were - my son Michael was born in 1970 - and it was difficult to leave Connecticut and go three thousand miles to California. And teaching school, I wasn't making much money. Now, I leave my wife along with my son. I'm missing my son and I'm missing my wife. And instead of try to work a part-time job in Connecticut, when I wasn't teaching, I had to take summer off. I wasn't making any money, so I was writing articles for Joe Weider. But I wasn't getting paid in a timely fashion, and I didn't have enough money to buy my supplements.

I started to get kind of homesick and negative, because I just didn't have the money to continue to stay out there without Weider paying me in a timely fashion for the articles I was writing about myself on how I trained. So, Arnold saw this negative attitude in me, which he wasn't going to allow anybody to have around him for very long - to be negative - because you're going to drain him and drain his strength by complaining or acting negative. He doesn't want to be around people like that. That's why he continues to be so successful. So he said to me, "Don't worry about it, Mike. I'll go to the office in Woodland Hills and get you your money." He said, "But I don't want to hear any more whining. I never met a Jew who is a quitter."

Here is a guy whose father was in the Nazi Army in World War 2, and he's talking to a guy who's had almost his entire nationality and religious group annihilated by Hitler. And he's telling me the only reason Jewish people have been able to survive is because they didn't quit. They didn't give up regardless of the Holocaust, or anything else you would be reading between the lines of that statement. And that is something, since 1970, I will never forget. When I get down or depressed or negative, I always think about those words which Arnold said. He said he's never met a Jewish quitter and I'm not going to tolerate you acting this way. It was sort of, without getting slapped in the face, a verbal wakeup call that has worked well for me for the last forty years.

Arnold won the Mr. Olympia 1971 in Paris and again in 1972 in Germany. You weren't present at the show, but did he talk to you about these two contests?

Mike Katz: It's interesting that there is some footage of the show in Essen against Sergio. I have seen it. I just don't know who owns it. I'm sure if I've seen it, thousands of people have seen it. I know that film exists. It was not a fancy film; it was probably 8mm. It was probably filmed by a handheld camera. Like in the movie Pumping Iron, I think either (Danny) Padilla or (Ken) Waller had a little handheld camera that they were filming with when Ed Corney was doing his posing routines. So, those little movie cameras existed back in the '70s. Sergio did a most muscular pose and turned, they were both facing the judges. As I remember, Sergio really believed he was better. I think that if he was better it was simply because Arnold wasn't in the good shape he could've been in. But I think Sergio felt he was going to win the title back.

He turned away from the judges and turned directly to Arnold and hit a most muscular pose at Arnold. It was the first time I've ever seen Arnold not have a comeback, you know, verbally or facially. He had no comeback for that most muscular pose. As if to say, "What can I tell you? He's in shape." Now, whether Arnold believed he should've won, or gave him credit for being in great shape, what was on Arnold's face was priceless. Because I never saw him so dejected or looked sort of... maybe you would interpret the look different than me. Maybe Arnold would say you don't know what you're talking about.

I wasn't there, so from a 8mm film I can't tell you who was better, because you've got to go through the judging, and it didn't show any of that; it just showed Oliva hitting the most muscular pose totally disrespecting Arnold. And it didn't matter that they were in Essen, which is Arnold's backyard. I mean, obviously, if I wasn't in my best shape and I was looking for any means possible to win, you can't say it's not an advantage to me in my own country. Just like it would be a home game in soccer, or your hometown when you're fighting for the world championship, that the crowds and the officials are kind of going to give you an edge. So, it was a long time ago. My recollections are: Arnold didn't look happy about that most muscular pose that Sergio threw at him.

According to Sergio Oliva, "People are still talking about Essen '72. Even Arnold himself said that he didn't win, that it was nothing but politics...but they gave it to him. After the contest, Weider put the promoter out of the promotion business." The French bodybuilder Serge Nubret was also a prominent bodybuilding event promoter in the business. According to Oliva, Nubret also was put out of business by

Weider because he did not want to run events like Weider with the placing predetermined. Arnold has admitted he sometimes went too far in his quest for being number one. "Of course you were competitive. Of course when it came down to the pose off and when it came down to who brings the best body in on the day of the competition, yeah, I was the most competitive," Arnold recalled decades later. "But now since I'm wiser and older, I thought many times maybe I went a little overboard. But, you know, that's the way I did it then. That was my thinking process then. And, you know, you can't go back and change it, but sometimes I regret it...."

Sergio retired competing in the Olympia after that, didn't he?
Mike Katz: Possibly, he did. I don't know whether he went to another organization with Dan Lurie, or if he just got disgusted saying: you know what, Weider wants Arnold and that's how he's going to promote his products. And no matter what I do, I'm not going to win. I've served my purpose to Weider before Arnold came. Weider tried to get Draper to beat Sergio, but that wasn't going to happen. Obviously, he looked to see if I would be the one to win. Because if you had at the time, before Arnold was ever Arnold, a guy like Larry Scott, who was 6ft and 250, not 5ft 5 and 190 - if Larry Scott had ever been 6ft 2 and 250, 260, like myself and Arnold, it's interesting that he (Joe Weider) would have had the desire to continue Larry Scott. You wonder if Weider would've had the need to go halfway around the world to find Arnold to try to beat and compete against Sergio for marketing standpoint. It's just interesting.

I think anybody would've looked and said, "You know, who can I market my products best with?" And it's not always potentially who the best person is, that's why when you take a look at the covers of the magazines, they're not always the best guys on the cover. It's about the people who would buy your magazine, that's why the covers of the magazines have the people they have on them. So, Scott was too small; Draper wasn't good enough; I wasn't good enough genetically. So he had to go and find someone else. He, obviously, went to Europe. And it was smart for him, because he wasn't looking to reincarnate Reg Park, who was already great. Joe couldn't take any credit for building Reg, because Reg was Reg, and Bill (Pearl) was too old, he was coming to the end of his career. Chuck Sipes wasn't good enough. So who could've been good enough? There was no Flex Wheeler back then. If America had Flex Wheeler back then, Weider would have gone to Flex Wheeler and Arnold probably wouldn't have ever come here, and who knows where he'd be now.

So, it's all interesting to me. That's something I've not talked about before, because as I get older sometimes I think of things when you ask questions, you know. And, again, it's "would've, could've, should've". In America they call it a "Monday morning quarterback" - which means: if the game was on Sundays, you could talk all you want about Monday. Arnold got married, he was the governor and he's a billionaire and God bless him. It's just funny how the history is and the opportunities one has, and Arnold got the opportunities. And Flex got the opportunity, but Flex never cashed in on an opportunity to be seven, eight or nine times Mr. Olympia, because he just didn't have what Arnold had. So you've got to even commend Arnold more, because it wasn't that Arnold was the best, he made himself to be the best. He did whatever he needed to do to make sure he continued to be on top. You've got to admire that. I do, anyway. I admire the "I'm not going to lose" attitude. Everybody in the world could be a just little bit better if they believed a little bit more like Arnold.

Did Arnold talk to you about growing up as a youngster, what was life in Austria like for him?
Mike Katz: I'm sure that from what I read - I'm sure you read the same stories - he never talked to me and I never really got involved in psychologically wanting to know about the treatment of his father, mother and brother - I never got into that. I know that, whether it's true or not, I heard that he was kind of a hellion, which isn't bad, you know. I'm sure Switzerland and Austria are pretty conservative places, and you've got a teenager like Arnold. In Southern California it's perfect, but I don't know if it's perfect in Zurich or in Munich or Essen or Graz, where things are more conservative and people are much quieter. I mean, Arnold's personality, it's a good thing he came to Southern California, because I thought of many times that if he went to New York who knows. I mean, he could've got shot! Going to Southern California, everybody was doing their own thing and there were different religions on every street corner. It was love and peace, the Vietnam anti-war movement and different cultures.

Southern California was like a great place for a free-spirited person. I remember once when we were in a supermarket in Santa Monica, he didn't want to wait in line. Obviously, at the time he was pretty brash. We had a 15-pound roast from the butcher, and he shot-putted the 15-pound over the top of about six people's heads and it splattered down on the cash register, where you get checked out at the supermarket. There's about six to eight people in line. Arnold wasn't going to wait because he was hungry. He wanted to go home and cook the food. And the people said that's cool, no problem. Because they saw how big he was, he had the Austrian accent - the German accent - nobody was going to screw around with him. In New York if he did that he probably would've got shot. But in Southern California everybody was cool about it. It was one humorous story after another.

Can you culminate more on hanging out with Arnold in the 1970s?
Mike Katz: We were so tired because we'd train twice a day. Believe me we were so exhausted. One of the stories is that he never believed that my chest was as big as it was, he always made fun of me. Like, I have to relax, "You have to relax, Mike. Big Mike, relax." He would tell Franco, "Mike never relaxes, his chest is always sticking out of his clothes. He was always worried that the buttons on my shirt would pop his eye out. So whenever he came near me and saw my chest, he would always put his hands up to his eyes to make sure the button did not pop off and blind him. We were so tired from a morning workout, him and Franco lived together, we had lunch and then we took a nap. I found out later that he came over with Franco because they wanted to see if my chest would really go down if the buttons holding my shirt together would really relax - and they didn't! So he knew I wasn't holding my breath trying to make my chest look bigger, because when I was sleeping it was the same size. He said, "It's so much safer when you wear a tie." Because when I have a shirt and a tie, the buttons won't deflect off the tie and hit him on the eye. He was a character.

After Arnold initially pursued the movie industry, you kept up your friendship. Did he talk about the fame he was finally achieving beyond the confines of the bodybuilding world?
Mike Katz: He was in a movie called Stay Hungry. It only lasted about a week in the movie theaters. It was with Sally Fields and Jeff Bridges. And Sally Fields at that time was in a television show called The Flying Nun. Like a Nun in a Catholic church. It was kind of a goofy thing. The Nuns would wear something and she could fly. It was a cute show on television for years. But Sally Fields, who has become an Academy Award-winning actress, wanted to break out of the Flying Nun television character and become a movie star. And the first movie she made was with the famous Jeff Bridges, who later made True Grit, which was the John Wayne movie. John Wayne made that movie years ago and Jeff Bridges has recreated the film. So, he was a famous actor. There was a bodybuilding scene in the movie, and Arnold got his best friends to come down to Birmingham in Alabama for a week and film with him in the movie. So, he sure didn't forget us as his friends and hasn't forgotten us today as well. I got a card from him and Maria during the holidays.

Did you talk about religion, was he religious in any way, shape or form?

Mike Katz: No. No. I don't know if anything's ever been written about religion and Arnold, or a conversation he had about religion.

What do you remember when Arnold was on the brink of fame in Hollywood?

Mike Katz: I definitely remember when he did Conan. I guest posed at a contest in Canada in Victoria, it was a famous show and I think they still have it. Arnold was a guest poser and I was a guest poser. I can remember working out with Arnold and he was practicing the sword. Because in Conan he had to wield this big heavy gladiator-type sword when he was fighting. He was doing a lot of choreography work with this big sword when we were training. That film, Conan the Barbarian, at that time I was coming to the end of my career, in probably 1981 or '82. I guess it was '82 - Waller placed lower and I placed just a little bit higher than him. But I went in the contest and I had been drug tested to prove that I was drug free and that I could compete against the athletes who were not tested, and that was my motivation. I beat Waller and I got him back for the t-shirt incident in Pumping Iron. I retired in '82. My son was twelve years old, I had had enough of going around the world being away from my kids.

Having been a friend of Arnold's, what are some of the most significant memories that come to mind?

Mike Katz: I think anybody who is successful, I mean, who has been really successful in life, whether it's a teacher or doctor, an attorney or an athlete, success can come in many different forms. But what he possessed, which I've tried to possess - and why I think I've been somewhat successful - is I don't let negative feelings get the best of me and enter into me. I've got blinders like a racehorse. I've got tunnel vision and blinders on, and I'm focusing on what is important to me to attain. And whether one day I wanted to be an actor or a politician or a millionaire, billionaire, I've accomplished everything in my life that I wanted to accomplish. It's not, like, I'm ready to die, I've got grandchildren that I'd like to see grow up - three little granddaughters. But I rest easy in reference to what I've attained and what I've achieved and to thank Arnold for it. Again, I had some of the qualities because I played football professionally before I met Arnold. So I couldn't have become a professional football player at the highest level if I wasn't positive and not coachable and if I did not have a good attitude.

So, I had that at the beginning and Arnold helped to support me. And how I knew I could continue to stay successful and be able to achieve the dreams I had in my life. So, if people look at Arnold for those reasons, sort of like: he came in with no education, couldn't speak the language, and here he becomes world famous like Muhammad Ali, like the Pope or like any famous president. And the question here is: if he did it, then what's your excuse? Why aren't you doing it to some reasonable level? You're not going to be a billionaire. You won't marry a Kennedy. You may not make movies for $30 million a movie, or be a governor. But in your own way, you can be a better parent; you could be a better husband; you could be a better person in your workplace, if you have the qualities Arnold and successful people, I think, like us have got. That makes the whole world better, if people would just believe in that and listen to that.

AL SATTERWHITE

Al Satterwhite is a professional photographer who has photographed for some of the top mainstream magazines. He photographed Arnold on numerous occasions. He is the author of several books and lives in Los Angeles.

You photographed for some prominent magazines, including Life. How did you get the opportunity to shoot Arnold back in the 1970s?

Al Satterwhite: I met him in 1974. I think it was probably around June. I'm not sure of the exact month. I had an assignment, I think from a European magazine, to photograph him at Gold's Gym - in the original Gold's Gym. I went and met him and took a few pictures. It kind of expanded over a few weeks that I spent with him. I didn't know much about bodybuilding, anything at all, really. So it was new and different and really interesting for me. And I didn't know anything about Arnold at all, either. He hadn't done any films yet, so he wasn't very well known, didn't attract much attention anywhere he went other than he looked pretty much awesome.

But he was really nice and a gentle personable person. He was fun to be around with. He had a good sense of humor and didn't take himself too seriously, and it was a delight to be around him and photograph him. I would spend a day or two with him, then some time with the labs and then two or three more days with him. It was over a period of three or four weeks. Usually, you might shoot the same person for three or four different magazines, three or four or five different times. Time or Life magazine, they would call up, or through my agent, and assign me to shoot. So it was pretty much always assignments.

Did you photograph him on the Santa Monica Mountains?

Al Satterwhite: Yeah, I think it was up in the mountains, we went skeet shooting. One day, with him and a friend of his, whose name was Roger, he was Mr. USA, we went up there to do some skeet and maybe trap shooting also. Arnold had obviously done it before because he knew the people. They just had the best time. I think you can tell from the photographs, they're joking with each other - missed shots and the shots that they didn't make. It was kind of a fun afternoon.

When shooting Arnold, did you detect anything which reflected the way he posed for the camera - did he have specific posing routines?
Al Satterwhite: I don't think so. When he was working at Gold's, he had whatever methods he used. He went from one machine to the next machine and actually helped a few other people who were working out at the time, helped correct their form, or held the weights for them. And he would, obviously, look in the mirror and check his own posing. Then he would go back to working out again.

Can you recall the atmosphere when photographing him on Muscle Beach?
Al Satterwhite: Yeah, down in Venice at the boardwalk, where Muscle Beach is, they have a weights gym where the bodybuilders workout. And it's pretty open. Some people would stop by and watch. A lot of people, to them it was new and different. Depending on who was there and what they were doing, they would sit down and watch. One day, when we were out there - Arnold and I - he was working out on one of the pieces of equipment there, and another photographer was shooting pictures of him also. So Arnold kind of stopped what he was doing with me and he sort of posed for the other guy, gave him a couple of different poses and then went back to working out where I was photographing him. And the other photographer stayed around.

Arnold asked him to leave, but the guy kept shooting pictures. So he turned to him, and in his thick Austrian accent he said, "Do you want me to stick that camera up your ass?" So the guy turned around and left, and we kind of laughed about it and went back to working out and taking pictures. I mean, Arnold looked, at that time, certainly intimidating, but he was kind of like a pussycat. He wasn't really going to do anything to this guy; it was kind of a joke. Then probably an hour later, he was working out on another piece of equipment and this little girl came up to him. I don't remember what she said, but he stopped what he was doing because he just loves kids. He went over and he talked to her, and he flexed a muscle for her. And they had a conversation together, couple of moments in between working out.

When you were shooting at the Gold's Gym, did the gym attract people such as Hollywood personalities back in the days like it does today?
Al Satterwhite: No, I don't think so. Because it was kind of removed from the Hollywood area. And down in the Venice area, I never really saw any Hollywood types there; mostly people who were very serious about bodybuilding. They would support each other and help each other out with different pieces of equipment and whatever muscle groups they were working on at the time. I remember Roger Collard, who was Mr.

USA, he and Arnold were pretty good friends at the time and palled around together.

What was Arnold like on a social level, did you spend time hanging out?
Al Satterwhite: Yeah, sometimes after he would workout in the morning we would go to this Mexican restaurant which was nearby. And he would have either a late breakfast or an early lunch, and we kind of would sit there and talk. I remember I was asking him about bodybuilding, because I didn't really know anything about it. I don't really remember much in way of conversation, but it was pretty pleasant and easygoing. I went over to his apartment once, he had a business, where I guess he was advertising courses in the back of some of the bodybuilding magazines about how to work different parts of your body and different muscle groups. I don't remember how many different ones there were and whatever amounts he was asking for them.

He had a secretary who would come in and open up all the envelopes and then deposit all the money and send all the pamphlets out. So he was making money. And at the same time, he was investing it in real estate. When I met him, I think he owned one or two apartment buildings in Santa Monica. So, I got the idea very quick that Arnold was pretty smart - especially in business. He was not your average person, surely not your average bodybuilder. I guess most people think of bodybuilders as all muscle and no brain, he was pretty smart and you could see that right away.

What do you think were the misconceptions behind bodybuilding in the 1970s, it wasn't a widely exposed sport?
Al Satterwhite: I don't think many people knew about it at all. If they saw somebody who was built like Arnold, I mean, it was pretty impressive. I mean, I asked him once where he got his clothes from, and he said he had to have them made, because he couldn't fit into normal ones. His arms and legs were just huge! Most people, and I was among them, didn't know anything about bodybuilding. I didn't see any negativity at the time, and the movie (Pumping Iron), which I saw later, certainly helped up the bodybuilding. I mean, it showed - particularly on backstage - that one Arnold had a great sense of humor, and two a great ability to be able to psyche out his competition. He was brilliant at doing stuff like that.

What were his best qualities as a person, human being and a driven person?
Al Satterwhite: I got the feeling he knew what he was doing, and he

had a goal in mind and he was not just going to sit back and let nothing happen. He was very exceptional in that, just like ((Muhammad) Ali, they both had a total awareness of their abilities and they could push it much further than anybody else and go beyond just being a bodybuilder, but being a humanitarian and a person capable of doing other things, which they both pretty much proved. Arnold still has time to prove even more yet.

How would you sum up his personality overall?
Al Satterwhite: At that time, he had a great personality, he was fun to be with. He could carry on a conversation on pretty much any topic. Just an all-around guy. A lot more than you would expect. He had a pretty thick Austrian accent then, but he was certainly able to get ideas across and communicate in a great way. I think that's why he has got as far he has, even in politics, which was kind of a difficult field.

What is the most fascinating thing you ever saw him do?
Al Satterwhite: Obviously, it was impressive to watch him workout and lift weights, because I'm a guy who weighs 150 pounds, he could probably lift me easily. I think the thing which really got me about Arnold was his inner-play with other people, especially kids. He had an ability to touch anybody. He could talk to a guy in a suit, or he could talk to a little girl who just didn't know what he was all about, and that's kind of why everyone liked him. He was such an easygoing guy, who had a great sense of humor, a great sense of humanity. He never seemed to have any of this "I'm the greatest", or "I've won Mr. Olympia many times therefore I'm really somebody big" - that never ever came into any kind of play.

BILL DOBBINS

One of the most prominent bodybuilding journalists, Bill Dobbins worked closely with Arnold on several projects in the 1970s and 1980s, collaborating together on Arnold's Bodybuilding for Men and The New Encyclopedia of Modern Bodybuilding. Dobbins, who lives in Los Angeles, is a former editor of FLEX.

How did you get involved with Arnold?

Bill Dobbins: Well, I've known Arnold since 1975. I used to workout at the original Gold's Gym, the one which was in Pumping Iron. It was a very small place, and there were a lot of really famous bodybuilders there. I felt sometimes, like, if you've ever seen the cartoons, little creatures staring around the forest trying to avoid being stepped on by the dinosaurs, that's how I felt. Because there wasn't much room there, and I had to stay out of these guys way, because they would've kicked me out. But Arnold trained there, that's how I first got to know him. Later, I became the founding editor of FLEX magazine, and Arnold was looking for someone to do a book with him who knew something about training. Because his biographer, who was a very good writer, tried to do an exercise book with him but didn't really know much about training. So Joe Weider recommended me, and Arnold and I got together and did Bodybuilding for Men.

What were you both aiming at with this venture - commercial or culminate on the confounding factors surrounding the sport - because bodybuilding wasn't as big as today in those days?

Bill Dobbins: The principles of bodybuilding are the principles of bodybuilding, whether or not there's an audience of a thousand or a million. When we did Bodybuilding for Men, it was meant to be a general interest book. Something which was accessible to anyone who wanted to workout. But then Arnold decided that what he wanted to do was the definitive book for someone going to the gym. He described it to me: he wanted anybody from somebody going into the gym for the first time to the Mr. Olympia competitor to be able to look in the book and learn something. So, it was about a thousand pages of comprehensive information. There's two versions, the first version was really an attempt to create something which was really an encyclopedia. There was a book at the time out by Bill Pearl, which was the biggest book in bodybuilding that existed, it was more of a catalog. It was a catalog of training exercises; it didn't really explain very much. Arnold wanted something that was more comprehensive that explained more, and he used his own personal experience as possible to illustrate what was in the book.

Arnold said he made the sport more acceptable when he promoted bodybuilding in the mid-1970s. He told Playboy, "I didn't say the kind of things that put people off." In the old days, bodybuilders bragged about eating two pounds of meat and thirty eggs a day, and how they had to sleep twelve hours a day and abstained from sex and so on. "And I said to myself, 'Who the fuck wants to be part of that kind of sport?' First of all, it was not accurate. And second of all, if you want to make people join a particular activity, you have to make it pleasant-sounding." Coming to America had allowed Arnold to develop a discerning mind. He realized promoting bodybuilding was just like promoting anything else. He continues, "You make it fun. I talked about diet, but I said I eat cake and ice cream as well. I said I stay out nights and I have sex and do all the things that everyone says you shouldn't do. I said all you have to do is train three times a week for forty-five minutes to an hour and you will get in shape." It didn't take Arnold long to grasp the American shrewdness to promotion and marketing, skills he came to be recognized for.

Can you culminate on some of the photo shoots you did with Arnold?
Bill Dobbins: Honestly, although I've shot all the top male and female bodybuilders over twenty-five years, rarely ever did I shoot Arnold. When I got really active with the magazine, he had retired competing. So I wasn't shooting him competing. When we were putting the photos together for the book, mostly he used the pictures which had already been shot that were in file. And when he did do photo shoots, he didn't want me shooting; he wanted me writing. Because a thousand-page book is quite a lot of work. Of course, we did it twice. So I actually only shot on rare occasions. Although I observed many photo shoots. Arnold was a highly experienced guy doing photos. And if the photographer knew what he was doing, he'd have a great time shooting Arnold. If he didn't know what he was doing, Arnold would straighten him out.

Arnold learned a lot from Joe Weider pertaining to business and utilized his shrewdness in this area. Emboldened by his mentor's business approach, Arnold ventured into mail order business. Can we talk about the mail order business which Arnold ventured into?

Bill Dobbins: Joe and Arnold were sort of collaborators, to help and make each other very successful. I would have to say that there's a talent for business, just like there's a talent for bodybuilding - it's almost generic. I don't think anybody ever taught Arnold how to be a businessman as much as they just gave him examples to learn from. I'm sure that seeing how Joe Weider was able to use, for example, mail order in order to sell products influenced Arnold. Because I remember going up to his office quite late in his career, when he was already a famous movie star, and there was a section of a room set aside for mail ordering - his t-shirts and other things he was selling.

So, even when he was making millions as a movie star, he would continue to sell products, because that was part of his business. I think Arnold's always kind of moved on to be famous, but not abandon the things that he already had going. In the same way, when he became a movie star he didn't abandon bodybuilding, he still had the Arnold Classic and still contributed to the magazines. So, one thing I point out to people all the time is: if you have something successful going and you want to move on to something else, that doesn't mean you have to abandon what you already have going for you. You simply expand and include the old with the new.

Arnold and Joe's relationship included Arnold contributing to the magazines, what kind of a relationship would you say they had?

Bill Dobbins: Joe and Arnold had a very long relationship, it's taken up many, many different forms. I'm sure they had all sorts of trade agreements. I'm not aware of the exact deals that they made, but certainly there had been trade deals like that done. I'm sure there were other types of deals done. Joe had a very complex business, and Arnold grew into a very successful man. So, I'm sure their relationship was multifaceted.

Did you accompany Arnold to book signings and meeting the fans in the early days, when your first book came out?

Bill Dobbins: On our books, Arnold did very little on that. Arnold had a national audience through the TV talk shows. So Arnold wasn't a person to sit at the desk and sign his name. But he did go out and promote the book on television quite a lot. He's always been someone who could get on whatever television show he wanted to, and that's where the real mass audience is.

Any social moments that come to mind at Venice after training at the gym?

Bill Dobbins: There were times I traveled with Arnold, both on commercial aircraft and also I've flown on his private jet. The thing about Arnold is, whenever you go with Arnold it's always about Arnold, as you would expect. I think if you were dealing with any major star, everything centers around that person. I've sat with Arnold at his house and we've just talked about sports, or about anything else, just like regular people. But once you get out in any situation, Arnold is so much the center of attention, that sort of becomes what the whole thing's about. It's very difficult for Arnold to be in public to go through an airport, to be in a restaurant without attracting a great deal of attention. I've noticed that he's learned to walk through a crowd, walk through an airport and focus on where he's going and not paying any attention to people asking him things, or want things from him, or trying to talk to him. Because if he did he would never get anywhere. And Arnold is a very practical guy.

He learned early on that the only way to go somewhere in public is to just go. And I've seen other celebrities who have more problems with that. For example, Lenda Murray, who is eight-times Ms. Olympia, there's been a few times I was going with here at a contest and I would be in a hotel lobby and it would take her forty minutes to get across the hotel lobby. Because people keep wanting to talk to her. And I just had to accept the fact that Lenda's nature is she doesn't like to say no to anybody. And so I would just have to stand around waiting till she finally got clear, so we could go wherever we were supposed to go. But that didn't happen with Arnold. In the old days, he would just go and nowadays he has a lot of security people who make sure he goes. Otherwise Arnold would never get anything done.

You've mentioned you've sat with Arnold at his house. What kind of atmosphere was there in his private surroundings behind closed doors away from the public persona?
Bill Dobbins: I've known Arnold for a very long time, and he's gone through sort of major changes, sort of what he's like. When I first met him, he was kind of a brash young bodybuilder. He liked to shock people and liked to play practical jokes. He was very playful and outgoing. Then he became a major movie star. And as that went on for twenty years, he became more and more, how would you say, surrounded by that kind of a thing. He evolved, as everybody does, he got older for one thing. I mean, we're talking about long period of time. But when he was a major movie star, he was much more formal and not interested in as much shocking people and playing jokes and things like that. Now when he became a politician, he's also a father to teenage children, I just find it has mellowed him out tremendously. I find him easier to deal with now than ever before. As I say, he's matured, he's experienced and

he's also been in a job where not everybody he's dealing with is trying to kiss his ass.

Remember Arnold has always been the most famous guy in the room and everybody catering to him. When you are the governor of California, you've got a lot of people who are not trying to kiss your ass; they are opposed to what you are doing. I think because Arnold is so good at learning new things and he is, of course, older and he has teenage children and all of those things, I think he's kind of become a much more mellow personality. He's perhaps more aware of other people and other people's feelings and much better at dealing with them. As I say, Arnold learns things and he's learned to do this. I actually like him better now. I think having done his incredibly difficult job, being the governor of California, has allowed him to grow that much more.

What's the most compelling conversation Arnold had with you?
Bill Dobbins: I wrote an article called How Arnold Thinks for FLEX magazine, and I didn't show it to Arnold first; I just wrote it. A few months after that there was an event in Northern California, with Clint Eastwood, where Joe Weider and some other people were donating equipment to gyms that Clint Eastwood was putting together for young people. I went up for that and Arnold was there. And he came over to me, and he said, "I really liked that article you wrote. As a matter of fact, I sent it to Germany to be translated for the German magazines." He seemed to feel that I understood him pretty well. The things that I wrote in that was, for one thing that as big ego Arnold might seem to have, he's one of those people who thinks about himself all the time, but he's very confident in himself and he pays attention to other things. He's very effective, because he's paying attention to who people are, what they're like and what they want.

He's extremely good at deciding what he wants and then taking the steps to get what he wants. He's very practical and very realistic about that. As I say, he pays a lot of attention to who he is dealing with. He's very aware of what the circumstances and realities are, what's possible and what isn't. When he was a competitive bodybuilder, he would come in backstage, all these other bodybuilders were wrapped up into themselves. Arnold was looking around to see what was going on and how he could benefit from the situation. He had the confidence not to pay that much attention to what he's thinking and feeling, but looking to see what other people are thinking. As a result he was able to respond to a situation better and faster than the other bodybuilders, because they were all wrapped up in themselves.

Also, what Arnold has always done since I've known him is made pretty good amount of money. In the early days, when I dealt with him when he was making a lot of money, he just rented a place, he had a very nice car but it was an old Mercedes. He didn't spend a lot of money on himself. He's not really materialistic that way. He put his money into fine art, which is, by the way, one of the things he directly learned from Joe Weider - to invest in fine art. That's specifically something he learned from Joe. But he was also buying apartment buildings and shopping malls and things like that. Afterward he made so much money as a movie star that he was able to buy pretty much anything he wanted to, but he wasn't really ruled by these things. Arnold's not the sort of person who measures success by what he owns. He's not like Elton John, who just seems to like buying things. He buys what he wants but he's not ruled by it. He's not dominated by that.

So the other thing is, Arnold is like many really great athletes. He is highly intelligent without being terribly intellectual. Somebody once talked about Michael Schumacher, the Formula One champion, saying that he was smarter than anyone, but he wasn't lost in his own thoughts, he was feeling what the reality is of driving a Formula One race car. Arnold applies his intelligence to achieving whatever his goals are, he's not interested that much in thinking about thinking. He's not that interested in the kind of things I do, that sort of creative things such as writing and photography, whatever. He's got a more practical businessman's approach, or an athlete's approach. His attitude is: if he needs something like that he'll hire the right person to do it - which is why he hired me to write his books. He loves working with James Cameron. He used to talk about James Cameron all the time, as an example of someone he approved of. Because James Cameron, apparently, is just an incredible person who sets a goal and then goes on achieving it. That's, of course, what Arnold's like. So, not only did Arnold get to do The Terminator with Cameron, which he was very happy with, but he approved of him as an individual. Apparently he and Cameron have a lot in common.

Did you ever go to any of the movie sets to shoot pictures of Arnold?
Bill Dobbins: I think once or twice. Not very much. One thing Arnold is very good at is compartmentalizing. I noticed when I would go over to his house or office for a writing session, when he was involved in something, whatever it was, he'd have some materials, documents or whatever, he would very carefully put everything away. Put them in the folder, put them in the files and he would clear his desk. Then he would work with me. I noticed when I first met him, he would be in the gym and he would workout, he would totally focus on working out. Then when he left the gym and went somewhere else to do business, he would then turn his mind totally to that. A lot of the bodybuilders like thinking

about bodybuilding twenty-four hours a day, it's kind of always on their minds. Arnold would think about what he was doing now, and then he would move on and concentrate on the next thing.

When Arnold was working with me on books, I did a lot of writing with him for the magazines; occasionally I did photography. Each of these things, he would focus on. I never socialized with Arnold a great deal. That wasn't our relationship. But I was invited to his bachelor's party before he got married. So there have been some social occasions. But basically when he was working with me, he was focused on books. When he was making movies, he was focused on the movies. So, I would not automatically be included in that unless he wanted me to do some work on a movie set or some other place, and he would call me up and say, "I need you to come over and spend two hours." But it was work-related. I didn't hang out with Arnold. I was never entourage.

Arnold became an icon that most bodybuilders would aspire toward. Can you tell me about the fan mail he received at the pinnacle of his bodybuilding career?
Bill Dobbins: I really have no particular opinion on that. It was long time ago and I don't remember any discussions on that. As I say, when Arnold was dealing with me we focused on what we were doing. I just observed. And he did get a lot of fan mail and he did do a lot of mail order. But I can't tell you exactly what his reaction to it was. Occasionally, things would come up. For example, it didn't have to do with fan mail but his opinions on things. A few years ago, Sports Illustrated published a very derogatory article, and really bogus, about the fact that some bodybuilders had been involved in murder, specifically Bertil Fox. Of course, Bertil hadn't competed in twenty, twenty-five years when he committed murder. So it wasn't, like, he was active in bodybuilding. But this woman wrote an article in which she locked together two or three different situations in which bodybuilders had been involved in killings.

You're talking thousands of bodybuilders in over a period of over forty years, and they came up with two or three examples. I think if you were to survey British football, you'll find more people guilty of crimes than.... Arnold pointed out that if he was running bodybuilding, he would have public relations - he had publicists, he knew how that worked. He said he would have found out that Sports Illustrated was going to run that article. He would have had somebody putting pressure on them to keep it honest and make sure that the material was accurate. And he would have had counter articles and interviews done to protect the reputation of bodybuilding, because that was really distorted kind of accusations. Again, it's another example of Arnold being aware of what's going on in the world and having a very practical approach to how he would handle it. But, of course, he wasn't running bodybuilding. He was very dismissive of the fact that bodybuilding, on most levels, does not have the same sort of public relations that almost every other sport does. And to this day, they still don't. So, he is aware of those things. But about the fan letters, I can't tell you about.

What is your opinion on when Arnold pursued the movie industry, it helped put bodybuilding on the map attracting the attention of people in droves as well as putting the sport on a wider mainstream and global stage?
Bill Dobbins: It certainly publicized bodybuilding. I don't know how many tickets sold in the bodybuilding contests, but in terms of public awareness of bodybuilding, absolutely. I mean, if you look at every sport, when there has been a major superstar it's promoted the sport. Going back to Arnold Palmer, Billy Jean King, Bruce Lee in the martial arts. Bruce Lee is a perfect example. Bruce Lee was to this day the only major martial artist to universally become famous. Bruce Lee was famous in the '70s - still is famous today. He's a total icon. And Arnold's the same way. Tiger Woods was doing that for Golf until he ran into marital problems. The point is: an awful lot of kids have got into bodybuilding because of Arnold. I hear all the time that as soon as they got into bodybuilding, they bought The Encyclopedia of Bodybuilding and that was their Bible.

When I was the editor of FLX, when I worked at Muscle & Fitness, I've always been aware that when I'm writing something that there's some kid next Tuesday who is going to go in for a chest workout and he's going to be reading what I wrote. I have to try to tell him exactly what he needs to do, not just the facts, but enough to tell him the complete information. Remember if I give you three numbers of a five-number combination lock, I'm giving you accurate information, but I've not told you enough. So you have to be careful when you're writing "how to" stuff. You could tell somebody enough as well as just being accurate in what you do tell them. I'm very, very conscious about that. And Arnold was totally behind that - that was his attitude. He remembered when he was in the '60s, when he would go into a gym and he would need to know how to do a certain exercise. He wanted to really know how to do it. So the Encyclopaedia has really helped people in that way.

I've worked with Arnold on his columns for Muscle & Fitness and FLEX as well. It was the same thing: how do you tell people what they really, really need to know and something that would work for them? Not just do something that looks good but does really help. Anyway,

Arnold is by all means to bodybuilding what Bruce Lee was to martial arts. And the interesting thing is that in both these cases, you had people who were really deserving of that; they weren't just hype, they weren't creatures of publicity where you see that. In some cases, you see a lot of people who are known for martial arts and they're not martial artists. Someone like Jean Claude Van Damme, who was never a fighter. But Arnold was Mr. Olympia and he did dominate bodybuilding. He was a person who deserved to be an icon.

Do you feel bodybuilding became the core base which he used for his future success as a movie star and a successful businessman? In your own words, can you elaborate on this?

Bill Dobbins: I don't have to use my own words, Arnold has been very clear about this since the beginning. Arnold by nature is a very disciplined and structured person. When bodybuilding came along it suited him perfectly. Because to be successful in bodybuilding, you have to be very disciplined and very consistent. You have to have to get up and do the sort of same thing every day for years, and you have to learn to do things correctly. You have to learn what works and apply that, and frequently that amount of discipline is difficult. So you have to really focus on it. Arnold has always said that bodybuilding taught him how to focus and concentrate and how to develop personal discipline in order to achieve what he wanted. And he used exactly the same kind of discipline and concentration in each of the things he did throughout the rest of his life.

Again, by nature he is this kind of an organized disciplined person. I used to go over to Arnold's place and it always looked like the maid just left. You come over to my place, and you can see the last five things I've been working on, because they're spread out all over. With Arnold, you would walk in and you'd think the housekeeper just walked out the door, because the place is just perfect. He's very disciplined that way. Bodybuilding gave him the structure to really focus like this and learn how to put this in practice. He has always been adamant in interviews saying that the bodybuilding was the basis of the discipline he learned to apply to everything else he did.

When Bruce Lee first went to Hollywood, nobody wanted to talk to him. Nobody would believe this guy, martial artist, who was amazing, how could he possibly be of any interest to the mainstream public? And look what happened. You know his story, he had a very hard time being recognized. He had to be in The Green Hornet. You remember he was in a James Garner detective movie, Marlowe, in which he played a part. Can you imagine Bruce Lee losing control of himself and jumping off the balcony by accident (in the scene), that's pretty silly. When Arnold was first being taken around by the Pumping Iron people, nobody in Hollywood wanted to pay attention to him. He had a funny name, he was this big guy with an accent. He was in a detective movie about Philip Marlowe, in which he played a muscle guy, he played the guy who backed the gangster. His big scene was him taking off his shirt, showing his muscles and how big he was. He was in exactly the same situation like Bruce Lee, people like producers had no idea what his potential was. So Arnold and Bruce Lee have a lot in common that way.

JON JON PARK

Reg Park's son Jon Jon Park had the opportunity to develop a close friendship with Arnold, which can be traced as far back when the Austrian stayed at their home in South Africa. Today, Park is a gym owner in Los Angeles.

Before Arnold actually met your father, he wrote to him as a fan, because he fervently idolized him. Can you tell me how they met, which lead to a friendship ensuing?

Jon Jon Park: Yes. I believe the story goes, according to Arnold, that he walked into a magazine store in Austria in his hometown of Graz and there was a bodybuilding magazine, a Joe Weider bodybuilding magazine, and there was a picture of my dad on the cover. He was very intrigued. And he saw all my dad's Hercules movies. My dad had made five at the time, in early to mid-'60s. He decided to train and mold his physique on my dad. When I first met Arnold, I was ten - I'm fifty-three now - so it was forty-three years ago, when he first came to South Africa when he was nineteen. Actually, I was nine, so he's exactly ten years older than me. So, we're going back to 1967. What happened was, in 1966, it was the year after my dad won his third Mr. Universe, he was doing an exhibition in London. And the promoter of the show said to him, "There's a young kid here who's just won the Junior Mr. Europe, you're his idol and he wanted to meet you."

Of course, he introduced my dad to Arnold. And at that stage, my dad would bring the top star every year to South Africa to do a series of exhibitions. In South Africa, they would tour the country during the Christmas holidays, which was summer in South Africa. They would go to all the little towns and all the beaches, and they would have local contests in each venue. They would come there, and there would be Mr. South Africa in Johannesburg, where the star would do an exhibition at the end of the show. So, Arnold knew that my dad would bring these guys to South Africa every year, and he said to him, "When will you bring me to South Africa?" And my dad said, "Well, if you win the Mr. Universe I'll bring you." The following year he won the Mr. Universe in 1967. He came down during the Christmas time of that year and spent at least six weeks with our family in South Africa. That's pretty much how the relationship started.

Can you talk about the people Arnold was staying with in England - Dianne and Wag Bennett - back in the 1960s before he ventured out to America?

Jon Jon Park: Wag Bennett was actually the promoter of that show, where he introduced my dad and Arnold. I know that he was actually staying with them in their home at that time. There is a very famous picture in Arnold's book The Education of a Bodybuilder, and the picture has been published in numerous magazines over the years where he's wearing a tank top with a large letter W on it, which actually stood for Wag's gym. Because at the Bennetts' house in London, they had a gym there as well. The picture of him with the tank top and my dad talking to him, my dad's wearing a cardigan. I know that subsequent to that he went and stayed in the United Kingdom several times with Wag and Dianne Bennett, and he kept up his relationship even when he went to the States. So, I think Wag also helped him and saw that he had a lot of potential. So, when he came to South Africa he had a lot of potential, he was big and had a lot of muscle mass. But he didn't have much definition, but did get it later years. He was a little weak in his calf area. My dad was actually known for having phenomenal calves, and he said to Arnold, "If you get your calves up, you'll be the greatest bodybuilder in the world."

My dad always used to train first thing in the morning, because he was running four gyms at the time, so he would begin his workout before the day started. At five o' clock in the morning, he would go to wake Arnold up - every morning. Of course, Arnold wasn't accustomed to it at that stage. The first time he woke him up, Arnold said, "Where are we going?" My dad said, "We're going to workout." They used to train every morning at five o' clock. They would do calf raises up to 1,000 pounds, squatting early in the morning 450 to 500 pounds, which he wasn't used to. I think he learned a lot. I think the intensity of his workouts certainly increased, and he applied pretty much what he learned from my dad to his training principles. He said he wanted to be Mr. Universe. My dad said to him, "Well, don't go for just one Mr. Universe, but win as many as you can." And the rest is history, as they say.

When your dad was in England in around 1966, your dad and Arnold went around England guest posing and competing. Can you shed light on this, please?

Jon Jon Park: They weren't competing, because my dad was a professional and Arnold was still an amateur at that time. And when he came to South Africa, he had just won the Amateur Mr. Universe. Then he turned professional. I believe they may have done several exhibitions throughout the United Kingdom.

How did Arnold fit into the environment the first time he went over to South Africa?

Jon Jon Park: My dad brought Arnold out to South Africa several times to do exhibitions, and they kept up their friendship. And he would later be a guest at his show, Arnold Classic, in Columbus in Ohio. On numerous times, he was actually a master of ceremonies. The first time he came to South Africa, he could hardly speak a word of English. He was absorbing everything he could from my dad. I was a youngster at the time. We treated him like a family. Everywhere we went, we took him with us. I remember when he first arrived in South Africa; he arrived in a coastal town of Durban. My dad brought him back to the beach. He was really white, because he hadn't been exposed to the sunshine. Somebody asked him if he could take a picture of him, so he started posing at the beach. And the next thing, there was a crowd around like you can't believe.

They had local restaurants just next to the beach. The vendors walk up and down the beach selling soft drinks, sandwiches and hamburgers, that's how they make their money in the summertime. The beaches were crowded and there was a guy walking and shouting, "Cold drinks! Cold drinks!" Arnold could rarely understand English, he said to my dad, "What is this 'old drinkz'?" My dad said, "No, he's saying 'cold drinks'." Because here in America they call it "soft drink". He had the opportunity to come to South Africa in 1974 to do an exhibition. Then he came again in 1975 when he competed in Mr. Olympia, which my dad was the master of ceremonies. On both occasions he stayed in our home. He would go with the family to where we went - restaurants and the movies - it was great.

There was a time in South Africa in 1975, after he won the Mr. Olympia, there was my dad, there was Arnold, my mom's brother John Isaacs - who took my mom to meet my dad when they first met - he ended up becoming two-time Mr. Universe, there was Franco Columbu - Arnold's oldest and best friend - and Bill Grant from America, who was Mr. America and Mr. World, and they had been there to compete in the Mr. Olympia. There was a photographer, a long-time friend of Arnold's, one of his oldest friends called Albert Busek, they were all staying at our house at one time. My mom was cooking for these guys who had a huge appetite. Arnold loved her cooking, he actually said jokingly, "Come back to America and you can look after me and cook for me. I need to find a woman like you." He really became a part of the family. Then a number of years later, my sister came to the States for a while. And her and Arnold saw each other and dated each other for a while. So there's been a long-time family relationship. I don't see him much these days, but once in a while we bump into each other. But being the governor, he certainly had a lot on his plate.

Early stage of Arnold's career, in the late 1960s leading to his peak in the sport, did he effervescently have any conversations with your dad which reflected his desire to become a worldwide phenomenon?

Jon Jon Park: He set his goals. He said to my dad that after bodybuilding he really wanted to follow in his footsteps. He said he wanted to get into the movies. And, of course, when he came back to South Africa, a number of years later after having stayed in America for a number of years, he was completely different. He was polished, he was articulate and, you know, he had a full command of English. He was just more sophisticated and polished. He actually shared with my dad that he had a list of things he wished to accomplish, which he crossed off one by one. He wanted to get into the property business among other things.

My dad said many, many years ago that he felt Arnold would get into politics, long before Arnold even made it public. Arnold never even really discussed it with my dad, but my dad felt that it was going to be natural for him, because he was just so driven. In fact, my dad said he was the most driven person that he knew. He felt that his articulation and his drive would be natural for him to get into politics. In fact, when he was elected governor he called my dad in Johannesburg, and he said to him, "The first person to call me was Nelson Mandela." So, my dad said to him, "And who are you calling now?" He said, "Well, I'm calling you because that's where it all started." My dad was kidding around, they had a very good relationship. They respected each other. I think Arnold regarded him very much as a father figure. When he passed away, he made a speech, because he was his mentor and a father figure.

In 1970, he issued my dad a challenge to compete in the Mr. Universe in London. My dad actually had retired from bodybuilding competition, but he accepted Arnold's challenge. Arnold at that stage was living in California, sponsored by Joe Weider as a fulltime bodybuilder. My dad was running businesses. There was almost a twenty-year age gap between them two. But my dad accepted his challenge, and he beat my dad by half a point, which was quite an accomplishment. He said he wanted to give him the opportunity to compete against him and issued him the challenge. He was asked many times if it was great to compete with my dad when Arnold entered. He said, quite frankly, it wasn't really about ego, if it wasn't for him Arnold wouldn't have been an Arnold. Arnold made it clear on many occasions that he got into bodybuilding and was inspired by my dad.

When the 1975 Mr. Olympia in South Africa took place, a country where certain people were subjected to the vilest racial epithet possible, how big was bodybuilding in that country in those days?

Jon Jon Park: Well, at that stage bodybuilding was pretty big. I mean, my dad really put bodybuilding on the map in South Africa. By bringing the top stars over, which he did, people were able to keep up with the sport. The whole bodybuilding scene, and, of course, the magazines we had. So, Arnold established it in South Africa by being there, bodybuilding had certainly grown. So, when Arnold came out there in '74, he said he would like to hold the Mr. Olympia in South Africa. Arnold was very much liked by my dad and asked my dad to get involved in the master of ceremonies. And the Weiders asked Arnold to have a conversation with my dad. My dad wasn't really a Weider bodybuilder when he started off. After he won the Mr. Universe, there was a knock on his door. And the late Ben Weider was there, who ran the political side of the International Federation of Bodybuilders.

Ben came to my dad and said we'd like to sponsor you. It was to their advantage, which, obviously, they were very, very successful and it became the number-one federation in bodybuilding in the world today. They said they wanted to sponsor him. And he appeared in a lot of the magazines and different covers. He went to the States in early '50s, maybe '55 or '56, and worked for the Weiders for a while. But then they had a falling out through his late father. My father's late father felt he didn't need them (Weiders), and so my dad never really had anymore association with the IFBB. But fortunately, he did keep a friendship with the late Ben Weider, and I think it would've been a more positive effect on his career. But, you know, he was young, his father interfered - and Weider actually said that. But, anyway, my dad agreed to be the MC of the show in South Africa. At that stage, they had a 200-pound class weight and over 200-pound class weight. But also going as far as the movie Pumping Iron, they decided to make the movie.

Obviously, Arnold was the star of the show, but they (producers) wanted to set up a competitor thing between him and the up-and-coming Lou Ferrigno. Well, Lou was still very young, he also had a lot of potential like Arnold in his younger days. But he didn't have the polish and certainly wasn't as muscular. Arnold completely psyched him out onstage. He just wasn't polished to compete against Arnold, so he came second. Franco Columbu beat Serge Nubret in the under 200-pound class. Then they had the overall category afterward, which Arnold won and Franco came second. After that they just did the open-class weight, which is how it should be on the professional level. He won the Mr. Olympia for the sixth time and decided to retire. They made some movies with him later, one of it was Conan the Barbarian, which was his first proper movie. He had made one earlier in New York, which the Weiders pretty much set up, which was a bomb. It was called Hercules in New York. At the time, he couldn't speak English properly and the movie didn't do well.

Then he decided to make a comeback in 1980 for the Mr. Olympia. He was training very hard for the Conan movie, and he felt he was getting in good enough shape to compete against with whoever competed at the 1980 Mr. Olympia in Sydney, Australia. Many felt he didn't deserve to win it because of his condition, the judging was advanced, he was releasing more and more water from his physique. There was a guy called Chris Dickerson who came second. Some said he should've won. And finally he retired after that. He won seven Mr. Olympias.

At the 1975 Mr. Olympia, what was the atmosphere like at the show? Any backstage stories after or before the show which you would like to expatiate on?

Jon Jon Park: They also held it in combination with the Mr. Universe, which was held a day before. So a number of guys who had entered the Mr. Universe and who'd won competed in the Mr. Olympia as well. The whole city, which was Pretoria, was just taken over by these bodybuilders from all over the world. Unlike the Olympia today - it's just Mr. Olympia. Those days, it was Mr. Olympia and Mr. Universe in one venue within two days of each other. And they did that on several occasions I think. But that may have been the last one at the same venue. So, it was a wonderful atmosphere. Because those days, in the '70s, there was a lot more camaraderie with the bodybuilding than it is today. They don't have the same camaraderie (today). All of the guys used to train at the same gym at the same time and all supported one another. So the intensity in the gym was fantastic. There was just this atmosphere with all the top guys working out in the gym at the same time. But nowadays it's not like that at all anymore. It's almost like a bodybuilding expo so to speak. Then after the Mr. Olympia, Arnold stayed on in South Africa. And with my dad, certain venues that my dad had organized, they did certain shows around the country, Cape Town, Durban and back in Johannesburg in the end.

When Arnold's movie career started to prosper with the release of The Terminator and Commando - in the mid-1980s - can you relate any stories pertaining to your father visiting him in California and seeing him advance in a new career?

Jon Jon Park: Yes. My dad visited California on several occasions, because my mom's brother lived there. Then I immigrated to the States in 1985. As a result of me being here, my dad would come over quite regularly. Every time he came over, him and Arnold would meet up together. They would meet each other at the gym and eat together meals. They always kept in touch. I went to several of Arnold's premieres. The after parties were where the atmosphere was. I mean, here in America when they have a premiere they all go out. You get a choice of wonderful food, you see all the who's who walking around. And they give everybody when they leave a bag, which always has some goodies like a t-shirt and a cap, maybe some perfume for the ladies and cosmetic products. So, you know, they go all out. It's pretty exciting to go to these events and rub shoulders with all the top stars. I mean, anyone who is anyone in Hollywood, you see them there. Of course, Arnold was a very, very big box office, a huge box office, which I think was the platform for him to become the governor.

I wasn't sure what he would do after he left the governor's office. I thought perhaps he'd continue the movies, production side of it. I think he'll carry on running the Arnold Classic every year, because it's such a huge, huge thing. It's the biggest sporting festival in the world, a three-day event, barring, of course, the World Cup and the Olympics. But it certainly is up there, one of the big sports events, because it's not just bodybuilding that they have, but other fields you're involved in. They have mixed martial arts, they have wrist wrestling, powerlifting, weightlifting, you name it, it goes on and on. So, the whole city of Columbus is taken over for approximately three days. My dad did go on set when Arnold was doing Terminator 2, he spent a day with him on the set. Once I immigrated to the States, my dad and my mom would come over quite regularly. They were always the guests at the annual Arnold Classic. In 2001, he gave my dad the Lifetime Achievement Award at the Arnold Classic.

What's the most significant advice your dad gave Arnold?
Jon Jon Park: I think what Arnold learnt from my dad was the importance of his family. Because from my understanding, Arnold didn't grow up with a close family. Certainly not to the extent what my dad had with my mom, myself and my sister. I think he was very impressed that at the end of the day, there's a time where we all sit down as a family and we talk. My dad would ask my sister, how was your day at school? He'd ask me, how did you perform at the athletics? I was a competitor, so I used to workout every day. I think that left a mark and the importance of the family to Arnold.

Secondly, my dad emphasized to him, he said, "OK. Go and win the Mr. Universe. But instead of one, go win as many as you can. Do not just be satisfied with achieving a goal and stopping, but just keep going as long as you can." I think the third thing was, you have the sky as the limit. He said to him, "You can do anything you wanted to as long as you set your mind to it." Just with determination and hard work it all pays off. It certainly has. Getting back to the Arnold Classic, in this little town, Columbus, I think they get over three hundred to four hundred thousand people in two, three days - unbelievable. The whole city is taken over by bodybuilding, weight training, martial arts, fantastic effort, unbelievable. They have a huge expo. And the booths, there are over a thousand booths there.

Your father ran a number of gyms in those days as businesses. Do you feel Arnold's business acumen kicked in as soon as he moved to America?

Jon Jon Park: Most definitely. I think Arnold is a very, very shrewd businessman. One thing, the secret of success for people, and Arnold took advantage of this, is that they surround themselves with successful people - with the best. I mean, Joe Weider has a huge, huge art collection which he's had for many, many years. He taught Arnold an awful lot about the art business, which Arnold invested in. He got into the property business, he only chose the right people to be involved with. And he's worked with people, he's a very astute businessman, very calculated and he doesn't do anything without thinking. He just doesn't rush into it. With his head first, he makes calculated decisions, wise decisions with the right people, the right money people, the right property people, the right legal advice; all the best in these fields. That's how he became successful.

To be successful in anything, you've got to learn from the best in their fields, and he certainly has. I think his drive is really the thing; there are not many people with that drive. Being a politician is not an easy position, because not everyone is going to like you. But he seems to thrive on that power. Certain things which are challenging and certain goals he has, he's never left, he seemed to be very resilient, even if it doesn't go his way.

When Arnold became the number-one movie star in the world, did your dad and Arnold get together and exchange thoughts and stories about the movie industry?

Jon Jon Park: Mostly on an annual basis, once a year, and it was normally at the time of the Arnold Classic. My dad would come to Los Angeles, either before the event or after the event, and spend time with me and my family. He would see him in Los Angeles and in Columbus. Often times he'd invite us out to meals, when my parents were here, or to his home for meals. So, he always made a point of seeing him and spending time with him. When my dad passed away I was in South Africa. Arnold called our home. I told him that when I get back to America I want to hold a memorial. And he said to me, "Look, if there is anything your mom needs I want you to let me know. And I want you to see me as his second son." I told him I want to have a memorial service when I come back to the States, because my dad certainly knew a lot of people. He said, "I would like to host it." It was done at a hotel here in Santa Monica, and there were over five hundred people at the service.

Arnold got up and talked, people were really pleasantly surprised, because when he spoke there was no ego whatsoever; he was talking like he was the young kid meeting his idol for the first time. He was extremely humble. He basically spoke about his early experience with my dad, and how my dad had given him so much encouragement. He said he had called my dad in South Africa, and my dad had said, "How are you?" He said he was deflecting it off himself. He said he didn't only teach how to love, but he taught people how to die and that he died with dignity. He said if it wasn't for my dad, if it wasn't for Reg, he wouldn't be here today. That's a pretty much powerful statement coming from a guy in his position as the governor of California in a room of five hundred people. He left a big impression on everybody. To call my home and say to me, "I want your mom to think of me as a second son," I think that sums up his relationship he had with my dad and how he felt about my dad's family.

Arnold made a speech at Reg Park's memorial in December 2007 at the Fairmont Hotel in Santa Monica. With great veneration and gleefulness, Arnold reflected the magnitude of influence his idol had on him, "He has had an effect on millions and millions of people. I mean, we don't really know exactly how many people he has affected. But I'm just one of them, you know, the impact he had on. When I think back, when I was walking down in Graz in Austria on the street and I saw this store that sold jeans and different clothing - American clothing, all American stuff - and there was a muscle magazine - there was a few muscle magazines in there - and Reg Park was on the cover. And I was looking, and I looked at the slides if the photograph maybe appeared, but it didn't. It was a shot of him standing there with his hands on his waist, as Hercules! And it was (written) on there 'Reg Park: Mr Universe', and how he got into the movie business. And I was fascinated by that and bought the magazine and read it from front to the back. It was in German, and it inspired me so much to finally realize what I wanted to do in life. So it was because of that I started to do bodybuilding. I was fascinated by the stories inside, how Reg trained and all this."

CHAPTER TWO

FRIENDS AND COLLEAGUES

CHARLES GAINES

Charles Gaines, an author and journalist, was one of Arnold's closest friends. Gaines wrote the classic Pumping Iron book and the documentary of the same name - as well as Stay Hungry novel. Gaines' close friendship with Arnold allowed him to observe the man behind the legend.

How did the concept for the Pumping Iron book come about?
Charles Gaines: I had written my first book, which was a novel called Stay Hungry. And after the book came out, it was bought for a movie by a director named Bob Rafelson, a well-known American director. He directed Five Easy Pieces and lots of other fine films. Anyway, he bought the rights to Stay Hungry. Stay Hungry is a novel about bodybuilding, and in the novel there's a character - a main character - named Joe Santo. Bob and I started looking around for an actor who could play Joe Santo, but we just couldn't find any actors who were as big as they ought to be. In the meantime, I had been reading muscle magazines, because it was part of the research I was doing for Stay Hungry. And I kept seeing stories about this new Austrian who had just come over to America, who was Arnold Schwarzenegger, and how he sort of set the new gold standard for bodybuilding so forth. So I got curious about him in terms of whether or not he'd make a good possibility for Joe Santo.

So I got an article assignment from Sports Illustrated magazine to go down and write a story about a bodybuilding competition in Massachusetts, and they asked me to find a photographer to go down and photograph it. I had not met George Butler yet, but I talked to him on the phone. I called him up and asked him if he wanted to take pictures at this bodybuilding competition for this article I was writing. And he said yes. He came and we went. At this competition, which was called Mr. East Coast, we kept hearing about Arnold Schwarzenegger. One of the guys there who was in the competition knew him. We found it interesting, both George and me, so we got another magazine assignment for OUI magazine, which is now defunct in America, and went down to the Brooklyn Academy of Music for Schwarzenegger's second or third Mr. Universe competition.

At that competition, we met him and talked to him and we were impressed by him. I told him about the movie and my novel. I asked him if he was interested in being interviewed by Bob Rafelson. He said, "Yes, of course," and so forth. So, at that contest - Mr. Universe contest - I think it was 1970, '71, George and I both were really impressed with Arnold and thought he could be a big star if he was handled right. Anyway, we went back home and I went out to California to write the script for Stay Hungry with Rafelson. Arnold was living there. Bob had him come over to his house and interviewed him. Bob told me afterward, "No, I don't think so. He's too unpolished. I just don't think, unless he can learn to act." I kept on telling Bob he's perfect and that we should use him.

Anyway, to make a long story short, after about a month looking at and interviewing all kinds of Hollywood guys, minor actors who happened to be bodybuilders, we couldn't find anybody who was right. Bob decided to take a chance on Arnold and hired him. That movie was shot in 1973 or '74, in Alabama, and it starred Arnold. That was the first movie Arnold ever made, other than a movie called Hercules in New York, which was a little film which was not really good. Stay Hungry was the first legitimate movie that Arnold made. It starred Arnold, Jeff Bridges and Sally Fields, and it won a bunch of Golden Globe Awards. It's still sort of a cult classic, and Arnold did very well in it. It was directed by one of the truly great directors of the 20th century - great American directors. He did very well, he did well enough to win a Golden Globe for Best First Time Actor. And working with Sally Fields and Jeff Bridges, who were both pros, I think was a big help to him too.

Anyway, Bob came down to visit me when they were filming in Alabama. There was another guy down here, who's still a very good friend of mine, who lives in California. He was at that time a young entrepreneur who started a waterbed company, different things in California. He had some money and he was a little bit of a playboy. George had met him at Cannes. And this guy had expressed interest in producing a documentary movie about bodybuilding, which was a concept George and I had been talking about for some time. In the meantime, George and I went to an editor in New York named Dan Green, while we were actually filming Pumping Iron. We had been to my editor, the guy who had published Stay Hungry, a man named Sam Richardson, at Doubleday. We had gone to Sam Richardson and said we'd like to do a book on bodybuilding - a non-fiction book on bodybuilding.

He said my book had been quite successful and he wanted to have me stay with Doubleday. But he said, "I think it's a lousy idea. I don't think anybody will buy a book about bodybuilders." He said a lot of bodybuilders are homosexuals, you know. Bodybuilding at that point was not what it is now. It was considered as a sort of a sleazy occupation, and it was kind of under the overcoat of the society at that point. So not many people wanted to touch it. Anyway, we saw four or five publishers, but nobody would buy it. But we ran into another guy. My agent had given up, he had really given up trying to sell this book about bodybuilding, because nobody would do it. So, this guy that I met was an agent, and he said, "I like this idea. I'll take it on and I'll guarantee you I'll sell it for you." So George and I went to his office, and he got an appointment for us with Dan Green, who was at the time one of the top editors at Simon & Schuster.

Dan just saw it. He was one editor out of six, seven or eight that we had seen. He saw the book and said, "I think you might have something. I'll take a chance on it. I'll give you the money you need to fly around and do the research." So, that next summer, I guess it was the fall, right after the film Stay Hungry finished shooting, George and I took off and spent about five or six months on the road all over the place tracking bodybuilders. A lot of it was down in Santa Monica, California, Gold's Gym, and a lot of it was in European countries too. And we produced this book Pumping Iron, which was an immediate hit. George was a great photographer, and the photographs were wonderful.

A number of celebrities got behind it, and George had the foresight to hire a terrific public relations guy in New York and this guy really made a meal out of Pumping Iron. I mean, really took it to the next dimension and got all kinds of celebrities involved. So the book became a bestseller. In the meantime, we had been - George and I and this guy Jerome Gary - talking about making a film out of the book, loosely based on the book. So, when the book came out and was a success, it made it easier to raise the money that we needed to make the movie. George and Jerome were the two producers of the film, and it was their responsibility to raise the money. Between the two of them, they raised whatever the budget the film was, and the film went on from there.

Arnold and Lou Ferrigno, who were the two major stars of Pumping Iron, they had competed together at the1974 Mr. Olympia. Did you cover this competition when Arnold beat Lou?
Charles Gaines: I covered a lot of them, because I was a judge, an IFBB judge. I was a judge for many of those competitions, and I judged at least four Mr. Olympias. I was in New York when Arnold beat Louie. What Louie had going for him was fine. I think I'm right about this, at that point he was the largest competitor ever in the Mr. Olympia contest in terms of both height and weight. I think Louie in his prime weighed

something like 265, 270 pounds, which was 30 or 40 pounds more than Arnold weighed at his top weight. Louie was much bigger than Arnold. He had more muscle mass than Arnold did. But he had a lot of glaring deficiencies that Arnold more than made up for. He didn't have the symmetry and the proportion that Arnold had. His legs were a little bit weak, he was not a good poser; Arnold was a great poser.

I think more importantly than any of those things is that Arnold was so intelligent. And by that I mean Arnold had a huge advantage over all of his competitors in all of his competitive life because of his mind. And what that mind allowed him to do was not only to train harder than most of his competitors, but to psyche people out, to figure out what their weak points were and how to exploit those weak points on the posing platform. And this is dramatized in the film Pumping Iron. I saw it happen at more than one Mr. Olympia contest, when Arnold was pitted against Louie or Serge Nubret or Sergio Oliva or Franco Columbu, Frank Zane or Ken Waller, or any other people who had set for beating Arnold. He could always find in those people a psychological flaw, something they were afraid of or ashamed of, knew they were deficient in, and then he would work that. As I said, it is dramatized in Pumping Iron.

You know where he has breakfast with Louie and Louie's father, and he begins to work on Louie, "Maybe next year you'll be right for the competition. You're just a little bit too smooth." Louie was smooth, he had not been as cut up as he wanted to be and both Louie and his father knew that. By bringing that up a few days before the competition over breakfast, he was trying to get into Louie's mind that Louie's not quite in the shape he would like to be in, not as cut as he would like to be - that the guy's already been beaten almost. Arnold had a phenomenal capacity to psyche people out like that. A phenomenal capacity to outpoint them, when he was on the posing platform in the pose-offs - the judges give a lot of credit. When you've got five guys doing the pose-offs, then you have two guys to pose-off, Arnold always won those pose-offs even if he wasn't the best body out there. He usually was by the way. But even if he wasn't, like in some of the later competitions, like the one in Australia with Mike Mentzer. I didn't go to that competition, but I read a lot about it, heard a lot about it. George was there.

But Arnold was probably not the best body in that competition. I mean, there were probably guys in that competition who were more cut and in better shape. A lot of people felt that he didn't deserve to win it, but he won it because he's smarter than everybody else. And being smarter than everybody else certainly has advantages if you're not the top body in the competition. If you are the top body in the competition, then you don't really need it, but it's a good edge to have on everybody. Louie was gone, he was gone. At the time, not a lot of people know this but he had a little bit of speech defect. He's a big guy, but he's shy and he didn't like to talk to strangers. His father did most of his talking for him. When he did talk he sounded a little funny, because of his speech defect. Louie was never dumb! He was quite a bright guy, in fact. And, you know, later his movie career proved that he could be quite confident. But he just wasn't smart as Arnold, but that's no insult. There's very few people in any line that are smart as Arnold.

So, when I think back on the series of competitions that they had and their relationship in the film, what I think of is a pro Arnold who's been through at that point and seen it all, done it all, knows how to win on fifteen different levels. And a young very talented guy, who didn't know how to train that well and took a lot of bad training advice from his father, with a hero-worship thing going on for Arnold, but also made it acceptable to be conned by and psyched out by Arnold. Arnold, more in good nature than anything else, didn't mean to insult or hurt Louie. But it was just his nature, just, you know, con him all the way to the bank.

Let's talk about the 1970 Mr. Olympia, when Arnold was crowned Mr. Olympia for the first time. Famously, Arnold was able to utilize a trait - sly manipulativeness - to get the edge over his competitors. What are your recollections of this monumental achievement, which laid the groundwork for his bodybuilding achievements?
Charles Gaines: I covered that. That was the turning point for Arnold in bodybuilding. I think he was surprised that he got beat by Sergio Oliva in 1969, and I think he made up his mind then that he's never going to be beaten again. He realized that he hadn't done the work he had to do. Sergio was huge! He was as big as Arnold and had a great body, great proportion, great symmetry, great muscle mass - everything was terrific. He just outworked Arnold, he just looked better. He said he was never going to get beaten again by Sergio or anyone else. He went back out and he had Sergio onstage where he paused against him during the competition, and then out-posed him. He knew he had to put some muscle on his legs, because Sergio had fantastic legs. Arnold's legs at that point were still a little bit weak. He went back and worked his legs. His back got harder in the next competition. He got more cut up and he worked on his pausing.

In 1970, he looked every bit as good as Sergio did, but he also worked on his pausing, so he knew he could blow Sergio away in posing. He also did the same psychological thing that I was talking to you earlier in reference to Lou. In the pose-off, when Sergio would go into his most muscular pose, Arnold would go to a double bicep, which was his best pose. And he psyched Sergio out during that competition as well. Arnold was smarter than everybody else, and he used his mind to help him compete. When he was in the pause-offs, he hit a bunch of pauses. Then Arnold says to Sergio that's enough, we've done all they need to see, let's go. Sergio walked off and Arnold starts to walk off, then Arnold, with his great big grin, starts posing again. Sergio had already left the stage. So he got five to six extra poses that the judges kept seeing after Sergio had already had gone. There's no rule against that, there's no law against it. He wasn't breaking any rules, he was psyching the other guy out, that's what he does.

Obviously, Arnold won the Mr. Olympia again in 1971 and 1972. Joe Weider offered Sergio $1,800 to compete in the 1973 Mr. Olympia, but he dismayingly declined. Why do you think Sergio stopped competing in the prestigious Mr. Olympia competitions, what's your opinion?
Charles Gaines: Sergio was a great bodybuilder. He was older than Arnold. When Arnold came on the scene, I think Sergio just thought: I'm never going to beat this guy, so I might as well retire. That would be my guess. I didn't really know Sergio. I just met him a couple of times, never had any conversations with him. So I don't really know what he was thinking, but that would be my guess. It was held in New York at the Brooklyn Academy of Music. Serge Nubret was expected to win, possibly to beat Arnold. But Arnold, again, psyched him out. Arnold joked around and he never got nerves before his competitions. Even after South Africa, when I was a judge for three or four years, seeing him backstage he never got nervous. Most of his competitors got real nervous before the show, but Arnold never let anything bother him.

You and Arnold became close friends. What is one of the most stimulating conversations you had with him?
Charles Gaines: We've been friends, we still are friends, since '68. We had a lot of conversations. One that stands out in my mind is when we were doing research for the book Pumping Iron. George Butler and I were practically living in Santa Monica, California, and we were spending huge amount of time with Arnold. I remember one day we were driving back from Woodland Hills, which is where the Weider magazines were based. George and I had rented a car. Arnold was in the backseat. George was in the front and I was driving. I asked Arnold, and it had been in my notebook to ask Arnold this question, which I had never asked before, I said, "Let me ask you something. I know it's going to sound strange, but have you ever thought of your body as a work of art and yourself as an artist? In other words, Michael Angelo had his clay. Do you ever see yourself as a sculptor? And your body has been the material that you're trying to work with?" He had a long, long pause in the backseat - silence. He said, "No, I've never thought of that. But

now that you mention it, it's a really good analogy."

Then he just started spinning off this whole thing as we are driving, and he said, "It's interesting, because I can look at my forearm and I can say by two weeks by the time competition happens that forearm needs to be half an inch bigger." He said, "Just by eating and exercising, I can cause that half inch to happen." He said, "I don't even have to think about it consciously. I look at the forearm and say in two weeks you're going to be a half inch bigger. Then I eat and I exercise and two weeks later that forearm is a half inch bigger." He said that's a good similarity to how an artist works. And another similarity is that an artist has to be incredibly honest about his work. He has to be able to look at the painting, sculpture or whatever, and say, "That's really not the way I want it to be; I've got to make it better." He said, "I think that one of my strengths as a bodybuilder is my honesty, that I can look at myself and say my calves...."

He had a big problem with his calves for a long time, before he got them up to where he wanted them. He said, "I could look in the mirror and say my calves are not what they need to be. I can be ruthlessly honest about it, then I can put in the work that I need to put in. Most bodybuilders won't or can't. I can put in the work that I have to in order to get them there." So, he said, "Yeah, yeah." The more he thought about this, the more he kept finding analogies. He finally said, "You know, it's brilliant! That's exactly what a bodybuilder is like. I'm exactly like a sculpture, and my body is like a material of a sculpture in that I bring it up to the vision that I have for it and put my heart and soul into it." From that conversation on, Arnold used that analogy over and over again. I mean, you'll see it in half of the interviews he has given about bodybuilding - not about movie acting - he talks about how a bodybuilder is a sculpture and an artist of his own body. I think that was one of the most interesting conversations we had, because it kind of lit a light bulb in Arnold's head that went on to be a gigantic spotlight.

Do you feel there was an evolutionary process which took place as far his personality is concerned? Do you feel a personality transition took place, and what was the contrast between the era when he was a bodybuilding star to when he became the biggest action movie star?
Charles Gaines: I would say yes and no. I think Arnold came to the United States with all of the essential psychological armor he had, which is to say that he was ambitious from the beginning. He knew more or less what he wanted to accomplish. In fact, he told George Butler this. I think he came over to this country knowing the good strokes of what he wanted to accomplish. He wanted to be the best bodybuilder that there ever was. He wanted to make a lot of money. He

wanted to become famous as a movie star. He wanted to marry a beautiful and rich and famous woman. The only part of what he has done with his life that I don't remember him having said he wanted to do when he first came to this country is the political part. That might have been a part of his plan too. So, in a sense very little psychologically changed about Arnold the time he got here until now.

But on the other hand, quite a lot has changed. Because there were a lot of subtleties, a lot of things that allowed Arnold to make use of. He came over here with this fierce intelligence and fierce independence and one of the greatest bodies ever given to a human being in the history of the world. And a fierce willingness to work, fierce discipline, all of those things going for him. What he didn't have is a sense of how to put all that together. And another thing he didn't really have was taste. I think what Arnold has done is to acquire that good taste. I don't mean being wise and charm and things like that, because he's always had good taste in that regard. But I mean in things like art, clothes and how to dress, how to speak, how to carry yourself. All those things, he pretty much had to learn from scratch. And he was the quickest learner that I have ever seen.

He learned things unbelievably quickly. If he saw something you did that he liked, the way you carried yourself, the way you spoke, the way you dressed, drank wine, or how you smoke cigars, or any of this, the next day he "owned" it. He would study you, and the next day he would be doing it. He'd be going to your tailor, and he would be buying the wine from the guy you bought your wine from, and smoking the cigar that he saw you smoking. So, he developed an incredible curiosity and ability to learn and develop that into yet another weapon that he had over you.

To answer your question, I don't think he changed psychologically much. I think he came over with all the essential tools that he needed to do what he needed to do. Which are, in my mind, very, very high intelligence, a very high curiosity, an incredible discipline and a willingness to work hard to aid him in what he wanted to become and what he wanted to accomplish. He's often quoted the title of my book, when people ask him his secrets to success. He says "stay hungry". That was the title of my first novel, the first movie that Arnold ever had been in. That's what he's done: he's stayed hungry. He stayed competitive. He's kept eating one thing after another, all the way down the line and all the way to where he is now.

When Pumping Iron was being made, Frank Zane, who was one of the most intelligent bodybuilders, made a rather sarcastic remark, "Why don't you call it Pumping Arnold?!" It seems like there was a competitive element going on between Arnold and Frank.

Charles Gaines: Frank Zane is a great guy and happens to be a good friend of mine and was quite bright. As you say, as a bodybuilder he was quite intellectual. He was well-read. He and his wife Christine at that point had a fascination with Buddhism, writings and philosophies and so forth. Very interesting people. Frank also was one of the early experts on nutrition. I think at the time, when he started to hang around bodybuilders, they didn't know as much about nutrition. Frank was in the vanguard of group of bodybuilders who took nutrition very seriously. He really understood it better than most. He understood supplements better than most and so forth. He was older than Arnold. He had been a star before Arnold got to this country. He was a small man, small boned and not very tall, with a beautiful physique. I mean, he really was one of those bodybuilders who ever had more symmetry and proportion in his body than 98 percent of all the bodybuilders.

But because he was small, he was not able to put on the kind of muscle that these small guys have now. Nor do I think Frank wanted to, because he was more of an artist, he had a lot of proportion and symmetry. So, he never was in a position to beat Arnold and I think that probably caused Frank, if not jealousy, a little bit of mild annoyance, because he had been a star before Arnold had got here. And he knew he will never win a Mr. Olympia, or a Mr. Universe contest against Arnold after Arnold did get here. Because Arnold was so much bigger, so much more heavy. Arnold also had a lot of symmetry and proportion. So I think Frank, as I say, might have from time to time been annoyed about Arnold of how really big he became and how everybody paid so much attention to him, and, therefore, conversely a little bit less attention to him. But on the whole, they got on very well.

And because they were two of the brighter of the then bodybuilders, they had more in common than Arnold had in common with most of the rest of the guys at Gold's Gym. Frank was a regular at Gold's Gym. They were quite good friends. I wouldn't say they were real, real close the way Arnold was with Franco, but they were good friends and they respected each other and they admired each other. Arnold admired Frank's posing. Frank not only had a beautiful body, but he was a beautiful poser - next to Ed Corney, who may have been the finest poser in bodybuilding. Arnold admired that. He admired his mind and he admired his body. Frank certainly admired. They were good friends, but they were never, never - at least in my memory - great best buddy types.

When filming the Pumping Iron film, how was Arnold like to collaborate with?

Charles Gaines: He was great to collaborate with. He had great suggestions. Of course, he knew the bodybuilding world way better than we did. He was very helpful. In terms of making the film from day to day, he was tremendously helpful and always fun to be with, fun to work with.

Can you reminisce on some of the more social moments you shared with Arnold?
Charles Gaines: I went to lots of parties with Arnold. The thing about Arnold is he's always himself; he's not a different person at a party full of movie stars than he is at Gold's Gym. He's always himself. He's always in tease. He always loves to tease people. He's always got a great sense of humor. He's always kind of the life of the party. He never pretends or tries to pretend to be anybody he's not. He's always himself. I think the most remarkable things about - one of the most remarkable things - Arnold is that he has an absolute rock-hard confidence in himself.

Most of us, if you and I went to a party full of A-list movie stars, or went to a party before the Academy Awards or whatever, we might be a little bit shy or a little bit different than we are in everyday life, a little bit quieter, or maybe a little bit louder, who knows. Arnold is always the same, no matter who is with. He's always the same. He's never impressed by anybody, whether they're politicians or movie actors or whatever. He feels he's as good, as big, as smart as everybody else in the world and there's no need to be self-conscious. I would characterize him at parties, the main characteristic I would say is that he is always the same in person. And secondly, that he's always the life of the party, because he loves to have a good time. He loves to kid people and joke around, so he's great at parties.

Were you invited to Arnold's wedding and did you go?
Charles Gaines: Yes, I did. I went to the wedding. It was a great wedding, you know, it was held at the St. Francis Xavier Church in Hyannis, Massachusetts. We were there for three days, I think. We went to the bachelor party and all the different parties before the wedding. And then the wedding itself was in a small church and the reception was back at the Kennedy compound, there were all kinds of people there. There were also some people who were not that famous but were going to be famous, like Oprah Winfrey. That was the first time that we'd ever met Oprah Winfrey, she at the time had a TV show in Baltimore or Washington someplace - nobody had heard of her. It was kind of an odd wedding, because Maria has such a huge powerful family and I'm not sure that they were all that sure that Arnold was the right person for Maria.

At that point, '87, he was already becoming a movie star, but he was a bodybuilder. He was a Republican; they were all Democrats. I think there was a certain amount of doubt on the part of some of the Kennedys as to whether or not this was the best choice for Maria. And you could sense that quite a bit if you paid attention to it. Otherwise it was a beautiful day. I remember the food was unbelievably good. The bands were great. Arnold had one of those Austrian suits with kind of a long skirt, green jacket with a kind of button kind of thing. He had a bunch of Austrian friends there, so it was a combination of Austrian and Kennedy, Republican and Democrat, movie stars and politicians. It was an interesting combination. It was a tremendous amount of fun.

From the perspective of the East Coast elite, Maria couldn't have picked a more outrageous person to marry - an Austrian bodybuilder from Venice Beach who'd attended community college, a leading political reporter Robert Salladay told me. But Arnold knows how to deal with larger-than-life personalities. He knew the secret is to not feel intimidated and to give back as good as he got. When he first met Maria's mother, he told her that her daughter had a "nice ass" - he wasn't afraid of the family, and they respected him for that. Many years later, Arnold said, "I never saw myself as a guy that could settle down. I was always very derogatory about the station wagons that people used in the '60s and '70s, with the dog and the cat and the kids screaming - and now I'm driving around with the dogs, the puppies, the kids screaming in the back, the wife in the front seat, trying to calm everyone down."

Can you tell me about visiting Arnold at his home, when he was in the peak of his movie career, and was he more inclined toward being a family and homely guy?
Charles Gaines: His family life has always been wonderful, and I think that was partially function of Maria. She has such a big close family, and that's what she wanted for her family. She also was born into a famous family, but the family managed to keep their privacy. They insisted on privacy and people not violating their privacy. So, the very few times that I visited Arnold at his home, and there was not many, during the time he was a movie star, I would say that it was just like being in a normal family. His kids were not spoiled. They're all wonderful kids; they're not like brats like some movie star's kids tend to be. They're really brought up well and well-disciplined by Arnold and Maria. They were just little gentlemen and gentlewomen - they couldn't be nicer. They had a great relationship with Arnold. There were always dogs around. I would characterize his family life as being informal. I've had dinner at his house, and we would just sit around and bring out the food

and the kids are there. Just have conversations like old friends, smoke cigars and drink some wine. To answer the question, his family life, to the extent I've experienced it and knew something about it, was quite informal, quite happy and completely family-centered.

How does a Hollywood celebrity father bring up his children so they have a "normal" upbringing, and not be distracted by the sheer wealth and status which can sometime deviate the children from experiencing normality? Arnold grew up in Austria with no refrigerator, his mother bathed first, then his father, then his older brother and he was the last one. By the time it was his turn, the water was black. He grew up in an environment where the rod was not spared. His rebel attitude did not bode well with that of his father's mentality. According to Arnold, "There was no food in Austria. My mother had to go around with us to various farms until she got enough food and sugar and stuff." There was no TV and phone in the house he grew up, and no bathroom in the sense we know it today.

Arnold has four children with Maria: Katherine, born 1989; Christina, born 1991; Patrick, born 1993; Christopher. born 1997. On the subject of bringing up his kids up, Arnold explains, "First of all, it is a big challenge. And you can't undo it. You try to concentrate as much as you can to make them grow up normal. Still, you know they see the big house than the other kids have, they see more cars and they see there's money there and all those things. It's a different ball game. So what we do is, we are very strict with certain things. For instance, I insist they wash their own clothes, that they make their bed every morning, they turn off their lights every day. I teach them that, because I went through it when I was a bachelor. I did everything myself. I want them to do that." Arnold's own upbringing was intense, and he had an unhappy childhood being rejected by an ungrateful father. Joe Weider says, "He didn't talk too much about it, but he told me personally that his father was rough, didn't treat him so good."

Arnold has lived a life which is far from being mundane; he's inordinately been an active individual. Did you and Arnold share any interests and hobbies away from bodybuilding and movies?
Charles Gaines: We have different enthusiasms; my enthusiasm had to do with the outdoors. I'm a fisherman, bird hunter, hiker and I like to canoe. I could never get Arnold interested in any of those things. We did do a television program for ABC, I forget what year it was, that I directed and produced and George Butler co-directed with me. We got

Arnold to come out. One of my great interests in life has been grizzly bears. We got Arnold to come out and do this TV show. We went into Ellison Park to track grizzly bears. That was about the only time I've been with Arnold in terms of interested in the kind of things that I like (other than bodybuilding and movies). I don't care a thing about cars and motorcycles; the things that he tends to be into. So, I don't recall any conversations about those kinds of things.

What was Arnold like as a traveling companion?
Charles Gaines: We traveled together a lot. In South Africa and in Europe. We traveled together in London. I remember London in particularly and Paris on the way to South Africa. Then we traveled together for the documentary I was talking about. We traveled over Wyoming, making that documentary about grizzly bears. It was great fun traveling with him. This was mostly before he got famous. Also, I flew around with him when he was the head of first George Bush's fitness program - whatever it's called. He had a plane at that point, he had a jet. He picked me up and we flew around for a number of days. I went with him to talk to these governors about the program.

I remember we flew down to see Bill Clinton when he was the governor of Arkansas, but he was late and he had his secretary to tell Arnold that he'll be half an hour. We sat there for half an hour, then he called back and said tell him I'll be there in another half hour. Arnold got tired and we left. So we never met Clinton. But we saw lots of governors and flew around to try to get the governors to embrace the fitness programs in their states. It was a lot of fun. We had been on the road flying in his plane. I've traveled with him lots. Being with Arnold is always the same, it doesn't matter whether you're traveling or at his house, or in a restaurant or at a party, he just pretty much sucks up all the oxygen in the world. And you are on his conversational schedule, and you're doing whatever it is he wants to do. It's always great fun, always amusing and always rewarding when you're with him on any of these occasions.

What was the core concept of President Bush's physical fitness program, for which Arnold became the head?
Charles Gaines: The aim was: American kids are in terrible shape, they were back then and they are still now. That was something that bothered Arnold, it bothered me. It was big back in the '80s and '90s. I also had a lot to do with that, to try to help kids and adolescent fitness levels improve in the USA, and this was one of the things that Arnold wanted to do as the head of the program. It was called The President's Council on Physical Fitness, and he (Arnold) was the head of it. He had been

made head of it by George Bush. One of the things Arnold wanted to accomplish was to improve fitness levels around the country for young people. He figured the best ways to do that was to go see all the governors in the states - every governor in every state, fifty-two states - and talk to the governors into starting state physical fitness councils, that would go down the grassroot level in the states and get kids on fitness programs in the schools, which would be funded by the states. So, that was what I was doing with him.

I didn't go to all fifty-two governors, but about five or six with him. But he went to all fifty-two. Arnold would say, "Governor, your state has got terrible fitness levels for kids. I want you to get them improved. I want to give you an incentive to get going. A State Physical Fitness Council and the National Physical Fitness Council. I'm going to help you out with it." And the governors, almost all of them, said yes. So, I went back to Hampshire - I lived in New Hampshire at that time - and started the New Hampshire State Physical Fitness Council. We were quite successful, as I think most of them were. So, that was the point of the thing that Arnold was doing.

Were you in the presence of Arnold when he was with the first President Bush?
Charles Gaines: Yes, I was. The first physical fitness day that they had in Washington, right after Arnold had been named the head of The President's Council on Physical Fitness, George Bush put on a big physical fitness day on the lawn of the White House. I was there. I remember Randy Travis was there, the singer. I got to meet President Bush.

Having known Arnold and being a close friend of his, what it the most significant memory that stays with you?
Charles Gaines: I don't know, it's kind of a blank. The most distinctive thing about Arnold, and I saw this over and over with him in all kinds of different circumstances, is his ability to create a dream for himself and then making it happen. I'll tell you one conversation. I did an article for Men's Journal, a cover article, when he was running for governor of California. I called him up and we had a long conversation on the phone. This is the result of that conversation. The trick in bodybuilding is to be able to turn a normal body into a competitive piece of art that is going to beat other pieces of art. That's the trick, that's what bodybuilding is all about. It is to take a normal body and turn it into an abnormal body according to a set of aesthetic criteria, and allowing it to compete with and win over people who try to do the same thing. So there's an element of brawn in there, there's elements of imagination in there and there's a tremendous element of will in there.

Another thing about Arnold, when I was talking to him about this article, you look in the mirror and be ruthlessly honest with yourself about what you see there and then decide by one to twenty seconds: I have to weigh 6 pounds more, my biceps have to be two inches bigger, or whatever, whatever aesthetic demands you want to put on yourself. Then you go out and accomplish it. Well, most people in their lives, they might come over to America from Germany and say to themselves: I want to be the best bodybuilder there ever lived; I want to be rich; I want to be famous; I want to be a movie star; I want to marry a rich and famous wife; I want to go on to be the governor of the biggest state in the country. Most people could say that sort of thing to themselves, but they could never make it happen. Because they don't have the discipline, they don't have the vision and they don't have the talent. You've got to have so many things in order to do that.

So, the point I'm making is, what Arnold did was to take the sort of the magical transformation that a bodybuilder goes through in changing his body with will and discipline, changing his body into a thing he has only in his mind. Arnold did the same thing with his life! He looked in the mirror when he got to America, and instead of saying his bicep has to be two inches bigger, he said I've got to learn these things in order to become a movie star. I've got to meet these people. I've got to be in these things. I've got to take these classes. And then through his phenomenal unheard of willpower, he just went on and did it. He did the same thing for everything else in his life. So, in a way Arnold's life has been all of these pieces. Because the same things that allowed him to become a great bodybuilder have allowed him to do and use his mind, his will, his imagination and his vision of himself to become anything he wanted to become. I think he's really unique among 20th century people. He's kind of a completely self-created human being. He took raw material and made it into what he wanted to be.

GEORGE BUTLER

Many acknowledge George Butler, born in the United Kingdom, to be responsible for starting Arnold's film career when he produced the classic Pumping Iron. A photographer and filmmaker, Butler became a close friend of Arnold's and got to know him personally.

George, you were the mastermind behind Pumping Iron, how did this all start?

George Butler: I had an assignment from Sports Illustrated magazine to do an article on bodybuilding contest in Massachusetts. I went there with Charles Gaines, who went on to write the book Pumping Iron; I took the photos for the book. We noticed that the crowd was going crazy over the bodybuilders, and we decided to do a book. One thing lead to another I guess. The last overseas assignment that magazine gave us was to go to Baghdad to cover the Mr. Universe contest. Once we finished the book and when we turned it in to the publisher, they rejected the book and said no one ever will be interested in Arnold Schwarzenegger. They were wrong.

What kind of personality did Arnold project when you were filming him in Pumping Iron?

George Butler: He was very quick, very eager to learn and very good at what he did. Very ambitious. He worked very closely with us at that time when we did the film. He was an ideal collaborator.

In your opinion, what was some of the more interesting footage you shot?

George Butler: It was all interesting. He holds the screen very well. We shot about a hundred hours of film, and Arnold was very cooperative. So we got a lot of good footage all over the world. We shot in California, Connecticut, Massachusetts and South Africa. Arnold was very helpful. There's a scene where Arnold went to the zoo in South Africa, where they were keeping some Rhinos. I was very nervous, because Arnold was very transfixed with this big Rhino, but that scene did not make it into the movie. Let me give you another example. I filmed some footage with Arnold and Mike Katz, Mike Katz was part of the movie Pumping Iron, and they were doing Roman chair sit-ups. I remember Mike Katz saying, "This is the most boring exercise I've ever done," and Arnold laughed at him and said, "It's perfect for me, Mike. I sit on the Roman chair and do those sit-ups, and I take the extra time to think how I'm going to make my next move."

Of course, Lou Ferrigno was the other prominent bodybuilder who appeared in the film. What influenced your decision to have him play one of the main roles?
George Butler: Well, I was very insistent to have Lou be in the movie, because at 6ft 4, 270 pounds, he was a giant and he looked like he could beat Arnold. The rivalry between Lou and Arnold was visible. There was Serge Nubret, who was a French bodybuilder who lived in Paris. There was Mike Katz, who was a professional football player. There was Ed Corney, who was a professional surfer. There were a lot of interesting people in the movie, including Franco Columbu, who is a chiropractor. We all got along and had a good time and shot very good scenes for the movie.

Can we talk about how you got the film financed, what obstacles lay ahead?
George Butler: Everyone thought it was a crazy idea for a movie. Everyone said, "George, you're wasting your life making a movie about Arnold Schwarzenegger." I stuck to my guns and we made a very good movie, and that's where I overcame most of the obstacles. It was very difficult to finance, but eventually we got it done. Most people thought that bodybuilding was a ridiculous sport - that was the enemy. So the more exposure the movie had, the more cities we went to and the more interested the people became. Eventually, I think the movie caused hundred thousand gyms to open up around the world and bodybuilding became a bigger sport than jogging, but it all took time.

The overall cost for Pumping Iron was $400,000. Jerome Gary, who was one of the producers, contributed $25,000, $110,000 came from then Butler's wife. This was a very modest budget for a film which filmed for three or four months. Butler was short on money, he went to a lab called DuArt Lab in New York after coming back from filming the initial parts of the docu/drama. He asked for credit from the lab, which was a standard practice when you produced a film. Butler asked the owner if he would give him a credit of $15,000. After Butler told the lab that the credit was for a bodybuilding film, the owner asked whether it had anything to do with Arnold Schwarzenegger. Butler, of course, said yes. He was denied the credit. The reason behind rejecting the credit was that years earlier, the Lab had done work for Hercules in New York, but the company never got paid, which amounted to $30,000.

When Pumping Iron was released, it was embraced beyond the confines of the bodybuilding fraternity. One reviewer in a prominent newspaper wrote, "Mr. Schwarzenegger is the central figure in Pumping Iron, an interesting, rather slick and excessively long documentary about the small but intensely competitive world of bodybuilding. The first thing the outsider realizes, watching the film, is that the object of all that weightlifting is neither strength nor prowess, but appearance. Mr. Schwarzenegger calls himself a sculptor of his own body. You look in the mirror and see you need a little more deltoids to make symmetry. So you exercise and put more deltoid on. A sculptor will slap stuff on."

It's generally considered that Arnold's exposure to a much wider audience through Pumping Iron, which was no doubt a seminal film, lead to open doors in Hollywood. Would you say you were responsible, to a degree, for this?
George Butler: You must remember Arnold made three movies before he made Pumping Iron. One was called Hercules in New York, which failed in the United States, it was a total flop. It was a ridiculous movie that got no distribution. Arnold should not have done it. Then there was a second movie called Stay Hungry for United Artists, Bob Rafelson was the director, Jeff Bridges and Sally Fields were in the movie. And it, too, was a failure at the box office. And it took Pumping Iron to come along and elevate Arnold to a much higher plain and the national interest in Arnold. He went on a wonderful publicity campaign in New York, and it all worked out very well.

More than twenty years later, at the height of his fame, Arnold was on the David Letterman show promoting Terminator 2. Letterman showed a clip of Arnold's first movie. "I cannot believe it!" Arnold laughed as the audience joined in hysterically. "I have to tell you, every single time I come to this show there's some kind of a surprise. I said to myself, 'What could it be today?' There you have it, a movie I tried to hide for centuries," laughed Arnold. "It was the first film I had ever done. I just got off the boat basically. I could not speak English. They dubbed my voice. I didn't even know what I was saying, it was dubbed. And it was one of those dream stories, in a way, you say to yourself, 'This is true, there's such a thing when you come to America someone comes up to you and says, 'Do you want to star in a movie?' That's what this was." He said he was ecstatic and had made $3,000 doing the film. Arnold had come a long way from his initial exposure into the film industry and was now polished and the highest paid star in Hollywood. By now, his whimsical persiflage was apparent as he became accustomed to being interviewed on major TV shows.

You were a photographer and shot Arnold. Can you tell me about some of the photo sessions you did with Arnold?

George Butler: Arnold was always willing to be photographed and he loved the cameras. I took my camera and my lights everywhere I went. I took about five thousand photos of Arnold. The photos worked out cool.

Your relationship with Arnold went beyond the confines of business. You and Charles Gaines developed a close-knit friendship with Arnold and became very close friends with him.

George Butler: Arnold and Charles Gaines and I were very good friends. We always had a good time together when we joined forces. We traveled a lot together. We did the book and the movie, and Arnold helped a lot, because he was always willing to talk to someone we introduced him to, he enjoyed the whole process. When the movie came out, he did hundreds of interviews and he wanted more. The premiere of the movie was on January 7, 1977, in a hotel in New York. There were a lot of celebrities at the theater, which was near Fifth Avenue. There were lots of news people and lots of television cameras. It was a very successful premiere because we got a lot of attention. A lot of people turned up to come and see the movie. The book that we did and the movie that we did spoke to the audience outside of bodybuilding. The project was successful because we succeeded in making Arnold famous, when people had no interest in bodybuilding, and he handled it very well.

Would I be right in saying some of the scenes in Pumping Iron were dramatized. Arnold has said some scenes were made up and dramatized to make it more interesting, can you elucidate on this?

George Butler: All of the scenes in Pumping Iron were true to the sport - truth in the scenes from the movie. He wanted to move bodybuilding into an acceptable arena. And everything in the movie is true to the individual. Nothing in the movie was pure fiction.

Arnold, when promoting the 25th anniversary of the film explicated, "Every time anyone sees Pumping Iron, they will come away, you know, loving the movie, being inspired by the movie. But at the same time,

120

they ask themselves, 'Wow, I mean, was all of this stuff true? I mean, Did Arnold really psyche out Lou Ferrgino? Did he really not go home for his father's funeral? Because it was shortly before the competition, was he really that cold that he'd say, well, forget that, he's dead already. I'm not going to bother with that. I'm going to focus on my competition. Is that true?'" Over the years, these are some of the questions which some fans have been bothered about. Arnold has said it's important to clarify there are certain elements in the film which resonated with the truth. Such things as the competition and the outcome of the competition, and the arduous intensive training, which was shown which the bodybuilders went through, and the sacrifices that the athletes make to reach the top. Also the dietary practices and supplements.

But there were certain things that were not true, admits Arnold. This is why the film is not a documentary per se, but more appropriately labeled as "docu-drama". Because certain things were created in order to make it more interesting, because it was very clear that the only way the money could be raised for the movie was to make it more dramatic. Arnold explained, "All the investors always said, 'Look, the training is terrific and what they are doing is terrific and all this. But how much can we look at this footage of them doing squats and chin-ups and sit-ups and all this? It's boring. Even though it's exciting to them, it's boring for us to watch. So therefore let's create some drama, some conflict. Let's create a villain, let's create a hero....'" So various things were created as they went along. It's also interesting to note that Nick Cohn, who wrote the smash hit movie Saturday Night Fever, which propelled John Travolta to fame, modeled the Italian family on Lou Ferrigno and his family.

There were certain controversial elements attached to the movie, like Arnold smoking marijuana cigarettes. He seemed to be quite open in those days, conversed frankly about various controversial issues. Can you expound on this, please?
George Butler: Arnold behaved the way he always behaved. There's nothing in the movie that cause the police to arrive and arrest him for smoking a joint. That's just part of life. I can't think of any other controversial elements. In various newspapers, there's been a score of articles about things that were in the movie; but there never were. So they (writers) were just wasting their time.

Did you have any new projects you wanted to work with Arnold on after Pumping Iron, and what did the general public learn about the sport and Arnold after being exposed to Pumping Iron?

George Butler: The truth of the matter is, after I finished Pumping Iron and went on to make other movies, Arnold was, obviously, making his own movies. I was working on a movie somewhere for some time, and Arnold was working on a movie in Indiana. I hadn't seen Arnold for a while, the last time I saw him was here in New York, he seemed very well. I went to a lot of dinners with Arnold and birthday parties to his house. I went to his wedding. You have to remember we were close friends.

Everyone changes when they become a big star, and Arnold's life has taken about his work, whenever I see him we talk same as we used to talk in the good old days. It's (Pumping Iron) a father and son story, about Lou Ferrigno and his father, about Arnold and his father, who, as you know, by then had died. It's a story about fathers and sons. Arnold is absolutely the epitome of the American Dream. He came to the United States with nothing more than a gym bag and no money in it, and he's become one of the wealthiest people in California, if not the United States. He's been a bodybuilding champion. He's been the governor of California. He's been a movie star. He's quite extraordinary. We did some television work together and made a show for ABC TV. There were several things I'd like to have done with Arnold over the years. Essentially, I make my own movies now.

BARBARA BAKER

Barbara Baker was Arnold's first girlfriend when he immigrated to America. She cultivated a personal relationship and got to know the real Arnold. Baker recounts her relationship with the man who would become the biggest star in the world.

You and Arnold met in 1969 at your workplace. Can you shed light on your first meeting?

Barbara Baker: Right. What happened with meeting him was, it was the year between my junior year of college and my senior year, and I worked in a delectation - a Jewish delectation - that he came into at least once a day if not twice a day. So, just as he came in frequently, all of a sudden I'm sitting at the counter eating lunch, eating French fries, he just came over and said, "You are so sexy. I must ask you out on a date." I was a college girl, little sorority girl. I had never been spoken to like that in my life, and it was a feeling to me and I gave him my number. It took a week or so to go out, but we did and really had fun on the first date.

How was Arnold adjusting to the American lifestyle when you met him, did you detect any austerity in his attitude?

Barbara Baker: His language was at a really low level. So his communication had to happen with a lot of body language and asking questions. So with that element and from my end, I kind of felt I could be the English teacher and have fun with it. And then on his end, he loved everything. He loved American politics, he loved the American movies, he loved the American beaches. People were so nice to him that he had instant friends, of course, surrounding the bodybuilding world. He struggled financially. Joe Weider was a very hard person to negotiate with. But you never really had the sense that he ever worried that he never had enough money. But he really didn't have very much money at all, but he still was able to have the life he wanted to have.

You were not into bodybuilding. Did Arnold relate his dreams and ambitions to you in those early years?

Barbara Baker: No, I was not part of the bodybuilding world at all. You know, what's funny is he really is somebody who was so much into

123

the moment that he didn't really talk on a daily basis about long-term goals. It was always about building his body for that day, for the upcoming contest which was next. So it was probably a two or three-month plan to get the goal of building up his body, and then overall goal. I think he just wanted to keep developing contacts, networking, writing letters, getting to know as many people as he could. He had realized in the value of networking.

In his mind, he may have known more about what he wanted to do with that than he said, but really none of us from those days can remember him talk about big dreams of being a businessman. Not even owning a gym like, say, the Jack LaLanne chain we had. He just felt it would just unfold. Even his movie career. I'll tell you that I never really heard him talk about it except through his fascination with Steve Reeves. So there was kind of an understanding that he would love to be the next Steve Reeves, but that was never going to happen. So it didn't really need to be discussed, because they weren't making Tarzan kind of movies anymore. Again, he just kept doing his best in the moment of now. I'm certain he had a strong believe that it will pay off some way, somehow, but I didn't quite see how it was going to.

Did Arnold talk to you about his childhood of growing up in Austria?
Barbara Baker: He did, a lot. He was very much Austrian. Even though he had a difficult childhood, he was a highly individualistic child that his father, in particular, didn't understand. Our childhoods are so pivotal to our lives, so he couldn't help but tell stories about his brother Meinhardt and various stories about his father being so demanding and his mother indulging him a little bit more. And his other friends, their father's would be surrogate fathers to him. They gave him more attention, they gave him more acknowledgment than his own father did. So there was a huge struggle that went on with his father, really, to the point when I met him there was no desire to see his parents frequently. He felt he had to do it out of duty, but there was no real loving desire to see his parents. So, when he would go over for contests, he would attempt to see them. And then suddenly it was too late, because his father died of a heart attack quite young. His brother died first. It was like all that was left was his mother from his childhood. When he was aged, I would say about twenty-four, those deaths had occurred, that's pretty young to only have a mother left.

Arnold had cultivated a desire to become an athlete when his father took him to Graz to see Johnny Weissmuller, the Olympic swimming champion and actor who became best known for playing Tarzan.

Arnold's father was a curling champion and had a penchant for sports, and he instilled a love of sports in his sons; he encouraged his young sons to compete in soccer, which was the popular sport in Europe, boxing and skiing. At the age of ten, the young boy joined a soccer league. Arnold later wrote in his semi-autobiography The Education of a Bodybuilder, "I still remember that first visit to the bodybuilding gym. I had never seen anyone lifting weights before. Those guys were huge and brutal." Arnold started lifting weights for his legs to strengthen his legs for soccer. The bodybuilders started paying attention to just how hard the young man, who at the time was fifteen and weighed 150 pounds, was working out, squatting with fairly heavy weights. According to Arnold, the bodybuilders at the gym encouraged him to pursue bodybuilding.

Do you feel that Arnold had to prove himself to his family, especially his father, because they weren't really keen on bodybuilding and they wanted him to get a proper job?
Barbara Baker: They sure did. I think he was in such a habit trying to get attention from his father that it has worked itself into his personality. I really think his drive was so dramatic in getting attention from his father, and acknowledging he was at least as good as his brother Meinhardt if not someone really special. So, yes. I think his whole life was about driving for that attention from his father, now it's patterned into his later life.

In Austria, it was a pre-requisite for all men to serve in the military provided they met the standards of fitness required. In late 1965, Arnold joined the military and was assigned to a tank unit stationed near Graz. After having expressed to his father his desire to drive a tank, his father helped him to enlist in the tank unit. The same year, Arnold was prepping himself for a bodybuilding competition. Although the Army denied his request to leave to enter the competition, he deserted to compete and won the trophy. After returning he was thrown in the military jail. Subsequently, he was allowed to train during his year of service in the military.

Arnold's father expected him to pursue a career in the military. Disappointed in their son's career choice, Arnold's parents could not understand why their son would not want to pursue a normal career path and get a job like anybody else. Arnold remembers, "My parents would just never understand it, they would say, 'Why don't you get into soccer? I said, 'I'm a soccer player but I like weightlifting better now. I want to be the youngest world champion in bodybuilding.' 'Bodybuilding? Why bodybuilding?! What are all those pictures on your wall here of these naked men all oiled up with little posing trunks, what's going on?' Disillusioned by her son's obsession with a sport which required scantily men to show their bodies, his mother went to see a doctor. "My mother went to the doctor and said, 'You've got to talk to this guy, there's something awfully....' We didn't have a therapist but it was a house doctor, and he would come out and he would talk to me. 'Tell me about these pictures on the wall? What's the story here with these men?' I would be explaining, and then he would say to my mother, 'He is very ambitious, he has big goals. I don't think there's anything wrong with that.'"

Arnold's brother died young, his father favored his brother. How would you define Arnold's relationship with his brother, did Arnold convey pacification?

Barbara Baker: Yes, the father definitely favored the brother - he was firstborn. He was a naturally good student. He was probably a more naturally all-around good athlete. They did things together like ice curling, which was I guess a special sport in Austria, you know, when you're living in the snow climate. The father believed in competition. So he always set it up that Meinhardt or Arnold had to be the better one in whatever activity they did. So it was never really about the sake of having fun; it was who could get the biggest handful of flowers for their mother on Mother's Day, or who could run the fastest. So, you know, Arnold always felt, being the youngest, he never could be better than Meinhardt. Meinhardt was a year ahead of him and did everything bigger, better, wiser, smarter. So that doesn't give a lot of room for having a loving relationship. So, no. As they were alive, there was more conflict than there was resolution.

His father inculcated his sons with a sense of duty. When Arnold's father passed away, you say Arnold showed little empathy. Was there any vestige of sympathy, why did he miss the funeral?

Barbara Baker: He really did make a very conscious choice that it wasn't good timing for him. He had shattered his knee in Australia in a competition. So, he had come home from that. Once he got home from Australia, maybe even at the airport in Australia, it was really bad timing - his knee had gone out on him. He got a phone call that his father had died. This was in early December. It's not, like, he had the surgery right away, because he was trying to postpone having the surgery. He had a miserable journey coming home because he was in crutches. But there's a secondary plot to that too. He really did not feel the obligation and the love of needing to be there. He figured his mother had the rest of the family there, and there was no warmth Arnold had felt for his father, so he already had missed his father - the missing had already occurred. So, to go home to show that he was going to miss his father, he really felt that his father had sort of abandoned him and the relationship I would say had already been severed.

Did Arnold have a tender side to him? Of course, being an athlete, he was a macho guy, did you see any side which wasn't perceptible to the outsiders?
Barbara Baker: I'm sure people have heard some of the sweet and tender stories that he would do for people. Certainly the bravados and the macho side, the gym, teasing the buddies, that dominated 95 percent of the time. But definitely there was a soft side to him, where people he really loved and cared about, whether it was my mother or me, even a little old lady who he saw fall off a bench in the park, he would run to the rescue and see if he can help. He loved to tease people lovingly. He would love to brush my hair. There was a side to him which was very kind and soft, and he really appreciated that side to him. Throughout his adult life, he continued to show that for certain people. He had a lot of surrogate fathers. And one of them was Mits Kawashima, who lives in Hawaii. He is ninety-five years old right now. I didn't get a Christmas card from him, so I'm not sure if he's still alive.

Arnold was so wonderful to Mits. And even as governor, he would call him to make sure he was OK. Before his wife died, Arnold made sure he had all the care in the world - the best. I don't want to say hospitalization, I'm sure he didn't pay for that, medical bills, but he made sure that she was healthy and happy as he could be as she was dying. He did that for quite a few people. Artie Zeller, the postal worker and the photographer that took his pictures. Again, when Artie was dying, he made sure that he had absolutely everything he needed. So he's really been there for his lifetime friends as they come to their deaths. He still supported them, he's been good to their needs. So, yes, there's a very tender side to Arnold.

Arnold was obsessed with his sport; you wanted to settle down and get married. Can you relate any conversations you both had reflecting this issue?
Barbara Baker: Well, they were fairly constant. Probably for the first year, you're typically dating, and my world was such that if you dated for a year you got married, because that's what all of my college friends were doing. But for him, I guess culturally, his upbringing and maybe in

different parts of Europe is that you didn't really have a need to get married. If you loved one another, you can live together and maybe someday you would get married when you wanted children. But for him, that wasn't now. So, once we started moving in the second and the third year, I was starting to get extremely impatient and worried and thinking I wanted to have children. I'd say at least once a year, there was a serious conversation, "Where's this going? Where do you want to go? I desperately want to have children and we have such a great relationship." It just went nowhere. As people today get into those kinds of relationships, when the man isn't ready - or woman - or one of you, it can't happen. He couldn't really explain himself well enough to me that I understood it. So I was really frustrated that we weren't getting married, but I wasn't strong enough to leave him.

You were both together for six years, what is the most strange conversation you had with Arnold?
Barbara Baker: Yes. Actually, one that occurs to me is where I was absolutely shocked after we had broken up, we really did maintain a beautiful friendship and we would still meet for lunch. So, I went to Santa Monica, by now he owned an office building along with his apartment building. I don't think he owned the restaurant yet, but there was a restaurant he liked to go to frequently. And he's sitting there telling me - this would be 1977 or '78 - he said, "You just wait, I will be the governor of California." And it came so out of nowhere. It was such an impossible thing to say, that you'd out of most people just laugh at him. I felt, because he was with Maria Shriver then, maybe he's going to learn something about how to get into the political arena. It did take him probably eighteen years or so when he said that, so he was off by a number of years. But to think he predicted that he would be the governor of California, it was a shock. I drove home that day thinking: I don't believe what I just heard. What if my ex-boyfriend becomes the governor of my home state?

Barbara, please can you reminisce on spending time together - did Arnold go out often or was he the type of a guy to stay in and watch a movie?
Barbara Baker: I would say he was a much of a doer. And it wasn't like a party scene, like today's youth would do; it was more dropping in on his bodybuilding friends, talking and laughing. And it wasn't even like drinking. He might have a beer here and there, but it wasn't a party situation. I almost think he would have a cup of coffee in the evening as opposed to a drink. A cup of coffee and a little tiny dessert. But we would do that with Italian friends, or Jewish friends, and there usually

would be couples, long-term married, and they would have this hospitable open-house policy. So, there was a lot of that, spending time with friends. Or he and his friend Franco Columbu, that you probably know of, the three of us, again, would go out to a restaurant and go to every movie. There was hardly any movie that was made which we didn't go to see.

We spent a lot of time with my family, who lived about half an hour away. Usually, we'd go over every Sunday and have dinner with my family. And just laugh and maybe play a little poker, just wear silly hats, and he would laugh and tease. He loved getaways, whether it was going up to Santa Barbara, Palm Springs, just day drives. You could be gone for one night - he loved getting out of town. But he wouldn't let it disrupt that much, because he was so driven to be back at the gym and back to his schedule. But he was a goer and doer and loved meeting new people. He really liked it if they could advance him. Again, that takes us back to the networking.

Would I be right in saying Arnold's mother for the first time visited America in the early 1970s, how did she settle down with Arnold in a new environment?
Barbara Baker: After his father died, I would say he already bought his apartment building, so she stayed with us in a rented apartment. So I would say that was probably 1972 or '73 at Christmas time. She stayed for quite a long time, maybe for six weeks. You know, he didn't spend much time with her, he visited her there (Austria) certainly. I had met her there by then, when I went to Europe with Arnold once. She was a very simple village woman and didn't have any kind of disposable income. She came over here with a very simple heart and a really closed pocketbook. And I know that it was a little bit really hard for him, because she was so Austrian and he was so American. So it was almost like he had a cultural conflict with his mother.

Eventually, she really learned to have a better life. She had a boyfriend for fifteen years after Arnold's father died, and they had a wonderful relationship. She, and even Franz, would eventually come over. This is after Arnold and I broke up, but our friendship allowed me to know that she and this man had a great relationship. She developed her personality, she was a lot more fun, she was looser. Arnold could help support her financially, so she wasn't as worried and nervous about her finances and she really started blossoming more in her personality.

Arnold kept in touch with his mother and cared for her very much, he would often send gifts to his mother when she was living in Austria.

Arnold related a story once saying his mother told him to write "gift" on the package whenever he sent a gift so she wouldn't have to pay tax on the imported package. Once he sent a package with a pearl necklace. Complying with his mother's wishes, he wrote "gift" on the package. When the package arrived in Austria, the authorities confiscated it. Because gift means poison in German. According to one of his closest friends from Germany, the deepest and saddest moment of Arnold's life was when his mother passed away in August 1998. Arnold didn't show it too much on the outside, it may not have been perceptible to the outsider, but inside he was suffering. "As a lifelong friend, I could see that his mother's death really got to him on a deep level," recalled his friend.

When you visited Austria with Arnold, how did you find the experience?

Barbara Baker: I would say it was in the summer of '73, I don't think it would've been '74. We went over for a couple of weeks, it was for an exhibition in Belgium and Germany. So it was more that he had these business deals where he would get paid for his exhibits. In Germany we were close to Austria, so, of course, it was an opportunity to go and see his mother. And what had happened by then, of course, you can't call her a sister-in-law because she and Mienhardt never got married, but Erika was really like his sister-in-law. She had a son named Patrick. We went to see all three of them and just had the most loving, wonderful, sweetest and kindest time. It was really a joy to be there, being in his mother's home and the home he had grown up and meet his little nephew, who now, of course, work's for Arnold as a lawyer. So, it's really ironic to see that child, who had been fatherless, taken on by Arnold all those years later and now living in Santa Monica and working for his uncle.

Like any relationship, there must have been tumultuous times with your ups and downs. Can you tell me what these were and how you came over them?

Barbara Baker: Well, I think I would go back to the conflict of how we each perceived marriage. So, other than that we really were compatible, we had a good time together. I do recall being dismayed by a little bit of sarcastic side to him that was hurtful to other people. So, sometimes his nature, I felt it really hurt my soul. It's, like, you have got to learn to be kind to people! You can't go hurting people's feelings for your own pleasure. So that definitely was a source of conflict. But mostly it was my selfishness, I just wanted to get married. And so any of the ups and downs would affect my emotional nature. I was so depressed I couldn't make myself leave him. It was more my issue, I was caught in the relationship. I couldn't stay and I couldn't leave. It was really, really tough.

Did Arnold have a penchant for fashion or anything else other than his sport?
Barbara Baker: We're talking in the early years, as he would say today, "I collect everything." There's not one thing that man doesn't collect. But at the time, no. He wasn't into clothes, he pretty much looked like a slob, like a gym slob. He was a monomaniac. Bodybuilding was pretty exclusively it. It doesn't mean he wouldn't like to go skiing or horseback riding or driving his cars fast or hang out at the beach. I mean, all of that aliveness was in him. It was business, business, business, learning how to develop his business; his bodybuilding courses; develop his body; win contests - apply that to better business. And how he could make more money through exhibitions, through selling more courses to negotiating his contract with Joe Weider. So, the years I knew him, it was all around bodybuilding as a vehicle to become a businessman.

What food did he favor?
Barbara Baker: He certainly was a protein person, as they were in those days. It was the protein powder, with the raw eggs and the protein drinks. Then in the morning, little steaks, kind of eggs in the morning - scrambled eggs or boiled eggs - cottage cheese - it was protein. Any way he could get it in there. Vegetables, salads, he and the other guys, they wouldn't want too much carbohydrates so they would have almost nothing on their salads, maybe vinegar and oil. But he had a little weakness for sweets, especially when it wasn't training time. He would have his apple strudel, which was his favorite. And he loved my carrot cake, that was the favorite thing. I had a special recipe where I would "hand" the carrots, and would take that to New York when he was competing at the Mr. Olympia. I even made a cake in California and physically hand-carried it to New York, so we could have it to celebrate his win in New York City. It was pretty repetitious. He was very protein driven.

What kind of restaurants did you frequent with Arnold?
Barbara Baker: We went to Zucke's Delicatessen so many times, that's where we met. We lived very close to it, so we would either walk over or drive over. That was totally a second home for us. They kind of knew what he ordered, so they would bring it to him without even him requesting it. We would go out for Chinese food a lot of times with Joe Weider. That was an unusual taste for him to venture into - Chinese cuisine. It wouldn't take him so long to get a little tipsy, so it was funny

sometimes seeing him have one beer. And, you know, I guess even though you're that big, if you're not used to alcohol it could get to you, and he could be really, really funny.

Did it ever surprise you that Arnold went on to become so famous around the globe?
Barbara Baker: Well, I don't know, if you've personally known somebody before their fame, it is really odd, because they're just the person they are. And you like them and you laugh with them and you know them. They're really like this person you're hanging out with. OK, fine, the reason you like being with this person is because they're so exciting. So, that's how I perceived Arnold, that he was the most unusual person that I ever met. He was just incredible fun to be with. He was the life of the party. Yes, of course, with that came narcissism, so life was all about Arnold 100 percent. And most of the time, that was OK with me, because I was included in everything and it was really great fun.

So, I never would have pictured how far it would have gone, because I had a small enough mind that I thought, "Hey, this guy really could have a successful chain of opening up gyms." And that's kind of where I was going with what I could see him doing if I kept it in the same domain that he'd been training in. So, to see him venture out in real estate, I got to witness that even being with him when he bought his first apartment building. I'm thinking, "That is absolutely amazing. He didn't buy a home, he bought an apartment building where six other people are going to have their homes within his home, and he's going to own their homes too. I definitely thought this guy was really unusual, so I imagined him to be wealthy. I figured he will be a real estate mogul, that will be something he'll do on the sidelines with the money he will probably make off the chain of gyms.

Then after we broke off, he ended up buying this office building in Santa Monica and really restoring it. Actually, it was Venice, well, they're kind of one and the same. But Venice was really rundown, and by Arnold buying this office building, he upgraded it. All of a sudden, I felt he was very much at the core of restoring the bad part of Santa Monica. I thought, that's powerful! That's really huge that you'd take a city that's so famous and rundown and being part of the restoration process. I kept seeing him buy more expensive homes. Of course, at the end of our relationship he had already been working on two movies - Stay Hungry and Pumping Iron - and that was the fact why we broke off, because I felt: OK. This isn't going to change. Arnold's not going to marry me now, just because he's going to quit his bodybuilding career, he's going to be now married to an acting career or whatever else is going to come in the way. I did see him in the Stay Hungry movie, which came out after we had broken up. We were together of the filming of it, but we split up during it.

The Hercules movie before that was such a joke that I never expected that he could succeed in that industry. The Stay Hungry part was a little weird. I know he won awards for it but, I mean, I just didn't see that was going to result in a big acting career. In Pumping Iron he kind of looked like a goofball. When he hit the big time with Conan, I couldn't believe that he was becoming a household name. I'm hearing it on the street, strangers talking about Arnold Schwarzenegger. And in my classroom, where I taught students, they would say, "I like Arnold." And it just seemed everywhere I turned around, I started hearing his name. But they didn't know that I was in any way related to this man's life. So, that continued forever and you get used to it. It still continues and you get used to it. But there's something very surreal about knowing a human being who once was a normal person and now they're completely iconic, you know. They're known worldwide, not even in a small little arena, it's just pretty phenomenal.

How would Arnold relax at home and kill time?
Barbara Baker: I don't think he'd know the phrase "killing time". He would watch a little bit of television, like the news, at the end of the day. And our last year together, we had a terrible gasoline crisis in the country, he was really focused on that and the politics at the time. So, he certainly had an avid interest in keeping up with the news, international news, state of California news, American news. But it wasn't really killing time; he really wanted to know what was going on in the world.

Did Arnold have a penchant for any particular TV programs?
Barbara Baker: You know, isn't it funny that he loved movies so much? But unless there were reruns of cowboy movies, he really liked the Western genre. I can't think of anything that was valuable enough for him to look forward to see on television. Remember television wasn't as advance in those days as the productions they do today.

You were a teacher, we know Arnold enrolled in college, but what was he exactly studying and how did this help him?
Barbara Baker: He really wanted to work on his English, so he started at the Santa Monica Community College. He struggled and he was not a natural student. So, getting the writing down and everything else, but it was very helpful that I was there, being an English major. So I could tutor him more or less. So, from Santa Monica College, he then started taking classes at UCLA. But in there there's adults, or people who are continuing education programs, because he wouldn't

have had the units or the grades to have gotten in as a regular student in UCLA. But he did do a lot of work in there, whether it was philosophy classes or history classes.

Then somehow he had enough academic resume that the University of Wisconsin gave him a degree; they're very creative in how they give you credit for your life experience for your education that you have had. They arranged to deal with him where he could go back to Wisconsin. I think it was for some classes he could do by correspondence. It's not a world that I really know very well, because I have a more traditional history with how education works, or you take classes on the campus and you go to them and they are credited. But in his case, he pulled it off and got his degree in business. I'm not really sure what the title would be, but I think it would have to be a B. Then after that, he got countless PhDs, honorary PhDs, from various colleges. So, for somebody who was not academically oriented, he does have a resume to show - it's very interesting.

Did you see Arnold in the 1980s and 1990s, when his movie career peaked, as he basked in his newfound fame?
Barbara Baker: Yeah. We really did maintain a friendship, most of the times I'd say it was on the telephone. I think he would just get lonely in the hotel rooms, making movies and stuff, and he would probably have a list of twenty or thirty people he felt like calling. Because Arnold is really not a person who likes being alone. He would call frequently enough when he was on the road. I can't tell you whether it was once every month, two months, six months, it changed over the years. But certainly we kept up that. And occasionally I would go down to visit him on a movie set. I went down when he was making, I think the Belushi movie (Red Heat). So, things like that would happen.

Then in 1992 or '93, he invited my mother and I to a really big art exhibit that he had thrown at a museum in Los Angeles. That was really sweet. As late as 1992, he extended this formal invitation to my mother and I. It was a great night where we had a wonderful reunion to see old friends. Then I got married in 1993 and it was interesting that the phone calls did start dropping off a little bit more after that. It was much more rare that I would hear from him. But we still would keep in contact, but it's less when he became the Californian governor. I think that his world is so ascended into this...at this point I just don't see a real need for us to speak with one another. But the feelings are fine, you know, we're good with each other. It's just that after a while you do grow apart. I think we might have hit that place.

Do you feel Arnold, from when you knew him when you were together in the early period and Arnold at the height of his fame, went through an evolutionary process as far his character or personality, and did you perceive any elements of pompousness?

Barbara Baker: When I interviewed him for my book, I really left the office sad that day. Remember it's all subjective, it's just me and how I perceive it. But I feel when you get that famous, most people are so locked off by your protection. Your security guards, your office staff, everybody is there to protect you so that you won't get killed, so you won't get burdened by the use of your time. And I could see that his life was so large and so small at the same time. It seemed to me it would be a real burden living like that. So, as a process maybe he has developed more of a harder shell in protection. He's lost the spontaneity that a freer life would allow you to have. I think anybody might have fallen into this kind of situation, although I don't know any other famous people, so I can't compare. But I just have to believe that that's going to be a certain direction for anybody who becomes so famous that you are openly no longer openly accessible to the public, you're more of a robot.

A lot of controversial stuff surfaces when someone becomes famous. Arnold had his fair share of negative media, especially when he was going to pursue politics, which may have become an inextricable problem. What are your views and was it something you were surprised about?

Barbara Baker: Well, as I explained going on Fox News network when all this came out, Arnold is certainly no saint, he has loved women his whole life. Certainly in my time, he had a more open morality about what constituted fidelity, the need to have it. So I knew that Arnold really had reached out to plenty of women in his life, and I watched his flirtation even when I was with him thinking: that was really inappropriate, why did you do that? But on the other hand, these women would reach out to him. They would expose their breasts to him, they would go offer their bodies to him. It's incredible, even way back in the 1970s, what women were capable of doing. So, I think he got so used to women being.... He's got two perspectives: on the one hand, he completely respects a woman who is worthy of his respect. But on the other hand, if you're going to put yourself in to being just raw meat for him, he's going to treat you like raw meat. And sometimes he's going to miscalculate, and he's going to treat somebody poorly who should've been respected.

I' thinking with that it ended up happening sometimes, there was just a big mismatch that he said the wrong thing to the wrong women at the wrong time and he went too far. But I don't think he's 100 percent to blame for it, because the women had fed him this all his life and also exploited him. So, I don't know, he just got himself into a really big mess. But nothing stuck, he sort of was tough throughout the whole deal and escaped. I think there were a few little lawsuits, but I think they went away, really, nothing stuck while he was the governor of California that really mared his reputation. Since that time, when I even asked him during the interview, he goes, "We've learned! We've learned!" It's, like, "We've learned?" How interesting to phrase it in that way. He and his committee decided that Arnold better keep his mouth shut and not be flirtatious around other women.

Can you tell me about how your book materialized?
Barbara Baker: When we broke up, 1975ish, and maybe the next summer we'd meet for lunch, and all of a sudden, actually, we went for dinner one night and he said, "You're the one. I don't want to write any more books, you're the one. You should write the book on me, you're the one who knows me." I always wanted to be an author my whole entire life, and I felt, "Well, I don't know what I would really say, but I'm going to give this a try." So that summer, I wrote a little booklet that was very poorly written, about a hundred pages. It became more like an elevated diary or journal that sort of pretended to have some kind of a plotline in it. It was just really awful, but I'd done it and I never threw it out. I tried to get it marketed at the time. But one, it was terrible. And two, he wasn't famous enough yet. So it sat in my file. Twenty years later, or whatever, I thought I just need a new creative outlet, because I had to quit my painting hobby because it was damaging my back too much. I thought: what would not hurt my back? Maybe I could write, sit at a computer.

So I talked it over with my husband. He was, like, "What? You would want to bring Arnold into our daily life?" Little did we know the writing of the book and getting it published would take six years. As long as time I spent with Arnold, that's how long it took to write and get the book published. There you have it. And Arnold wrote the foreword to it. It was really a nice completion and closure. Just looking at how our lives were separate, we met, then how my life went on in his shadow whilst he's become what he has. And I'm just sitting here as a little school teacher, you know. There are a lot of people who care intimately about what he's really about. A lot of the biographies are great - Larry Leamar's and Doug Hall's books. I mean, they did what they could for what they had without the feeling on the inside. But I could really get my feelings come to the surface and try to express him in a way that I thought more roundly about his personality.

Having known Arnold on a personal and intimate basis, do you feel anything the media misses?

Barbara Baker: That's about your toughest question yet. Everybody in the world already know almost every single thing about him. I just don't know if there's anything I haven't shared, or so much I could say would be speculation, because I can't prove anymore because we don't have that intimate relationship.

What would be your most enduring memories of Arnold during the time you spent with him?
Barbara Baker: Instantly, I had the picture of us meeting his nephew for the first time, just poignant bond that developed. That was like the birth of his fraternal feelings when he met Patrick, who was probably two years old. So, just seeing his tenderness, that was a surprise because I didn't know that he had that side. I don't know him as a father. I've not met his children, but I have to believe, even though he's known to be strict, he's probably incredibly tender, funny and really, really a good father.

JAMES LORIMER

James Lorimer is one of Arnold's closest friends - a friendship that can be traced as far back as four decades - and a business partner. Lorimer, who early on in his career served as a FBI agent, is the promoter of the annual Arnold Classic.

You and Arnold joined forces back in the 1970s, can you tell me how you got involved and how the friendship ensued?
James Lorimer: In 1970, I was promoting the World Weightlifting Championships here in Columbus, Ohio. And in connection with the World Weightlifting Championships, I obtained television coverage from Wide World of Sports programing here in the United States. I knew I wanted to have an addition to the World Weightlifting Championships - a Mr. World contest. So, I promoted the Mr. World contest that year, because it was going to be the first time bodybuilding and weightlifting were on international TV, right here in Columbus in 1970. So, as I put the contest together, I identified the top six bodybuilders in the world. Among them were, of course, Sergio Oliva, Franco Columbu, one was a new young Austrian who had just come over to the United States.

And I called Arnold and told him that this was going to be on a national TV program. He said he understood the importance of that and he very much wanted to be there - the event was in September of 1970. He said that the day before your event - Mr. World contest - is going to be the day before on Saturday, and I'm scheduled and I've made a commitment to participate in the Mr. Universe event in London, England. He said I don't know how I can make your event on Sunday. I said, "Well, if you compete in the Mr. Universe contest on Saturday evening, and go directly to Heathrow airport right after the competition and get the last flight out of London for the United States, we will meet you by private plane in New York City and bring you to Columbus and you can compete here." He said, "Well, if you will do that, I'll do that."

So, in September 1970 he won the Mr. Universe competition in London on Saturday evening. Then he got the plane and we picked him up in New York and he came here and competed in front of four thousand people, in connection with the World Weightlifting

Championship and the Mr. World contest. He beat Sergio Oliva that evening on our stage for the first time. After the contest, he came up to me and said, "This is the best competition I have ever been in. When I compete and I'm done competing in the sport of bodybuilding, I want to go into the promotion side of the sport and raise the energy of the sport up and professionalize the sport making it a great sport worldwide." He said, "I'm going to come back to Columbus, Ohio, and ask you to be my partner." I said, sure. I didn't know who he was, really. So, the next five years he won everything. He won the Olympia every year.

And in 1975, he won his last Olympia, as you may know, and he stopped by on his way back from South Africa in '75, and he said, "As I told you five years ago, I'm done competing now and I want to go in the promotion of the sport. The next year we'll hold the Mr. Olympia here in Columbus, Ohio, in 1976. And if you will help run the competition, I will help get the athletes and help get the sponsors. And we're going to raise the cash prizes." He was still only making $1,000 in cash prize, when he won in South Africa. He said, "The first year, we'll raise our cash prizes up to $10,000," ten times whatever was being made. And he said, "In three years, we're going to have it up to $100,000 in cash prizes for the athletes." We shook hands and thirty-five years later now, on a handshake, we're still partners. We did everything we said we'd do. The first year we had ten thousand, and three years later we had a hundred thousand in cash prizes. We've expanded over the years, as you know, we're giving $500,000 in cash prizes, still promoting together all of these thirty-five years later.

Can you tell me what the core concept of the Arnold Classic is?
James Lorimer: Absolutely. We ran the Mr. Olympia contest for several years very successfully, and then the Weiders suggested that they wanted to run the Mr. Olympia contest in Europe. So we then began running the Mr. Universe contest. And during the 1980s, we ran several international contests in Europe, but then in 1988 Arnold said, "Really, we've been running the Olympia contest and some years we've been running the Mr. Universe. I think we should have a contest which carries my name - the Arnold Classic. So in 1989, we ran the first Arnold Classic. The reason for that was, again, a title that was his; nobody could take it away. And every year since 1989. This will be our twenty-third year that we have ran the Arnold Classic, raising the cash prizes up every year.

In the early 1990s, while Arnold was the chairman of the United States President's Council on Physical Fitness and Sports, and I was on that council with him, and at the time we began to get more opportunities to work with a number of other sports like martial arts, gymnastics and the like. So in the early '90s, we began to expand the Arnold Classic weekend to include other sports in the weekend. Each year we've added some different sports. So, now twenty years later we have the largest multisport event that we know of anywhere, which involves athletes from seventy-one nations competing, eighteen thousand athletes competing in forty-four different sports and events. Olympic Games in Vancouver usually had six thousand athletes competing in about eighteen events. We had hundred and seventy-five thousand people who attend the weekend, plus booths involving seven hundred booths with exhibitors around the world. So it's a huge, huge event. But it's become a huge event because each year we've added new events in a twenty-year period.

Driven by an immense desire to succeed and an unparallel determination, Arnold cultivated a no-lose attitude. He has stated that he would do anything possible to achieve his goal and put his mind and focus wholeheartedly into fulfilling his ambitions. "When I used to do seminars on how to become a champion, I would always ask people, 'Why do you want to be a champion? Or, 'What do you want to accomplish? Or, 'Why are you training?' And if a guy would get up and he said, 'Well, I want to train because I think that if I get muscular and I feel like I'm getting the definition, then maybe I can enter a bodybuilding competition.' I said, 'Sit down, if you think this way, you're going to be a loser, you're never going to make it, because there's no maybe. You've got to get up and say, I want to be a champion, and I'd do whatever it takes, the amount of hours it takes, the posing, this and that, the visualization, looking at training footage, I'm looking at motivational books, reading this and reading that, whatever it takes, I would do it. That's the answer I want to hear from you.'"

What was Arnold's vision, ultimate vision of achieving goals promoting bodybuilding and fitness?
James Lorimer: Well, the original vision, of course, was to do everything we could to enhance and professionalize the sport of bodybuilding, which is his first love. And, of course, as he moved through his career, he's become very much involved, always involved and committed to bodybuilding. At the same time, acknowledging the fact the whole physical culture movement involving many sports is very important in our society. We have great problems with child obesity and the like, so his vision has gone from the focus on bodybuilding to a focus on the entire sports community. How do we bring more opportunity and more fun for youngsters to compete in a wide range of sports?

Because there's a sport there for everyone. One of the Olympic sports we have in our program is archery. We have thirteen hundred archers come into the Arnold Classic. Archery is, you know, an Olympic sport and so is fencing, gymnastics, weightlifting. And all the Olympic sports that we have in the program. We focus very much on the Olympic sports now, but also other sports like cheerleading and the like, which add to the opportunity to participate and compete. It's a combination of all the sports, adding a sports festival feeling to the weekend.

In 2011, at the Arnold Classic, Arnold expressed his admiration for mixed martial arts. The sport which has enjoyed immense success and has become part of the annual expo with many stars and companies promoting themselves in Columbus. "I just love to watch the fights. I think they're very entertaining, and you get a kind of a combination of things," the bodybuilding legend told a reporter. "You get inspiration because they're in extraordinary shape. It's entertaining because it's fighting. It's just like basic stuff, just like the Gladiator days. They don't have as many restricted rules...tap, which I think people enjoy. And they have great personalities, they all can talk very well, they can explain what they've done, why they won, why they lost. It's also very important, so you get involved with different personalities. And the whole thing is just organized very well. It's show business - it's sport and show business. I think that's what you need. People love to see it there and have a show and spice it up.... I watch every one of the fights, yeah."

What is Arnold's role in attending the event?
James Lorimer: For the past thirty-five years, Arnold has been here every year without fail. He makes a tremendous contribution to the weekend and advice throughout the year, especially on that weekend. Because I told you about all the different competitors we have and the booths we have at the expo, and he has a full weekend of moving around. He goes to every competitor site, he goes to all of our major sponsors' booths at the expo. He participates in the award ceremonies and recognitions throughout the weekend. We give twelve college scholarships on the weekend, and he participates in the awarding of the college scholarships in various sports. So he's very much involved, has very much output and is very much committed to the sports festival.

As a business partner and a close friend, what is the most intriguing conversation you've ever had with Arnold?
James Lorimer: I think one of the most interesting things about Arnold

and myself, an interview I had with a Time magazine writer a few years ago, she called, like you did, and interviewed me for quite a while. The last question she asked was, "What is the one thing that distinguishes Arnold Schwarzenegger from anybody you've ever known?" And I said, "I feel it's his capacity for enjoyment." I said, "Everything he does, he seems to enjoy. And that's not in just from a humanistic standpoint necessarily, but it's just from a pure joy sense. And if he doesn't enjoy something, he isn't likely to do it very long, that's for sure." So, after that conversation with that writer, I called Arnold and told him what she had asked me, and he said, "Well, that's interesting." He said, "Because if she asked me one word that I would use to describe myself, it would be 'joy'." Here is a guy who defines himself in terms of joy. And that's part of his charisma, that's part of what comes through to people. Here is a man who is enjoying life to the fullest. And it speaks to us! We all can relate to a person who is feeling that way about life.

Just recently I called him, and I said, "Arnold, I Google you every day, and in the political environment it's so nasty. They are always coming after you." I said, "How are you feeling about that?" He said, "I'm loving every minute of it. I'm enjoying every minute of it. The challenges are so great, so fantastic. I feel I have an opportunity to give expression to everything I've learned. And I'm doing the best possible job I can. But the opportunity to give everything I have to a mission is very, very rewarding, very, very enjoyable to me." Again, if I was standing in what would normally be a very, very troublesome environment for a person.... I think it's an attitude toward life, an attitude of mind and the attitude of joy that distinguishes Arnold to anybody else. That's also, to respond to your question, a very interesting conversation with me about Arnold how he sees himself.

Arnold says, "To me, it's fun to have a movie come out and make $500 million worldwide. It's not fun to get beat up by some creature, or be in Predator and freeze my butt off. I think in general, what I do with my life, everything that I do I have fun - or otherwise I don't do. Every movie that I made, I had some fun. Every work that I do, whether it's working with the Special Olympians - I have fun." In early 2011, Arnold told a prominent magazine, "I can only operate to the utmost and to 100 percent of my potential if I have no safety net. Because it's only then that I'm at my peak. That's one reason I never did TV shows - I didn't want to have that security. What I liked about being governor was never knowing how a meeting would end. The legislative leaders could leave and destroy you to the press. Or they go out and compliment you. So you don't know. You don't know the way the people go. One year they like something, the next year it's number seven on their priority list. So you just never know. That brings excitement and spice to life. And that to me is the difference between living and existing."

Arnold is also known for being a facetious person.

James Lorimer: He's a part of a joyful atmosphere and joyful attitude that he has. He's always good with a line to come up with in respects to any situation. He's always fairly critical of himself, he can make fun of himself. And a lot of his humor really has a political pitch to it. But I can think of so many humorous things that would be really significant in political environment in the US. When Arnold was the chairman of the President's Council on Physical Fitness and Sports, I traveled with him quite a bit. Because he went to every state in the United States and meeting with the governors and educational leaders, telling them about message about fitness. I remember one time, when I was in his own jet when we went to Washington DC. He was going back to California, and I asked him, "Would you mind dropping me off in Columbus, because you're flying over Columbus?" He said, "From how high?" I was at Arnold's and Maria's wedding and I gave the reading on behalf of Arnold's side of the family. Ted Kennedy gave the reading from Maria's side. Arnold said he selected me to be the reader because I was the only one of his friends who could read.

In 2010, at the Emory Commencement Address, when Arnold received his honorary doctor of laws degree, he joked, "And finally, the Kennedys would think that I am successful. Finally, Maria can take me home and meet her family, finally! It's a truly honor to stand before you here on this joyous day as your commencement speaker. I was also to go and give a commencement speech in Arizona, but with my accent I was worried they're going to deport me back to Austria, so I canceled that idea right away." The audience laughed as the governor expressed his light-hearted side and was in his element.

How would you describe him as a family man, irrespective of the mistakes he's made, away from the public eye?

James Lorimer: He's a tremendous father, caring dad, very much involved in his youngsters' life. Of course, he and Maria have been very protective of their family, which is important in the political environment. But he is absolutely a great father, and the family did things together, went skiing together and sailing and did just about everything. It was a great family. There's two girls and two boys (born to Maria), and that's a good size family with a lot of caring and a lot of sharing.

His movie star status propelled the sport of bodybuilding into a much more mainstream arena. What are your sentiments on this?

James Lorimer: There's no question about it, he's the most iconic figure that ever competed in the sport of bodybuilding. He's always identified in the public mind as a man who came out of the bodybuilding culture, so that has been a tremendous help to our sport giving it legitimacy. A man who could go on to be worldwide one of the top movie stars in the world, and still go on further from his bodybuilding background to become governor of the largest state in the United States. That shows quite a bit about the fact, the discipline and training and the experience in his early career of bodybuilding certainly did nothing but help him. And he got into one of the great fields in which he attained a high level of achievement.

When he initially became famous, winning all the coveted titles in bodybuilding, did he talk to you about pursuing even bigger things which went beyond the confines of his beloved sport, which may have been imperceptible for some?

James Lorimer: You have to understand that Arnold was a goal setter, and he consciously sets goals five years out. That's, of course, one thing which distinguishes him from other people, too, because a lot of us just go along. But he says setting a goal gives him a track to run on. He knows where he wants to go. He knew that he wanted to go in the movie field. He bridged over from the bodybuilding, starting off with bodybuilding-related movies then going more over to the straight action films. But I also knew very earlier on he found a great and abiding interest in politics. And in the long run, he was going to go into the political field. So, he also makes his plans and he's moved from one pathway to the other with a goal in mind, always.

Arnold has also been involved in charitable ventures, would you care to elucidate on these?

James Lorimer: He's involved in a number of charities. Of course, he established his own charity called The After-School All-Star Charity, which is in thirteen major cities in the United States. It's aimed at children in the inner cities. They have periods from 3 p.m. to 6 p.m. every day after school, giving them places to go and activities to participate in. This is a major, major charity of his. Of course, the Special Olympics, which the Shriver family has been involved in for many years, is another major attraction for him which is aimed at the disadvantage young people throughout the world. He's traveled worldwide in support of the Special Olympic program.

Can you explicate, from the perspective of a close friend and a business partner, how you perceive Arnold as far as an entrepreneur?
James Lorimer: He proved very early on, because of his discipline and training, that he is an extremely successful businessman. He owns a great deal of real estate, he's had heavy, heavy investments. Because of his success in the film industry, he was able to invest in real estate. And he is positioned financially so that he wouldn't have to work again - he's got the income. The fact of the matter is: he's been like that for some time. All the time he was the governor, there was a salary that went with that job - about two hundred thousand a year - but he never accepted any salary in the seven years he was the governor. So, he's economically independent, because of the great business judgment he used earlier in his career building on his film advantage. So, it's a beautiful business partner to have.

He's trying to do a lot of good now. He's not necessarily motivated by money. Arnold is the best possible friend you could have. His attitude shows you what kind of a man he is, on a handshake thirty-five years ago we still have that partnership thirty-five years later. We've been part of each other's lives for all those years. I've been there for every major thing that has happened to him, and he comes into Columbus, Ohio, for all our events, several of our birthdays and activities like that. So, from a close personal friend you could not have a better friend over a lifetime than Arnold, and I've been very blessed and very fortunate to have that friendship to enjoy. I'm encouraging him to continue to be involved in the world of physical culture and sports promotion, opportunities for that to move forward worldwide.

JOE LEWIS

Joe Lewis, an extrovert personality and training partner of the late Bruce Lee, was voted the Greatest Karate Fighter in History. The former actor and ardent fitness aficionado met Arnold back in the late 1960s. Later, both men were in the same acting class in Los Angeles.

Joe, did you come into contact with Arnold for the first time back in the late 1960s or early 1970s?

Joe Lewis: I met him in the first year he came to this country. He came here in '68. I met him right in the end of 1968. He was living with a buddy of his, Franco Columbu. Joe Weider had brought him over to this country to pose for the magazine, and he was paying him to live here. They told me that all he had to do was work one day a month for Joe Weider. They were to take pictures, and it was kind of nice. Arnold was going to college. They lived in a little apartment, Arnold slept on the top bunk and Franco slept on the bottom bunk. They just had two really nice bodies. I walked with them to their place one day after they finished the workout. The first thing they did is that they ordered a pizza to eat. Junk food! You know, when you're training so hard you can eat anything you want.

Years later, in the mid-'70s, he actually joined my acting class in Hollywood. Eric Morris was the acting coach. He was more of a loner; he didn't really hang out with the guys so to speak. He was kind of like me, I didn't like hanging out with guys, either. People didn't think he was real friendly. It could've been the fact he needed to learn the language. He probably went through the same nonsense that I did in the film industry: if you want to do a movie, you better get rid of those big muscles. You've got to get rid of the accent. Because that's what they did to me. Then the kid named Jean Claude Van Damme and Arnold came along and said, "Well, you can have the muscles and you can have an accent and it doesn't matter, you can still do the movies." But that wasn't how it was when I went through Hollywood. Bruce Lee had the same problem. They said, "No Chinese guy is going to be taken on by any major studio to become a big film star." So he had to go to Hong Kong to get started. Arnold was lucky.

What was Arnold like in the acting class, did he possess an austere style?

Joe Lewis: The classes that he and I were in met once a week. I was taking private lessons on the side, because you get a lot of extra knowledge that you can pick up from the coach. He was studying what they call "method acting". It's the most difficult form of acting. It's more for, like, stage than it is for preparing you for the actual film. For some reason, I don't know how he got involved in the class. I don't know who recommended him to go there. But he had a persona, an image and reputation, which he can use rather than a lot of that acting preparation stuff and go right into doing films. He was like kind of Clint Eastwood, Charles Bronson and John Wayne. They weren't what we would call "character actors" like Lawrence Olivier and Robert De Niro. Whilst actors such as Arnold and Clint Eastwood are what we call "personality actors", they play themselves on screen. If you watch their roles, they're the exact same character and the only thing that changes is the plot, the wardrobe and the storyline. So, Arnold became what we call a "personality actor". And what's interesting is, personality actors actually make more money than the real authentic character actors.

Did he relate his ambition in class, as far as what he wanted to pursue and achieve in the movie industry?
Joe Lewis: No. You're not allowed to do that in class. No one cares that much about what you're doing professionally, whether you're doing commercials or you're onstage or you're doing films or television. There are some famous people in class, for example, but nobody really cares, so you don't talk about those things. In class it's 100 percent you're there to train, and it's all about training. An acting class has nothing to do with getting you jobs, or send you up to be hired to do a movie or anything like that. So nobody talks about that stuff. You'll have famous people in class, sometimes you'll have a famous writer or producer or a director come by and visit the class because, especially people who are casting, they're always looking for new talent. I don't know how Arnold got discovered outside of that. He did that Pumping Iron film and he did that real low-budget film Hercules in New York. That just kind of catapulted him into the big time. But, you know, a lot of actors are poor. Back then in the early '70s, Arnold was doing really well with his mail order. He was doing mail order bodybuilding stuff. I heard he was making at least $300,000 a year, even way back then. Of course, now he's worth millions of dollars.

You had an interest in weight training and bodybuilding, was there ever any inclination to talk about this subject?
Joe Lewis: I would talk to the guys who competed in the Mr. Olympia contest, or the Arnold Classic. They would tell me, if you don't do

steroids you're never going to be a world-class bodybuilder - they all do steroids. That's kind of interesting, because they keep that hush, hush. Then if you talk to the experts, they say if you train hard and you're dedicated then anybody can become a champion. That's not true. World-class bodybuilding, world-class powerlifting, in my opinion, is 97 percent genetics. For example, if you're not born with long muscles, you're never going to be a world-class bodybuilder - you've got to have long muscles. Number two, if you're going to be a world-class arm wrestler, then you've got to have the long tendons, the large thick tendons, what they call "the bicep tendons". For example, my bicep tendons are an inch thick, that's incredible. When I had my muscles measured by some physicist at the University of California, they told me that my muscles were two- and-a-half times as dense as the current Mr. America. That's kind of important.

It's no secret that Arnold has admitted to using performance-enhancing anabolic steroids, when it was legal to do so. He said he used them for muscle maintenance when cutting up; not for muscle growth. They were helpful in maintaining size, while he was on a strict diet when preparing for a competition. Years later, the talk show host David Letterman asked Arnold on air, "If you had to do it again, would you use steroids, do you think?" To which he replied, "No. I think that drugs, the name already says 'bodybuilding', you know, this means you build your body and that you build your health and you want to stay away from any kind of drugs. And I always tell people on seminars, you must create the body without the steroids, without the drugs. No matter what it is, if it is acting or anything else, drugs are temporary." He said bodybuilders experimented with them and it was foolish to do so.

When asked whether he could have achieved the same results without steroids, Arnold replied, "Absolutely, oh, yeah. It would take maybe an extra half year or a year. But it's such a small percentage you get, and then when you stop taking it, it goes back to normal, you know. It really is just a temporary thing and it doesn't pay off in the end." In those days, you could go to a physician and merely say you wanted to gain some weight and take something. And the physician would advise the athlete to take the steroids for six weeks before the competition, and this would be safe. The dosage which was taken by bodybuilders back in those days in comparison to what is taken now was less than 10 percent.

Did you spend time socializing with Arnold in the early days, when he was settling in and competing in the sport?

Joe Lewis: We had a mutual friend who brought us together. I don't know if anyone who really socialized with him. I got along much better with Franco Columbu. Dave Draper and I were pretty good buddies, he did that Don't Make Waves movie. I think he beat Arnold in a physique contest early, just like Frank Zane beat Arnold when Arnold first came over here. Because Arnold had that big bulky body that was very popular in Europe, but that wasn't very popular in this country back in '68, '69,'70. Arnold was kind of a unique figure; he was a man's man. But he wasn't necessarily somebody you could befriend easily, because he was kind of a loner. He was always working. I remember he talked about how he only slept for four hours at night, and that that was the only sleep he needed to get. And that means you're up twenty hours every day. You could get a lot done if you're up twenty hours working every day. There's not that many people that have that kind of pace. So he was kind of like a unique person that's just very different than all other men.

Were you surprised when he became a big movie star? He wasn't exactly the best actor in the pure sense of the word, but he became the biggest box office draw?
Joe Lewis: No, but John Wayne wasn't, either. Bruce Lee wasn't, either. But that's not what makes money on the big screen; it's your persona. It's that ability on the careen and the presence and the energy that you project which affects people emotionally. And they're not been affected by how good an actor you are. So, there was something that they could identify with him when they watched him on the screen, and that was the special energy which made him a big star. I was shocked!! Because first of all, his accent was very strong. I'm thinking: what kind of role could you get? You can only get the roles where you need that accent. And then it's kind of hard to put him on the screen, because when you're in front of the camera you always look 20-25 pounds bigger than in real life. I'm thinking: how are you going to get any roles unless you play a role of some kind of a bodybuilder? So, he kind of changed Hollywood in a way, he made Hollywood his world.

Was it ever suggested to Arnold to change the name Schwarzenegger? "A lot of things were suggested to me, believe me, from changing my name, to changing my body, changing my accent, and all of those things," Arnold told an interviewer when promoting his 1985 high-octane movie Commando. When he made the transition from bodybuilding to the motion picture industry, the industry fraternity felt that those obstacles were an impediment and would hold him back from ever becoming a major player in the movie business and achieve the

149

status he had achieved in bodybuilding. "But I felt that, you know, if anybody could pronounce Gina Lollobrigidia and all those kinds of names, I felt they can also pronounce Schwarzenegger," remarked Arnold. The ambitious actor said he had no special interest in getting rid of his accent, remarking that if you were born somewhere it was almost inevitable to have somewhat an accent. As for the physique, Arnold affirmed that eventually people would comprehend that his body would be fashionable enough and appealing that it would be considered an asset rather being an impediment. It, of course, became the norm and almost a necessity to have a well-developed physique in order to play a heroic role in the action genre.

How much of a motivated individual was Arnold? A lot of people say he had an immense level of motivation, and he just wanted to be a big movie star rather than the best actor?
Joe Lewis: It's true, it's true. He wanted to go beyond bodybuilding. When I met him, when he was going college every night to study economics and business, because he knew that's where the money was. That was his real passion. Then when he became the governor of California, they had bankruptcy problems in that state. But he was real good with finances and money and marketing, and that's an asset a lot of politicians don't have. Most politicians come from law school. They don't teach you how to motivate people, they don't teach you how to run a business in law school. So, he was unique and different in that respect. I don't know what his real passion is now; I'm kind of curious.

I was talking to his wife on an airplane, we sat together, about four years ago. What was interesting is we talked about him about the acting class with Eric Morris. But I was kind of curious as to what next Arnold would do when he left the office. Will he really go back to acting? Does he really want to go back there, or is he just going to retire? He's a businessman, he owns a lot of property in the Santa Monica area, California - that's part of Los Angeles, right on the beach. I heard rumors that he's worth close to $600 million. I don't know if that's true or not. I think his real accomplishment in life is, that all the young people he motivated around the world, not so much with the movie acting, but with his bodybuilding accomplishments. For example, I get guys saying, "You were my idol when I was a kid, thirty years ago." I get that all the time. So I know he's getting at least ten times more than I am.

When Arnold was on the brink of finally reaching the fame he craved for, in the early 1980s, he did tests where he would walk down New

York's Fifth Avenue and would stop strangers. He would ask them if they recognized him. Some people would say they knew him as Mr. Olympia from watching Wide World of Sports. Then Arnold would ask them another question, if they knew him for anything else. Then he would go to another person. Two years later, he would repeat this process. This time one person would say he recognized him from the movies, whilst another saying because he wrote a book. He reflected, "It's not accurate information, but somehow I always know where I am at." One person who was close to Arnold once said Arnold was always complaining in the early days, because people came up to him bugging him for autographs.

One day, a man from another state, who Arnold and his companion bumped into at an airport, started to converse with them. But the man wasn't aware of who Arnold was. According to the companion, Arnold couldn't leave it alone. Arnold spent the entire trip explicating who he was and his connections to people. Arnold was featured in Time magazine, and he showed the man a copy of the issue. Then he told the man that if he ever came to Los Angeles and wanted to go to the Playboy mansion, he could get him in. "Everybody likes to be wanted and needed and appreciated and loved, and all those things," Arnold said in one interview just before he was catapulted to fame. "Some people only have it in a limited way, you know, by just being loved by the family or by their children or by the brother, whatever, the wife. Some people like more than that, and I'm one of them."

Did you bump into him at the height if his movie career, and did you see any change in the man you first knew?
Joe Lewis: Yeah. I'd see him and say, "Hey, how you doing, Arnold." One time, I met him at the Arnold Classic bodybuilding contest. He was sitting with Joe Weider, and his wife and Weider's wife. I just walked up to him and I just said, because his two daughters were taking karate lessons with an instructor I knew, "How are your kids?" You talk about the little stuff, you don't talk about making movies, you don't talk about bodybuilding, none of that stuff is important. You know, when you've done it all it's no longer of any importance. You just talk about personal things. He became, in my opinion, more humble than he was back in the late '60s when I first bumped into him.

You, of course, knew and trained with the late icon and one of the greatest icons of the century Bruce Lee. Did you ever talk to Arnold about Bruce and share your experiences?
Joe Lewis: When I met Bruce Lee, he wasn't that much into the

bodybuilders and Arnold wasn't that famous. I was with Bruce Lee from '67. Arnold didn't get really known till he beat Sergio Oliva in the Mr. Olympia contest in 1970. So my thing with Bruce Lee did not come up. I mean, Bruce Lee has a lot of fans who are famous people. Today, for example, Mike Tyson thought a lot of Bruce Lee. Klitschko brothers, the famous world champion boxers, think a lot of Bruce Lee. Famous basketball player in this country - probably the best basketball player in the world - Kobe Bryant was a Bruce Lee fan. So it's kind of odd talking to Bruce Lee about other famous people when he was going to become probably more famous than they were.

What kind of an acting student was Arnold, was he a fast learner and did he blend into the class quite well?
Joe Lewis: No. Because in bodybuilding, you're taught to insulate your emotions. In an acting class, he was going to.... One of the key things to work on is to get you to open up emotionally: they want to see you cry. They want to see you look embarrassed. They want you to be humiliated. And they want you to show that - don't insulate that from the outside world, because to be an actor you must be able to show all those colors of the rainbow. And that's very difficult for a fighter, and it's very difficult for a bodybuilder. Because in my opinion, a lot of the bodybuilders, all that muscle around the body, to me it's insulation, it insulates emotionally mostly from the outside world. So one of the reasons he was in the class was to break that barrier. The more appealing you're emotionally, the more interesting you're going to appear on the screen. You don't want to see a person on the screen who's one dimensional from the beginning of the movie to the end. His voice never changes, there's no fluctuation in his emotion; there's no fluctuation in his voice; there's no fluctuation in his attitude. People who are uptight and afraid to show their emotions, they're not going to make it on the screen. So, I thought Arnold was smart that he went to a class which was designed to teach you to open up that way and to show those emotions. That's what method acting is all about.

Did you two talk and see each other often?
Joe Lewis: I had my friends when we met, and he had his friends. So it's not like I was looking for a new friend, and he wasn't looking for a new friend. Little things. I remember once when we walked into a magazine office, it was called Inside Kung Fu, and he saw me on the cover of the magazine. And he told the publishers, "Hey, that guy's got a good body." Little things like that. There wasn't a lasting relationship; we were more acquaintances and not really what I would call "friends". So, if I bumped into him today, I'll say, "Hey, Arnold, how's it going?

You were supposed to give me a Lifetime Achievement Award a couple of years ago." They forgot to call me up onstage when he was up there presenting awards, and that kind of peed me off a little bit. But I would never bring that up to him and say, "Hey, Arnold, remember you were supposed to give me an award?" He doesn't know what awards he's suppose to pass out. The promoter doesn't tell him.

And wherever he goes around, now it was kind of hard to be around him, because he was married to Maria Shriver, who is part of the Kennedy family. Everywhere she went, she had two Secret Service agents with her. Now I think she's free of the Secret Service. But when Arnold became the governor, you've got a Kennedy with two Secret Service and you've got a governor of a state with Secret Service. So wherever he went, there was an entourage of six or more people around him at all times. So it's kind of...you can't just walk up and say, "Hey, Arnold, how's it going, old buddy?" You have to realize that. Then you've got all the hangers-on, photographers and the news reporters, and they get first contact because the promoter wants to use Arnold to make money. And to make money, he's got to do a quick interview here and a quick interview there and then move on. Times have changed.

I remember seeing Sylvester Stallone at the Arnold Classic a couple of years ago. He's pumped himself up with weights, and everybody thinks he's done steroids, but that's no one's business. Arnold had a crowd of people, wherever he went there was, like, twenty people around him, like bees around a flower or something. And I'm thinking: would you really want to live like that way? Because if you've got to go to the bathroom to take a leak, you'd say, "Hey, you guy's mind waiting here? I'm going to go in by myself." When you're sitting out eating, you want to eat in peace at an event; you don't want twenty fans walking up to you trying to shake your hand. How many germs are you going to pick up putting your hand in this guy and putting your hand back on the food? So, there's a certain kind of...that you want to grant celebrities.

When I see Arnold or somebody - I know Jack Nicholson - I'm not going to approach him. I'll make eye contact and he'll make eye contact with me. I know Lou Ferrigno, who worked with Chuck Norris at one time, and I'd say, "Hey, how's it going?" If Lou saw me walking in the hallway, he'll say, "Hey, how's it going, Joe?" If I see him at a contest, and he's sitting behind a booth and he's signing autographs - twenty bucks an autograph - I'm not going to walk up to him and say, "Hey, how's it going, Lou?" Because he's got two or three guards who'd say, "Hey, get in line." So I'll look at Lou and he'll look at me. I'll wink at him, he'll wink at me. And it will be, "Hey, I'll see you next year." That's just the way it is. Probably the same thing with Arnold. To me, it's like: hey, I just want to go out in public, do my job, come home and turn the TV on. Not have an over-long conversation just because they are a celebrity.

Did you train Arnold in martial arts, and can you relate any conversations you both had pertaining to the martial arts?
Joe Lewis: No. He did an article in Black Belt magazine about six or seven years ago. In the very first paragraph, he said that he trained with me and Chuck Norris. Now, I don't know if he said that for real or the magazine just says he said that. But I gave Jim Lorimer, who was his partner, the magazine and said to him, "How about having Arnold sign this for me?" Jim threw the magazine away. So, when I saw Arnold that night, the night before, I'm backstage at the Arnold Classic and Arnold's entourage come walking in backstage. As soon as Arnold sees me, there's about hundred and fifty people and I'm back there with Bill Wallace, Arnold yells out to everybody, "Joe Lewis!! Joe Lewis!! Champion of champions!! He makes a scene straight away. I know why he's doing that: to make everybody jealous. But that's three decades of friendship, it goes way back.

So the next day, I asked his partner to have that magazine signed. I don't get autographs, but I thought it's kind of neat he's used my name in there. If he wants to tell people he trained with me, let him say that, you know. I don't know if he's got any martial arts training outside of films...who taught him to work that sword for the Conan movie. Now, he must have some interest in martial arts, because he and Maria had their two kids taking karate lessons. And he felt that was kind of neat, because that's something I've talked to him about. You have to keep in mind that, how much time does he have to take lessons and learn how to move a sword, or take lessons on how to throw a kick? I mean, if you look at pictures of him, he probably doesn't have time to workout anymore.

ERIC MORRIS

Perhaps one of the most prominent acting coaches in Hollywood is Eric Morris. His clients have included Jack Nicholson, Johnny Depp and Arnold Schwarzenegger. Morris first got together with Arnold when he was preparing for his Stay Hungry role.

Can you tell me how and when Arnold came to you for acting lessons?
Eric Morris: Jack Nicholson recommended me to Bob Rafelson, who was directing a movie called Stay Hungry with Sally Fields and Jeff Bridges. Bob Rafelson called me, he was going to cast Arnold. You know, it was about Mr. Olympia, it took place in the South. He told me that Arnold had not done any movies except that documentary Pumping Iron and would I work with him. I said, "Well, how long do I have?" He said, "About twelve weeks." I said, "That's a very short time to work with somebody and teach them my system, my work." He said, "Well, you come very highly recommended to me, so would you at least meet with him?" I said, "Of course!"

So I met with Arnold and we hit it off. We got along very well from the beginning, and we worked for about nine weeks together. I found out all about his life, about certain things that he could use as choices, etc, etc. Then he went to Alabama to shoot the film. He did very well and he won the Golden Globe Award for the Promising Newcomer. Bob Rafelson called me from Birmingham very early morning once, it was five o' clock here, but eight o' clock there. He apologized because he'd forgotten what time it was here. He said, "I thought I'd call you and tell you Arnold's doing really well. And I'm very grateful to you, Eric, for the work you've done with him. He's incredible." So, that's how it started.

After he finished this film, he began to work with me in my classes for about a year or nine months. After that he kind of went out. I guess the rest is kind of history. But he was with me for eight or nine months in class, and I worked with him privately. Recently, a couple of years ago, he called me and asked me if I'd work with his daughter, who wants to be an actress. She wanted to work on weekends, but I don't teach on weekends, so that never worked out. But I told him I finished my book - The Diary of a Special Experiencer - and he said, "I want to write the foreword." I said, "Arnold, you're the governor of California, do you have time to do that?" He said, "Send me some information and I'll write something. I want to do it!" So he did. The last book that's in publication, he wrote the foreword to.

What was he like in the acting classes? Did he earnestly pursue coaching and what was your impression of him?
Eric Morris: Well, you know, he was very committed. He was very good and we did a lot of stuff. He was very vulnerable in some of the exercises, and he did a scene or two in class. I really always believed Arnold was very talented. He chose to do action and adventure films. If he wanted to do serious dramatic films, he could. First of all, I think he's the smartest human being that I have ever met in terms of intellect - he has a mind like a steel trap. He took to the work very well. And then he visited my class after he had been out of it for a while. He said, "I love the work you do, Eric. But the kind of work I want to do, I really want to do action and adventure. I'm an athlete and I want to do those kinds of films." So, I wished him well and he went ahead and created a career in that area. I don't see him very often, certainly, after he became the governor. But I am in touch with him in terms of I know how to reach him if I need to talk to him or something like that.

Arnold seemingly was looking for adoration through fame. Can you recall some of the dreams and goals he related to you pertinent to making it in the movie industry?
Eric Morris: He wanted to do action and adventure films. He came to me one night and watched a class. He said he liked the work I did; but the kind of work he wanted to do was physical. I wrote him a letter once. I guess it was a documentary; somebody introduced me to a documentary. I said, you know, if Arnold wanted to play Hamlet, he could do it. I mean, with an accent or no accent. He certainly could fulfil emotion. He wrote me a letter saying, "Well, Eric, I'm a little too old for Hamlet, but if I ever do Macbeth then you can come and coach me on that. I think that was very humorous, he's got a great sense of humor. His career was mostly about action and adventure (films). I had the feeling that after he is released from the governor's office, he might return to acting. I thought he won't return as an action and adventure hero. I thought he would probably want to do serious work. He told me once, when we were having coffee in Cafe Roma in Beverly Hills, he said the kind of acting he wants to do is character acting, like the actor Armin Mueller-Stahl. He's a German actor. He said I'd like to do scenes like that. And I thought if he goes back to acting, he'd probably do much more serious and meaningful and dramatic type of work - and he's capable of it.

Did Arnold ever give you the impression that he admired any particular actors? He expressed that he admired Clint Eastwood and Sean Connery.

Eric Morris: The only thing I could tell you about that is that he never mentioned any of those people to me. He did say that, as he got older and matriculated out of the action and adventure, he'd like to do characters like Armin Mueller-Stahl, the German actor. He did the movie Music Box with Jessica Lang. He's a very good actor, a character actor. He's much older than Arnold, but I think Arnold kind of admired his work. But he never mentioned Clint Eastwood or any of those people to me.

Even though Arnold didn't let on to his acting coach, he had long admired Clint Eastwood well before he even immigrated to America. And he hoped one day he would have a career just like his hero. Arnold said, "First of all, you have to understand that Clint Eastwood was, like, my inspiration. I remember when I first came to this country, there was, like, John Wayne, Clint Eastwood and Kirk Douglas; there were two, three guys like that that I really admired and I wanted to have a career like them. And Clint was one of those guys that I always thought, even from the Westerns he had done before Dirty Harry, I want to be like him. I wanted to have like his career and do this kind of movies. So, obviously, he had already impacted me that he was the motivating force for me to come to America and to get into acting in the first place."

What advice did you impart on him in your role as the acting coach?
Eric Morris: After working with him, I told him he was capable of doing really serious, meaningful work. When he came and watched a class and said that he had decided to do action and adventure work and that he was very physical, I encouraged him to do that. That's the direction he went into. When I had coffee with him in Beverly Hills at Cafe Roma, he did say that he would like to do more serious and dramatic work later in his career, that was before he became governor. I thought when he leaves the governor's office, I don't know what he's going to do. Whether he's going to continue with politics or not. If he returned to acting, I thought he would return as a serious actor, serious dramatic character actor. That's what I thought. And I hope if he did that I can work with him. He was very effective in class.

Do you think he is the epitome of the American Dream?
Eric Morris: Are you kidding! He came to this country without any

money in his pocket, and he's become a multimillionaire and a super movie star. Are you kidding, the epitome of the American Dream? I would like to have a dream like that. I'm pretty successful, you know, but that's some American Dream.

Arnold received the 1847th star on Hollywood's Walk of Fame on June 2, 1987. "Well, I think this is the first time a Schwarzenegger has been on the Hollywood Boulevard represented on a star," Arnold told a reporter. "It was like a dream of mine. When I first came to Hollywood, I walked up and down Hollywood Boulevard and I saw all those stars. And I said, 'God, this must be incredible, to be one time forever on Hollywood Boulevard.' You know, with an ego like mine I saw it possible." He advised, "Well, for those young girls and guys that have dreams, it just shows to you that dreams can become a reality. Set a goal, believe in it and go for it." By now he was a star in the motion picture industry, he proved that everybody with a dream and a lot of perseverance had the opportunity to make their dreams a reality. Arnold says, "The question really was: how do you come to America as an Austrian farm boy? I grew up in very poor circumstances, so there was no way that an Austrian could ever go to Hollywood and become really big."

Can you tell me about the more social side to your relationship with Arnold?
Eric Morris: Actually, he sent me a couple of people to work with. I had dinner at one time and we talked. And I talked on the telephone a couple of times. And he volunteered to do the foreword to my book, and he did. I talked to him and his secretary, he asked me to participate in a couple of documentaries. I can't remember if he asked me or they (producers) asked me, but I did participate in two or three documentaries on Arnold. Then there were a couple of other ones, one from England. So, I appeared in three or four documentaries on Arnold and talked about him in those.

Once in class, Arnold complained that no one liked his accent. Can you elucidate on this and tell me exactly why he was disconcerted on that particular day?
Eric Morris: He came in one night very angry. I saw him sitting there and I could tell he was angry. So I got him up onstage, and I said, "What's going on, Arnold?" He said - in his accent - he had just had a very disappointing interview with an agent - this was before he did one of his action and adventure movies. He said, "I'm pissed off! They don't

like my accent. They don't like my body. They don't like...." I forget what else he said. He said, "To hell with them! I'm going to be a superstar." And everybody laughed and applauded him. Then he did an exercise in class where he recreated a Christmas morning in Austria. He was playing with some of his toys and he became very vulnerable, it brought tears to the eyes of everybody in the class. He was recreating a Christmas morning when he was a child in Graz, Austria. It was so effective that it brought tears to everybody's eyes in the class. Arnold is a great man, he's a good guy. If he loves you or he likes you, he'll do anything for you.

Arnold was aware there was a natural pressure to conform, to do things the way they had been done before. However, he always felt the only way you make an impact is by being unique and break that barrier by doing things that have never been done before. If people had followed the flock by changing their name, he believed maybe he should be different. Basically, he thought he should venture into the unknown and do things differently. He said if everybody had gotten to the top with a perfect American accent, maybe he should be the exception and be the first one who didn't. His determination and drive to succeed at all costs was apparent right from the start.

What would you say were Arnold's attributes and vulnerabilities, plus points and minus points, when you were teaching him the craft of acting?
Eric Morris: He was very receptive. He was very bright and he understood the work immediately. He's a very sensitive man, you know. He plays all these action picture heroes where he kills people and all of that, but, you know, Arnold is a very, very sensitive man. He's a very loving man. I don't know that a lot of people know that. He's a very, very deep, sensitive, caring human being and I love him. I would still say that if he wasn't a movie star and he wasn't the governor. As a man and as a person, I love him.

SVEN-OLE THORSEN

Sven-Ole Thorsen is part of a close-knit group of friends of Arnold Schwarzenegger who share a commonality in that they hang out and know the man personally like no one else. Originally from Denmark, Thorsen moved to Los Angeles in the 1980s.

Before you immigrated to America, how did you meet Arnold and become close friends with him?

Sven-Ole Thorsen: In 1978, a cinema owner in Denmark who owned a theater told me that she had invited Arnold Schwarzenegger for the premiere of Pumping Iron and if I would go into business with her and pay half of the cost. And I said, "Of course." In those days, I had started a gym, which still exists in Copenhagen. And later, she came back to me and said that it was too expensive to invite him. I said, "Let me pay the expenses." Then when he came to Copenhagen, we picked him up in a 1926 Rolls Royce. We gave him a tour of Denmark. Then he disappeared - last ten minutes of the movie. Outside they had two double-decker London buses to bring all our guests downtown Copenhagen. We had ladies onboard the buses dressed in t-shirts which read "Arnold is Numero Uno", which were the t-shirts from Pumping Iron. And we served champagne. In my gym, we had set up three hundred chairs for the press. He came and he gave a great speech and a great seminar.

Back then the sport of bodybuilding only existed in Denmark in two or three gyms, but then it exploded. I started off the Danish Bodybuilding Federation in 1979, and when I stopped in 1981 we had many gyms in the federation. So by his visit, he actually created the foundation for the sport of bodybuilding, and we turned into friends. The same year, I went with Arnold skiing in Austria. And then I went to Los Angeles for some martial arts championships I was involved with, and me and Arnold went to a meeting with John Peters, who was writing Conan the Barbarian. In those days, I was kind of a big guy. I was 330 pounds. So when John saw me, he asked for me to give him a famous Viking name for his picture, Conan the Barbarian. I said Thorgrim. So, the next year I got a phone call from John, he wanted to hire me and take me to Spain to play Thorgrim in Conan the Barbarian. He also asked me to bring nine other Danes.

So in 1980, I went to Spain for seven months with my friends from Denmark, all champions in track and field, weightlifting, powerlifting, boxing and martial arts, and we worked seven months in Spain. That created a relationship which lead to the second Conan picture, which we did in Mexico for six months. Then for the third Conan picture, Red Sonja, we spent four months in Rome. So, when I immigrated and came here five years later in 1985, I'd done three American pictures whilst still living in Denmark. The only person I knew in Hollywood was Arnold. So I called him and he invited me to come and play a part when he was shooting Commando. I arrived in '85 as the Strongest Man in the World. I was quite huge. I was 340 pounds.

So Joel Silver, the producer of Commando, invited me to work on Commando for three months for $22,000. But I had to be a member of the Screen Actors Guild. From then on I was in the business. Actually, I came here for the sunshine, not really for the movie business. But when I wrote my memoir, Viking in Hollywood, I realized that in twenty-six years I have done over a hundred movies and TV shows. When we did Conan the Barbarian in Spain in 1980, which lasted seven months, the last days of the show Arnold said to us that his dream one day was to become the president of the United States. That's what he said in 1980.

Conan the Barbarian producer Dino De Laurentiis left his native Italy to pursue a Hollywood career in 1976. Edward R. Pressman, also a producer of Conan, recalled, "We signed Arnold to a three-picture deal, which called for him to be paid $250,000 for the first film and the same for the sequel. The movie turned into a monster hit, and we sold our sequel rights. I'm sure Arnold was able to negotiate his salary for the sequels." Conan the Barbarian set the stage for the bodybuilder-turned-actor to becoming one of the biggest and highest paid movie stars in cinema. Scripted by Oliver Stone, on January 7, 1981, principal photography began in Spain.

Arnold has stated that he really knew that they had a winner on their hands when the movie was screened. It was beyond anything he expected. He affirmed that he would be able to make a leap forward giving him the chance to make a transition from being a bodybuilding champion to being in the international arena of show business. Arnold had cultivated such a positive approach to life and a burning desire to succeed, he exclaimed, "I've never been wrong yet with my instincts, and they tell me this is going to be a really big film, a whole new phenomenon." Equipped with determination and an unparalleled hunger for being accepted beyond the confines of the bodybuilding arena, he said he didn't care what it takes and if he had to take one year out of his life and be an animal - work hard - he would do it. He firmly believed this film was going to be unbelievable for him.

Arnold's agent had arranged a meeting with the Italian producer, his agent was hoping Arnold would be cast in Flash Gordon, a part which would later go to Sam Jones. Both men arrived at De Laurentiis' office in Beverly Hills. Arnold witnessed a diminutive man sitting behind a large desk; the desk took up most of the space in the room. Arnold asked, "Why does such a tiny guy like you need such a big desk?" The producer incensed by the remark shouted in his thick Italian accent, "You have-a dah accent! You cannot-ah be in-ah Flash Gordon!" Arnold was immediately thrown out of the office by De Laurentiis. Arnold's agent was furious with his client; he had spent four months setting up this meeting which Arnold blew in under two minutes. The agent furiously told his client, "Schwarzenegger, you idiot! Mark my words, Arnold, you will never amount to anything!" How wrong was the agent.

After the initial mishap and disastrous first meeting, Arnold did get signed up. The producer flew to London to meet and sign up the director Ridley Scott. However, the British director told the Italian producer that he'd love to do the film, but he couldn't do it with Arnold Schwarzenegger; he needed an "actor". As we know, John Milius ended up directing, who later, because of his differences with De Laurentiis, refused to direct the sequel and Richard Fleischer was brought in.

Often things didn't go to plan when filming Conan the Barbarian, Arnold had his fair share of mishaps. It inflicted a seemingly series of injuries on Arnold. Arnold recalls when filming one of the scenes which involved a wolf, "There's a wolf the second time we shot with it. And sure enough everything that could've gone wrong, I somehow got to the place where I supposed to climb up and couldn't find my first step. The next thing I knew was this wolf jumping on my back, ripping me down from the top of the rock, and then falling down and injure myself at the front. It was right in front, right in my face. And the animal trainer was luckily right there on top of it....This was the first few stitches. This was still in the morning, it wasn't noon yet, and the first day of shooting I had already got my first few stitches with the medic there. In Spain it's not the doctor who comes to stitch you, it's the medic...."

Another scene which required a medic to intervene was when they filmed the vulture scene. Arnold explains, "It was actually a real vulture leaning over to me, but then pulling back. Then we picked it up, the vulture which had died mysteriously, and I bit into the neck." He vividly remembered this because right after that the medics ran up to him and gave him something to gargle with, because there was a danger of getting really sick. Because it's the real thing, except it was now stuffed, but it was all primitively done.

Conan the Barbarian cost $17 million to produce at the time, which was a big-budget action and adventure fantasy film. Regardless of the budget or critical appraise, it grossed around $70 million worldwide. John Milius praised his actor, "If I had movie stars, veteran actors with inflated egos, they never would have done what my people did. Arnold's a great man. He's very disciplined, the closest thing to Conan in real life. He has built his own character and career just like Conan did. He was willing to work endlessly, training with a sword, practicing his lines until he was sick of them, every day, the physical conditioning, the horseback riding, the philosophy." Apart from the work which was needed to polish his acting skills, Arnold often found romantic scenes to film difficult. He once said, "The love-making scenes, they were very, very difficult. It's so strange when you're used to doing these things within the privacy of your own four walls, and then all of a sudden here we are naked with hundred and twenty horny Spanish guys breathing down our necks, and we're not even sure who they want to get a look at, Sandahl or me."

The movie received ambivalent reviews. Vincent Canby wrote, "Conan the Barbarian is an extremely long, frequently incoherent, ineptly staged adventure fantasy set in a prehistoric past. One has the impression that it cost a lot of money, though not all of it is on the screen. One is never unaware that one is watching a lot of extras trot around Spain wearing goat hair, jogging shorts and horns on their hats. Conan the Barbarian contains plenty of ambitious scenes - episodes of magical transformations, battles in which skulls are split if not lopped off - but it's not engaging even on a primitive level."

The weekly entertainment-trade magazine Variety described the movie in its December 1981 issue, "Director John Milius does a nice job of setting up the initial story. There is a real anticipation as Schwarzenegger is unveiled as the barbarian and sets off on the road to independence. But for whatever reasons, the actor has a minimum of dialog and fails to convey much about the character through his actions." Regardless of Arnold's acting performance, which may have been wooden as some critics may have perceived it, the movie was a big success at the box office. He had improved, and nothing came close to the extreme amount of talent vacuum he possessed in his first flick Hercules in New York.

After Arnold immigrated to America, his subsequent investments, mainly real estate, enhanced his reputation for shrewdness. Did Arnold already have properties and restaurants when you moved to America?
Sven-Ole Thorsen: During the '80s, Arnold started to buy the whole building there. We created together a Cigar Night, which took place the first Monday of the month. We had people who came over for dinner

and we traded cigars, which became extremely popular. Some movie stars, movie directors and producers were standing in line to get into this intimate kind of cigar event. He worked with a gentleman in town and they owned a lot of real estate on Main Street in Santa Monica; they had several properties there. Also, he built his own office in his own building on Main Street where he also had a restaurant called Schatzi on Main. He recently sold that building for, I think, $40 million or something.

Can we talk about Red Heat, Sven? You have a fight scene in the snow with Arnold. Can you tell me more about working on the film with Arnold?

Sven-Ole Thorsen: Absolutely. Red Heat was a movie where all the interior stuff was shot in Hungary. And most of the exterior shots, for the snow and stuff, were shot in Moscow and Austria. So, in the opening sequence we are in Hungary, the interior shots in the sauna with all the naked women, we have a fight and fly out of the window. But then all the snow scenes, after jumping through the window, were shot in Austria. Because there was no snow in Hungary. So it was shot in two sequences. The interior in Hungary and the rolling down and fighting in the snow was all done in Austria. And the sad part was that it was so cold there, so our stunt coordinator, Bennie Dobbins, who was a close friend of Arnold and me, unfortunately died because it was so cold. In the movie you see there's a special credit for Bennie Dobbins. That particular day, we stopped filming and Arnold and I took a walk smoking a cigar. And actually, Arnold and I cried with tears because of Bennie Dobbins death. Because he had been trying to protect us from freezing in the snow, by doing that he had a heart attack.

Can you tell me about choreographing the fight scenes with Arnold? And what was the cast and crew like on this movie, were their elements of melancholy or was there always high spirits pervading?

Sven-Ole Thorsen: First of all, Arnold liked to work with me because I never hurt him. We had sword fights in the Conan pictures, and later on different fights in different movies, so we coordinated our stunts and fights pretty well. Because I didn't have a stunt double, because I'm playing myself. It worked out pretty well. When there's a big crew that goes to another country, three or four hundred people, it's like a military operation. So, when you come to Budapest with all those people, later in Austria, it's like an army coming, the whole army. At the same time, it's like a traveling circus. So three, four hundred people are like one big family. Very often in situations like big movies, it's not so much based on people's talent - which is good to have, a hairdresser or a makeup person or an actor or stuntman - but it's all about how you are to be with socially.

Because very often when you work together with people for seven, eight months you need to have good chemistry. So talent is very often secondary, whilst social behavior is more important. Because you have to work with people, very intimate, different countries, living in hotels. So, if there's too much bad chemistry it influences the production of the movie. When you're hired to do a job, you do it! When we did Red Heat, every morning at four o' clock it was wakeup time. It was wintertime, we went to a gym which was in a basement. We had gloves to workout with. Then we start work at six o' clock in the morning. So the discipline you have from being an athlete is going to make you a good team player on the movie. Because they can count on you, you're there on time, you're prepared, you are willing to go all the way and you don't mind doing it again and again and again. So discipline is a big factor.

You played a security man in Arnold's The Running Man, how did you get this part? What was it like to work with Arnold on this movie?
Sven-Ole Thorsen: One day I was called in to meet the director, and there was another man who was a bad guy, he had had a fight with Muhammad Ali, he's a tough guy, very tough guy. I'm sure if you investigate his name, you'll see his resume. Anyhow, now the director says to me, "OK, you guys go ahead and start threatening each other." The other guy was more experienced than I was, he really put his face in my face and was spitting on his lips. He chewed my ass! I was so shocked I was almost speechless. So, finally after threatening me with all kind of verbal attacks, my reaction was, "If you touch me you're dead." And based on that, I was hired to play the part in The Running Man. That was my casting. It was a little unusual way of getting a job, he put two guys up against each other and wanted to see who is the toughest, and according to him I was the toughest. Because I stayed calm; he didn't know I was shocked and he liked my reaction. Strange way of casting people, but that was the director's choice.

First of all, everybody in town likes to work with Arnold, because he pays attention to every employer who is working on the movie. Meaning, if one of the grips has a birthday there's a birthday cake, there's a birthday gift, there's a speech from Arnold and there's a song. So the crew and the cast, they really love Arnold because he's a team player. He's very considerate, has a great sense of humor and makes it fun to make movies. It's always fun because of his personality, he's a very charming gentleman and very easy to work with. He never complains about eighteen-hour days, or never complains about being cold, never complains about being uncomfortable.

He actually told me once that what he loves the most in life is to work on a movie, because there is a call sheet every day that showed you what to do that particular day. He likes that. He likes to be told what to do without thinking. So, every day you get a call sheet telling you what to do. He's very easy to work with. He's probably the best guy to work with, because I've worked with Sean Connery, Mel Gibson, Steven Seagal. I mean, all the big stars I've worked with, Clint Eastwood, Chuck Norris, Jean Claude Van Damme as well.

The Running Man was directed by Paul Michael Glazer (Starsky and Hutch), and produced by Keith Barish, who would later team up with Arnold for the Planet Hollywood venture. A common denominator in a Schwarzenegger movie is science fiction. Arnold had read the novel and liked the concept. He said, "I think it's a great, great concept that Steven King came up with when he wrote his novel. And I was very, very happy someone picked up on it and made it into a script and decided to do a film, and decided to put that much money behind it and really go all out and really make it as good as possible. And when I read the novel, I said I hope someone is going to make a film, because I would like to play Ben Richards. And two years later, you know, I heard about it that it's going to be made into a film, and I got the job. So I was very delighted over it." Sven was one of the few friends Arnold looked after by having him in most of his movies playing bit parts. Another former bodybuilding friend and training partner says, "As he grew in the film business, he gained new friends and some of the old ones were set on the sidelines. He gave his roommate Franco a small part in The Terminator, but that was it. As far as using any of us as actors, it never happened for some reason." Being in a unique position, some would say he could've done much more for some of his friends and somewhat elevate their careers.

You worked with Jean Claude Van Damme on Hard Target. Did Arnold and Van Damme ever have plans to work together on film projects?
Sven-Ole Thorsen: When we did Predator in Mexico, Joe Silver, the producer, had hired Jean Claude Van Damme to play in a blue outfit playing the monster. They photographed it in the blue suit, and upside down and stuff, so later on the CGI can put the monster, the Alien, in the Predator. But Jean Claude Van Damme had claustrophobia. So after a week of work, he was whining and complaining, so Joel Silver fired him and promised him he would never work in town. Then a year later, he became a star himself. Very skilled martial arts guy with a lot of talent. But there was never any thought of him and Arnold working together. Then later on, Jean Claude Van Damme had his own career.

Being involved in the Hollywood motion picture industry and being a close friend of Arnold's, what's the first premiere you went to with Arnold?

Sven-Ole Thorsen: Actually, it was in Copenhagen for Conan the Barbarian in 1982. And as you know, he was charming and the press liked him. I can't remember in detail, I think that was the only movie I went with him for the premiere, actually. There is a very interesting story I would like to share with you. I worked for a couple of weeks on the movie called Twins. I'm on the screen for maybe only thirty seconds. But as an actor, member of the Screen Actors Guild, you get residuals. So, next year I got a residual check from Twins; I got $15,000 and I was so proud of that. So, when Arnold was visiting me for a cup of coffee a couple of days later, in my little apartment, I said, "Hey, can you believe it? Thank you very much for having me in Twins. Because, look, I got a check for $15,000." He said, "Great." Then he said, "I never see my residual checks, but I think I remember one. I think it was from Twins and I think it was either $14 million or $15 million." For Twins Arnold made about $17 million based on residuals, the movie made five hundred million worldwide. I have made, since that movie, I probably made $400,000 in residuals.

Twins was the first movie where Arnold was paired with his co-star Danny DeVito. Both men pulled it off and Arnold really was able to show a rather homorous side to his character, which wasn't intrinsic to this movie alone, because he continued to make comedies. Can you expound on this side to Arnold which he portrayed in this movie?

Sven-Ole Thorsen: Arnold has a great sense of humor, and he loves to pull practical jokes on people. And all those years I worked with him, I always pulled practical jokes on Arnold. And for him now to actually be himself, in Twins he was more like himself, more than any other movie. He was very relaxed and very much himself. Because when he is himself, he's an extremely funny guy who loves practical jokes. That's probably one of the reasons why he likes me, because if people are too serious, they take themselves too seriously. I'm there to put a practical joke on them in a second. They had a great relationship, they laughed a lot. Danny DeVito is probably one of the most skilled actors in town. Everybody likes to work with Danny DeVito, because he's very professional and he's also very sweet and very funny. But I can't recall any particular situation for the moment.

Ivan Reitman, who had directed such hits as Ghostbusters, recalled how he first came into contact with Arnold. Arnold walked up to the director in the lobby of a club and asked him if he was the "Ghostbuster guy". The enthusiastic actor told him that he could be a Ghostbuster. Reitman, at first, seemed a little puzzled, but realized what he was trying to convey was that he was capable of doing comedy films too. When Arnold made his first comedy Twins, there's no doubt the studio was taking a risk. Arnold was stepping into a completely different genre to what he was known for.

But he's always believed in taking risks in order to achieve monumental heights. As he explains, "I think that if you think along the way you're not going to fail, then you're blind. Because there's no one that I've ever met, no matter how successful they are, that haven't said that they had their failures along the way. You have to. I mean, the only way that you really know that you can lift 500 pounds is if you're willing to fail. So if you're afraid of failure then you will never grow." He believes the people that go the furthest are the people that really don't care if they fail or they succeed, they're going to take the risk and pursue what they want to. "Because that's what you have to do," he says. Although Arnold primarily is associated with action genre in the movie industry, he was able to make a transition into comedy, which may have been a huge risk for a one-dimensional actor. He often parodied himself and enjoyed the experience of testing his metal and endured and came out a winner with the immense success of Twins and Kindergarten Cop, the two comedy flicks which were enormously successful.

Arnold cultivated a penchant for Hummer jeeps, can you expound on the story where you went car shopping with him once?
Sven-Ole Thorsen: When we did The Running Man, we filmed a lot of the times at night in Fontana steel mill. Most of the shooting for The Running Man was at night, so during the day me and him went to different car dealers who were selling Porsches, because he wanted to get a Porsche for the right deal. After visiting for three months maybe fifteen, twenty different Porsche dealers, I said to Arnold, "This is ridiculous, why don't you call Porsche in Germany and have them make an 'Arnold Porsche' for you?" He said, "Sven, you don't understand. I want to deserve it when I buy something. I can buy an airplane. I can buy a yacht. I can buy an Island. But I want to feel when I buy something that I deserve it."

Now, he was doing The Running Man for four months and hustling and visiting car dealers. When he finally found a deal which was to his liking, he probably saved $5,000. He felt he deserved to give himself a car. So he's not a guy who just buys stuff, you know. Once he said to me some years ago, "Sven, there's so many millionaires in town, but there's not too many billionaires. And I'm actually a billionaire." I said, "Good for you." Also he uses phrases from his past like he wants to stay hungry. Meaning, even though he could buy anything he likes, he feels he has to do some work before he gives himself a gift, like a car or whatever. A very healthy way of thinking.

Arnold also enjoys motorcycles. You often, along with Arnold's other close friend, Franco Columbu, enjoyed riding with Arnold.
Sven-Ole Thorsen: When we did Raw Deal, in the movie there's four motorcycles and Arnold's riding a Harley-Davidson in Raw Deal, which was shot in North Carolina. After the movie was done, one day he called me and Franco to his home and he gave us one motorcycle each, Harley-Davidson, which both were used in Raw Deal. After that he had several hours of enjoyment on Sundays riding the bikes off to a place in Santa Monica Mountains called Rock Cafe, where thousands of people are on Harley-Davidsons who are meeting on a Sunday to hang for a cup of coffee and gossip and stuff. So we had a lot of pleasure riding the motorcycles.

Arnold had a motorcycle accident in 2001. Do you feel because of his bodybuilding it helped him to recover more rapidly?
Sven-Ole Thorsen: The thing is, if you're physical, if you're an athlete, if you have an accident you kind of roll yourself out of it, you know kind of how to fall and react. Him being an athlete, it probably saved his life a couple of times when he had accidents, yes.

Arnold put on parties, what celebrities and people attended these house parties? And what would be one of the most significant anecdotes you remember?
Sven-Ole Thorsen: July 30, 2010, it was his sixty-third birthday and I was invited. There was a big crowd, there were sixty people. And in his speech, he told the people there, who were at the party, most of the people who have been with him from the beginning, me and Franco, also his heroes Clint Eastwood and Sylvester Stallone, and, of course, people from his office in Sacramento, so the people at that particular party were people who have been around him since he came over here. I worked with Clint in a movie called Pink Cadillac. So, when you kind of hang with those kind of people, who are superstars, they actually act like normal people. They have the same needs of being complimented, of being loved, so there's no difference between a person who is a superstar and a normal person; they're just average people who have a kind of an unusual job. They're all very nice people, very highly

educated and low-keyed. There's no star stuff there; you talk to them like you talk to normal people.

And that's one of my advantages of being a Dane; Danes are not easily impressed. I mean, if you see the Queen going somewhere in Copenhagen, it's no big deal. So for me, the only time I was impressed by meeting a so-called celebrity was some years ago - 1988 or '89. There was a fundraiser for a Californian politician. Ronald Reagan was supposed to be there, so I was invited there. Three months ahead, I had to give my passport to the Secret Service. Then before the fundraiser, there was a little get-together in the VIP room. There were about twenty-five security people and maybe twenty guests, and me and Arnold were standing there side by side. Then Ronald Reagan came up with Nancy. He talked to Arnold about his wedding, and then Arnold introduced me. When I shook Ronald Reagan's hand, I said to him, "My name is Sven and I'm from Denmark. It's a great honor to meet you, because I'm a big admirer of you and your country." Then Ronald Reagan said to me, "What do you want to do here?" I said, "I want to be an American." He said, "Then you have no problem. I'm your friend and Arnold is our friend."

From then on when we went home in Arnold's limo, I was sitting there and got my right hand out. I said, "Arnold, you know what, thank you very much for allowing me to meet Ronald Reagan, because I actually shook hands with a person I can decide if I have to live here or not. I actually shook hands with the most powerful man in the world." So that was impressive. I said to Arnold, "I don't think I'm going to wash my hand for the next couple of days." It was really an experience for me to meet and shake hands with the most powerful man in the world, which is the president of the United States.

Arnold himself became a US citizen on September 17, 1983. "I was born in Europe and I've traveled all over the world, and I can tell you there's no place, no country, more compassionate, more generous, more accepting, more welcoming than the United States of America," Arnold proclaimed two decades later. "As long as I live, I will never forget the day, twenty-one years ago, when I raised my hand and I took the oath of citizenship. You know how proud I was? I walked around with the American flag around my shoulder all day long." Arnold broached at the Republican Convention in Madison Square Garden, "In school when the teacher would talk about America, I would daydream about coming here. I would daydream about living here. I would sit there, watch for hours, watching American movies transfixed to my heroes like John Wayne. Everything about America seemed so big to me, so open, so possible. I finally arrived here in 1968, what a special day it was."

Did you often go shopping in Beverly Hills with Arnold?
Sven-Ole Thorsen: There's a place in Beverly Hills called Cafe Roma, which is owned by some Italians. And that's a place where I used to go to, because it's very European, very relaxed and all kinds of people from the movie business come there. Then there's another place we go to smoke cigars called Havana Room. That's the only two places I go to in Beverly Hills. I'm not a guy who goes to Beverly Hills, because it's kind of an unreal world with all the fashion shops, you know, it's not my kind of life. I'm kind of low-keyed. I don't go to so-called Hollywood parties or Beverly Hills arrangements, it's a different world. I never really participated in that. Even though people think if you live here, live in Hollywood, it's all rock and roll - which it's not. It's a lot of very hard work, and when you socialize in town, in Hollywood and Beverly Hills, it can take all your life. So you're more focused on being seen than actually working. So always try to avoid that kind of scene.

Can you tell me of the most thought-provoking conversation you and Arnold had?
Sven-Ole Thorsen: I did Dancing with the Stars, and the week after I came out of my last surgery, which was for my right hip - in two years I've had six new joints put in my body, two new knees, two new hips and two new shoulders - I get a phone call and Arnold says, "I'm in the neighborhood, may I come by for a cup of coffee?" I said, "Sure." So in my alley, there were two SUVs with eight security guards, and Arnold came in and gave me a cigar and said, "Give me a call sheet, what's going on?" I told him, "I'm going to Denmark." He said, "Are you crazy? You've just had surgery." I said, "No, Arnold, this is a smart way of...you have to train every day six, seven hours." He said, "You know, that's maybe a good idea."

So I said, "What is your call sheet? Now that the governor thing is over shortly." He said, I'll quote what he said, "Sven," still believing what he said in 1980, that he wanted to be the president of the United States, he said, "Sven, if I cannot be the president of the United States, or if I cannot be the secretary of state, I want to be 'Mr. Green' of the world. Because if I go up for a Noble Prize, I want to have a Noble Prize." I said, "Good for you." I thought that was the most intriguing thing I ever heard from Arnold. Even though it's impossible for him to be the president of the United States, based on the Constitution, he still believes he can be the president.

On his birthday party he's playing chess with Franco Columbu. And even thugh Arnold only has a king left, but Franco has a king, queen and a bishop and a couple of others, Arnold's still moving his king believing he could win. Stallone wants to say goodnight, he's standing there waiting to say goodnight, but Arnold's so focused and so occupied, still being able to beat Franco even though the odds were one-to-hundred. It just shows his strength that he never gives up and always believes in himself.

Another situation, actually, when we were in Mexico working on Total Recall - I also worked on The Hunt for Red October - I'm flying back from Mexico to Los Angeles and on one of the trips I'm flying with the producer of Total Recall Andy Vajna and also Arnold. Andy Vajna is now talking to Arnold about how he wants to do Arnold's next big Terminator picture, "What can I do to make it happen?" he keeps saying to Arnold. Arnold looks at me and says, "What do you think, Sven." I said, "To start you can take over the fucking airplane we are flying in." Arnold looks at him and says, "What do you say to that?" Then there was a handshake, it was Arnold's airplane, and Andy was producing his second Terminator picture. It was kind of fantastic that my little crazy idea became a reality. It was one of a kind.

Hard work and persistent reflect the depth of Arnold's character, and his unparalleled desire to achieve the ultimate and reach heights which mere mortals can only dream of. Can you exemplify how he is able to thrive on achieving what he sets out to?
Sven-Ole Thorsen: I think when he did the first Conan picture, that really showed a great character there. I think that he had the most pleasure working on that picture, because there is a lot of camaraderie, it was a long shoot. So, I think it's actually my favorite movie that I have worked on, and I also think that's Arnold's favorite movie, even though he hasn't said anything directly about which movie he liked the best himself. It's always interesting to work on a movie, very often you're on locations all over the world. An Arnold movie is a special movie, because as I said to you, they all become kind of family members - it's one big family. I mean, for example, they love Arnold because he gets on with the average Joe; he doesn't pretend to be a superstar, he's just a guy.

I always used to say that people like Arnold come around every thousand years. There's a certain person who has a higher call than anyone else. Because if he can say in 1980 in Spain that he would be the president of the United States, that's kind of an unrealistic thought. Also, for example, when he said to me one day, "I think I've found my wife." I said, "So, yeah?" He said, "I haven't met her yet. But I'm going to go after Maria Shriver, because she's a Kennedy." I said, "Good for you." A couple of years later, he married Maria Shriver. I was one of the best men. When he does the opening sequence in Conan the Barbarian with the sword, he'd been training with Yamasaki with the sword, who was a sword expert in town, for over a year. So when he does that with the sword, it looks like a top professional.

When we did Red Heat, he supposed to speak in a Russian accent, he had an Austrian accent, for a year he started to learn how to have a Russian accent. When he did one of the Terminator movies, where he hangs out on a truck with a shotgun and he used a six shooter, he practiced that in his backyard for six months. So when he does stuff he goes all the way. And he is able to focus 100 percent and have a tunnel vision. There's another skill he has, which is kind of unusual. Every time he has to go from one set to another set by a car, he power naps, even for five minutes or two minutes. That's one of his biggest skills.

Another example, when he became the governor I was flying with him to Sacramento and back to Los Angeles. When we got back to Los Angeles, I said to him, "Hey, look how big Los Angeles is. In reality, Arnold, now you are the governor, is that kind of a dream? I mean, now you're the kind of a king of a country, you're actually the leader and governor of one of the most important economies in the world, six or seven in the world. I mean, how do you feel?" He said, "Sven, I believe I have one talent only. That is, when I believe, it happens. I believe I can fix California's problems, and for that matter United States of America's problems." Can you imagine a person can say that? He's one of a kind. Every thousand years, I believe a person is born with a higher purpose and he's one of them. He's not done yet, there's much more to come. I was at one of his speeches at his birthday party, where Maria said, "I know everybody here likes to ask Arnold what will he do after now not being a governor end of the year. That's why I love him. I never know what Arnold's going to do next." She said, "By the way, two days ago he told me we should have a birthday party." I got the invitation two days earlier. I never know what Arnold's going to do.

Any last words on your friend?
Sven-Ole Thorsen: I think what I said earlier, I cannot come up with a better explanation, that I believe every thousand years there's a person born with higher purpose than the average person. And Arnold is one of them. Jesus was another one. And I really mean that. Even though I'm always the guy that kind of tries to make him humble, even though he is humble, but he speaks big words. And, again, every thousand years there's a person born for a higher purpose and Arnold is one of them. He's the kind of a guy whose charisma can't be explained, when he

comes into the room he kind of takes over the room. That's one of his biggest assets: his charisma. I think that's something you're born with, and I think he's one of those guys with the charisma which goes beyond what you can't explain.

Arnold Schwarzenegger poses at the Cannes Film Festival, 2003.

Bodybuilding days, 1977.

In his signature role in The Terminator, 1984.

Sylvester Stallone and Arnold Schwarzenegger pictured at The Expendables Las Vegas movie premiere, 2010.

With wife Maria Shriver, Footprint Ceremony in Hollywood, 1994.

Doing the tango with Tia Carrere in True Lies, 1994.

At the premiere of Batman and Robin with director Joel Schumacher and co-star George Clooney, 1997.

President Obama speaks next to the governor at a meeting in Los Angeles, 2009.

The governor's first press conference after the election at the Century Plaza Hotel, Los Angeles, 2003.

The governor meeting Prime Minister Tony Blair outside 10 Downing Street, London, 2007.

CHAPTER THREE
FILM FRATERNITY

MARK LESTER

Mark Lester directed Commando in 1985, the film which became an Arnold classic. Lester's credits include Showdown in Little Tokyo, which starred Dolph Lundgren and the late Brandon Lee. He's worked on many action pictures as a director, writer and producer.

How did the concept of Commando come to materialize, and how did Arnold come on board for this project?
Mark Lester: There were two original writers, Mathew Weisman and Jeph Loeb, they're on the credits, (both) associate producers, and they gave the script to Joel Silver. I met him at a party at the Playboy mansion. He said he had this great script. I said, "OK, let me read it." He said, "If you read it, you'll never do the movie. Let me just tell you the idea." So he pitched the whole idea to me. I said that sounds great, and Schwarzenegger and I said we're in. So, then we hired Steve de Souza to write the script. It was pretty much different, because it didn't have comedy in the original script. It didn't have the one-liners, so he wrote the draft and it was really well done. That's how it all started, preliminary first draft of the script. He was brought in right after that. We went to the producer, who pitched the concept of the movie and told him the whole story with the writer, and then Arnold signed on right away after hearing the story. So, he was involved right from the beginning, from the whole script writing to the draft. He was involved from the beginning.

What was Arnold's personality like back then?
Mark Lester: That was a thing, in the meeting he was a very fun guy, always telling and cracking jokes, very charming personality. But he hadn't been seen in movies yet other than the Conan movies, and then he did The Terminator. And that's when I said that this character should just be like who you are, you should be cracking jokes and having fun and still be the commando. So it's kind of a cross between Terminator and James Bond kind of thing. That's what developed the screen personality, where he had this charm and humor, which went with the action.

How was Arnold to direct?
Mark Lester: He was unbelievable to work with. He was like using a

model, he followed instructions perfectly and he was extremely cooperative. He wanted to do all of his stunts, so he did all of his own stunts. There was one scene where he dresses up as a commando on the beach before going for the final attack. He had a knife fight. Because he was confident, we had to do it in closeup. He even wanted to do that himself, but I tried to convince him not to, and that was the only time he got hurt. He really wanted to do everything, fighting to glass stunts, he was very excited and jumping. He was very exciting and cooperative. He had a lot of different ideas. One of the things people don't know about is, he wanted to pick up one of the guy's arm after he cut it off and slap him with his own arm. I think that went a little too far. But that was the only time we had a discussion about what not to do.

Were there obstacles in shooting the scene at the shopping mall?
Mark Lester: We had to shoot it quickly, because we had used it all night long when the doors were closed. So we had all the stores opened up and all the extras throughout the mall. But the interesting thing there is, when Arnold swings across the galleria there is no net. He swings across the elevator. So we hired a circus trapeze artist but he was so tiny and small. I said this is never going to match. He said don't worry I'm going to swing moving so fast that no one will know it's me. That was done by a stunt double trapeze guy. That was the most concerning thing. He got up there and swung across and landed on the elevator perfectly, that was pretty amazing because there was no net or anything.

Can you tell me about Arnold socializing on the set and any intriguing anecdotes?
Mark Lester: Nothing like that happened. People always call me, when he was running for governor, and ask, "Who did Arnold seduce on the set?" I said, "No one." Someone said, "The service girl said she had sex with Arnold." I said, "That's impossible, she was ugly." He never would have.

What I meant was, how did Arnold socialize on the set?
Mark Lester: Oh. He hung out with a lot of the bodybuilders that came. There was a trailer filled with weight equipment, and they all hung out and lifted weights between the takes. They were all smoking cigars with Arnold. It was a lot of fun. That's basically what he did between the scenes.

Can you shed light on some of the more intricate action scenes, there were a lot of machine guns firing and explosions?
Mark Lester: We blew up three buildings, they had to be built on the

beach. And the Californian Environmental Laws, three days before we were to shoot the scene, wouldn't let us because it would...and the beach water ocean. So we had to find another place, we used a beach which was owned by Will Randolph Hearst, the old newspaper mogul in the '30s. He owned a beech, so we had to quickly go there - there were huge barracks on the beach - and make that major explosion. There was no CGI and animation in those days; we had to do it for real. We have Arnold running from the explosion near the building, and the explosion goes flying toward him and he has to dive for cover. This kind of stuff, you don't need to do anymore because they have CGI. But in the '80s, it didn't exist. So we and Arnold had to make actual major explosions.

Were there any particular scenes which were an impediment to shoot?
Mark Lester: There was a scene in the shed which was really hard. Even though it was a small little scene, where he had to kill, like, six people very quickly with garden tools. That was a hard scene to choreograph, getting all the timing to work with and kill so quickly with different tools in the shed. That's the scene that he wanted to pick up the arm and slap one of the soldiers. And the other scene, which was with the plane, was really difficult because we had to shoot it at the actual airport. In those days, when they used the airport to shoot they'd shut down the runway. So we had a plane out there, and Arnold had to get attached to the wheel, and we had a very complicated sequence with the airplane. Again, there was no CGI, so we actually had to have this huge wheel apparatus brought up to the airport, which was attached to a truck. And then we had to run it down the runway. It was all very complicated. It would be easy if you put it against a green screen and put the airport behind it. Back then we had to actually do everything practically.

Did Arnold get involved in other aspects of the film beyond his role of an actor?
Mark Lester: At that time, no. He basically concentrated on the acting. His haircut and his character, that became famous in the United States. In the '80s, people wanted to cut their hair like Arnold's in the movie. That was more about the cut than makeup of the hair. And in shooting, he wanted to make sure his body was right, the muscles flex a certain way; he was very meticulous about all those things.

He wasn't an actor, let's say, of the caliber of Jack Nicholson and some of these other actors, he was an action man. Did you encounter any problems pertaining to filming dialog scenes with him?
Mark Lester: It was written for him, so I had to do it many, many times.

It was mostly written with one-liners; there weren't a lot of long lines. It was written very much for him, so there weren't any issues like that.

Commando is one of the best action movies Arnold made, which imprinted his image on a generation of Americans. Do you feel this movie was the perfect vehicle to catapult Arnold into global stardom? **Mark Lester:** Yes, this was the vehicle. This launched his entire career, because in The Terminator he just played a robot. This was the picture that launched him into the action movie career that he had. People could see he was really a very good actor as well. Then he did things like Kindergarten Cop, where he just played in comedy films. But from this movie, it launched him into Total Recall and all these big action films. Without Commando, I don't think he ever would have had the big career as he did. We never had a premiere, the movie was finished a day before it hit the theaters. At the studio, we had a rough cut of the film and we had a big screening for the studio executives. They said the good news is we love the movie but the bad news is we're moving the release date to November right away. So we only had forty-five days to finish the whole thing, edit the movie and do everything. So, I mean, literally the prints were done two days before it opened up in the theaters. There never was a premiere in the United States.

Commando was released on the big screen in October 1985 in America. Five months earlier, Rambo: First Blood Part 2 had been released which went on to gross a staggering $300 million worldwide. Commando, with a budget of $10 million, grossed $57.5 million globally. The marked difference from the box office receipts was evident who was the number-one action star at the time. When asked about how his film Commando differed from his nemesis' Rambo: First Blood Part 2, Arnold stated, "It's a different movie. Mine is a battleground right in Los Angeles. Stallone's battleground is Vietnam. His is a very politically oriented movie, and mine is not at all. Mine is humor oriented. You can laugh and you can have a good time with it, and I don't take myself seriously in the film, either. I believe in comic relief, otherwise the whole thing becomes too intense and too heavy."

Franco Columbu had trained Sylvester Stallone for Rocky 2. The producers asked Columbu if he was willing to train Stallone and get him in shape for Rambo. Sly called Arnold's best friend and stated that they had seven weeks to get in shape, and how were they going to achieve this. Columbu's biggest concern was the fact he would probably not have complete control over Stallone, because the star loved to be the boss and had an inclination to do things his own way. Columbu clearly stipulated if he was going to train Stallone, then he had to have total control as the trainer. He even went as far as drawing up a contract in which it was stipulated Stallone was not to take anything without Columbu's approval - that includes steroids, vitamins and minerals. The bemused Rocky star looked at the contract and asked what all this was about. Anyway, Columbu proceeded to get his client in brutal shape and defined in seven weeks. He explained to his client that if you take steroids, you get pumped up but you don't get defined, hence the producers won't be happy.

Alyssa Milano, who played the young daughter, remembers, "I'd never worked with someone so large in my life. I found him intimidating." Arnold looked ripped and toned in this classic, which has become a fan favorite. More than twenty years later, Joel Silver remarked he was watching a movie he made twenty years ago which seemed so simplistic to him as he looked back. He says he was so childish back then, and everyone has evolved now. Nevertheless, Commando has become one of the classics of the action genre from the 1980s.

What was Joel Silver's relationship like with Arnold, and what was his sentiments on the finished movie?
Mark Lester: Oh, he loved it. He loved the movie. I mean, he did Predator later with Arnold. Everyone got along with Arnold, he was a great person to deal with. You'll have to ask Joe.

What do you remember the most when you look back at when you initially teamed up with Arnold?
Mark Lester: The funny thing was the night before shooting, we had dinner at the hotel before we went on the set the next morning. Arnold says to me, "I'm scared to death." I asked him why. "The first day of shooting, I'm always scared to death." I said, "So am I. Everybody is until we get the first shot, then we're OK." But I was kind of surprised to hear that. There were just two of us there. He became a big star, and I think he got more involved, that's what I hear, with different pictures with the technical aspects and production. And he had a lot more control of the various pictures than at the time, which was one of his first movies.

How would you define Arnold's Commando from a historical perspective in the genre?
Mark Lester: Commando is considered as the finest action movie of the '80s. Myself, I was always thinking at the time like John Ford who made all those Westerns people didn't...he didn't know those Westerns

were classics; it's only years later they became classics. Now Commando plays almost every week in LA and on American Movie Classics. So, it's considered, what everybody likes about the action movies of the '80s, Commando to be the major action movie of the '80s, and in every magazine and so forth, and there's websites devoted to it on the internet. They're even making a remake - 20th Century Fox. It's considered as a classic action movie of the 1980s, and I'm proud to have done it. At the time, I didn't know I was making a classic, we were making an action movie. It's now that people consider that to be a landmark film.

After working on the movie with Arnold, did you continue to see him and stay in touch or did the friendship dissolve?
Mark Lester: We stayed friends, even to this day. He's a very nice guy. He was busy as the governor, but I'm sure I'll see him again. We usually used to meet in his restaurant in Venice. I saw him with his wife at the Cannes Film Festival five, six years ago. And Maria and him, they told me Commando was their favorite movie that he made. They consider that's their favorite movie he's made. Maria likes it too.

BILL DUKE

Bill Duke was born in New York, he is known for his physically imposing frame. He appeared with Arnold in Predator and Commando. Duke has appeared in many Hollywood movies, including Sister Act 2 and Hoodlum. He continues to act and direct.

You worked with Arnold on Predator, but also had worked with him prior to that.
Bill Duke: I did a movie before that called Commando. Joel Silver was the producer on that. And we got a long very well. Joel Silver did Predator also. The most impressive thing was that he (Arnold) was a professional, in other words, very gracious, no ego. It was, like, let's move forward, let's get the work done. And as a result, the crew and cast were like that. He had a sense of humor and was a very good person. At that time, I think he had retired from the bodybuilding world and he was getting into the movie business. I think he was really beginning to move in as an actor. He was a good person and a good collaborator and a professional.

Anything you would like to share pertaining to filming Commando?
Bill Duke: When we have our fight scene, where I die in the movie, I told Arnold, "In real life I'd kick your butt." He said, "Yeah, but it's a movie and you get killed, so die!"

Can you tell me about filming Predator in Mexico, I believe the shoot was done under harsh conditions?
Bill Duke: We filmed in Mexico and we filmed in Pacific Palisades. We had a great team of people, that part of it was possible. But when we were in the jungle, that part was not easy. For the first two weeks that we were there, they had netting around the place where the catering was, but still bugs got in our food. So we told the caterer that we refuse to eat the food because there are bugs in it. And he said there's nothing we can do, because we were in the jungle. By the end of the second week, we were eating the bugs and we caught something.

Did you have time to socialize with Arnold, was the hotel far from the location set?

Bill Duke: Well, Arnold didn't socialize very much because he's very disciplined. He had to get up early with the other guys and be on the set, let's say 7 a.m., he and some of the other guys would get up at three or four o' clock in the morning, and they would go for a run for at least, I would say, an hour and a half. Then meet back and workout in the gym for two hours. And then they would eat breakfast, then go to the set. I couldn't do all that all the time, because they were much more disciplined than me. But it was a real challenge. But they did that seven days a week.

What were some of the obstacles and extremities the cast and the crew had to endure when filming the movie?
Bill Duke: Heat, humidity, spiders, scorpions, snakes, we had diarrhea - anything possible, we got! Because we were in the jungle. When we would go back to the hotel at night, everything was pretty much OK there. One day, something had broken down and we all got sick. It was a very difficult shoot.

In the past, Arnold has said it was a survival story and it was physically demanding. Can you define Arnold's professionalism, he's someone who never complained, his professional ethics set an example for everyone when working on Predator?
Bill Duke: Arnold is a professional. Arnold is the kind of person, no matter what the problem is, he doesn't complain. He deals with it. And with his leadership, everybody did the same thing. In other words, he was the star of the show, but he had no better condition than anyone else. And after we go, everybody followed his lead, because they had great respect for him, also because of his leadership. So we were all in the same kind of cage together, he didn't ask for special treatment, he didn't ask for anything. He simply did his job as an actor, and it was a very god example for the rest of the cast and crew.

In your opinion, what were the most demanding or stressful scenes to shoot which required maximum physical exertion?
Bill Duke: Oh, yeah. Well, you know, the jungle affected us. When we were trapped in the jungle and blew everything up, we had to do that scene repeatedly. There was a lot of running up and down the hill in the sweltering weather, we had uniforms on. I mean, that was all real, the weather was one hundred degrees with humidity.

Was there a lot of hanging around in the jungle?
Bill Duke: Everybody had a good time despite the obstacles, that's number one. But the main thing is, the irony of the conditions. In other

187

words, we were playing these soldiers which were in this jungle situation, but our conditions were no better than the guys we were playing. In other words, snakes, scorpions, spiders, you know, it was, like real. The conditions were so real.

John McTiernan directed Predator, who also later went on to work with Arnold on another movie.
Bill Duke: John McTiernan is a good director, he was a wonderful guy. He did a great job I think. One thing that you might not know is that the Predator creature that you saw was not the original creature in the picture. The original creature was more adept and smaller. He had a suit where they could put green screen special effects. It was very hot and the humidity, and several times the person playing the creature actually passed out. The producer said if you pass out again I'm going to have to fire you. The name of that person was Jean Claude Van Damme.

John McTiernan believed Arnold had the potential to be another John Wayne. McTiernan had been warned that he'd have to do hundred and twelve takes for Arnold to get it right. But they didn't do more than nine, and four of those takes were for camera problems and two for Arnold and another actor for breaking out laughing in takes. Prior to filming, Arnold had lost over 25 pounds, which made him lean and better fit into the role of a special warfare operative. Aside from the extreme conditions, the cast had their light-hearted moments to get them through the filming. Jesse Ventura suggested to Arnold they should measure their arms, and the winner would receive a bottle of champagne. Arnold told the wardrobe to tell Ventura that his arms were bigger than Ventura's.

Would I be right in saying co-star Sonny Landham was unstable on the set, and as a result a bodyguard was hired to protect the cast and crew?
Bill Duke: Sonny Landham is a great human being. He had trouble sleeping, so when he didn't sleep he would go up to the clubs. So they hired a bodyguard to watch him to make sure he didn't get into trouble or anything.

As far as conversing with Arnold, what do you remember which made an impression on you?
Bill Duke: I'm into education and I have helped kids in education. I asked Arnold one time, I said, "If you were giving advice to young people for them never to give up on their dreams, what would you say?" He said, "Bill, very simple. Tell them to stay hungry." Arnold is a

professional and money is not important to him, what's important to him is he does the best at what he does. I think his standards are excellent and got him to superstardom. Whether it's acting, whether it's producing, whether it's being a politician, whether it's being an entrepreneur, he has values and he wants to be the best at what he does. I think it's not competition outside of himself; it's an internal competition. He always wants to be the best at what he does. It's not your standards, it's his standards.

Did he talk to you about bodybuilding or working out? There were some big guys in the movie, notably Carl Weathers, Sonny Landham and yourself!
Bill Duke: I was working out but those guys have a different standard. I mean, they worked out three, four hours a day! In other words, the workout ethics is three or four hours a day, the average person works out an hour and a half. These guys worked out! I mean, hardcore working out.

Did Joel Silver frequent the set and what was his vision for this movie?
Bill Duke: Joel came on the set all the time. He flew from the US and came down to Mexico all the time. In the original script concept, it was written from an animal rights point of view. The original writer wanted the script which showed how people kill, how they hunt animals. He wanted people to know how animals felt being hunted. So they wanted it to be an animal doing the hunting. Now the man is being hunted and killed, like we hunt animals all the time. But we don't think of them of anything but animals, because we don't consider them as important. They wanted to make people feel how animals felt, and that's how the whole idea came about.

The movie did well when it was released. Would I be right in saying Arnold went to get married during filming (February 25, 1986) and the production was halted?
Bill Duke: I don't think the production was halted, but he did go to get married. But we kept shooting. The premiere was wonderful, the people really, really loved the movie. It was a big major action film in the jungle, and with the special effects. Some people hadn't really seen something like that, you know. It was really well-directed. And people like performances, so there's nothing negative that people responded to. Arnold was the kind of a person to take on the leadership role, not what he said but what he did. He never complained. He always was prepared. He didn't put down other actors. He was famous by then, he also was a

human being. A lot of people in that situation don't have the great class or professionalism that he has, and they have the tendency to feel that they're better than other people. He was never that way, ever. He's not one of those idiots that throws it in people's faces. Personal depth of a human being.

When promoting the movie, Arnold recalled, "The only problem I had was I had to leave after three weeks of filming Predator. The schedule was really strange. So I had to leave the shoot and I flew to Hyannis (to get married), and they wanted me to come right back to film in the jungle. How do you explain this to your wife now that you have to go back to working in the jungle right after your wedding? So I took Maria to honeymoon to Antigua, and I explained to her this is a beautiful vacation site and all that. She was very excited to go down, and little did she know she'd end up in the jungle in Mexico where we were shooting the film. But it was a fun honeymoon."

After Predator did you keep in touch with Arnold or did you both part ways?
Bill Duke: We still keep in touch. I had a premiere of a film in Sacramento, Arnold changed his schedule and attended my premiere. He came to the movie and I was really grateful for that, because he is very, very busy. He had another appointment but canceled that appointment and came to see my film, which I really appreciate. I really respect him and have a really high regard for him for as a human being and he's a great guy and a person.

VIC ARMSTRONG

When it comes to stuntmen and stunt coordinators, Vic Armstrong is without a doubt one of the greatest ever! Armstrong worked on Conan the Destroyer, Total Recall and Last Action Hero with Arnold. He also worked on the Bond and Indiana Jones movies.

You worked on Conan the Destroyer with Arnold among other movies. How did you linkup to work together?
Vic Armstrong: I had just finished Indiana Jones and the Temple of Doom, and Raffaella had called me to go out to Mexico in June. I went out there and finished the job. Then she said, "We need you to do another film with Richard Fleischer, and we'd like you to do that one. It's called Conan." So I went straight from Mexico to do Conan. That's how I got it. I had a wonderful time there in Mexico. I love Mexico. I've done a lot of films there. We had a great time at the Churubusco Studios and all over the place - loved it. It was fabulous. We did a lot of films together after that, because Raffaella used to like to keep the same crew together, the same special effects, the production and everyone. We went on and did Red Sonja with Arnie, and it was very good,

Arnold has been immensely passionate about making movies and thoroughly enjoyed the experience. When working on Conan the Destroyer, he said, "It's like being a little kid again in many ways, and doing the things that maybe you were not allowed to do as a kid, you know, stabbing people with a sword and killing them with an axe and stuff like that. And at the same time, acting wise it's challenging at the same time. So it has these two opposites." Arnold said he didn't take many things seriously. For him, making movies was a fun thing to do. As a matter of fact, he said many times that it was his best paid vacation he'd had in his life at the time of filming Conan the Destroyer.

Can you tell me about meeting Arnold for the first time?
Vic Armstrong: He was fabulous. I met him when he was in the wardrobe having his wig fitting. I went in and introduced myself. He

was great fun. I used to box and train at the time, so we used to workout every day together and go to dinner together. He hasn't changed at all. Actually, he was a wonderful social character with charisma, but really tough. In Mexico City, which is 8,000 feet, after work we would go out running and training, he was just amazing. He's an amazing strength of character. He's a good guy and good socially as well.

What was it like working with Arnold on the scenes on Conan the Destroyer, he valiantly despatched assailants in the movie?
Vic Armstrong: He was very collaborative, because, obviously, he's a big man so very difficult to double. So he did a lot of stunts himself. I did a percentage of them, I had a stuntman there in case we needed him. But, because - as I say - he was doing it bare chest, you can't double that figure, you know. I worked very close with him, training him to do the sword fights and the horse riding, we taught him to ride. And the sword fighting, we'd rehearse every day with swords. He was just fun. We would discuss it and work out all the fight scenes and treat him as a stuntman. He'd come with the boys and we would work it out together, and because he knew he had to do most of the fights himself because of his physique.

The film wasn't without it's mishaps on set. According to Grace Jones, "I hurt a lot of people with that stick, yes, seriously. I clobbered about five guys and sent them to hospital." Arnold found it quite hard to work with Jones, who was as real as they come when it came to filming the fight scenes. But he praised her performance and enthusiasm which reflected reality. He sedately exclaimed, "I have done a lot of fight scenes in the first movie with stuntmen, dangerous scenes, and falling off horses and jumping 40 feet and everything. I would rather do all of those things together than do one fight scene with Grace Jones, because she really takes it seriously! But she looks wonderful on the screen, because she really gets into the character."

Jones said the match between Arnold and her was fantastic, because there was so much of being physical and because of the great sense of humor, and they had a lot of laughs. The movie was released in June 1984. This sequel to the original Conan was moderately successful domestically and very successful outside of America, as was the case with many of Arnold's movies, grossing $31 million domestically and a further $69 million internationally. When filming, Arnold had remarked, "I really hope there is a Conan Two, Three, Four, Five, Six, Seven and on and on and on. As a matter of fact, I visualize myself doing Conan when I'm eighty years old with a big gray beard or something like that."

Arnold was asked by Dino De Laurentiis to do him a favor by doing a cameo role for another sword and sorcery movie he was producing called Red Sonja. This movie introduced a Danish model-turned-actress Brigitte Nielsen - Sandahl Bergman also co-starred in it. Shot in Italy in 1984, the B-movie flopped taking in less than half its budget costs. It was critically panned because of its bad acting and bad characterization. Arnold has said Red Sonja is the worst film he ever made. "Now when my kids get out of line, they're sent to their room and forced to watch Red Sonja ten times. I never have too much trouble with them," bemused Arnold. Although Arnold was asked to appear in an extended cameo by the producer - producers cashing in on the success of Conan - he was unhappy when he discovered he had been given top billing.

Can you relate any social moment in Mexico away from the set?
Vic Armstrong: One night we went out, and he used to eat very wisely, you know, vegetables and salads and steak and red wine. Then we'd finish with some tequila. Then during the evening, I had agreed to go play tennis with him in the morning. At seven o' clock the next morning, I woke up with a terrible headache. The phone was ringing and it was Arnold. He said, "Where are you? I'm on the tennis court waiting for you!" I was like, oh, my God. He was on the tennis court, so I had to go play tennis.

What were the most arduous stunts on that movie, it was an action-packed movie with a lot of fighting?
Vic Armstrong: Most of the stunts are difficult, because he couldn't wear any padding. We did one fight in a room where there were all mirrors. The mirrors smash during the fight with the Wizard, so poor Arnold's running around and there's broken glass exploding everywhere. There's mirrors exploding and breaking. That was very dangerous and difficult to shoot. And we had to keep the camera out of the reflection of the mirrors, and we had to break all the mirrors. All the actors are standing there with no padding on, because they can't wear padding because they had to show the flesh.

Were there any sophisticated stunts on Total Recall, the film which you both worked on which was a science fiction action and adventure?
Vic Armstrong: Yeah, very sophisticated stunts. In the end, we built the set vertically. Imagine the set being horizontal, take a horizontal set and stand it vertically. And you put the camera vertically beside it, when you look through the lens it looks horizontal. But for all the stuff where

Arnie's heading for space, it was really hanging from the ceiling, but it looks like it's hanging from a wall. So the ceiling became the wall. It's very difficult to do that on a diagram. But it was very tricky and complicated, it made the film much more realistic in the world we were dealing with.

Arnold had matured as an actor by this time, 1989, when filming Total Recall. What's your impression?
Vic Armstrong: Oh, yeah. When you think about it, Arnold is a very, very...I can't stress how intelligent he is. He's a very intelligent man. And he knew to improve and carry on in the business, he had to learn the business. Everything Arnold does, he does 100 percent thoroughly. So he had acting coaches, he watched films and he thought about his performances. I think he improved 100 percent from Conan to Total Recall.

Did he have any input which went beyond his role as the lead actor as far as directing or coming with ideas and putting them forward to the director or the stunt coordinator?
Vic Armstrong: Oh, yeah. I was stunt coordinating, and we did rehearsals with Arnold. We rehearsed together and we talked together. Anything that would make it better for the movie or for him, we would incorporate that into the fight routines. Then we would present them to Richard Fleischer, the director, or Paul Verhoeven, the director of Total Recall - it's a team effort.

What was Sharon Stone's and Arnold's collaboration like?
Vic Armstrong: They're great. The fight routines have all got to be rehearsed; you can't do them without rehearsing them. So I had good stuntwomen that could double her. My wife was doubling Rachel Ticotin. It's a team effort, you have to work hard at it and train together. Every film we do the same, they (actors) have to become stunt people for two or three weeks whilst they rehearse their actions and everything else.

Were there any stunts which didn't go to plan in Total Recall?
Vic Armstrong: No, not really. Everything was good. Everything worked out, if something didn't work out we'd change the action before getting around to filming it. But the time we get on the film set, everything has been rehearsed and perfected. So nothing was a problem on that. It's time and money to rehearse it properly.

Total Recall was also filmed in Mexico.
Vic Armstrong: Arnold threw a party for the whole crew one day. He

came up with this idea of giving everybody water pistols, squirt guns, so we had all these squirt guns on the table. As the dinner progressed and people drank more, we squirted these water pistols at each other. But, of course, at the end of the evening the water pistols were filled with red wine and vodka. So everybody was just squirting these things and going crazy, it was a mad evening. It was wonderful. Arnie paid for everything. I missed the premiere because I was working. I actually saw Total Recall in a midnight screening in Marble Arch in London. I never forget seeing it there, everybody was screaming and enjoying it in the middle of the night. It was wonderful. I missed the premiere unfortunately.

Arnold, a physical specimen, was cognizant of the hard work which went into stunts and the abilities of the stuntmen. Did you perceive him to be appreciative to the stunt fraternity?
Vic Armstrong: Arnold is a great supporter of the stunt world. He's always friends with his team, we're all part of his gang. We all work very, very closely together, because he knows from his upbringing what work goes into it. He knows it's an integral part of his movies and action, so he's always very, very aware of what's going on. Even since he became a governor, he still came and presented the World Stunt Awards. He presented me with my Taurus World Stunt Award. He's a great supporter of the stunt team and great friends with everybody.

You worked with Arnold on Last Action Hero, you did stunt coordinating. There were lots of stunts on this movie. Can you reflect on working on this movie with him?
Vic Armstrong: I only joined Last Action Hero at the end, when they were finishing. I was doing another movie and John McTernian and Arnold wanted me to go and do some stuff. So I did lots of little pieces that joined the movie together. So I'm afraid I can't take credit for all the movie. I was on it for about four weeks. I Remember I had Arnold on one sequence where he had to fall away from the camera about 100 feet, and we had a big swing set up. We had a 120-foot crane and a cable on it, and Arnie's swinging underneath it. He is amazing. I've gotta say he does anything you ask him to do, he's really brave.

Critics and fans alike didn't like the movie, what are your views on the finished film? It didn't do well as other Arnold movies, can the failure be blamed on the script?
Vic Armstrong: Yeah, I think the script was the problem; action was good, Arnie was good. The script just didn't get the people's imagination, it was too confusing I think. It wasn't what they were expecting to go and see.

Did you occasionally run into Arnold and keep in touch with him?

Vic Armstrong: We went to the opening of Planet Hollywood in London with Arnold, that was great. We opened the restaurant there. Everybody from the film industry was there, it was a massive opening.

PETER KENT

Peter Kent worked with Arnold for fifteen years on most of his movies as a stunt double. This lead to a friendship ensuing on and off set. Both men enjoyed a camaraderie, which went as far as visiting each other's homes for dinner.

How did you become Arnold's stunt double, when was the first time you actually worked with him?

Peter Kent: I went to Los Angeles with literally no experience. I was living in a YMCA, and I found some small magazines for casting. I went to one of the casting sessions, and they said we're looking for somebody for this little movie called The Terminator and we need someone to stand in for Arnold. So I went over to the offices and James Cameron saw me, and he said, "You're perfect, you have the job." He said, "By the way, do you know how to do stunts?" I thought if I didn't say yes to the second question, I wouldn't get the job. So I lied basically and got the job. Then basically, I kind of worked my way through it. The night that we went through the glass backwards in the nightclub, the stunt coordinator - Frank Orsatti - came to me and said, "Do you want wraps for those?" I had no idea what he was talking about. He looked at me and he said, "You don't have any idea what you're doing, do you?" I said, "No." He said, "I better help train you so you don't get killed."

There's no doubt that The Terminator cemented Arnold's spot in the action-brawn firmament. The Terminator is shuddery as the futuristic cyborg who kills without fear or mercy. It is safe to say that it was a happy accident for Arnold to portray the android assassin. James Cameron stated, "People at Orion passed the script to Arnold with the suggestion that he plays the so-called 'hero', Reese. He and I met, and neither of us felt very comfortable about him in that part. It had never occurred to anyone that he consider playing the villain, but that was the role he wanted! Now, Arnold is a shaven-headed, eyebrow less half-man/half-machine in a black leather jacket with wraparound sunglasses. It does break the mold of what people think about him."

Mel Gibson turned down the role and O.J. Simpson was considered.

Mike Medavoy, the studio head, had told Arnold that O.J. Simpson had been hired to play the Terminator and he should play the hero. Arnold remembers, "Basically, they were looking for someone to play the heroic character in the film, in the first Terminator, and they asked me to play the character and they asked to send me the script. And I had a slot open for spring and I want to see the script first, and I read the script and I immediately could relate much more to the character of the Terminator than the heroic character."

Cameron recalls that initially he didn't want Arnold, "I'll never forget walking out of my apartment and telling my roommate, 'I've got to go have lunch with Conan and pick a fight with him.' That was my agenda, because I didn't want him to do the movie. So I had to get in an argument and come back and say he was an asshole. But that's not what happened. I had lunch with Arnold, and he was so charming and so into the script and so amusing and entertaining that I totally forgot my agenda." Cameron remembers having a great time at the meeting, Arnold made him smoke a cigar, which made Cameron sick for six hours. The director says Arnold paid for lunch because Cameron didn't have any money and was with "this loser from Hemdale" who didn't have any money.

When you first met Arnold on the set, what was your first impression and working with Arnold on The Terminator?

Peter Kent: We were shooting in the Department of Water and Power in downtown Los Angeles. I went down there, they had a chair set up in the corner. The first thing he said, when I walked up to him where they had the dressing and wardrobe, he looked at me and shook his head and said, "Too tall." I thought I'd just lost my job, and I turned around and walked away. He was, like, "I'm kidding, get back here." We got along great. It was one of those things we were kind of like brothers right from the start. It was really a good relationship. In fact, my mother had said to me, when she found out that I had the job with Arnold, "Don't treat him any differently than anybody else." I didn't. And I think that was the success to it all. We got along well. I would tell him anything, if I didn't think it was right, or he was doing something stupid, or an acting thing which wasn't working for him, I'd say do this or that.

The darkly hued science-fiction movie The Terminator gave you your first taste of stunt work. Was there anything which you found to be much more intricate than you imagined it would be?

Peter Kent: Well, on the first Terminator there was some of the motorcycle driving, which we actually had a guy who came in and did some of the driving on that. I didn't have a whole lot of experience, I was physically body doubling him. So, really the toughest one for me was going through a window for Arnold, having never done it before. The rest of the stuff was doubling, walking with the machine gun and that kind of thing.

Would I be right in saying Arnold sometimes did his own stunts on his movies?
Peter Kent: Yes. He did. He did almost all of his own fights, which he was very good at. And he would do whatever he could get away with. Obviously, when he got more popular the insurance company which was funding the movie wouldn't allow him to do any more.

What was the next movie you worked with Arnold on?
Peter Kent: I worked with him directly after that on Commando. We shot Commando in Santa Barbara, California. We filmed in San Luis Obispo and then bunch of it in San Pedro too. Not much of it in central LA, we did a little bit onstage work there, but mostly it was outside of town. Arnold and Joel got along really well. I never saw them arguing. In fact, we did Predator with Joel again later on. Joel was always a really gracious producer. I remember I was getting really tired of eating the food in Mexico (when filming Predator), so Joel sent food from a deli from New York City. He had flown down about 50 pounds of stuff, including potato salad and all kinds of great American food that everyone was missing so much. He had it flown in privately for the crew, because he wanted everybody to be happy and be comfortable. It was a very nice gesture.

Commando had a lot of action and explosions. Can you tell me the precautions you have to take when filming such action?
Peter Kent: Oh, yeah. You have to be very careful. I mean, one of the things about doing stunts, when I had the luxury of working with Arnold, was with the safety factor. A lot of guys get pushed into things where the director says, "Hurry up!" or the AD says, "Hurry up, we've got to get this done!" And you're in a rush and put in a position where something happens and you get hurt or killed even. In my case, I was always careful and I watched everything, because I'd seen that stuff happened before. I was thinking, "It's not gonna happen to me." So I would watch what was going on, and if I didn't feel comfortable and felt that I was being pushed, I'd just get on the radio and call Arnold in his trailer and say, "Arnold, look, they're rushing it. I don't think it's safe." And he would say hand the radio to the AD and Arnold would say to the assistant director give him time, let him get what he needs. So that may have saved my life in some instances, I don't know.

I just know a lot of guys never thought like that, and a lot of guys get injured because of being rushed. A lot of those explosions are every bit dangerous as a car bomb in Baghdad. A lot of the times I would say, "There's going to be an explosion here." And they'd say, "OK, show me one." I worked with a guy named Tommy Fisher, who is a special effects guy, he was the only guy I've worked with that if he said you're safe standing there, I would believe him. Everybody else I'd say, "Please show me one. I want to see you blow that stuff up first." And they'd say, "Oh, no, we don't want to blow that up right now, we have to wait when they're rolling." I say, "No, I want to see it."

What was your experience working with Arnold on Twins, which had elements of humor thrown in, the movie which gave Arnold another dimension to express his character?
Peter Kent: It was a lot of fun obviously. I mean, working with Danny DeVito was a real treat. Danny kept it quite lively all the time and had a good rapport with everybody. Arnold and Danny DeVito threw a big party at the end of the shooting when we were in Santa Fe in New Mexico. I remember Danny and his wife Rhea Perlman who was there. All he did the whole night was drink tequila and dance. And on the very end of the night, Danny turned to some of the stunt guys and said, "Guys, do you still want to carry on?" But we had a 7 a.m. plane to catch that morning, I think it was 4 a.m. at that time. Danny took all of us to another nightclub and bought each of us a bottle of wine. And we walked around with beers in our hands until 6 a.m., and then we left for the airport totally drunk and climbed on the plane.

Arnold got on very well with Danny. I don't think anyone doesn't get along with Danny DeVito. Danny's got a fabulous sense of humor. Danny is a professional and he's been in the business for almost all of his life. He's one of those kind of guys he's always in a good mood when he comes on the set; he's always happy and he always makes people laugh. So he's very fun to be around with and a lot of fun to be with. Because Arnold is a joker and Danny is a joker, there were a lot of pranks, just goofing off on the set with Danny and Arnold. We were shooting in New Mexico, so it was a nice place to be away, beautiful location, nice artwork. Arnold and I took a trip to the R.C. Gorman, the famous artist factory there, and Arnold bought a bunch of very large faces and was also kind enough to get R.C. to lithograph for me "happy birthday" because it was my birthday at the time.

Arnold's collaboration with DeVito on Twins lead to further collaborations, and a friendship ensued. Arnold cheerfully recalled, "He was always insisting of smoking bigger cigars than I did, because he was short. But, anyway, we had a wonderful time, he was a great partner. We did Twins and Junior together, and he's a very talented guy, very talented chef, he cooked everyone lunch every day. The pasta, the Italian stuff, and with the wine in, sometimes we couldn't even remember our lines we were so drunk. And Ivan Reitman, who's another great Canadian director, who directed the movies, he was always upset, said, 'Guys, you're losing me money, you've got to remember the lines.' I said, 'I can't remember the lines now, maybe I said something wrong.' Anyway, me and Danny had a lot of laughs and a lot of fun on these movies."

Kindergarten Cop was another movie which allowed Arnold to express his lighter side. What are your recollections working with him on this movie?
Peter Kent: We had fun on that too. As they say: working with kids and dogs very much slows down the process. I think also the kids were, in fact, really great, they took direction pretty very well. And, in fact, sometimes they weren't required to take any direction; the director Ivan Reitman just wanted mayhem from them. But the kids' mothers, who were Hollywood moms who had been failed actresses themselves, were just miserable. They would be bickering backstage saying their son was the better actor, or their daughter was better. They would go to the director whilst he was trying to shoot and say, "Why doesn't my son have lines whilst so and so has lines?" He'd be, like, "I don't know what you're talking about. Your kid wasn't hired to have dialog. He's here in the background, he has a line later on in the movie. Why am I discussing this now?" It was pretty crazy, the going-ons behind the scenes of the moms was quite something.

We shot in Astoria, Oregon, which is a real great little town. I'm from the Pacific Northwest, so it was a real great taste of home for me to be back up there to so close where I live in Vancouver. But I had been in LA for quite a while and I missed the home thing. It was really a nice small town. The whole town turned up with open arms, it really helped us with the shoot. It was a lot of fun. One thing working with Arnold, whenever we went on location we always made sure we had a lot of fun. It was a very light-hearted film. There was a very good camaraderie between Arnold and Pamela, the woman who played his female cop counterpart. We had a lot of fun working on that film. It wasn't an action picture, so it wasn't as physically grueling as lot of the stuff we had done before that. So, it was just one of those kind of movies where it's nice to have some time to where you're actually working, but at the same time, especially me, I'm not out there getting the shit beaten out of me every day.

Oregon is a little town with great food and great sights to see. In fact, that town is where - and nobody really knows this story - Arnold saw a Hummer; he has many Hummers now. In fact, they named a wing after him in the factory. We were driving by the Army base, I think it's Camp Kirby, or something like that, or Reilly, I'm not sure which. Anyway, we saw the Hummers coming out of the base, and Arnold said to me, "Jeez, those look cool. I wonder what those are." And I was reading a magazine, a Car and Driver magazine, on set a couple of days later in my spare time. And there was an article in there on how AM General had one of their Hummers driven across Mongolia and China by a private citizen to test the vehicle out. So, I said, "Arnold, this is what this thing is." So I wrote away for him to AM General, and they sent us a video tape and a huge press package for the vehicle and it was then when he ordered one. So, basically I was the one responsible for Hummer being into the private sector, out of the military and into the private sector. I don't have one. Maybe if I hadn't written that letter to AM General and not got the press package, he may have just not paid much attention to it and it might have just gone by. But that wasn't to be.

In 1992, when Arnold purchased his first Hummer, which weighed 6,300 pounds, it kicked off a nationwide craze for the gas-guzzling behemoths. In a bid to work toward saving the environment, in 2006 Arnold gave up his fleet of seven Hummers, thought to be worth around $950,000. He kept one and reportedly spent $21,000 to get one of his Hummers converted to burn hydrogen. Arnold regularly bought and sold cars. Protecting the environment did not require one to be against large SUVs or trucks, he affirmed when he was the governor. Instead we should develop technology to cut down greenhouses gas emissions, because that was where the action is, he said. He believed that it wasn't the size of the car which was the issue. His collection of cars have included a Ferrari 360 Spider, a stunning jet-black Bentley Continental Supersports, a vintage Mercedes Excalibur and a Porsche 911 turbo.

Brian Grazier, the producer of Kindergarten, says Arnold was the dream star for a producer and a studio. Unlike many big stars, who are above such philistine concerns as marketing and promotion, Arnold was willing to do all the promotion and converse with the press to promote a movie and all the smiling you could want, the producer stated. Kindergarten Cop was a role intended to show the action man's light side, and he pulled it off safely. In preparing for his role, Arnold went to a real kindergarten accompanied by Ivan Reitman to get the feel and atmosphere of a real kindergarten. "Ivan Reitman took me into a real

Kindergarten to see how I communicated with kids," Arnold recalled. "The first time I went in there with a hundred of them, I was sweating. You say, 'Hi!' and they look at you strangely. You say, 'How are you today?' and they look at each other like you were talking Russian."

One critic described Kindergarten Cop as being somewhat violent and offensive. Entertainment Weekly stated, "The idea of the extremely big (Arnold Schwarzenegger, whose upper arms are larger than the average person's thighs) in comic collision with the very small (a kindergarten class) is rich in possibilities. But Kindergarten Cop, in which America's favorite lunk goes undercover as a teacher in Oregon to retrieve big drug money, is, above all, offensive and violent. Conan the Teacher turns the tots into something resembling Hitler Youth, with the kids (obviously too old for kindergarten) goose-stepping their way toward obedience and responding to boot-camp commands." However, this didn't stop the film from being a huge success grossing over $200 million, with a budget which was around $26 million.

What was Arnold's relationship like with the stunt guys and the crew in general, and was his appreciation of the hard work which went into stunts, which merits our attention, visible?
Peter Kent: Always good. The stunt guys would always kind of hang out together. The reputation John Wayne had with hanging out with the stunt guys, and I think Arnold was pretty much on the same level. He always liked to hang out with the guys and smoke a cigar. I was always to be found in his trailer. I had my own little room. So, whenever they were looking for me on set, they would always go to Arnold's trailer, or Arnold had a radio in his trailer so they would call for me there. I was generally in there, we were eating, smoking a cigar or drinking coffee or playing cars or reading a magazine or rehearsing dialog or something.

He was always very one for and appreciated his crew and would take a moment to say hi to everybody. He always appreciated it. When we did True Lies, when we were in Florida a couple of guys got hurt really badly, and he showed a lot of concern. When we shot Total Recall in Mexico, one of the stunt guys, Joel Kramer, doubled him on a scene where he supposed to get shot on the planet when the reactor explodes. I was working on the other side of the set, working with a different camera team, and so they said, "Joe, get into the clothes, we want you to go down on the slide and shoot on the planet." And something went wrong, and Joe ended up shooting about 30 feet above the air and coming down on his tailbone on the stage floor and almost broke his back.

And Arnold made sure...in fact, Sven Thorsen and I went to the hospital and went in and stole Joel Kramer from the Mexican hospital, took him down to a car, took him to the airport and put him on Arnold's private jet. The doctors were chasing us down the hall, trying to get us to let go and leave him, but we didn't want to leave him there. Because we didn't believe in the care of the Mexican hospital. So we actually just went in there and stole him out of there and put him on Arnold's plane and sent him back to Los Angeles.

Premieres in Hollywood. Did you go to the True Lies party?
Peter Kent: I also work as an actor and was working on a TV series at that time. Between my stunting career, I had actually started out as an actor. So many times after I finished doing the film with Arnold, I would go do my acting job. At that point, I didn't go to the True Lies premiere party. I did, however, go to the Total Recall premiere party, which was held on Sunset Boulevard at one of the nightclubs. That was a big, big party. I think by the time, a week later, it had generated many millions of dollars, so it was quite a big party. Everybody hangs out in their kind of groups together. Arnold never had a tendency to stay very long at a premiere party. He would come in, have a drink, have a cigar, walk around, say hi to a few people, do some photos and then usually leave. He wasn't the kind of guy to spend the entire night there.

What is one of the most thought-provoking conversation you ever had with Arnold. Firstly. pertaining to work, secondly, to life in general?
Peter Kent: My acting coach used to be a woman named Zena Provendie, who was the head coach at MGM for twenty-six years, and I had started to do Shakespeare before I even went to Los Angeles. Arnold used to call me the "Shakespearean stuntman". I was also a dialog coach for him. I worked with him many times rehearsing his dialog scenes for his movies, almost for all of his movies, especially later on. And I don't know if I would call it thought-provoking, but I just remember many times sitting with him up till three o' clock in the morning sometimes, working on the scenes trying to make them better. It's funny because we did one scene in Eraser, we worked so hard on that scene and when I saw him shoot it after we had spent hours polishing it, we shot it the next day in New York City, it was one of the best scenes I had ever seen him do acting wise. And unfortunately, it was deleted because the producers wanted to see more action in the story. In the final cut of the film, it's chopped off, which I was really sad about, because I was really proud the way he did that scene.

Can you tell me about the stunts involved in Eraser, and also about working with James Caan, Vanessa Williams and, of course, Arnold?
Peter Kent: Well, there was a lot of work on Eraser. I was getting blown

up running through fire, in the end, of course, I think you may have seen there's a scene where they're on the big shipping container. I ended up getting my top ribs broken and nearly getting killed. In fact, I got hit by that container, 100 feet in the air, and it went badly wrong. The container which was supposed to fall...we had a wire on our backs which would pull us away when the container would smash on the ground. It didn't. So now you have a three-ton shipping container spinning round and round, and it smashed into me. I ended up in hospital and was out of work for a while because of the injuries. We were all pretty lucky. There was myself, the girl who was doubling Vanessa Williams and the guy who was doubling James Caan. I think I sustained the worst of the injuries, but we were all pretty beaten up from that.

They were great to work with. I didn't get much time to talk to Vanessa very much, but I spent quite a bit of time hanging out with James Caan. In fact, in Vancouver not that long ago I was in a bar downtown having a drink with some friends, and someone slapped me on my back really hard. When I turned around, it was Jimmy Caan. He was in town working on a film here. But I hadn't seen him for quite a few years, so it was very nice. They (Arnold and James Caan) got along very well. Jimmy Caan was always trying to get the last word in a scene, they were always joking around. The director would say cut and they would still keep on acting, trying to add another line in there. He is a real joker and a lot of fun to work with.

Let's talk about the stunts in Terminator 2, which were a lot more sophisticated with intricacy attached to them compared to the first one.
Peter Kent: I was the first guy ever in the history of stuntmen to wear sort of a Mission Impossible type mask made out of latex and glued to my face, so I looked more like Arnold. In fact, if you look at the motorcycle jump coming off the bridge, you could see it's not him, you can tell it's not Arnold's face 100 percent, but it looks like him. That's me wearing a mask, which I wore for sixty-six days on that movie - it was hell. Every day I went in, there was a four-and-a-half-hour application every morning, and I wore it for twelve, sometimes eighteen hours a day. It was very, very hard on the skin. Usually, now all of that stuff can be done with computers, but it was pretty tough back then. And there was a lot of work on that show. I think I worked sixty-six days; Arnold only worked forty-two or something.

I remember James Cameron coming over to me one morning, when we were shooting in the steel mill in Fontana, shaking me awake in a chair and looking at me and going, "I have beaten on some stunt guys in my career, but I have never beaten on anybody like I have beaten on you." He said, "Go back to the hotel and go to sleep."

It was just relentless on that, I was working on three different units sometimes. I would work on the main unit, and then I would have to jump in my car when I finished on there and makeup and go across town, or to the other side of Los Angeles for another shot and then back somewhere else.

It took six months to make Terminator 2 and a cast and crew totalling nearly a thousand people. As always, Arnold had a positive attitude when it came to work. He said, "Whenever you work hard, it doesn't mean you can't have fun. I mean, of course we were freezing and we were shooting down in Fontana in the steel mill and did a lot of those scenes there. We did a lot of night shooting and it was uncomfortable, but we always had fun. Because I think that when you work and you do scenes that you know will look great on the screen and people get entertained by it and all that, I think you have fun doing it."

The Terminator in this film adapts certain human characteristics. Linda Hamilton recalls, "He had this wonderful moment where he smiled at John (Edward Furlong). The rushes were hysterical. But Arnold went for it, and I really appreciated that dedication." Edward Furlong's voice had to be re-dubbed after filming, because his voice broke during the shooting of the film. Arnold merely had a total of seven hundred words of dialog. During the course of working on the movie, Arnold said he'd never play an evil role again. When released in 1991, with a budget hitting the $102 million mark, the film grossed over $519 million worldwide (earning $204.8 million in America). The first Terminator grossed $38 million with a budget of $6.5 million in 1984.

How would you define James Cameron and Arnold's relationship working on Terminator 2?

Peter Kent: James Cameron, they say he can be a difficult guy to work with. I've always gotten along with him, because we're both Canadians. I know Arnold and James had a good rapport. I think James is a very exacting director and knows what he wants, and he's not going to play around or fool around in getting that. And some actors have thin skin, so they are taken by that or they get offended by that and then they don't want to work with him, because they say he's difficult. I don't think that at all. I think James Cameron is very exacting and he's a brilliant director. I think if he feels he's got you on the run so to speak, then he'll work on that. I never had a problem with him. He would give me shot sometimes, and I would go right back at him, you know, and say, "Fuck you, Jim," and we'd just laugh at each other and carry on. I think Arnold and Jim had the same kind of relationship, they would make jokes. Everybody worked hard on that movie, everybody! From the craft services to the driver, it was really an intense six-month shoot.

Did Arnold suggest certain things and collaborate with the director or did he merely do what he was told?
Peter Kent: He would say I think we should try this, or I would like to try this, and always they would do it. He would be accommodated, and they would look at it later on in the edit suite and see if it, in fact, worked or if it didn't work.

What was the most gruelling movie Arnold and you worked on, which really demanded a lot of physicality?
Peter Kent: It would have to be Terminator 2, for me, anyway. I know for him as well it was very difficult, because in the scenes in the steel mill he had a very, very bad cold and he was sick quite a bit. But he never quit, never stopped, never took a day off, because we knew we had to get it finished. Between him being sick and tired, falling asleep in the chair coughing and stuff but still getting up and doing the shots in that freezing cold. It's in a steel mill, it looks like it was molt and metal and you would assume it was hot, but it's not. None of that metal is real, it's all done by lighting. The place is actually like a giant refrigerator, it was freezing cold in there. It was a tough shoot, and six months of it relentlessly.

Can you tell me about any conversation you had with Arnold regarding bodybuilding and working out on the set?
Peter Kent: Yes. I had many conversations about bodybuilding with him, because I had to look like him. Once I started working with him after Commando, I started training hard with him. I would meet him every morning at World Gym in Venice, California, and we would have our morning workout and go for breakfast; that was a pretty much ritual every day. Then, of course, on set he would always have his gym with him - he had a mobile gym - which would be set up somewhere, whether it was a big trailer, like a big truck trailer, or whether it would be in a convention hall in the hotel. But always we were working out. Many times I would be very tired from having taken a beating all day long doing stunts, then Arnold would say, "Peter, are we going to the gym now?" I'm like, "Are you fucking kidding me? I can barely drag my ass across the room to get into a car to go home, and you want me to go train?" There were times when I would actually sneak off the set when they were wrapping, I would take off, because I knew if he saw me he would try to drag me into the gym. I was too exhausted to go there.

Anything you would like to share working out with Arnold at World Gym in Venice, which is a hub for bodybuilding?
Peter Kent: Oh, God. I mean, there was always something going on. There were always some tricks being played on each other, the bodybuilder guys, a lot more so when he was competing. Basically he would come in the morning and we would do the workout, ride the bikes and then take off and go for breakfast or lunch. Sometimes there wasn't a lot of shenanigans going on, not like in the bodybuilding days. Back then there were all kinds of stuff going on. You read all about that in the bodybuilding magazines, I'm sure.

Did you converse with him about anything else other than work and training? Would you say Arnold is the epitome of hard work?
Peter Kent: I think all you can say about him is, whatever he puts his mind to he does, that's all you need to say about him. It was usually work-related or fun-related or something like that, I never really had conversations about life, no.

How did you end up working as the stunt double of Arnold on Raw Deal, what recollections do you have about working with Arnold on this movie?
Peter Kent: I just became part of his deal. He would just request me and I was part of his package. I was there all the time. Raw Deal was a fun shoot. We were in North Carolina, Dino De Laurentiis, who has passed away, was there, too, at the studios in Wilmington, North Carolina. I remember when we first got there, and Dino wanted to show Arnold his brand new boat that he had just got made, custom-made - beautiful mahogany boat. So we all came down to the dock, myself and one of the other stunt guys and Sven Thorsen. Dino was standing on the dock with his friend, and he's, like, in his Italian accent, "Arnold, see my new boat." Arnold's, like, "Nice, Dino, let's see the keys." He took the keys from Dino and we all jumped in and we roared way from the dock. We were gone for the whole day waterskiing in Dino's new boat. We came back five o' clock at night, Dino was still sitting there on the dock looking quiet. Arnold just tossed the keys to him, "Very nice boat, Dino. Thank you." And we just walked away.

Dino De Laurentiis had given Arnold his first major role in Conan the Barbarian, which was the film which propelled the bodybuilder-turned-actor into the forefront. When the Italian producer passed away in 2011, Arnold was among the many personalities at his funeral. In his speech, Arnold said, "He never feared failure, and this is the only way you can be successful in life." At the funeral, which was attended by a long list of Hollywood names, Arnold talked about how the producer had inspired him, and he stated that he had unbelievable memories of the producer. Arnold also expressed that De Laurentiis had also taught him to be courageous, smart and to have a big heart.

Making movies means living a compressed life. Was Arnold and the crew accustomed to traveling on shoots staying away from home, and can you elucidate on Arnold working on Raw Deal and how he spent his time away from the set?
Peter Kent: There was a little bit of everything there, the driving stuff. I remember Arnold tearing the transmission out of two of the cars from the driving scenes, which was a good laugh for everybody. There was a lot of work on that show, but not so much for his character, but a lot of the other characters. His character had some fights, etc, a bit of driving, but there was a lot of work for the other characters. You get used to it, that's why you kind of become good friends, because you know each other, you work together, you've known each other for a long time, you trained together. When we finished working, we would go back to the hotel and we would workout in the hotel gym. Then we would go have a shower and get cleaned up. Then we would go out and have dinner, and then maybe go back and read the script a little bit, go to bed and do it again. That was basically the extent of it, you know. Every night you just tried to get out and do a little something, just to keep your sanity; not just sitting in the hotel room staring at the walls. We always hung out with each other. I would cook for him many times. My mother ran a boarding house when I was a kid, so I learned how to cook at a young age. So, Arnold always appreciated a home-cooked meal, and a lot of times if we had access to...I'd make him my famous spaghetti sauce, which he used to love.

What do you remember about Arnold as far as his lighter side on the set?
Peter Kent: Arnold had a scene in Raw Deal where he had to come down the stairs in his suit and light a cigar in front of the camera and look really cool and walk toward the lamp. We waited until he rehearsed it, then we went to the box of cigars they had and we put an explosive in the cigar. So, we waited when they rolled the camera. He comes down the stairs looking very swell like Cary Grant, and he pauses there and sticks his lighter out straight up the cigar and takes a puff on it. He takes two steps toward the lamp and brings it up to take another puff, and the cigar exploded in his face. The director knew straightaway who it was,

the director was John Irvin. And in his English accent, he shouted "Peter!!! Where are you!!!" yelling for me, I took off, ran and hid. It was really funny. The cigar just disintegrated on camera. He didn't keep that in the outtake.

One of the things Arnold did in Raw Deal, unlike other films he had shot, was to make his character very much resonate with his real-life personality. Always on the forefront when it came to the action scenes, he said, "One of the things that you, as a main actor, have to do is to be able to trust the special effects department. And, of course, what that basically means is, when he comes to you and says, 'Arnold, I would like you to do the scene although 10 inches away from your face glass would explode.' Then you say, 'Wait a minute, glass would explode in my face?' He says, 'No, the way it's set up it will explode away from your face.' And you look at the guy and say, 'Sure,'" looking at him unconvincingly. It was Arnold's belief that if you were known as an action star, the most imperative thing you do is to make sure the action is believable and that the audience got to see your face. He advocated the need for the action star to do most of the action himself. Of course, he said you would use a stunt double on things which you could not do, or if the stunt was life-threatening.

You worked with Arnold on Jingle All the Way, which was another comedy movie. What can you recall as far as spending time with Arnold on location on this movie?
Peter Kent: I did. I didn't do a whole lot on that. I think I did about four or five things. At that point, I was starting to work myself away from doing stunts. I was getting ready to go back to Canada at that time, because I had been injured previously on Eraser. I went to Minnesota with Arnold and worked a little bit on that film. He wanted me to come and do dialog rehearsals with him, because there was quite a bit of dialog in that film and it was more of an acting role than an action role. I had been hurt on Eraser, so at the point I kind of had decided I wasn't going to do much more in the stunt business. But Arnold came and - I was rehearsing with him at home, anyway - he said, "Look, I'd like you to come on the road with me to Minneapolis." There were some minor stunts, photo doubling stunts where I didn't need to hit the ground so hard. I had been still sore from the damage I had received from Eraser. So I was mostly there working on the dialog with him.

I stayed in the hotel with him and rehearsed dialog with him for the whole time. Every night we would sit in his room, and we would go over the dialog and I would rehearse with him. Basically that's why I was really there for. As far as the movie itself goes, it was fun working with the cast again, some great people. It's always fun when you go out of town to work, you're out of LA. We were some place where there was snow, there was a lot of snow. It was a nice change as opposed to being in LA where the sun is shining all the time. For me especially, I'm Canadian-born and I love the snow. An Austrian guy named Danial Donai came in who was doubling Arnold, most of the flying stuff in the flying suit.

What are your recollections about The Running Man, which is set in a totalitarian society?
Peter Kent: The Running Man was a tough one too. The only thing I can really remember is it was a lot of night shoots - a lot of late days. I do remember that I really enjoyed working with some of the cast on that. Paul Michael Glaser, who played Starsky in Starsky and Hutch, was the director on The Running Man. I really like Paul Michael Glaser, he's a nice guy.

Did conversations with Arnold ever lean toward expressing his desire of becoming the biggest action movie star?
Peter Kent: I don't think we ever had a conversation along those lines, but it was evident what was going on for both of us. I watched him, I learned a great deal working with the man, put it that way. Not only on set but being with him every day in his trailer for fifteen years, I saw a lot of things going on, how to manipulate.... No. I wouldn't use the word "manipulate", just how to make the business work to your best advantage and how to do it, really. I learned by watching him. We never really had any conversations about what direction he was taking, because that was self-evident.

Did Arnold tell you what his favorite movie was?
Peter Kent: I think Terminator 2 by far.

What was the toughest stunt you did on an Arnold movie?
Peter Kent: I think one of the bigger ones was getting on the truck in Terminator 2, climbing out of the little truck, running across and jumping onto the big rig. Climbing up and shooting the windshield out and turning the rig over to the side, which was all done in one take. And we were traveling, it was very dangerous because if I had slipped and fallen off the truck, I would've been run over by the big rig - all eighteen wheels - at least nine of them on one side. So it was one of those things where we rehearsed it a few times until we found the right speed.

Because the truck was shaking so badly by being pushed by the big rig that I couldn't even get across the back first.

When we finally got it, we were going for lunch. Everybody was, like, OK, break for lunch. It was two o' clock in the morning. I said, "You know, Jim, I'm not hungry. My stomach is in a knot right now, I'm so psyched. Can we just shoot this?" And Jim turned to the crew and said to everybody, "The man wants to go now," everybody was going to lunch, "we're going to shoot this right now." I think that was really awesome of him, because he could've put me off by saying let's just wait and let everybody eat. I wasn't being selfish by wanting to do it. I really, really wanted to get it done. I felt in my own mind I had it right. I was ready to go and I didn't want to wait any longer. I just wanted to make sure we got the shot right, and we did! We got it in one take.

Did you visit Arnold at his residence, what was he like away from the cameras and work?
Peter Kent: I went to his house many times, many, many times. And he would come to mine for dinner sometimes, or he would come over we would rehearse the script. In fact, I would workout with him. Some mornings instead of going to the gym in Venice, we would just train at his house, because he had a full gym set up there. So we would train in his gym and then have some breakfast out on the patio, and maybe sit in the Jacuzzi for a while, then rehearse the script. Like I said, I worked with him on the dialog level as well. I had been an actor long before I became a stuntman. He was never - with me, anyway - a much different guy on the set or off set. We always got along the same. I can't really say there was much of a comparison there. I think everybody's a lot more relaxed in their own environment at home. He would just be in a pair of shorts most of the time, or even a swimming suit, and we'd be out on the porch eating, having a coffee or smoking a cigar or sitting in the Jacuzzi.

Arnold had purchased a home in Pacific Palisades in 1986, the year he got married. Pacific Palisades is a coastal community, nestled between the Santa Monica Mountains and Santa Monica Bay. Later, he bought three more houses to form a compound; four large homes on five wooded acres near Will Rogers State Park in Pacific Palisades. He sold one of the properties to Maria's cousin. The Schwarzeneggers put two of the houses for sale for just under $18 million. Among the sellers of the individual houses the couple bought to form the compound were actors John Forsythe and Daniel J. Travanti.

In September 2004, professional golfer Dennis Watson and his attorney wife Susan Loggans bought one of the properties from the Schwarzeneggers. Back then it was listed for $7.95 million. However, Loggans demanded compensation for construction defects that the Schwarzeneggers allegedly failed to disclose to her before the sale went through. Loggans claimed the swimming pool and tennis court were damaged and the moldy walls, and her husband exclaimed it would cost $150,000 to repair; he said that the whole thing had been a very unpleasant experience.

Martin Singer, the Schwarzeneggers' lawyer, denied his clients had failed to disclose the precise condition of the property. Singer said, "My client had representatives involved in this transaction, and whatever information was known was disclosed. Watson said, "Governor Schwarzenegger is a very informed and powerful person, and we expected him to act in a decent way. He has not done so. We have given him every opportunity to resolve this with us, but we feel that his lawyers have just been playing around. But California law is pretty clear about disclosure. If you know something about your property, you have to disclose it, simple as that. That was our expectation. The governor has acted in an appalling way toward my family." In 2011, Watson put the property for sale for a whopping $23.5 million.

What was your memorable or happiest moment with Arnold?
Peter Kent: I think one of my happiest moment was being finished in Terminator 2. I was so exhausted and so tired. I had to go have water drained, my elbows from landing on the ground, even though I had elbow pads on, landing on my elbows on the decking in the steel mill. I was just so happy for that movie to be over. I was so exhausted that I think I slept for almost a week straight, because I was so tired. So, I think that's probably one of my happiest moment, finishing T2.

Did you both frequently talk on the phone after you finished working on the movies?
Peter Kent: I was in a film with Hulk Hogan, Mr Nanny, I played the bad guy. I played the German character Wolfgang. I remember calling him up, because I needed some German (words) that I could say which wasn't very, very bad language, but something I could direct to the kids - because it was a family movie. I remember asking him some questions about some stuff, what to say to a child, what I could say to him in German which would work, but not be telling him to fuck off. Arnold called me back giving me a list of things I could use. It was good. I pretty much was with him every day for almost fifteen years. Sometimes we would do two films a year, each film was either three or six months,

so you can imagine that's nine months in the whole year working with the guy and rehearsing and training with him. So I spent a lot of time with the man and learned a lot from him.

We became really good friends, and we're still friends. We talk quite a bit, he congratulated me with the birth of my boys and sent some photos up and signed them for the boys. It was really a great time, it was one of those things in everyone's life where you sort of take a look back and say, "OK, that was then," and use what you've learned and move on and keep going in life. I learned a great deal from working with him, from every angle, from how to be behind the camera. I worked with some of the best directors in the world: Walter Hill, James Cameron, Ivan Reitman, some great directors. So I've learned a great deal about the business, not only from a business standpoint and Arnold's standpoint, but I've learned a great deal from a filming standpoint, and the directorial and editorial standpoint, and a screenwriting standpoint. All the aspects of movie making. Because I worked with him close to fifteen years, I was privy to some really great artists in the industry, and it's all really, really helped me a lot in what I do now. So I'm grateful for that.

TIA CARRERE

An American actress, singer and former model, Tia Carrere came into prominence with her appearance in the comedy Wayne's World. She also appeared in Showdown in Little Tokyo and has co-starred in many movies. In 1994, the Hawaiian-born actress was cast in True Lies.

How would you adumbratively define Arnold's and your own character in True Lies?
Tia Carrere: Let's see. True Lies was a huge film, it was just an honor to be part of. I played Juno Skinner, a rather shady art dealer of ancient antiquities, who is really a threat for terrorist activity. I guess that's the only way to put it. I'm also sort of a terror for Arnold's character, Harry Tasker. Unbeknown to his wife, Jamie Lee Curtis, he's a spy, and unbeknownst to me as well. I'm basically trying to buy and sell arms for terrorists, funded by my art dealership. I don't think of myself as a villain; people characterized me as a villain. I think more of myself as a very dubious businesswoman with rather questionable moral accomplish. But I am basically a businesswoman, not necessarily a villain per se. I think it was fantastic in that he didn't have to play like just one side of the tough cyborg or the tough soldier. In this role, he got to show charm and humor, and self-effacing humor, and I thought it really humanized him. Because he's such a larger than life, powerful figure, in this film he was able to be a little more vulnerable, funny, charming and a little softer. It was a perfect balance between the two.

The plot was similar to a James Bond movie, wasn't it? Arnold is a big James Bond fan and finally got to play a formidable superspy!
Tia Carrere: Jim Cameron wrote the script. I mean, it's very Bond. People come up to me all the time and say, "Aren't you a Bond girl?" And I say, "No, you're probably thinking of True Lies," which is very Bond in its storyline, because he wears a tuxedo and he has a hidden camera, the crew and the van following him around. So it's very much like James Bond.

In 1992, when Arnold and James Cameron were having breakfast at his Schatzi restaurant in Santa Monica, Arnold brought the concept of the script, originally of the French film La Totale, to the attention of James Cameron, which had a bond theme to it. Arnold says, "I loved the Bond movies. I think the Bond movies really set the base for all the other action movies, because it had everything." A big Bond fan, Arnold would now be able to play a role which resonated with Ian Fleming's character. "I'd say the beginning Bond movies, the later ones were not that great anymore, but the beginning ones with Sean Connery and also the other one, Roger Moore, and there was the other character who played the Bond character, there were some really good ones.... But they had great humor, terrific action and always bigger than life things. I mean, it was wonderful. I think there's a lot of things that you can copy from that."

What was it like working with Arnold on the movie?
Tia Carrere: I love working with Arnold Schwarzenegger. He and Jim Cameron both have such a work ethic; they're on the set eighteen hours a day. So you really can't slack off around them, because they are there. And a lot of movie stars go hiding in the trailers or whatever, but no, he and Jim Cameron were around the set 24-7. They're just wonderful people to work with. Arnold and his crew of stunt guys that he worked with all the time are great friends, and it's really nice to see someone so loyal to their friends.

Can you relate any hilarious incidents on the set pertaining to Arnold?
Tia Carrere: Oh, yeah. It was funny learning to do the Tango with him, because he's a guy who can't do the Tango. But I think he did a wonderful job. It's necessary for him to have strong shoulders and a very straight back, and he's got that natural posture, anyway. So he was a wonderful tango dancer. But I made a mistake once - and only once - doing my lesson in my bare feet, until Arnold stepped on my feet, and that was it. I was like, "No! Oh, God." Another time, everybody would be sitting on the cast chairs on the set, his crew of stunt guys that he worked with all the time, like I said, they'd be sitting there talking and then one of them would sneak up behind the other one and do some sort of a prank. And once somebody lit a fire underneath the bum whilst they were sitting there. And you see the seat's slowly heating up, until you see them jumping for their lives. That was very funny. Just like child pranks. But it was two o' clock in the morning.

Did you and Arnold find any obstacles whilst shooting any of the sophisticated scenes, which required meticulous planning?
Tia Carrere: The hardest scene was the scene with the helicopter. I had

just taken Jamie Lee hostage into my limousine, and my driver drives away and the helicopter lands exactly where the car was. So, we rehearsed it and all the stuff. But during the take, and everything's going off, huge, huge scene, and the car wouldn't start, the limo wouldn't start. It was really dangerous, because the helicopter was going lower and lower. Me and Jamie Lee jumped into each other's laps, and I picked up the walkie-talkie and said, "Stop! Stop! The car doesn't start! The car doesn't start! Lift the helicopter!" So that was a quite frightening moment.

Every Arnold film has action. Can you culminate on the action-packed scenes?
Tia Carrere: Yeah. The most amazing one that I saw, which took us days to shoot, was the scene where, it's like every single explosion has to go off in tandem one after the other, the factory blows up then Arnold jumps into the water to save himself. That was a very complicated thing. The setup for that, it wasn't going right, so they had to do it again and again.

What did you learn about Arnold's personality?
Tia Carrere: I would say he's a great student of life. I never went to college; I learned everything from traveling the world and speaking to people. If something interested me, I would read up on it. What strikes me about Arnold is, he has a lot of that. I think he's got natural curiosity. He's a perfect example of the American Dream. He has achieved what is possible to achieve in America, if you work hard and apply yourself, and I really admire that about him. My favorite conversations were about working out. I went to his sixty birthday and he's in amazing shape. On the set he had his workout trailer. He said, "Hey, go, you can use it if you want to workout." And this is important, it's the basis and the foundation to everything else and that work ethic what carries him through.

Arnold, who has been known for being primarily an action man, was he able to evince the caliber of his acting skills?
Tia Carrere: I think he was terrific in True Lies. Mostly because he and Jim Cameron have a great relationship, and they have shorthand to their work. So, you know, Jim would know what to say to Arnold to get the response out of him. Arnold's work in the film was terrific. I think he got the tone of the comedy perfectly. It's, like, he's in on the joke, he has a very sort of an impish nudge and a wink to his performance. I think it's great. But I think definitely Jim Cameron is a great director and they have a great relationship, so he's able to get that. Arnold's got a very fun-loving personality, you can see it through Kindergarten Cop to Twins and every number of things. He likes to have fun, he's got a little

nudge, nudge, wink, wink, sort of aspect to him that is just delightful.

I think the performance in True Lies was a combination of the fun-loving characteristic to his personality, as well as Jim Cameron's direction right in the right spots. He's a wonderful director. I loved working with Jim Cameron. He empowered every actor on the set. For me, I'm, like, fifth on the call sheet, I'm not Arnold or Jamie Lee, but he would ask me, "What did you think of that performance?" He would show it to me and I would watch it back. He took the time. I would say, "You know what, may I try this different thing?" He would say, "Yeah, that sounds great, do it." He's very collaborative and open with his actors, and I think that's why I think he gets such great performances.

Arnold got on well with Jamie Lee Curtis, but when she was being cast he wasn't too sure about her being casted. Can you tell me more about Arnold working with her?
Tia Carrere: I never saw any divisiveness whatsoever. I just saw them getting along great. So I've never heard that before. I never heard that story, so I can't speak on that, I don't know. I think Jamie Lee is a great broad, like in the old movies you see Betty Davis and Joan Crawford. These are broads. They are tough, strong female characters. Jamie Lee is a very strong woman who's playing a great role in this film. It was great to hang out with her, because I like it how she is...she's a broad. You know, it's cool. She can hang with the guys and hold her own, let's put it that way.

James Cameron wasn't sure whether Jamie Lee Curtis and Arnold would get on. Arnold wasn't too sure about having her play the role and made it clear to the director. According to James Cameron, "I didn't know how Jamie and Arnold would get along. Arnold loves to goose people when he first meets them. Jamie goosed right back and they were off. There's a chemistry about them together. They're both totally vulgar." Tom Arnold, who played Albert Gibson, cultivated a close friendship with the star on and off set. "It was great, because I had great chemistry with Arnold off camera and so we just carried that on to the camera and then it turned out good," he explains. "We just had that kind of a relationship where I'm giving him a hard time, he's giving me a hard time, and, you know, we just played that out there. And I genuinely like Arnold, and my character really likes him, too, but he gives him a hard time."

Can you tell me about shooting the scene where you have taken Arnold and Jamie Lee Curtis hostage?
Tia Carrere: That was fantastic, the scene was something else. That

scene, the torture room scene where Arnold and Jamie Lee are locked in the room, was the craziest day of shooting ever. Because it was the day after the huge Northridge earthquake in Los Angeles. It was a huge earthquake, buildings had collapsed. I mean, apartment buildings, it was a big deal. The day after we were shooting in this huge warehouse, about three miles from the epicenter of that earthquake. And, of course, the only thing that matters is what's on film, because no one else in the world knows that that's happened three miles away from where we're shooting. And everybody's freaked out, and every few seconds the whole building would go du, du, du, du, rumble with aftershock all day long. And who had all the dialog? Me! It was quite something. I had all these monologs talking about the torture to Jamie Lee and Arnold.

But that really tested my focus as an actress, it was frightening. I mean, the ground wasn't really still most of the day. The only thing that mattered was, you keep your eye on the ball and you do your work. No one in the world knows that the day after one of the hugest earthquakes in California we ever saw, we shot right by the epicenter of this earthquake. And actually, after I had completed my scene that day, they evacuated the area because of a fear of a gas leak. So it was quite a day, everybody was freaked out. But the show must go on, and you just keep your concentration and you keep doing it. I've not told this story before. That was one of my favorite scenes of all the films I did, which was kind of funny.

When True Lies was released by 20th Century Fox, Arab American advocacy groups protested in various cities around the country. The film depicted Arabs as anti-American zealots, which members of the Islamic community found to be offensive. But to some, the portrayal of Middle Eastern terrorism was and is in some respects accurate and topical. Tired of Hollywood portraying them as terrorists and criminals, some Muslim spokesmen exclaimed their groups were angry at what they saw as a lack of depth in the movie's Arab characters. "The film is a work of fiction and does not represent the actions or beliefs of a particular culture or religion," said a spokesman from the studio. The purpose of the protests and demonstrations were so that people can be inoculated against this kind of xenophobia before seeing the movie. Ibrahim Hooper, of the Council on American-Islamic Relations, added that his group was not opposed to the portrayal of Arabs or Muslims as villains, as long as there are positive portrayals also.

Did you attend any parties with Arnold, or were you invited to any parties which Arnold often threw at his home?

Tia Carrere: Going to the premiere was just amazing, it was. All the publicity and the personal appearances we did after that, it was just a huge wonderful film to be a part of. I can't remember anything specific about parties or anything. I went to a birthday party at one of his residences. It wasn't like tons of people, it was, one thing that struck me, and always has, about Arnold is that they're all about family and friends. They could've had thousands of people, but it was a very intimate gathering and people you see time and again in his life. He's always a very loyal friend to the people who are in his crew, and that's what strikes me. A good solid family man that keeps his friends and loved ones close to him. You saw that at tributes over and over again.

In 2002, Arnold purchased a newly built home in the gated and guarded community in Brentwood Country Estates in the Mandeville Canyon area of the Santa Monica Mountains. This seven-bedroom, 12,000-square-foot residence, which sits on a 5.9-acre hilltop, was listed for $11.9 million back then. This is where the Schwarzenegger family resided. Arnold's long-time close friend Franco Columbu also resides in Brentwood. Arnold believed when you have a partner who is in a profession, the nice thing is an exchange of ideas. When you come home end of the day, you don't merely talk about yourself pertaining to what you did. Reflecting on the day's events, Maria would tell him who she interviewed and what she learned. And Arnold absorbed and learned from that. When they sat at dinner, they would have the most stimulating conversations. It was a two-way street.

"There is no boss...my wife sometimes tries to make me believe differently," Arnold said. "I know for sure the way it really is." The Schwarzeneggers was a close-knit normal family. Certain rules had to be adhered to, such as no phone calls accepted when having dinner with the family; kid's were not allowed to have their cell-phones at the table. Arnold tried not to bring his job home, he advocated spending quality time with his kids and family without any outside distractions. He also advocated to his eldest daughter to start the day early, saying that if you don't get up early in the morning (5.30 a.m.) then you weren't going to get everything in on the day. He told her that if you want to accomplish a lot, then morning was the time to start the day; you could get your training done and prepare yourself for the day.

ANDREW G. VAJNA

One of the leading Hollywood executive producers, Andrew G. Vajna has produced a plethora of action genre movies such as Red Heat, Total Recall, Basic Instinct 2, Terminator 3, Die Hard, Nixon, Evita, Escape to Victory and the Rambo franchise.

The first movie you produced with Arnold was Red Heat. How did the concept come about?

Andrew Vajna: It was an idea that was developed by Walter Hill, the director. He came to us with a concept: a Russian cop and an American cop working together to solve a case. Arnold could be the Russian cop, and we'd see who the American cop could be. He said, "What do you think?" We loved the idea. We talked to Arnold and he loved the idea. So we went forward and had the script written. Walter wrote the script, and we went on to make the movie with Arnold and James Belushi.

Arnold watched a 1939 film called Ninotchka to observe Greta Garbo's performance under the advice of Walter Hill, who advised him in an attempt to best convey to Arnold how he should capture the essence of his character. The director also asked him to lose 10 pounds for his role, whilst James Belushi was told to gain 10 pounds. Belushi and Arnold were an unlikely pairing. There were plenty of laughs on the set. "Arnold got me smoking cigars," exclaims Belushi. "We were in a police car in Chicago shooting Red Heat, and they roll the windows up on the car and between takes he would bring out his number two...and just fill the car with smoke and I turned green. What's the matter, Jim, can't you handle a little cigar smoke? And so he gave me one, that's what started it. I mean, I first threw up and got sick, but then I got pass that." Belushi remembers that Arnold smoked heavily. Belushi had two choices: cough or join in. He decided to join in. "He's a person who's hyper aware of how he projects himself to the public," the Red Heat star says.

Were there any obstacles when making this movie? Obviously, on a big-budget movie you're going to encounter hurdles and pursue to overcome them. What were your hurdles?

Andrew Vajna: I think the biggest obstacle was that we never really got permission to film in Russia. We wanted very much to have an authentic background, with the Kremlin and everything else, to say that this is Russia. The obstacle was: how do we get there? We had written to the government agencies to allow us to shoot there, but we couldn't get any answers. So we finally took it upon ourselves, and through a friend of ours, who was supervising bands - music bands - told him to come play in Russia. He said, "OK. I'll organize it for you." We went with him without any official permits or official papers.

We flew to Russia, and in three days did all the shooting and then left Russia. We got it, so that was fantastic. That was our biggest obstacle. Except for the weather. In Hungary, while we were shooting the snow sequences, because in Russia it was snowing so we had to match everything else in the movie, we had to manufacture snow everywhere. Then as we were getting toward spring, everything was melting and we had to keep moving further and further to the west. Because originally, we were going to shoot the snow fight sequences in Hungary, then we moved to Austria. And then we moved further into Austria, then finally we went on top of the hill where we were able to find some snow. The weather and the political relationships were the two issues.

What was your viewpoint of the final product?

Andrew Vajna: We thought it was great. We liked it very much, it did very well all over the world so we were happy with it. We felt it might have been a little bit funnier, could've been, but the director felt that he wanted to have a serious angle, so we had less of the comedy. So, we said fine and we let it go.

You were involved with the Rambo movies and produced them. Stallone was a big star, so was Arnold, in the 1980s. Did you have any conversations with Stallone or Arnold about their rivalry, a rivalry which became well-publicized?

Andrew Vajna: Sure. I mean, there was constant rivalry between Arnold and Sly in those days; they weren't really friendly as they are today. In those days, Sly was already an established star after Rocky and Arnold was still on the edge of stardom - not quite being there after Pumping Iron. Stallone was way ahead of him, and he picked Stallone as his sort of running mate, or as his example and tried to sort of catch up with him and surpass him. And I think he certainly caught up with him. He was able to maximize his popularity with the bodybuilding and with the movies he was doing that he was able to catch up with Sly.

So that contest I think kept him on the edge all the time, and to be better and try to compete. So the two of them were definitely rivals in those days. I'm sure we talked about it, but it was always with good intensions, joking. I don't remember what the conversations were, because it's twenty years ago. Working with Sly was great! I mean, Sly is a very talented person. People don't give him enough credit for his writing and directing ability. I think he's a really talented writer and he's a very, very talented director. He sometimes gets a little lazy as a writer, but he needs sometimes to focus on the paper and he comes out with something viable. But when he does do it, he becomes a real success and he's a very well-liked actor. I think he's got everything going for him.

It's no secret that for years Arnold and Stallone were competing for the number-one spot as the ultimate action hero and box office spot. It's quite interesting to note what a member of Stallone's entourage in the 1980s told Ian Halperin, author of The Governator, when questioned about the legendary feud, which took place more than two decades ago. His response surprised the author. "That was all bullshit," his source told him. According to the source, Arnold and Stallone were friends and were both in on the gag. He said whenever Arnold and Stallone got together, they'd be ragging on each other and insulting one another. It also happened at public events, he claims. Then they'd laugh about it.

He says he isn't sure who initiated the whole thing, but when Arnold made remarks in the magazines he was given the heads-up, or the whole concept was conceived by a publicist according to the source. Call it a trend or whatever, these days often celebrities make the headlines by orchestrating "stunts" to be in the public consciousness, which elevates their popularity and profile. According to a former member of Stallone's entourage, Arnold and Stallone were always friends. So could all this have been meticulously planned for the benefit of both parties? I guess we may never know. One thing is for sure, both men are friends and finally even collaborated together.

In 1990, Wendy Leigh who released the sensationalized biography Arnold, which basically was a derogatory look at Arnold painting a very unflattering portrait asserting his father's Nazi past, and Arnold's inappropriate behavior and claiming he used steroids. It was said that Stallone provided Leigh some devastating information about Arnold. The book mostly focused on dirt-digging and derogatory exploits. The highly deflating book was published by Contemporary Books. And certain sources even contacted the publisher saying they would reimburse the publisher what he had paid the author, and even claiming Arnold would do a book with the publisher if the publisher didn't publish the book.

Harry Poltnick, who was the publisher at Contemporary Books, recalled, "The caller suggested that Arnold would do a joint book with me if I quietly dropped the biography, retained the rights and paid the author off. In the other case, the caller, who was also very close to Schwarzenegger, said I would be reimbursed for what I paid the author, plus something extra, if I didn't publish the book. Nonetheless, Poltnick refused to accept the offers and the publication of the book went ahead. In 2011, Brigitte Nielsen's revelations of her liaisons with Arnold when they were filming Red Sonja were culminated on in her autobiography. Sensationalist books are often hyped to sell books, often offering one side of the story, often the motive being pure greed.

In the early 1990s, Stallone's movies The Specialist, Judge Dredd and Assassins, one by one, stumbled or disintegrated at the box office, which demoted the Rocky and Rambo star's career to normal stardom. These projects had once been whispered as potential Arnold Schwarzenegger vehicles. In 1996, Stallone expressed his disappointment with his agent ICM, he left them for another agency, William Morris, piqued somewhat by ICM's failure to procure the coveted role of Mr. Freeze in Warner Brothers' Batman and Robin - a role which went to Arnold.

Arnold told a magazine once in the mid-1980s, "I think Stallone, as far as I knew him, is extremely intense all the time, even when it comes to the gym." It was continuous competition for the Rambo star, claimed Arnold. "If you're doing 120-pound curls, he will say, 'I can do 130.' He's obsessed. And that carries through in the way he dresses, how hard he tries to belong to a charity organization." As much as I'm enormed and can resonate with Arnold's ambitious and goal-oriented philosophy, Stallone's work ethic and philosophy can nothing but inspire one also. Stallone says, "There are always goals. If you don't have a mountain, build one and then climb it. And after you climb it, build another one; otherwise you start to flatline in your life." He also possess a drive unparallel to most, always striving to reach new heights. "People think retiring is fun. Well, maybe, but if you have a certain kind of fire inside, there is no end in sight," Stallone says.

Interestingly, you knew Bruce Lee. Before he passed away, he received movie offers from a Hungarian producer, was this producer yourself?
Andrew Vajna: Yes, that's me. I was actually a friend of Bruce Lee's in the '60s in Hong Kong, when he made his first three movies, and, in fact, I had a deal with him to do his next movie. Unfortunately he passed away before that came to be, but I was a friend. We were working on a picture together that we were going to do. Actually, he bought my house in Hong Kong. I was living in Hong Kong at the time, and we actually

made a deal where he just bought my house as part of the deal he was going to do the next film. Unfortunately he passed away, so we're all very unhappy about that.

Total Recall was a science fiction movie, some critics saw as imprudent to glorification of violence, which was one of Arnold's most successful ones. Can you tell me how the concept materialized?

Andrew Vajna: This was based on a short story that we had acquired. And the script, I think Dino De Laurentiis owned it at the time. He wasn't going to make it, because he wasn't quite sure how to make. We acquired the script from him. We got Paul Verhoeven involved in reworking the script and we gave it to Arnold. And the rest is history - it was a huge hit. We shot the movie in Mexico. I think that one was pretty smooth going. I mean, the director and we had some difficulties in making sure we could keep the budget in control, because Paul likes to spend a lot of money. But I think ultimately, he was on his best behavior as far as this movie is concerned. We were able to bring it on budget, and Arnold's performance was great, you know. We built a star - Sharon Stone - in later movies. So it worked out pretty well for us.

I can remember the party afterward, it was a private club which used to be a Japanese restaurant, that's where we celebrated the - not the premiere - $200 million mark that Total Recall reached. And the party with Maria and Arnold and all the people that participated in the film, it was just a celebration, you know. I think it was very good. I don't remember the exact numbers now, because it was so many years ago. Arnold is a great salesman, he's brilliant. I remember one particular thing when we were doing, I think, Total Recall and we brought him to Cannes to promote the movie. We were a young company so didn't have a lot of money. So we didn't put a lot of posters all around the place. He said, "How do you expect to sell the movie? There's no marketing. You came here and you should be the most visible picture in Cannes. And here I come and there's nothing." And he was right! He's a good salesman, and he went out there and met up with all the distributors, he hyped the movie and he was very supportive in whatever he did. That was a great asset, because a lot of movie stars are not that way.

The first thing Arnold did was call the director Paul Verhoeven and said, "Remember when we met a few months ago after you came out with Robocop?" Verhoeven said he remembered. "Paul, you and I have to work together, you're exactly my style of directing, my style of visual looks, it's a visual feast watching your movies, it's so extraordinary. He said, 'Yes, I remember that.' I said, 'Well, I have the project for us now.'" Arnold felt that the switch from being powerful physically and then being put in a position of being vulnerable was such a stronger kind of contrast. He felt the character should be played by him, rather than someone that was ordinary kind of looking guy.

The actor and director cultivated a wonderful working relationship working meticulously. "I pushed him, you know, and I helped him," recalls Verhoeven. "I was laying with him on the floor...like this, or (saying) you have to give more action to this word, or push this a little bit harder, it has to be a little faster, don't be so slow, do it two, three, four times." The director says Arnold had no ego and was open-minded. He was able to look at his problems and mistakes, and was able to deal with that instead of saying, "They're not true. It's all fine. I'm great. I'm wonderful," recalls Verhoeven.

Total recall was attacked by the critics because of the sheer violence; some critics considered the film excessively violent. Verhoeven accepts violence on much a higher level than most other people do. For him, it's just another way of expressing things, his dreams or nightmares, etc, which he admits he basically is giving to the audience. "I felt it fit in perfectly well, the body count, because it was a very hectic kind of a movie," recounts Arnold. "But, of course, Paul I think gave them that cut so they have something to complain about, and then he would cut it down." Personally, Arnold believed violence on the screen did not influence people necessarily. He said he had watched violent movies all his life, but this had no negative influence on him. Total Recall was one of the most complex and visually interesting science fiction movies.

One reviewer wrote, "Fifty million dollars worth of exploding glass, blazing bullets, earsplitting noises and sometimes clever, sometimes gut-wrenching special effects say that Mr. Schwarzenegger is no figment of anyone's imagination except, possibly, his own. Total Recall is a thunderous tribute to its star's determination to create, out of the unlikeliest raw materials, a patently synthetic yet surprisingly affable leading man. Melding the ever-more-workable Schwarzenegger mystique with a better-than-average science-fiction premise, the director Paul Verhoeven has come up with a vigorous, super violent interplanetary thriller that packs in wallops with metronomic regularity. Mr. Verhoeven is much better at drumming up this sort of artificial excitement than he is at knowing when to stop." Total Recall, released in America in June 1990, which had a budget of $65 million, took in over $260 million worldwide; it was one of Arnold's biggest blockbusters.

Arnold initially refused to do Terminator 3, because James Cameron wasn't going to direct it. But Arnold was compelled to star, once again, in this third instalment of the classic series. Can you please shed some light on this?

Andrew Vajna: Yes, that's correct. We bought the rights to Terminator 3 from an auction when they were selling off the assets. I guess Jim Cameron was also interested in having Fox buy it for him, but Fox never stepped up to the line and we ended up getting the rights. Our intention was always to go to Jim to direct it, but he felt that we had stolen his baby. Even though we're the ones who made Terminator 2 and made it such a big hit, together with him, we felt that it was kind of the same family. But I guess he felt differently about it. He was very upset that we didn't let him know ahead of time that we were doing this. We, on the other hand, thought it was a great thing that we would buy it and have him direct it, and we would form some kind of a partnership that would make sense for everyone. But he was definitely against it.

Then Arnold said he's very close friends with Jim so he doesn't want to do anything against Jim's wishes. If Jim didn't want to make the movie, then he wasn't going to make the film. So we said OK, we are going to have to pair down and see what happens. In the long run, we decided to develop a screenplay. And we felt if Arnold read the script that he really liked, then he'll do the role. Because it was an important role for him in his career. And, in fact, that's what happened. He read the screenplay. He said I understand Jim doesn't want to do it, and he talked to Jim and Jim said sure, you should do the movie. Then we got together and made number three.

Arnold had approached his friend James Cameron in relation to directing Terminator 3, because Cameron had been overlooked to direct it according to some source, when he was approached by the producers. Arnold says, "I'm always optimistic when talking to directors. But it was very clear he could not commit to a certain time, and he was busy and had other things he wanted to explore. James Cameron is not a director so to speak, but much more of an explorer. And there is another dimension to his directing. I'm the last person to say, 'Hey, schmuck, you really let me down,' because I want people to move on."

Terminator 3 was originally to film in Canada. A lot of films were being shot there because of the great incentives. Arnold said he wanted to keep it in California, he asked the company what the problem was. The producers said it would cost $8 million more if the movie was shot in California. Arnold told them that they'd have to sit down and negotiate. Arnold remembers, "So we sat down and negotiated. I put in, out of my personal salary, I put money in. They said, 'OK, the producer should put some money in,' and they put some money in. And then the various different departments, departments that were cutting down some of the fees, and we came in with a difference of the $8 million." As a result of this, it created five hundred jobs in Los Angeles. Furthermore, the movie would be released a few months before he became the governor of California.

Arnold's Terminator character burned its way into the American consciousness, moreover, the world's consciousness. Why do you think the Terminator movies caught the public's imagination, it is a hugely successful franchise globally?
Andrew Vajna: It became a brand name. There are very few movies where you have a line "I'll be back" or "make my day" or "show me the money". There's maybe three or four or five movies in the world that have a tagline that everybody in the world identifies with. And Terminator had one of those liners, two of those lines were "hasta lavista, baby" and "I'll be back". Those are very simple things, but they totally identified with Arnold and the movies. So, it became a real big hit and it became a brand name; a brand name kids identified with and enjoyed as a character.

In your opinion, what was the marked differences between the first and the third Terminator movie, in terms of production values and box office receipts?
Andrew Vajna: I didn't do the first one. The first one was done by John Daley. I thought that the first movie set the groundwork really well for that character. For some reason John Daley didn't want to continue it, then we at Carolco started bidding for the rights and got them, paid a fortune for them. Then Mario (Kassar) and I separated. He went over to make the sequel number two, which was a big breakthrough in character and special effects for a sequel as a whole. Then, of course, we went out to take that one step further for number three.

In 2002, Arnold along with director Jonathan Mustow made a surprise visit at the Comic Con International. The star worked the podium like a pro and reminisced about going to a comic book convention in Austria when he was a child. As usual, with his buoyant nature he told the audience, "I can't reveal anything of the plot, but I've got to tell you a little bit of it. This is a really scary plot that we have this time. I'm coming back again from the future and arriving at the present in order to stop a very dangerous conspiracy - Enron. And, of course, the other thing that I can tell you is that our female Terminator is all made out of artificial parts. Every single part of her is artificial - just like any Hollywood actress." Arnold and the director answered questions put forward by the audience. Arnold stated working on this movie had been the most extraordinary experience, and that he was working his butt off, but also getting paid, he laughed. He also commended the director saying it was a great pleasure to work with such a talented director.

Out of all the movies you did with Arnold, which was the most gratifying experience?

Andrew Vajna: I think in the Terminator series. The movies we've done with him, I think Terminator 2 is the most liked movie. As far as which one is my favorite, that's also my favorite. I liked Terminator 3 a lot, but I think Total Recall was very interesting. So it's very difficult for me to chose from between those. I think all three of them were special movies in his career.

Having worked with and known Arnold for many years, can you tell me about the immense drive he has to succeed and his ability to reach higher plain?

Andrew Vajna: I think he's totally dedicated to his passion. His passion was bodybuilding and he became the best at it. Then his passion was to become a personality in the motion picture field, where it's most difficult to make it and he mastered that and became one of the most sought-after movie stars. So, I think it's his passion that drives him. I think he's totally dedicated to what he's trying to be successful at, and he would not allow himself to deviate from that for a moment.

Arnold developed this colossal persona which was projected on the screen. How would you define his off-screen personality having had socialized and worked with the man?

Andrew Vajna: I think he's got a great sense of humor, always the practical joker. He loves a laugh and he's a very good friend. He will be there to help you when you're in need and he'll reach out. So I would say those are the characteristics of a very positive personality. Planet Hollywood, they were huge fun parties and events. Hollywood was able to be present at a local diner. And it was a great combination of fun and happiness and just outgoing personalities that you don't get to see every day were there. Each opening was like a movie premiere.

Were there any movie projects you were pursuing with Arnold which didn't materialize? Was it hard to negotiate a deal with him and induce him?

Andrew Vajna: I was there for the beginning of it, then I left the company, but Crusade was the movie Paul Verhoeven and Arnold were going to do. Unfortunately the financing didn't come together. The budget was out of control, and they couldn't bring it down so the movie got canceled. He's tough, he knows what he wants and he usually gets it. I know it was always very difficult, he always knew what he wanted. He often didn't use his attorneys to get there; he often did it himself. He said, "Listen, don't worry about it. It might be a lot of money, but I will give it back to you in promotional value of the film. I will go out there and promote it." He always did that, and we were always happy with the result.

Can you tell me about your climb on the ladder of success?
Andrew Vajna: It's the same kind of thing as Arnold, my partner Mario had a tremendous drive and we had tremendous passion for the material for the films that we were doing. So we were dedicated day and night for years to make it happen. When you are putting that kind of dedication into it, hopefully if you chose well, the results will be there too. We were fortunate enough that we chose well and the results came.

In your opinion, how much of an impact did Arnold have on Hollywood and pop culture as an action hero?
Andrew Vajna: I think tremendous. I think people love him all over the world, because the Terminator character, as well as some of the other things that he's created - Conan, Predator - I mean, those were characters he mastered and people loved him for it.

MARIO KASSAR

Born in Lebanon, Mario Kassar is known for his collaborations with the Hollywood executive Andrew G. Vajna. He is the executive producer of Basic Instinct 1 and 2, Total Recall, Terminator 2, producer of Terminator 3, the Rambo movies and Red Heat to name a few.

Mario, can we talk about Terminator 2, how did you obtain the script? And what were the hurdles which were in the way of getting the film into production?

Mario Kassar: I was running Carolco, and I had a good relationship with James Cameron. I wanted to do Terminator 1 with him, but he was under contract. I think if I recall, in those days it was Orion. I read the script and I really liked it. I said to him that, if by any chance it doesn't go well with those guys, if it falls apart, you can come back here and we can do it here. But, obviously, that didn't happen and it was done over there. Then I went to the screening and when I saw it I thought, "Oh, my God! Whatever you want to do next, just call me." And then, as all sequels, it was a very complicated one, because the rights were, when he divorced his wife Gail Anne Hurd, following the divorce he gave her as a settlement 50 percent of the sequel rights - he had the other half. Everybody tried to do it, but it was very, very complicated. We tried to get Arnold, tried to get James, tried to get all the writers together and tried to do it.

And the budget, obviously, would have been very high because it was a very big idea. We're talking many, many years ago, not like now. Anyway, I got involved and made the deal basically with Cameron and Arnold. Then I had to go and make a deal with the wife of Cameron - Gail Anne Hurd - who basically gave me only the rights to one sequel for quite a substantial amount of money. But I had to take it because it was the only way. Then with Carolco, I made it. In those days, it was above $100 million movie. Of course, it was all over the place. But that's how expensive it was and that's how I was running the company into...whatever. Of course, everybody saw the movie and we know what it did, everybody loved it. And the rest is history about Terminator 2. It wasn't an easy thing to put together, because it took about a year and a half to put it together before shooting and everything else.

Of course, Terminator 2 was much more sophisticated than the first one and it did huge business. Can you reveal to me the budget issues surrounding Terminator 2, because it was the most expensive film ever made at the point?

Mario Kassar: Yeah. In fact, it was a little bit above the hundred million mark. I think it was hundred and eight or hundred and ten - something like that. We had sets in those days worth $17 million, which was enormous. We're talking twenty-something years ago. Those were sets that James invented and created. We tested them and we saw a lot of them before we spent money on them to make them. Then the rights were expensive. Cameron is not cheap and Arnold is not cheap. Then when James shoots, he shoots for perfection; everything has to be perfect. So it was a very expensive movie in those days, and as I told you before, I got a lot of heat from the media and everybody the fact that I was doing such an expensive movie. Then the movie was done and the results, of course, were great.

The absolute peak of Arnold's popularity came when Terminator 2 was released. Do you believe Terminator 2, which did more business than the others in the series, is renowned as far as a cult classic compared to the others?

Mario Kassar: Yes, everybody talks a lot about Terminator 2. Because it was a pioneer and the story was great and everything fit together perfectly. But it's always very difficult to please people. But we tried and we succeed a little bit in Terminator 3. And then on the fourth, unfortunately, we sold the franchise. And whatever they've done, it didn't really work out somehow.

Can you recount any conversation you had with Arnold when Terminator 2 came out which reflected the movie's success?

Mario Kassar: The good thing about Arnold is he knows exactly what he wants and he sees it. When he works with the director, in production, or whatever he's doing, he's 100 percent committed. He always has an amazing faith in the whole combination, between us, and mainly the director. He talked to James to do it. We all knew James did a great job. I mean, this was his baby. He did the first one, he knew what he wanted to do in the second one. I mean, you could see he already had it all plotted in his head - design storyboards and the effects ready. It was only a question of time and money. He was always upbeat about it, and when we went to the first screening - not the final cut but the first screening - you could see the smile on Arnold's face. He knew he had a big success in his hands. Everything was always very positive and nothing really at all...except on our point of view: we kept on seeing the budget a little higher than we originally had thought. The money situation was a little high, but we were expecting it. If you think about it now, it was cheap compared to the movies they are making now.

You were one of the people in the industry who pioneered the foreign market. When Terminator 2 was unleashed upon the world in the summer of 1991, can you tell me about going around the world with Arnold promoting Terminator 2?

Mario Kassar: We went and we promoted the movie; the guy's a publicity machine. He knows exactly how to handle the media. He knows exactly where to go, what to do and what to say. He's a magnet. I mean, he's nice to everybody. And actually, from all the actors I've worked with, he's probably one of the most who leans toward promotion that I've ever met. He is very good at promoting movies, and he loves to do it. He knows that end of the day, by promoting the movie he's also promoting himself, which is good for everybody. And he does do what he says he will. Because sometimes you get actors who tell you they'll do this, or they'll do that but they really don't do everything, or they become a little more difficult, or they get tired after a year of shooting, or they cut the schedule short. Arnold does it from A to Z and if he could do more he would do more.

With a ferocious appetite for marketing and publicity, Arnold set the benchmark for other Hollywood actors for global promotional campaigns. On the subject of global publicity, Arnold states, "You can be the greatest painter, but if you don't know how to market your work and showcase it in the right frame and the right gallery, how successful can you be? All this stuff is part of the business. It's marketing. So if you look at everything with that spin and acknowledge that you need this in order to be successful, that helps you. It helped me in my promotion of movies. I recognized that actors in the 1970s and 1980s never went overseas to promote their movies. I said, 'Wait a minute, the globe is our marketplace.' So I went to Italy and France and Spain and India and Japan and Australia, and my movies grossed two-thirds overseas and one-third in America. Normally, it was the other way around. But I was able to increase my salary and increase my partnership, because so much more money came in."

Arnold now was at the peak with his hard-earned box office credibility, he could demand the largest paycheck in Hollywood. Arnold involved himself every step of the way when it came to marketing, nationally and internationally. A Japanese journalist remembers interviewing the former governor, "Arnold Schwarzenegger was such a nice guy. He was in a room where he had to go to every corner for a different interview, answering the same questions. I felt sorry for him. He took my hand, patted it and said. 'Don't worry. That's what I am here for.'"

What was wrong with Terminator 4 compared to the original Terminator movies, was it a devoid of substance which was integral to the first three movies?

Mario Kassar: Well, we sold the franchise and we have seen that they did a little bit of different things. I think maybe there weren't so many.... When you're not involved, I wasn't really involved, we were far from it. So, there's new producers, new actors and new people than when you were in the business. I don't know, maybe the actor wanted to do something (different). I heard there were revised shootings, but I can't really confirm because I wasn't there. I had nothing to do with it. I'm sure they tried their best to make it a good movie, nobody wants to make a bad movie. But somehow, it's not maybe so bad, but it is not to the level of the first three and definitely not to the level of the second.

When you made Terminator 3, did Arnold advise you to buy the rights from Dino De Laurentiis, which were worth $7 million, but he said to you to bid $3 million for them?

Mario Kassar: No. I don't remember that at all. My recollection is, we paid for half of the rights, $7 million from the bankruptcy of Carolco, and that was only for half of the rights. And the other half were still with the, as I told you, James Cameron's ex-wife. So we took a big risk by just buying the half. Then we approached Arnold. He said I don't want to do it, I'll only do it if Mr. Cameron will direct. But James felt we had taken it away from him. I don't know if he was offended or something, we said we got it (the script) and we want you to direct it. But he didn't want to direct it. He said no - he didn't want to do it. Then we went ahead and told Arnold, "Look, I don't think James wants to do it." I guess when Gail heard that James wasn't doing it, and maybe Arnold wasn't going to do it, she said, "You know, I'll sell my 50 percent now."

And the minute she said yes, we went and bought her 50 percent and secured the whole rights. Then we said, you know, James and Arnold, we believe in the franchise and we're going to make the screenplay. We made it and we got Jonathan Mustow to direct it. We ended up with a good screenplay. At that stage, I wanted to have a woman Terminator in the movie, which we did. And we took it to Arnold to see and he liked it and he was on board. With the new director things started progressing, and we put the finance together. And those are the days when they had the German Tax Fund available. German-owned movie financier Intermedia Films invested with us, and we did it. And we made a deal with Sony and Warner and couple of other territories that we sold to independently, and the movie came out and did OK.

Some people found James Cameron hard to get on with, does this reflect the fact he's a perfectionist and extremely devoted to bringing the best out of people?
Mario Kassar: Yeah, he's definitely a perfectionist. Only if you try to interfere in his business. I mean, I go hire him because he's very good at what he does. If you're going to come and tell him what to do, then I don't understand why you hired him for. I mean, he's been proving film after film that he knows exactly what he's doing; he gets exactly what he wants and he does deliver it. If you try to put your fingers everywhere in what he's doing, then he's not a happy camper. He's kind of the king of the set, he runs the show. He's the captain, and he should be. I'm sure he's got his ups and downs, had some bad days and good days. At the end of the day, he's such a perfectionist that he wants everything to be perfect. When you look at the end result of the movie, you forget whether it was twelve months, six months or two months of making it. You forget all the dramas and the little stories, because you just look at the result and you forget about anything else that happened. You only see the good stuff. He is absolutely a perfectionist. His movies, they talk for themselves.

How did the concept of Crusade come about, which was going to star Arnold and be directed by the same director who directed Total Recall, Paul Verhoeven?
Mario Kassar: Paul Verhoeven was in my office one day. I've always been affected by these (historical) kind of stories, and Paul came up with the idea of doing a movie about Crusade. We got a writer, I don't remember his name now, but he was a writer, to write us a screenplay. And Arnold was on board. We had a very good screenplay, we met Arnold and we met Paul. We were scouting in Morocco to shoot. We were almost there, but unfortunately it didn't materialize due to technical and budget reasons. And the company at that time wasn't really in the best financial situation and I had another movie I was preparing for the company. But I could not really get a budget that I could maintain a certain amount that was agreeable to all parties, so unfortunately I had to stop it.

It probably was the wrong decision, but you know when you cannot financially do all of those things at the same time, and when you're not certain of how much the budget could be. Because sometimes they can go over budget, they always do, whether it's 10 percent, 20 percent or 50 percent. I really had no clear idea the way things would progress, for many technical reasons and whatever reasons. I don't remember them now well. I could not put my finger on the exact amount that I could predict for the budget. So I said I'll cut my loses now. I had to stop.

What exactly was Arnold going to play in this movie - which was touted as being the bloodiest historical epic ever made by some critics - and what was the core concept? You had meetings with Arnold pertaining to this project, what were his sentiments?
Mario Kassar: He was a kind of a happy-go-lucky kind of thief running around in this area, who by mistake ends up with the Crusade and becomes what he becomes. He was not a Crusader, nor part of any faction or political group. He just happens to be there doing something, and he's caught in the middle of all of this. And, of course, he makes the best out of it. We didn't know how the people would react. It's hard to believe that Arnold with that accent would be in that area (Middle East). Arnold was all for it. In fact, he owned the rights for a while. I don't know whether he still owns them or not. He was a big, big believer in the movie and so was I. I wanted to do it very badly.

Of course, there were also the studios with their own worry on how you handle the Crusade, because of the religion factor. You've got the Christians, you've got the Muslims and you've got Jews. It's very difficult to always be politically correct in things like this. So the studios were scared to touch it. They were really scared to release it. But in my mind, it didn't matter. If I was doing this then I would have enough advice, so I wasn't worried about that. After Carolco, I was looking if I could do it again with Arnold. But I think Arnold and Paul tried unsuccessfully to go to the studios to do it. But somehow it didn't work out, whether it was because of the budget or whatever.

What's the most intriguing or compelling conversation you had with Arnold?
Mario Kassar: The only kind which always stays in my head is when we were doing Total Recall. He wanted to get to a certain amount for acting. He called me very early in the morning - about six, seven or eight o' clock in the morning - and he said, "Mario, I want you to give me more than that. I want you to give me this amount of money and I promise you I'll promote the hell out of the movie. If you have to go and pay for promotions, it'll cost you, anyway, that amount of money. Because I'm trying to establish myself at a certain amount of salary." I thought about it for a second, because he keeps his word all the time.

It's usually against the rules in Hollywood to increase and put the salary up for an actor. Let's say he's worth $8 million or $9 million, and they all agree to pay more unless he comes out with a $300 million movie. And it becomes ten million, and they all agree to pay that amount. They don't compete on each other to pay more money - the studios to an actor. You know what I'm saying? When he called me, I thought about it for a second. I said OK, I'll give you nine (million dollars) and you promote the movie all the way as much as you can. Which for me was like money in the bank, because promotion is so important for a movie. I did that and he was very happy. I kept my word, and believe me he kept his word, because he promoted Total Recall like there's no tomorrow when he went on a tour.

Arnold became a commercial commodity. What was his agent Lou Pitt like to deal with?
Mario Kassar: When I dealt with him, his agent was a very nice guy and he was very helpful. But at the end of the day, Arnold makes his own decisions. But his agent is a...I don't know if I would call him a typical Hollywood agent. I mean, there was nothing special, he's kind of open. But he is a very nice man, a man of his word and he never played any games with us. He was cool, very nice guy.

After much introspection, Arnold no doubt clearly was able to ascertain the formula of success. What strikes you the most about Arnold?
Mario Kassar: Mostly his character, he's got an amazing character. I think when the guy comes to a meeting, he's always so prepared. He's done his homework, so he doesn't sit in the meeting and act like he doesn't know. I mean, he knows and he always asks the right questions to get the right answers. On the set, he knows everything, he's ready before, during and after and ready to do more. One thing about him is his persistence, when he wants to get something he will get it. He will go and do anything humanly possible to get it, and he does succeed at the end of the day. So, I mean, he has an amazing will of discipline. I mean, he's German so he's got that discipline and the persistency and the enthusiasm. For him, it's like nothing is impossible. Obviously, nothing is impossible, you can see where he's come from and where he is now. Oh, my God, he's come a long way, hasn't he?

Not everybody is going to be hungry, ambitious and intense as Arnold. Arnold has asserted, "Let me tell you, if someone told me something is impossible, I'd go out and do it. That's just the way I always was. I was told to my face, you're nothing but a giant muscle, you can't act, you have no future and you have an accent which is laughable. And that's exactly what my wife Maria said to me on our first date...." Arnold's rules of success encompassed visualizing your dreams and infiltrating beyond the limits. He continues, "Because it so important to know exactly what you want to accomplish and what you want to do. I mean, the key principles are, they brought me incredible success in several careers, from bodybuilding to acting, from public service to politics, simply the rules of work like hell, trust yourself, break some rules, don't be afraid to fail, ignore the naysayers and stay hungry."

CHUCK RUSSELL

Director of Arnold's Eraser, Chuck Russell's credits (director/producer) include The Mask, with Jim Carrey, A nightmare on Elm Street 3, and The Scorpion King, with Dwayne Johnson. Eraser was the last hit Arnold had before his decline at the box office became apparent.

When the concept of the Eraser movie came up, were you actually working with Arnold at the time on something else, and did you discuss the minutia of the Eraser script?
Chuck Russell: I was working on a pirate movie, it was a remake of Captain Blood that Arnold was interested in doing for Warner Brothers. And Arnold persuaded me, he had a script called Eraser. We discovered that the film Captain Blood was in studio development, so it was going to take a long time. This was all before Pirates of the Caribbean. And the studio wasn't sure about a big action version of a pirate movie. Arnold had come across this script called Eraser. I was very pleasantly surprised, it had everything at the time what I felt an action movie should be and something that was very cater made for Arnold.

The pirate film may have been a more difficult fit. So, we immediately began final script polishes and working out what was a very good production plan. Even then it was still a year before shooting. It takes time when you're dealing with films of that level of production. But I was quite pleasantly surprised. It's something you learn in this business: to develop films through. I've been very lucky in that I've never done a film that I haven't been very excited about. But to collaborate and work with a star, at that time Arnold was at the top of his game, but he wanted to have one more big hit, and that was another goal. He wanted to have one more commercial success in an action film that still had some fresh exciting ideas in it. I think what helped make that film successful was casting Vanessa Williams. It was a bit of a surprise for the audience - a good surprise. She was a good match for Arnold. She was an actress with a real grip of heart to her as well.

In this movie, the plotline was inclined toward more reality based. Because a lot of the movies Arnold did, science fiction was subsumed into the manuscript.

Chuck Russell: This was a little more reality based, it was broad action. You have to have some fun in an Arnold Schwarzenegger movie. And at that point of his career, I wanted to have some sense of humor along with the action. Arnold was a US Marshall in a witness protection program, who had to work on his own. Because in the story, there's a mole within the US Marshalls. I think it was a great idea for a character. He's so good at relocating his witnesses and creating new identities for them that he's one of the erasers. He literally erases people from the records in this modern day in every computer everywhere. And seeing him work as a rogue agent, it was the fun of the movie. There was a plotline that involved real guns, which was something that we researched and had found which was being developed. Which were magnetic powderless weapons and the most powerful. It's something on a large scale. The storyline was to keep that technology from falling into the wrong hands. This was really part of the story.

Can you tell me about some of the locations - New York, Washington DC, Warner Brothers Studios in Burbank - that you filmed at?
Chuck Russell: We set up in New York, which was really great fun as a filmmaker. We have Arnold trashing through the gates of the New York City Zoo that we actually built the front of in Central Park. It was quite spectacular having Warner Brothers' full corporation on this kind of scale of production. We also blew up a small house, which was built on a set which was ready for demolition. It was the opening sequence, where Arnold saves a mobster who had to disappeared and goes into a witness protection program. They were great, great fun. We had cooperation from New York. I think it really helped keep the film on a great scale. It's great about seeing Schwarzenegger crossing the street in front of the FBI building; we shot this in Washington to kind of give the film authenticity and create a setting that this kind of character would be familiar with. I just think it helps make the film kind of classy, gives it a classy setting. In a way, I wanted to do some honor to the US Marshalls, and even the FBI and CIA and the police agencies that do a great job. They're often the bad guys in the movies. So it was nice to make the US Marshall a good guy.

Would I be right in saying that the majority of the film was shot at Warner Brothers Studios in Burbank?
Chuck Russell: It was. One of the sequences, which is very well known from that film, which I think helps distinguishes it, is when Arnold escapes from a 747. James Caan plays the villain, a mole within the US Marshalls, and has Arnold at gunpoint. It was the kind of a scene I always wanted to do, and I've seen it done since. There's been some scenes in

other action films with the hero making that kind of escape. In that sequence, Arnold turns a seat into the jet engine, which puts the plain off-course. And he falls chasing a parachute; he has to catch a parachute. It was actually one of the best experiences I've had from the storyboard, from that point of concept, this was not in the original script.

I knew we had a lot of Schwarzenegger movies to live up to at that point of his career, and we needed one or two big action set pieces that I felt the audience had never seen before. That's the 747 that I had to campaign the studios for, they ended up being very happy about it. Basically, that was the trailer of the film, when the film was done. It involved some of the most spectacular stunt work an actor had done at the time. And Arnold, who was already in his late forties, did a jump on what was a new rig at the time. And a stuntman dropping almost full velocity on a cord, which has a very sophisticated breaking system. We went to the biggest stage at Warner Brothers, and on the door section of the 747 set piece Arnold did five takes where he dropped off to get this right. It was quite the pro at the time, only seven of them had used that rig. But he was going for it. We got a very good sequence.

What was Arnold like to work with, was he easygoing or malcontent?
Chuck Russell: Arnold, you, know, he's a very bright and competitive guy. He evolved a long way from the guy we all saw in Pumping Iron. Actually, after that experience I was not surprised, everyone else was very surprised when he went into politics, because he kept very quiet about that. He had an interest in political affairs. But people were quite shocked when he went into politics here in California. He was really almost like a producer on the show. He was smart enough about the system, how to work with the studio. He was always very good about our need for bringing in the proper experts and getting the scenes done correctly. I could totally depend on him. You're working with someone who already is an icon, and I was prepared to take him through to another hit. But I was surprised that he was so bright. He was really very strong on the teamwork that it takes to make a movie of that caliber.

So, when he went into politics, I already knew he had a talent for working with a team of people. I actually thought he would do quite a good job. Arnold enjoys himself, again, entertaining the crew if we're held up waiting for the lights or waiting for special effects. Arnold cares about everybody, right down to the guy sweeping the stage. I've seen him entertain the whole crew when we've been stuck at night waiting for an explosion to take place. We had a shot where we had to pop under the floor, because of the gun blazing, which was very difficult because of the awkward angle. He had to pop up breaking through the floorboards like a jack in the box. I can recall it was two o' clock in the morning, and we were still trying to get the shot done. He's just a tough guy; he's ready to do what's required. While we definitely used a stunt double, you can count on him. Arnold appreciated that I cared about his safety as much as I did. I think he's worked with people who imagine he is the Terminator; he's just a human being. Maybe has sore knees at two o' clock in the morning, but that's part of my job: to make sure and keep an eye on him.

Were you an executive producer on this movie as well?
Chuck Russell: I was. It's because of the development of the film. It's something that I started as a producer and putting the pieces together where you get the proper budget and get a script through to completion. I was working very closely with Arnold Kopelson, who was a producer on the film, getting that picture in front of the camera. Problems with filming at studios can arise, because there's many films in development and you want to get your film into production. It was actually fairly quick. It took us a year, which is actually quick in films, to take it from the original script to a final polish in front of the cameras.

What was the most challenging decision you and Arnold had to make when making Eraser?
Chuck Russell: There were various production decisions, but I think this was actually fun and great to make. It's hard work but it's what I love. So I'm very inspired to do it. The most difficult thing is safety. When you're doing this many physical stunts, that was still before a lot of the CGI was available, but we still did more of the stunts physically at that time. So, for me it's really running a safe set when you're doing the explosions and this much action. The filmmaking is fun, and when you tie it in with the special effects, it's the hard part to make sure they're safe and less dangerous as possible. And Arnold appreciated that. It's something where you don't want to break a finger, or something you have to be careful about.

Can you tell me about working with Arnold's two main co-stars, James Caan and Vanessa Williams?
Chuck Russell: Vanessa is a very charismatic lady, and in casting there's only certain actresses you want to see with Arnold. Jamie Lee Curtis was with him in True Lies. Vanessa, I felt, was another actress with a heroic sense about here as well. I think it's one of the things that captured the audience's attention. They were a very good pairing. There's a shot of Vanessa stealing Schwarzenegger's cigar at the premiere that was circulated in all the papers. That kind of captured their relationship as we publicized it in the film as well. When you make a

film, it's one of the important things. I really do believe in old style chemistry between the stars, and James Caan was part of that. It was really all three of them.

James was so great in The Godfather and movies like Gone with the West. He hadn't really been working for a little while, and I just thought: what has happened to this terrific actor? I talked him into doing the role and he had a great time. In a way, it renewed his career at the time. He went on to do a number of films and a very successful television series Vegas. James Caan was just a big character, a great actor, a prankster and a guy with a good sense of humor on the set. A tough guy! An old real tough guy. And it was fun. He's now in Entourage and in Hawaii Five-O too. His son is a terrific actor now. I still bumped into Arnold when he was the governor. I just saw him at one or two functions and bumped into him by accident almost, and he always takes a moment. This is what's great about Schwarzenegger. You asked me about him earlier - one of the things that I think really sets him apart - it's true of Tom Cruise, too, both Arnold and Tom are really very personable guys. They're high energy guys. It's something I noticed similar with both of them.

I did the publicity junket with Schwarzenegger, we did seven countries in eleven days. I've never done anything like that. It's all about Arnold's level of energy, and how hard he's willing to work for film or projects he believes in. So, his people had planned that junket. Tom Cruise almost invented this style of international publicity. Both of those guys have a work ethic and a kind of personal charisma. They'll take the time with the media, and they'll take the time with their many friends in their personal lives, with all the demands of being a lead in a movie. That is something, ultimately, the public realizes. It's just the energy level it takes. Arnold's a tough guy, and you gotta come to the table knowing what you're doing, so it's not easy. But I enjoyed it because of that element. He cares, and he cares about everything he does and every film he makes.

Vanessa Williams' agent had told her there was an invitation for her to read for the new Arnold Schwarzenegger film - Eraser. At the time, she was to go on a tour so initially said she wouldn't be able to read the script. There were financial problems with the tour, so she called her agent and asked him whether the invitation was still open. Williams said, "So I flew myself out for the audition. Read for Arnold Kopelson (the producer) and the director Chuck Russell. Then they called me back the next day and wanted me to meet Arnold and read with him. I flew back. Then that Friday, they called me back out to do a screen test. By the following Monday, I had gotten the part. I didn't realize that nobody wanted me."

Arnold's wife Maria had suggested Williams to the producers, but everyone else had their reservations. Because she didn't have the profile of a feature film actress. "Maria said, you know, thinking about people, Vanessa might be a good idea," Williams said. Kopelson wasn't familiar with Williams as a feature film actress, Arnold knew she was a recording artist and the director wasn't familiar with her at all. "So these are people that I had to convince," continues Williams. "I had to go in there and basically kick ass in my audition. I fought for the part and got it. So it wasn't offered to me on a silver platter at all. And they also probably didn't want me to do the single, because they didn't want it to be another Bodyguard (type film). They didn't want to have the same thing. But they couldn't deny the screen test, and I was prepared." Originally, in the script there is a relationship, but nothing is consummated in a scene. They rewrote the ending of the script and Williams and Arnold end up together. "Obviously, there's a commercial value when you do an Arnold Schwarzenegger movie.... He gets the girl too. He insisted, he cried like a baby, we had to change the ending," joked James Caan.

Chuck, can you tell me of anything you talked about which signifies his persona?

Chuck Russell: So many things. I think just that Arnold used to kid about Stallone. There was an old-standing competition I think from the '80s between them both. Arnold always used to kid about what Stallone is doing down the street. I think Arnold is a real man's man, and I enjoyed that. I'm from the Midwest of America, Chicago, and it's a little more of a tough guy city than California. So I enjoyed Arnold's big manliness, attitude about sports, working out, kind of the brotherhood of Arnold, the cigar club - that was the most fun: hanging out with Arnold at the cigar club. We often had support from James Cameron, who came in and gave us his thoughts on the script and was very supportive in general. So that's another Arnold connection from me. It's been interesting to see how great a filmmaker Cameron has turned out to be. Arnold has a habit where he'll test people. He doesn't mind testing. And he's got a great sense of humor. He knows his reputation in his film as a tough guy. I've seen him test people, when he first meets other people at the cigar club, in a very friendly, charming way. You have to kind of prove yourself to Schwarzenegger if you're going to sit down and have a cigar with him.

Eraser is a return to the formulaic action genre. It was apparent Arnold was contentious in seeing through how the final product looked and wasn't shy to offer his input, which went beyond the capacity of an actor. Whilst on set, one day he was walking and he stopped and watched on a small monitor showing a sequence of a dummy (stand-in for Arnold) in a parachute being approached by an airplane. The plane is supposed to hit him in midair. After watching the brief sequence once, he immediately noticed the dummy appeared to be higher above the ground later in the sequence than it was earlier. He exclaimed, "That's wrong. As he falls, he should get lower." Because the scenes had been shot with two different lenses, a technician explained to Arnold. Arnold not satisfied, he says, "That's fine, but the audience will notice the inconsistency and you can't hand out a brochure to everyone in the theater explaining that you used a different lens. You have to make it look realistic, like I'm getting lower."

What was the filming routine like from morning to night?

Chuck Russell: We start early and do rehearsals, and if there were action things involved we'd layout exactly where the rigs explosions would go. I'd explain everything to Arnold for bigger scenes, and I'd show him exactly what was expected of him, how we're going to design the stunt. He cared about the performance. I wanted a little bit more heart from him in some scenes. His relationship with Vanessa as well, there is a sense of protectiveness in actuality. I honestly think he was trying a little more in the acting side than he had done in some other roles where it was really about "I'll be back". So we spent a lot of time on that as well. He was going to do rehearsals, and things that I think he hadn't done too much of before.

That brings me to the next question: Arnold was and is known as an action man, some critics have the tendency to refer to his acting performances as "wooden". How did you perceive him in the dialog scenes and acting, coming from the perspective of a director such as yourself?

Chuck Russell: I expected him to have limitations, but I think when you're working with somebody who is already established with this kind of personality with the audience, you want to present him in his best light and give the audience what they expect. And he, like I said, spent a little more time in rehearsals and tried to come across a human being as well as an action star. I think he did achieve that. He and Vanessa in particularly. I had to allow time for him to workout with his weights. He had a truck with his weightlifting kit on it. He was determined to keep in shape, so he's got to put a couple of hours into that each day as well. So one of the things I had to make sure was that he had a break. If I was going to have an hour for the lighting to be set up, I would make sure to let him know it's his time to workout. That's one of the things with people like Arnold Schwarzenegger, where you have to give them a balance as an actor and an athlete.

The film grossed more than $234 million worldwide. After this movie, his movies at the box office started to decline as if the studios were no longer prescient. Can you tell me more about the premiere?

Chuck Russell: The premiere was at the Mann's Chinese Theater. I think the studio was holding their breath, because it had cost a little more than they thought it would originally. The original script had a lot of gun play. The 747 scene and the crocodile scene - which was shot in a zoo set - I knew I needed something more. Those were the two scenes that were unique. And it played so well at the screening at the studio and the premiere. Premiere audience are actually not that easy, it's stocked full of Hollywood people that are very critical. But the film has a lot of interest, old fashion heroism, and the audience really responded to that and responded to the humor in the film. Robert Pastorelli, who has since passed away sadly, did a fantastic job for the comedy. Robert was a very, very skilled actor, almost underrated but brilliant comedian. He had just the right touch, like a New York tough guy, mobster Arnold had embraced, who was sort of stuck onboard for the adventure. Pastorelli just did a spectacular job. He always fed Arnold the lines, real plus to the show and a great personality. The big moment at the premiere, though, was Vanessa and Arnold. Just the humor, the friendship and the camaraderie they had really played well on the screen.

Any after party moments?

Chuck Russell: This is how you can judge a film premiere: how many people come to your after party. The film was a real crowd pleaser so everybody was at the party. And Arnold was, of course, the center of attention. He knows how to play that. So, you know, this is what we set out to do. Arnold was at a certain point of his career where he hadn't had a hit in a couple of years, and the goal was to make that $100 million-plus hit. He knew then, he knew right at the premiere, that was when he first knew that it was a success. We could tell, he had the crowd.

One of the big thrills of filmmaking is you can plan, you can have a big budget and you could have a star, whatever, but you don't really know how it will do. The crowd decides, the audience decides. Critics tend to underrate action films and comedies. I don't know why. They assume they're easy, but they're not. Action acting is a very stylized kind of acting. It's very interesting to see which actors can pull it off. It's just not that easy. Arnold is Arnold because of his style. He actually is a brave guy. He actually is that disciplined of an athlete that it comes across that well on the screen - you can't fake it. It's very hard to double these guys, it's just as hard to double Schwarzenegger. Dwayne Johnson, 6ft 3, I found him very difficult to double him in Scorpion King. Nobody could swing the sword like Dwayne. We had a 20-pound sword, and this other tough guy couldn't move it. So these are macho pictures, and it takes a lot of heart to pull off those roles. I think the critics sometimes think they're review proof, but really it's about pleasing the audience. It's about pleasing the audience internationally, which is something I bare in mind. The story has to make sense, even when it's translated.

The film was nominated for an Academy Award for sound effects and editing.
Chuck Russell: We had one of the best mixing teams in the business, and we did something which was new at the time with all of the sound effects.

BRIAN LEVANT

Jingle All the Way was one of the comedies that Arnold made which flopped at the box office. Brian Levant, the director, is best known for directing the films Beethoven, The Flintstones and Are We There Yet. He also directed Jackie Chan's The Spy Next Door.

Can you tell me how you got together with Arnold to make Jingle All the Way?

Brian Levant: Arnold (after leaving the governor's office) told his agents that he was ready to accept roles again. He said that after seven years of CAA (Creative Artists Agency) asking him, "When can we put you back out on the market?" he said go ahead after his time in the office finished. Let's go back a little bit. The film was originally developed to star someone like Danny Stern from Home Alone. And somewhere along the way, someone at ICM - Arnold's old agency - read the script and thought it would be a good vehicle - a third comedy vehicle - for Arnold and Danny DeVito. Arnold read it and he liked it very much. Danny DeVito was directing a movie, so he couldn't do it. So we got Sinbad.

I was sent the script by Peter Sherman, who was then the head of the Fox movie division. I had worked with him in the television department there. I went over to San Francisco and I met up with Chris Columbus, who produced the film and was the director of the Home Alone movies and the Harry Potter films. We had a wonderful meeting. Then I went to the set of Eraser I think. No, the one with apocalyptic turn of the century...what was that one called? Peter Hyams film (The 6th Day). He was shooting that. We sat down and talked. We had a good meeting, and I told him how dedicated I was to family comedy and that I wanted to make this big epic slapstick film. He was gong ho, he responded to my energy and he listened very carefully. He's a very, very smart man. I don't think he gets the credit he deserves in that respect, you know. His mind is as well developed as his biceps. He finished over seven years of being the governor of the state.

His agent, who later became my agent, Lou Pitt and all of us said, "OK, let's do it." Basically, when I came on we had a release date before we had a script. So we jumped in on the script and started solving innumerable production issues that needed to be resolved. I mean, in the film, in the world of CGI technology 1995 was a long time ago, so we had to do so much of that more practical, a lot of wirework, a lot of costume design for the opening and for the Turboman set. We set in Minneapolis for a month and had to scout there. We had eighty-two days to shoot, the longest by far I've ever had. And on the backlot of Universal in July, we had one thousand two hundred extras who dressed for a Minneapolis winter in one hundred degrees in Los Angeles summer. But we had a wonderful time.

Arnold, it's interesting, you know - Jackie (Chan) too - Peter Morgan, the guy who wrote the last Clint Eastwood film and Ron Howard's Nixon, said an interesting thing about Clint. Ron Howard said that they were like sailors from a century who came to port now and again but lived on the ship. Their lives were on the set; they move from place to place, movie to movie. And that's really what their lives are about. Both Arnold and Jackie fit that description very well too. That this is where they spend undoubtedly so much of their time, surrounded by close associates and the people who help construct all their stunts, protect them and work with them and provide a fun environment around them. And this film was a prime example of that. Arnold comes alive on the set and behind the scenes of the camera, that was his terrain and he occupied it beautifully. I don't think he's ever gotten credit enough for his comedy work in the film.

We asked him to do a great deal more comedically, to wield many more comedic weapons than he had before. And things like Twins, where his silence and his glare, the things that we've come to know so well, and ferocious in action films and comedies became comedic. We asked him to play, really for the first time in his career, an unexceptional man, a normal stubborn dad. I believe he was very successful in carrying the story from scene to scene, in propelling the scenes, in playing a straight man, applying comedy and playing the action helping to find the balance between action and comedy, which is a very delicate thing to do. You want to keep it at a certain level, because it's a PG film - it's for kids. We had one big set piece after another. The man is so professional. The first day of work, he not only knew his lines in the entire script, but every character's lines in the script. He memorized the script before the first day of shooting.

Can you tell me about Arnold's and Sinbad's collaboration?
Brian Levant: We let Sinbad loose many times! And we let him run, and we wanted to. I felt Arnold was very adept at, we'd do things and shape them and edit them a little bit on the set, and Arnold was great about that. Despite the fact he memorized every line, he said, "OK,

we're going to do this and that." He was great about that, "Yes! Yes! Then I can do that." We'd say, "Good! OK! Here we go, let's try it!" So it was a very collaborative film. Chris Columbus, the producer, always had great ideas and everybody pitched in and we had fun. I think on the first day of the movie, we shot a scene with Sinbad and Arnold on the street and it went really well. There was a lot of improvising stuff, and it looked terrific and it had a real nice feel about it. The only time during the whole process of the film that I got a call from the head of the studio, he said, "Hey, that was great! Saw the dailies. Can't wait to see the whole movie!" I don't know if he felt like that in the end, but it was great at the time.

What would you say was your most memorable moment working with Arnold on the movie?
Brian Levant: When you're out with Arnold - and same with Jackie - in public shooting outside in the streets, you see how excited people are just to be in a block of him. How magnetic the personalities are and how they respond so positively to the crowd and the recognition. You never see Arnold and Jackie Chan brushoff anybody, they're gracious to everyone. Everywhere I go, I sometimes hear, "You know, I met Arnold, boy was he nice." You know they're a big star, but when you go out in the world and you see the reverence that they command, that's fun. That's really fun. We had many, many good days on the film. It's hard work working with animals, working with kids, working on wires, things that test your patience. Arnold was always in great spirit and very positive of the whole experience.

Brian Levant directed Jackie Chan in the spoof The Spy Next Door. Chan broke into the West after many years of being the number-one action star in South East Asia. Arnold had a cameo role in Chan's Around the World in Eighty Days, which also starred Steve Coogan. Chan remembers the lack of intuition with the Austrian actor who never lost his accent, "I've known him (Arnold) for a long time, from being partners in Planet Hollywood. I met him at a party and we talked, but not really deep talking, always just...'Hi, Jackie. Nice to meet you,' and then we sit down and talk about the business. The next time I saw him again, we were sitting in the bathtub and he said some jokes, but I didn't understand what he was talking about. And probably when I say something, he doesn't understand. He's a pretty nice guy."
Many celebrities go through a phase wanting to be left alone when they are hounded by fans and the media. They lose their privacy and complain. "That is movie star bullshit, loss of privacy," Arnold told

James Cameron's biographer Christopher Heard in 2000. "We all want people to come see our movies, we make a good living off of people knowing who we are, love to come watch our movies, every actor that dreams of being successful dreams of being famous - one goes with the other in this business - so to say, once you get what you dreamed of, that you wish people would leave you alone is fucking bullshit. If no one wanted to see you, or nobody was suddenly curious about you, then you would no longer have a fucking career and you would be back to saying, 'I wish people would ask for me again.' Any actor that wants his privacy back should stop making movies and move to a cabin in the fucking mountains."

Did you get a chance to socialize with Arnold whilst shooting the movie?
Brian Levant: We went out, when you're directing a movie just because you stop shooting it doesn't mean you stop working. So, yes, we did go out a couple of times for dinner and have some lunch in his trailer. And we'd work on things and talk. You know, it's a big job. Sometimes he had his family there and he needed to spend time with them. But we had a great time, we really did. I'm very heartened by the film's growing reputation, it wasn't a blockbuster by far when it came out. But since, it's proven to be tremendously endurable and a popular holiday film. I did a college speaking tour, and the only movie anybody ever asked me to sign for them was Jingle All the Way. Everywhere I went the kids had it. They said, "We watch it every Christmas. We love it. I grew up on it." It's surprising and gratifying and shows the enduring popularity of Arnold. I think the world was going to be excited to see him on the big screen again.

He's an intellectual person, what conversations did you have with him in which he exuded his intellectual side?
Brian Levant: Yes. I enjoyed talking politics with him. At the time, he was starting to become immersed in political thoughts - you could see it was on his mind already. We enjoyed discussing issues. And once again, I don't think people give him credit for developing his mind as much as the biceps.

Do you think Arnold became recognized and accepted beyond the confines of the action movie genre, because of the success of his comedy films?
Brian Levant: I think he was very lucky to team up with Ivan Reitman, who I did Beethoven for. That is a very, very smart man and knows how

to get the best out of performances. What he found with Arnold was that he could tap into people's expectations, of Arnold's behavior, and your expectations of comic effect. All he has to do sometimes is look at somebody and raise an eyebrow, and people would laugh knowing what's behind those reactions. And the simplicity of many of the things he did for Twins, the goofy look he has on his face after he has sex with that cute girl, you know, it's very simple and very unfettered; it's very clean and simple and makes great use of Arnold's personality and his natural charm. So, he was very lucky to team up with Ivan. Then he had a comic in Danny DeVito, who's an expert comic actor, and they did have wonderful chemistry and it was an unusual team. A team like Laurel and Hardy.

JOEL SCHUMACHER

Batman and Robin director Joel Schumacher was already friends with Arnold before they worked on this movie in 1997, which was critically panned by critics and fans. Schumacher's directorial credits include Batman Forever, Phone Booth and The Phantom of the Opera.

Can you tell me when you first started to work with Arnold, was it when you collaborated on the Batman and Robin film?
Joel Schumacher: It's the first time we worked together, but we'd known each other for a long time before that. We had coffees and had talked to each other about working together. We just never had the right opportunity.

Joel Schumacher was the motivating force for Arnold to get involved in Batman and Robin. Arnold explains, "Although I'd seen all the other Batmans and I have enjoyed them thoroughly, and was always interested in, of course, playing the ultimate villain in one of those movies, I didn't really think much about it until Joel Schumacher came to me and said that he would like me to play Mr. Freeze. I said to him, 'This sounds interesting, let me think about it. This is really a great character to play.' And Joel then turned to me and said, 'Just so you know that if you decide not to do it, I would not direct the movie. Because I can only do this movie if you can play Mr. Freeze. So what are you going to do, screw up the whole movie?' He made me feel I would make this whole thing fall apart if I'm not a part of it. So he made me feel like King Kong, so I called him up the next day and I said, 'You know something, Joel, I'm going to do Mr Freeze.'" Schumacher's second choice to play Mr. Freeze was Anthony Hopkins, third choice was Hulk Hogan, the former WWE star whose film career didn't really take off as he would have hoped.

What was your vision for Batman and Robin, did you feel Arnold's international fan base would propel the movie in terms of box office success? Arnold said it was very wise for Warner Brothers to have him in the movie from a marketing point of view.

Joel Schumacher: Batman Forever was my first Batman movie, and my job was to sort of refresh the franchise. So we made a much younger and sexier Batman with Val Kilmer, and Nicole Kidman. Jim Carrey, Tommy Lee Jones and Drew Barrymore, there were a lot of terrific stars in the movie. And then Batman and Robin was just, you know, a sequel made for one reason: to make money. I was expected to make another one. So we were trying to make a bigger, better one and I think the fans were disappointed. I think the first one, Batman Forever, was the biggest box office in the United States. That was in '95. I think Arnold has fans everywhere.

Can you describe his character, although known for being an action man he seemed to have been able to integrate humor into some of the characters he played during the course of his career?

Joel Schumacher: Arnold, even in his most serious action movies, usually has lines that are ironic or comedy, you know, he's a very funny man. I think he's always taken his characters and has used them with a couple of famous lines that seem like, you know, that he gets the joke.

What was the working relationship between Arnold and George Clooney like?

Joel Schumacher: They're two of the greatest guys in the world. You couldn't be working with anyone who is more fun, kind-hearted individuals. The whole cast got along great, because we had a lot of terrific people in the movie. I think it was a very complex character. It had humor in there and also in his lines, it was a mixture of many things together to make that character so that it had, you know, even though it's still a comic book you try to give it humanity. I think Arnold did. I think like a lot of villains he's misunderstood.

While working together on the movie, Arnold and Clooney had a drinking contest to see who would prevail. This took place at Arnold's restaurant, where he had a big dinner and several prominent people were in attendance. Arnold was drinking peach schnapps. Clooney recalls, "He was bragging that he could outdrink any Irishman. You don't do that. It's not right." Clooney had a couple of shots and soon realized the chances of beating Arnold were slim. "So I gave the waitress $500 to keep bringing me shots of water and bring him shots of peach schnapps," recalls Clooney. "Every five minutes, he'd be sitting there talking to his wife and I'd be like, 'Hey, let's go! Come on, super stud, let's go! I got him literally fifteen shots, and he was just sitting there (slumped over the table)." Clooney never admitted to Arnold that he had cheated.

What would you say were his strong attributes, having had observed and worked with him?
Joel Schumacher: Well, he's so prepared and he's so professional. People that worked with him, some people are an asset in the business. He's very dedicated, he's never late and he helps the other actors. He brings a wonderful camaraderie, he's very jovial on the set and he makes work fun. But none of this surprises me, because I know him as a man, and that's the way he is.

Someone like Nicolas Cage and Nicole Kidman, with whom you worked with on Batman Forever, can play verzatile characters. How would you define Arnold, he seemed to be a one-sided actor, would you agree?
Joel Schumacher: I don't know, you can't ever put Arnold in a square box. I mean, you never know what Arnold's going to do next. So I'd put nothing pass him. I think Nic Cage is like all great character actors, he could play the best of the best or the worst of the worst. I think Nicole Kidman could do that too. Because they're character actors, they're not just actors. I'm convinced Nicole could do Lady Macbeth if she wants to, or she could play the sweetest human being that ever lived.

Arnold played a villain in some of his movies and a hero in most. Can you tell me what you detected in Arnold when working with him in terms of the joy in making a movie?
Joel Schumacher: I think Arnold loves making movies and he's so good at it. So, I think he brings a lot of joy to it and he drives himself into the part. I don't think Arnold does anything halfway; I think he's an all or nothing guy. So, he brings a lot of energy and a lot of focus.

You also have known him on a social level.
Joel Schumacher: We're friends and I'm friends with his wife Maria. Arnold and I traveled all over the world promoting the movie, and we had a lot of fun together, night life. I went to his birthday party, I went to his fiftieth birthday party and his sixtieth. We're friends. He's the best advertiser in the world. He's a great marketer, and he goes into each territory and really sells the movie.

Were there any projects you or Arnold wanted to work on after completing Batman and Robin?
Joel Schumacher: He became governor. It was very late in the '90s

when I was doing different kinds of movies, so we didn't have any plans to work together at the time. Obviously, he had other plans, which I'm not sure what they were.

Critics panned Batman and Robin. Time Out Film Guide wrote, "The fourth Bat-flick finds this juvenile franchise running on empty. Oozing insincerity and perplexed paternalism, Clooney plays Batman as an irrelevant bystander. Screenwriter Akiva Goldman sets up a 'revenge of nature' theme, with Schwarzenegger's lumpen Mr. Freeze croaking interminable 'cool' puns ('chill')." No doubt the studio wanted to continue to capitalize on the Batman franchise and keep toys on the shelves. It seemed to have been scripted so much as run through the Hollywood script mill, where lines of dialog were reduced to a catchphrase. Despite the fact the movie received negative criticism from critics and the audience, the movie was profitable earning $238 million worldwide. With a budget of $125 million, all wasn't lost. After Batman and Robin, what path would Arnold's career take? Would the studios be willing to splash out another big paycheck? Arnold's name was attached to several projects, including a new film version of I Am Legend, remake of Planet of the Apes, and a film scripted by Quentin Tarantino which would see Arnold play an Austrian for the first time. However, none of these materialized, instead he would go on to make End of Days, a film which received negative reviews on the most part.

ADAM GREENBERG

A leading cinematographer in Hollywood, Adam Greenberg is noted for his work both in Israel and America. He worked with Arnold on Terminator 1 and 2, Junior, Eraser and Collateral Damage. His other credits include First Night, Rush Hour and Snakes on a Plane.

Can you tell me of your experience working on The Terminator?
Adam Greenberg: Arnold and me, we met on the set of the movie; we became very good friends from the very beginning. We had things in common: it was difficult to understand both of us because of our accents. It was difficult to understand him, and it was difficult to understand me. And we were the two foreigners on the movie set. We are friends to this day.

Arnold's character and script called for nonstop action throughout. He played a bad guy character, which became emblematic, and this made him the star of The Terminator.
Adam Greenberg: Yeah, the first movie, it is what it is: a guy coming from a different place and a futuristic idea. There was a difference between his character in the first and the second movie. I didn't do the third and fourth; I only did the first and the second one. The first one was done without money, very low-budget movie. It was very difficult to shoot the movie at that time. The Union was very strong, and they didn't permit you to do movies like this. But it worked out very well, the movie was accepted very well and I expected it would open a lot of doors for me. I became very popular at the time, everybody approached me to do exploitation movies. I didn't do them. I tried to stay away from it, always choosing movies with different subjects.

I tried to make him powerful. I tried to give him the visual look he had, I wanted to shoot him. I shot with the camera kind of being on the ground, very widening lens - 80mm lens. Arnold's not too tall, he's wide but shorter. I wanted to make him big and strong therefore I built special type of equipment, very primitive but it works well. You are able to put the camera on the floor and actually not look at the camera but look and operate this way. He liked it very much. And movies that he shot later, with other cameramen, he always asked them to do the lighting my way.

Because he looked good like that, his cheekbones are very strong. I think his head looked very powerful. I showed him a few times and he was very happy with it.

Did you get to converse with Arnold regularly on the set?

Adam Greenberg: I don't remember what I discussed with Arnold. To be honest with you, when we shot Arnold in the first movie, way back there was no equipment that we have today where you can see the playback. I don't remember us doing that in the first movie, because it didn't exist back then. I never discussed with him how to do things. To be honest with you, the way I work is I have my idea set up ahead of time, the way I want the movie to look and I stick to this, you know. I never discussed with the director the script or things like that. I tried a few times, but the directors are mostly involved in reading and actors reading the script. I tried a few times, very soon you immediately end up with very cold feelings from them, which means they don't think much about the visual. But with my experience with the visual, I'm into the visual, my job involves the visual side.

I'm a filmmaker. I come with an idea for the movie that would be a great look for the movie. I always work this way. I come very prepared for the movie. With Arnold, you know, he's a great guy, he liked what I did. He always liked what I did and complimented me. Later, in Terminator 2 and other movies, we had the instant playback. So he would come and look at it, and he could like it or not like it. He understood very well, he was always very cooperative with me. He understood what I was doing: to make him look like what he was supposed to look like - his character. He was always cooperative and understanding and patient. He's very disciplined.

Can you tell me about Arnold working with his co-star Linda Hamilton on the first movie?

Adam Greenberg: Yeah. Linda Hamilton. I think it was Terminator 2, he's in the garage gas station. In his movies he doesn't speak much, but in that scene the boy's standing and Linda was there. But he had about one page of dialog, which we did many times - maybe thirty-five takes. He had the piece of paper in front of him to read the lines. He said I'm a bodybuilder, not an actor. That's what he said. He knew his weak area, but he's a great guy and had a great sense of humor. I remember him and Linda, both of them, being very cooperative, but they worked opposite ways. She was with Michael, the other Terminator, in the first one. I don't remember any incident or complain between Arnold and Linda. But both of them were very cooperative. In the second Terminator, when he dies he's melting down. There was no tension between them that I can remember.

Linda Hamilton said after the movie came out, Arnold didn't mention her name in all the press interviews he did. Do you feel Arnold wanted to be the center of attention and ostentatiously endeavored to do this?

Adam Greenberg: Could be, could be. I'll be surprised, he's not that kind of a guy, you know. To mention names, it shouldn't come from him; it's the advertising and the producer's responsibility. Obviously, it could be that they pushed Arnold, the studio and the advertising, they want to make him the hero, they want to "punch" stronger, because he's the star of the movie. She does have a big part, she's on the screen. Naturally, he's the hero. He's the guy they're building up and advertising around him. So naturally they would lift him up and push him to build him up and promote him more than her. But I don't think Arnold is that kind of a guy.

The Terminator became unexpectedly a huge hit. Cameron's story and direction are pared to the bone and all the more creepy. The director demanded perfection from his actors. Linda Hamilton says Arnold is a team player and is just excited about other people's success and is a loyal friend. In the beginning, she had her doubts about her co-star. She recollects, "When we made the first Terminator, I was first naysayer. I was like, 'Arnold Schwarzenegger? I don't think so....' I was a complete snob." Hamilton was a serious actress who moved to Los Angeles from New York. Although The Terminator didn't make her rich, it definitely opened doors for her. "Here I was, working with Arnold, going, 'I'm not sure about this.' Eventually, though, I came around. He was a good guy."

Because of the minimum dialog Arnold had and the nature of his character, the two stars scarcely had scenes together with dialog. "We almost didn't act together in T1, because he chased me continuously," states Hamilton. "When he finally caught up, he was an endoskeleton! Arnold hung around the set a lot, though, and was a good sport. He still is. I don't think any of us guessed how big a megastar he would become. But he's a team player, doesn't keep you waiting and was very generous with his personal gym and airplane. None of that side interferes with his work. I can't honestly say hand on heart that Arnold is a wonderful actor. Yet he knows how to use his persona well and smartly." She says when it comes to merchandizing and marketing, you can't argue with him. Of course, Arnold mastered the art of promotion.

Were there any unusual incidents at break times that you can recall?

Adam Greenberg: He's a great guy. Arnold is very smart. He has his two legs on the ground, a great guy, smart and very friendly. He's like one of the guys talking to everybody and he tried to help everybody. Sometimes later on, when he became a big star - not in the first or second one (Terminator) - you had to wait for him maybe half an hour or forty-five minutes until he finished his chess game. If you interfered in his chess, he would not come on the set - you had to wait for him. Fifty people would wait for him on the set, because he's playing chess. Later on, he had a lot of power as an actor. Eventually, the studio gives a lot of power.

When the first Terminator came out, was Arnold incredulously surprised of the success of this low-budget movie?
Adam Greenberg: All of us were surprised. You have to understand that all of the people involved, I have to justify for myself, I think maybe myself, when I came to do the movie I had already behind me maybe thirty or forty feature films. Not television but feature films. I was all ready to go. But all the others, including Arnold, I think Arnold did one movie and the Conan films. Jim hadn't done anything, the producer Gail Anne Hurd had done nothing, she had invested the money, she financed Jim. She gave Jim $500 a week to keep him up - she financed him. But all the other people involved in this, they had previous experience.

When it came out everybody was astonished, and the people in town - Hollywood people - were astonished. Don't forget the movie was done for only $6.5 million; two million out of the six and a half would go to Arnold. So really the movie was done with not enough money. I think looking back, there was a lot of drive, including myself, everybody wanted to prove themselves, and on top of this Arnold and the director Jim Cameron. It was something new. Even visually it was something new. I remember I was looking to get a new metallic kind of look for the movie. This was a pleasure to work closely with, we came up with a different look. Today, every second movie is like this - with a metallic look. But at that time, it was something that I think had never been seen before, before any of this digital things, all that you see today. I think everybody was astonished, and everybody's careers built up from the result of this movie - there's no question about it.

Reflecting on the initial success of The Terminator, Arnold explained, "He's indestructible, no emotions, no feelings, can just eliminate anything that's in front of him. I think this is why the film became such a success. Because I think everyone has a dream to just be maybe for one day to be a Terminator, you know, just be able to really, I think that's why it became so successful. Because everyone wants to just be a

Terminator one day and take care of the 'job' , you know, the payback whoever did them harm or just to settle the score or just go out and take care of the 'job' and all those things. So I think that's what really is the fantasy in everyone." Arnold's friends had advised him not to pursue playing a villain, the conventional wisdom being that it would be bad for his career. However, Arnold believed he would give it a shot, partly because he found the script well written and the director was very enthusiastic and determined - two qualities he himself possessed.

Do you feel the character Arnold played in Junior put a dent on his image at the time? You have said, "Why is he doing this movie like this?" But the producers and Arnold seemed to be enthusiastic; they thought it would do well. What did he think about playing such a role? **Adam Greenberg:** Yeah. He did Junior with Ivan Reitman. I didn't talk to him about it, but the same director, Ivan Reitman, had done a movie with Arnold and Danny DeVito called Twins. It's a very funny movie. And if you put an actor like Arnold playing the hero, obviously, in a pregnant situation, it already becomes controversial with people and something which is unexpected, something shocking. Arnold was willing to shoot it, and he enjoyed it. I could tell he enjoyed it. I didn't discuss it with him, asking him why he was doing that kind of movie. The director was a comedy director, and I think the previous experience between Arnold and Danny DeVito in Twins worked out very well and so the contrast and difference between them two was like black and white.

Emma Thompson was in the movie too. They liked each other very much, and, obviously, Emma Thompson's a great actress. I like her very much. I remember she was a great actress and lady. I still have memories of her today. She liked Arnold and respected him very much. You see, Arnold is very likeable, you cannot not like him. You may not agree with him, but he has a good sense of humor and he's one of those guys he's nice to be around. In situations with Arnold whenever you go to a party, always there's a group of people around Arnold. He's a funny guy, nice to be around and people enjoy to be around him. I always go to parties for the movies I've shot. I'm not a party guy but I do go to them.

His wife Maria would come on the set. I don't remember his kids coming, but Maria did. And the movie we did in Mexico, Collateral Damage, which was a distant location, she would come there too. They had a private plane and she would come on the plane. But Junior was done here in town (Los Angeles). But she was always on the set sometimes. We stayed in Mexico in a very isolated place. I can tell you that ahead of time, the company Warner Brothers sent a lot of equipment to Mexico before the production crew arrived, before we all arrived. I think film negatives and many printers and faxes, a lot of stuff, they had an entire truck loaded, a big truck at the airport by air. They supposed to take the equipment to the location, but it was robbed. Some guys with guns came and told the driver to step down from the truck and they took over and drove away the truck with all the equipment and the negatives - everything disappeared. Then I came to Arnold, and I told him, "Arnold, I think you should think about it. They might kidnap you over there. You should have protection. Think about it."

I told him they could kidnap you for money - because he's from a very rich family. He was very thankful to me and eventually they hired an international protection team of guards in Mexico for the entire shooting. He was coming to the set with one jeep with guns ahead of him and another car in the middle and one behind him. They were guarding him twenty-four hours. In these places you disappear, they kidnap you. He's a very valuable man, they can take him and ask for anything they want. But she (Maria) would come on set. I don't remember their kids coming on the set, but the wife, yes. She was very friendly, but she was also busy, they have four kids. She's an independent woman.

Although Arnold had prevailed through his comedic roles in box office hits Twins and Kindergarten Cop, the role he undertook in Junior was perhaps putting it on the line. He said, "The great thing about it is you're so...you can't afford to play a woman or let the sensitive side to come out, because that is tougher to do than to play in an action movie and play a tough guy - that's easy. But I mean, to play the opposite of that, people always ask me, and the show asked me when I did the press junket, 'How can you do that?' You need to be secure with your masculinity to play a woman, or to play someone who plays a woman and to lay the pregnancy and all those kinds of things. You have to be very secure with your masculinity."

Arnold believed that the only way you know how far you can go is you stretch and take risks. "So I cannot blame any actor or any athlete or any businessman for taking risks," Arnold said. "The chances are you can fail." Arnold said he wasn't trying to be a woman being pregnant, but was trying to act a man being pregnant. He felt it was much more extreme, and because a man whims about this stuff, men are not as tough as women are. Arnold got to play an emotional guy in Junior. Maria laughed all the way through the movie. She also was able to resonate with elements in the movie which were total copies of her behavior when she was pregnant, according to her husband.

Can you tell me of the obstacles encountered during the course of filming Collateral Damage in 2001 in the jungle?

Adam Greenberg: Working with a foreign crew is one issue. In Mexico they have a very strong organization, and my point of view is when you ask for four, you get the whole. For example, on this movie we had hundred and twenty drivers. Technically other than the distance and location, you prepare yourself well, snakes and bugs and being bitten by mosquitoes. You have to prepare yourself well and have a special cream. The mosquitoes were a big issue.

Arnold would play chess in the jungle, is this correct?

Adam Greenberg: Yeah, he always played chess. He had an assistant and he taught him to play chess. He would be locked in his trailer playing chess, until there was a certain situation in the game where he could win. Once I took on his assistant, to try to see how good he was. I think in three or four moves, I gave it back to him. I beat him. So the story spread on the set about me beating his assistant.

Can you recall Arnold's working relationship with the director Andrew Davis who indicated that Arnold played a more reality based character in this movie, compared to his previous movies where he seemed to play a mythical action hero?

Adam Greenberg: Arnold is very disciplined, he would do anything the director asked him to do. He's very accurate. He discussed his ideas, he came with his own stuntmen and his assistant. For example, the first Terminator until Eraser, there were many scenes he shot with his assistant who was his double. He had a double in the first movie who looks like him. But with Andy it was pretty simple. Arnold's a hardworking guy. I think the bad luck with this movie came because it came out on 9/11. Let me tell you, I was in Hollywood and they were processing the film. I came that day to see the first print, to approve the first print. I came to the studio, this was the day 9/11 happened. They said not to release it yet. The timing was so accurate, opening for the movie for a long time. Then when it opened, I don't think the movie did very well.

By now, aged fifty-four, Arnold had already lost some of his box office luster, but he continued to command an extremely high salary. Talking about Collateral Damage, he said, "I got interested in it because I change in my career. Because for a change I don't play a cop; I play a fireman in this one, a heroic fireman." Two weeks after September 11, Arnold went to New York's Ground Zero where the twin towers came down. He visited the firefighters and rescue workers. He also paid visits to various fire stations and saw the shrines there. Each station had lost between ten and fifteen men in the tragedy.

Arnold says, "I have to say, I was so excited about the fact that I play a firefighter, because originally when they re-wrote the script, you know, there were people who said, 'Firefighter? Isn't it better if you are a CIA guy?' And I said, 'No. I think it would be more fun to play an ordinary man who saves lives.'" Arnold felt this was also heroic. He liked the idea of playing the ordinary guy. But then there was this doubt about and ambivalence: is this heroic enough? Arnold explained, "Then when this happened on September 11, I think now the world has a whole different picture of firefighters. So I was very glad I chose that, because it is a heroic profession. I remember I was big fan of Backdraft. You could see the things people were doing."

When Collateral Damage was released in February 2002, there were complaints from some Arab and Muslim organizations because of the sensitivity of the subject - terrorism!
Adam Greenberg: I'm not really aware of this. There might have been. The movie is about, when we shot it I don't think anybody came to the movie set to advise us the proper way to make the characters and the best way to shoot. All of us tried to do the best job we could.

When Collateral Damage was released there were protesters who criticized the movie because of its portrayal of Colombians as terrorists, some people felt it echoed the real-life events of September 11. One movie critic described it as: basically a silly adrenaline-pumper - albeit one that's reaped a gold mine of publicity thanks to September 11. Former mayor of New York, Rudolph Giuliani, was criticized for attending a screening of the movie. Originally slated for an October release, Warner Brothers put it back in the wake of the terror attacks. Arnold donated $1 million and helped to raise an additional $4 million for rescue workers' families.

Arnold broached on a TV news program that the bottom line was: you never can throw everyone in the same pot. And that this was a story about what America is doing to Colombia, and what Colombians, a few Colombian terrorists, are doing to America and as a result the damage it causes. The film flopped merely grossing $78 million worldwide and it cost $85 million to produce. However, Arnold would go on to command an even higher salary for his next and final major film, Terminator 3, for which he received $30 million, before making the transition into politics.

In your opinion, what are the manifold attributes of Arnold as a person and actor which reflected the primal life force which may have been apparent?

Adam Greenberg: On a private level, he is very loyal to his friends, you can rely on him. He's very smart and a businessman. Very approachable. Even though he is a big guy, the governor, or a big star and a very wealthy man, you know, he's very approachable - at least to his friends. Me and him go a long way back together, from the beginning from The Terminator and till he went on to become the governor. Obviously, he didn't work on any more movies (when he was in office) and I slowed down, too, but we stayed very good friends. He's very loyal to his friends, all of his friends. He invited me to Sacramento and we flew together on his private plane. He took me with him all day to San Francisco where he made a speech in front of four hundred and fifty people. I asked on the jet, "Could you believe one time you'd be the governor of this big state?" Because California is a big state. He said no. He's a very accessible guy, very good guy. He's speaking much more and he got coached in English. Arnold played well as long as he doesn't have too much dialog. He's better now since he became the governor.

As an actor, he's not a dialog actor. Can you recall any scenes he was having problem with dialog, was he just content on being an action star?

Adam Greenberg: Before I mentioned what happened on the second Terminator movie, where he said I'm a bodybuilder not an actor, laughingly. But when he shot movies, he never had much dialog, you know. For some takes, he would prepare himself ahead of time and he used a coach. The difference between him and other big star actors I've worked with, I've seen experienced big star actors, who sometimes took $30 million for a movie, taking long time on the set doing thirty-five takes on a scene. And they're Americans, it's their own language, but they couldn't do the proper delivery of the dialog. Because they didn't prepare themselves. But Arnold's a hardworking guy, with a coach he would come ready. Again, if you look at his movies he doesn't have much dialog.

He's better now because he's speaking more. He's very pleasant to be around and a very good guy. He's a figure, he will not be in any Shakespeare part - he is what he is, you know. I don't think he's a great actor. In certain situations his presence is good, but I don't think somebody will be shocked at his great acting. He will never be and he doesn't intend to be. He didn't aim to be a great actor; he's a personality. He comes there, you know, he can say two lines, I don't think he'll be....

Did you socialize outside of the confines of the studio and set?
Adam Greenberg: In his trailer I would come to check his makeup, etc, and when we flew to location sometimes I flew in his jet - he took me with him in his jet. I don't want to talk about it. I don't feel comfortable talking about it.

Were there any complications involving filming scenes for Collateral Damage?
Adam Greenberg: Acting wise, the interior was shot in the jungle there in Mexico, but whatever we could bring home onstage, we did it here. But still to make it look direct continuation from the jungle to here, he needed to make the acting. In acting he did very well. He has some scenes running with explosions all around, you never put the actor in some dangerous scenes, always do it with a double. In Eraser he's hanging on the plane on the wing and jumps with the parachute. We did that on the set. In the second Terminator, all the chases and everything's done, every time you have the actor doing such scenes you use protection, before the green screen was used in those days, it's done onstage.

Arnold's relish and fervor pertinent to making movies seemingly was apparent. Just how much did he enjoy making movies?
Adam Greenberg: Very much so. He got involved and had much interest all the way from throughout the shoot, so the end product will be the best possible. I remember on Eraser we had some problem with the director, and we had a meeting in his house here in Santa Monica on a weekend. We went to his house with one of the head of the studios of Warner Brothers to talk about the movie. We discussed what should be done and how it should be done. He was close to it right to the very end, to ensure he was very close to the project.

When somebody does very good, he expresses himself very well and congratulates you. I remember we did a scene in Collateral Damage or Eraser, I don't remember which film, we had fire in the building. It was in Collateral Damage, where he plays a fireman in New York. It's the very beginning. He appears as a fireman trying to put out the fire in the building. We did all this control fire on the stage, very small stage, but it was looking great and he came to me and said, "Adam, this is good." He stayed close to everything that was done paying attention and interest. Some actors don't have so much interest in what is done, or how it's done, but he does.

KEVIN POLLAK

Kevin Pollak is an actor, impressionist, comedian and game show host. He played Bobby Chicago in End of Days - directed by Peter Hyams. Some of the other movies which he has worked on include A Few Good Men, Casino and The Usual Suspects.

Kevin, you worked on End of Days with Arnold. Did you know him before working with him or was this the first time you both met?
Kevin Pollak: It was the first time I met him on the set. He was pretty wonderful, open and approachable completely, very gregarious and outgoing with all the crew members and cast members. He was very social and had an open-door policy on his trailer where you could stop by and say hello. He was very friendly.

Arnold said, "For me, it was very important, because I hadn't done a movie for a while, to come back with the right film. And so the right film, meaning a suspense thriller, something that is big, something that has a lot of production value on the screen, something that has a lot of stunts, a lot of action, a lot of suspense and all those things. Because here, I hadn't been on the screen for two years, so I wanted to come back with something really big with a big bang!" It was an unsuccessful and typical dark attempt to broaden his acting range. Although the Peter Hyams movie received mostly negative reviews, Arnold had, once again, pulled it off with strong international box office receipts, which ensured the movie wasn't a total disaster regardless of the critics being sentimental. With a budget between $80 and $100 million and taking in $211 million worldwide, financially it was successful because of strong international and DVD sales. Arnold pocketed $25 million for his efforts, matching what he received for Batman and Robin two years earlier.

You're a comedian yourself, with a great sense of humor. Was Arnold able to resonate with this?
Kevin Pollak: Well, there were moments, for example, when I would pass by his trailer - he had a separate trailer with workout equipment in

it - and I would pass by it and see him working out and I would make a point by showing him the big sloby cheesecake I was carrying back to my trailer from the catering service. I would make sure that he would see I was eating it whilst he was working out. There was playful nature like that between us.

But I will tell you one thing I did notice about him, not necessarily funny, but how political savvy he was, and not just about American politics. I remember being in a conversation with him one day on the set, and a crew member came up to us and said, "Hello, I have my cousin visiting me from Tel Aviv and she wanted to meet you." Arnold smiled and reached out to shake the hand of the relative from Tel Aviv, and he said, "Oh, yeah, Tel Aviv, you just had your mayor elected," and then proceeded to tell this person from Tel Aviv the three different candidates that were running and why the two lost that did lose and why the ones who won did in fact win. And I remember thinking: first of all, who else do I know that even knew there was a mayor raised in Tel Aviv last month? Second of all, of those people that I know that may know that, how many could name one candidate let alone all three? And have I ever met anyone who could then have told you why the candidates lost and what was wrong with their candidacy and their positions on certain issues that caused them to lose?

He wasn't showing off, he wasn't trying to impress this person from Tel Aviv; he was merely engaging them in a conversation as if he was talking about a local restaurant in Tel Aviv that he had once eaten at. It was a way of his relating to this person. And I found it beyond sort of impressive, rather this is clearly hugely important part of his life what may be a hobby to someone, which is to be politically aware on a world scale. It was beyond a hobby for him; it was a passion. It was one of the things I, of course, instantly remembered when I heard that he was running in California for the governor.

What would you say was the most memorable scene in the movie to work on with Arnold?
Kevin Pollak: Well, to work on it would be when we were actually in the helicopter flying over downtown Los Angeles with huge open-side doors that one can easily fall out of. This helicopter was making maneuvers, and Arnold was extremely comfortable while I was not. I remember he enjoyed my lack of being uncomfortable. I need to say that I'm not an action hero, and I made that clear to everyone when we were maneuvering a mile above downtown Los Angeles, so it seemed. Arnold has a tremendous sense of humor. So he thoroughly enjoyed the opportunity to suggest I was being a wimp and, you know, a girlie man.

What did you find the most intriguing aspect to Arnold?

Kevin Pollak: Just the generosity, you know. He had myself and my wife over to his house a few times, and we became friends. He was very open and generous and kind, that's what I remember. I think he was living in Brentwood.

Were there actually two endings filmed for End of Days?

Kevin Pollak: You're absolutely right, there were two endings. I don't remember the context. I kind of remember in one ending Arnold lives, and in the other he dies. That might be the difference between the two.

Gabriel Byrne was, of course, one of the co-stars. Was the filming schedule really hectic for the stars?

Kevin Pollak: Not hectic, it was a very big production so it was a long shoot - three or four months. But it was a very well-organized production. I knew Gabriel Byrne from working with him previously on The Usual Suspects, so we had a camaraderie and friendship before. So I enjoyed working with him again. It was great fun to be part of such a giant-budget action movie with Arnold, and he really was a tremendous host on the set. Like I said, he made everyone feel like they were part of the winning team. He has a great sense of competitiveness in him, which comes from being an athlete. He would always try to engage people in a game of chess in his trailer, and, you know, like I said, doing the action sequences with him, I just remember being teased a lot. I either couldn't run fast enough, or climb fast enough, even the way I held a gun, he would make fun of me. So he had quite a sense of humor during the shooting.

How did you perceive Arnold off set, you mentioned you went to his house a number of times for dinners?

Kevin Pollak: I would say he was a classic sort of patriotic character. They have several children, also with the gatherings at his house there would be a lot of children and families. To some people, he seems like a patriotic character, Father Christmas, depending on your perspective there's a bigness about him that goes beyond his physical attributes in sort of a gregarious personality. Again, it wasn't a surprise for me when I heard he was running for governor, because he's a leader by nature. To me, to be honest, it was also a sense of being in the presence of almost a superhero like superman. He's the closest thing to a live action superhero that I've ever experienced quite frankly that didn't seem like an actor but more like the real thing. And I think having been an award-winning and widely celebrated athlete himself, this had something to do with that. Also, being a self-made businessman. He made his fortune as an athlete long before he was in the movies, and he was buying and selling real estate. And he's a great businessman, way before he got into the movie business. All of that was wildly impressive and inspiring to be around.

In your opinion, do you feel he was able to ameliorate as an actor, because he was more like a John Wayne and Clint Eastwood playing one type of a character?

Kevin Pollak: Well, I think you just did. He always has been pretty much one dimensional like a John Wayne, where John Wayne eventually won an Academy Award for True Grit, I'm not sure Arnold's going to. He represented I think a time and a certain genre of film that appears to be a young man's game, although Stallone suggested otherwise with The Expendables.

Do you feel age was a factor when he made End of Days, and some of the movies at the time which weren't as successful as some of his other movies which he did, was this the decline of Arnold?

Kevin Pollak: You could make that argument, but I would argue that there's another flow. If you're that big of a movie star, there's always an even flow throughout the course during one's career, be it a Bruce Willis, a Stallone. If you get to that level, it's just a natural order of things that there will be highs and lows from decade to decade. You could say, well, he had a heyday in the '80s and early '90s, because there was a certain sensibility and to that kind of film. Can he reinvent himself yet again? I have no question in my mind that he is a one-of-a-kind personality on screen, and in the right vehicle....

After working with Arnold in End of Days, did you see him and keep in touch?

Kevin Pollak: Yes. He invited me to a couple of dinners at their home. Also, I have been invited to a couple of fundraisers for various causes, which he was helping with. Also, he called me when he became governor to say hello and to let me know how much he was enjoying the job. I'd say we've stayed in contact over the years.

What are some of the charities he was and is involved in?

Kevin Pollak: I'm not as quite as comfortable in talking about his charitable efforts. I feel I wouldn't do them justice in describing them in detail, because I know they're very, very important to him and without all the details in front of me I'd do it a disservice.

What would you say was Arnold's ultimate attribute on a professional level?

Kevin Pollak: From a professional level, I think he's a one-of-a-kind unique personality, and in the right vehicle I think people will always come and see a film starring Arnold Schwarzenegger. Because he represents a certain feeling that premade in most people, not only are you coming to have a good time, but there's going to be a sense of raw energy and action that he promises to deliver. And I think that's why when you mentioned some of the films that didn't do well, I think it was just a period that the consensus of the audience had drifted from that style, the same way a Western is a genre that comes and goes. Now you have the Coen brothers doing True Grit, and getting all these awards and nominations, when some people might have made the suggestions that the Western had gone on the waste side. I think the same is the truth. And I mentioned Stallone bringing back tremendous success with an action film with The Expendables. It was just a tremendous joy and a thrill to work with Arnold on End of Days. I would be equally if not more thrilled if I had another opportunity.

After End of Days, Arnold next rolled on to star in another science fiction The 6th Day. He plays Adam Gibson, a helicopter pilot who co-owns a tourist business, who comes to the realization that his life has been stolen from him when a clone has been created by a malevolent corporation. Adam Gibson is caught up in a conspiracy to provide replacement clones to wealthy individuals, who control the corporate cloning technologies. This movie attempts, within its action movie framework, to be a thoughtful examination of the cloning issue. It necessitated an approach different than the typical Arnold Schwarzenegger epic. The director Roger Spottiswodde, who directed the James Bond flick Tomorrow Never Dies, said, "Arnie was great playing against himself. He's great, so long as he knows you're going to have to do it (takes) hundred times he's happy - and I do things hundred and twenty times."

Arnold felt it was challenging being responsible for the two characters - Adam Gibson and the clone. He admitted the pressure is always on with every movie that you do. He also expressed that it was quite important they made sure they had a movie that gave you the subject of cloning, making it an issue. But also not dwelling on it too much, because they didn't want to make a serious movie about cloning, so people will be interested in touching the subject and the drama when they come home and see themselves.

"It's more inner strength than physical strength, because you're not really doing anything that heroic physically," Arnold expressed. "It's more having the guts and brains to figure out a way of how can we, instead of fighting each other, get together and work toward a common goal, which is to get our family back. In either case, I am my clone and think that it's my family, but it doesn't matter. We've got to save the family." He says it took intelligence and inner strength to do this. It was playing much more on that, even though there was a lot of action there. Again, Arnold was able to command $25 million for this movie, which, although, made its money back it was considered a box office flop.

KRISTANNA LOKEN

Kristanna Loken, born October 8, 1979, in New York, is of Norwegian decent. She is best known for her role as the cyborg T-X in Terminator 3. A former fashion model, she also started in Mortal Combat: Conquest in 1998. Loken continues to act and ventured into producing.

Terminator 3 director said you had the physicality required to take on Arnold in this movie. When did you meet Arnold?

Kristanna Loken: I believe it was on the set for the first time. I think there was a large and long series of auditions. I probably had to do different auditions before I actually got the job. I think it was my physicality, like Jonathan Mustow said. I'm tall, I'm 5ft 11, and I've always been athletic and I love the outdoors. Then from there on, I did the extensive training and I actually put on 15 pounds of muscle mass, you know, getting bigger and stronger for the role. I had always been a fan of Robert Patrick's performance in Terminator 2, and he was a real inspiration to me when I was doing all the auditions.

What did you and the cast and crew see in Arnold, which caught your imagination on the set working with him?

Kristanna Loken: Well, I think one of the...couple of things. Definitely, I learned a lot by working with him and watching him do the action, because he's such a pro at it. So by watching him I was able to glean a lot of experience. And also he's very, very gracious with his fans. He's very giving. And I think that's been one of the big things to his success. Because the fans are the ones that keep you going and go to see your movie. So, I could tell that it was very important to him.

Any intricate and sophisticated scenes you and Arnold filmed which come to mind which required meticulous planning?

Kristanna Loken: Sure. I would say the final action sequence in the bathroom, and then when we fell through the floor. That was really interesting to shoot. Because Jonathan Mustow really wanted us to be like two bulldozers going at it, so it was just pure power and strength. I thought that was a very creative approach and a new approach for the characters. The bathroom sequence was quite something. I mean, obviously, there are a lot of CGI shots in there, going through the different things in the bathroom and throwing me into the toilet and various things, it was quite creative.

One of the biggest challenges in this film for Arnold was fighting a woman. Loken was in great shape. "What was challenging about doing it with a woman were the fight scenes," Arnold recalled. "I had no training of how you grab a woman, how you throw her against a wall, how hard can you really pick her up and throw her, how hard can you hit her? I had to rely on Kristanna to tell me that you can go harder, you can grab me rougher, you can imagine a guy standing in front of you. It took five or six takes to get up to that level of rough handling her, because I felt uncomfortable with it. She was a great team player." Loken didn't mind taking some bruises and pains to make the fight scenes as realistic as possible. She put in a lot of energy and effort into making the scenes visually believable. She trained well with the stunt coordinators and proved she could handle the pressure.

Regarding Arnold's collaboration with the new director, what input did Arnold have and did he and you make any suggestions to the director?
Kristanna Loken: Frankly, their relationship - from what I can ascertain - they got along quite well. But I'm not really that privy of the ins and outs of what was said between them. But from what I could see, they collaborated very nicely together. As far as I'm concerned, for me Jonathan had a lot of faith in the choices I was making for the character, as far as my movements, and he really gave me free reign to do and create what I wanted and what I felt was appropriate for the character. So, he would usually say, "Go on, go ahead and do your thing." He really had a great believe in me.

Can you tell me some of the locations used for Terminator 3?
Kristanna Loken: We shot the movie in Los Angeles, the set was built on a soundstage. Part of the huge chase scene with the crane, they filmed part of that on an airplane hanger. And they really demolished it, they really destroyed it. So a lot of what you see when those buildings are coming down, that really happened.

Was Arnold in any way intimidating to work with?
Kristanna Loken: He was a very professional person overall, I would say. He definitely was also a practical joker on the set. He likes to make practical jokes, which were fun and funny. He really enjoyed and loved to play chess.

And with his stand-in between the scenes, he would play chess. I didn't really find him intimidating in that sense. Of course, I have a lot of respect for him as a fellow human being and with all his success. I think that I had done a lot of training and was ready for the job, so I gave it my all.

Another co-star of Terminator 3 was Claire Danes, who fondly remembers the thoughtful side to Arnold's personality. During the course of the shooting, the actresses' boyfriend's nephew had a Bar Mitzvah and she was invited to attend. Danes thought it would be cool if Arnold could do a short video recording for the young boy saying happy birthday and congratulations on becoming a man. Arnold was very cooperative and put together, in the words of Danes, "the most awesome Bar Mitzvah" video. Danes also recalls Arnold would also do a gag where he would put his thumb in his mouth and blow his muscles up. He would say, "Let me pump my muscles up," which Danes found impressive and thought it was really an amazing feat.

When asked if Arnold had a sensitive side, she said, "Yeah. Well, you know, he does surprisingly enough. He would give me a lot of relationship advise, some of it which was quite unsolicited, but he was concerned. Because, you know, I'm very connected to my boyfriend. I'm very much in love with him. He travels, he's a musician so he used to go on tours. So I get a little bit down. I get a little bit depressed and he observed this - he's perceptive. He said, 'Claire, what's wrong, what's going on?' I said, 'I don't know, I don't know.' He said, 'He's been away again?' I said, 'Yes.' He said, 'You're too co-dependent?' He would round me up, he could be a little pro-active. But I realize now, you know, his logic was quite... because one partner can't be more co-dependent than the other partner. You know, by definition that's why the 'co' exists before the 'dependent'." Danes says she really got along with Arnold and is a big fan.

Arnold grew up in a small village in Europe; you grew up on a farm in the New York area. You both had this in common. Did you exchange stories pertinent to growing up?
Kristanna Loken: Not really. He didn't really talk much about his past. I did, of course, spend some time with his family, his wife and his children, especially when we were doing the press tour all over the world. They came along for that. So it was nice to meet his family. But he didn't speak much about where he grew up.

What were the most challenging aspects whilst working with Arnold on the movie?

Kristanna Loken: I would say definitely keeping up the very strict workouts routine and diet that I had set for the film. It was tailor-made for me. I worked with a nutritionist and it was very, very specific. Including the three, four months prior to the shooting, then the eight months of actually shooting. It was a good year of having a very, very strict diet and workout regime. So it was a good physical challenge.

Arnold went back to the drawing board, getting himself in peak physical condition for his third outing as the Terminator. The star said, "It was very important to really prove that it is the same Terminator. So therefore my body, I had to build up again to the size the way I was in the first Terminator and the second Terminator. Because, again, the Terminator arrives from the future to the present totally naked! So I, again, went back to the gym, worked out for two hours, two-and-half hours every day, to really show I was in the same kind of shape as I was twenty years ago and ten years ago."

He had to train much harder on this movie, normally there's no real need to be in this kind of shape. He started training very intensely to bring the body back to where it was when he did the last Terminator movie. "That was a key thing for me - you have to get into that kind of shape so it's more believable that it's the same character," Arnold continues. "It's difficult; you have to have a lot of will and a lot of motivation." As in previous instalments, Arnold has a nude scene. After so many years away from the franchise, his feelings on the scene were, "Anytime you take your clothes off and do a nude scene, it's embarrassing.... That's why it was important to train hard. I went into the mode of training as if I'm preparing for a competition again." Arnold also gave co-star Nick Stahl an invitation to his gym, telling him he could use his 20-foot gym trailer. But after one look at the gym equipment, Stahl declined the generous offer and went outside for a cigarette instead.

You have said he'd open up to me in the makeup trailer, in terms of conversing, any conversations you both would engage in?
Kristanna Loken: Not that I can think of, on top of my head. Mainly, like I said, he liked to do practical jokes and he was very friendly. He enjoyed his cigars. He's a real cigar aficionado. All round he was a very relaxed and a likeable person.

When you did the press and the publicity around the world, where did you go with Arnold to publicize the movie?

Kristanna Loken: We went all over the world. I mean, we went to Tokyo, we were all over Europe, in the UK and numerous countries. We publicized on the Formula One race cars outside of London. We had a big premiere of the film in Cannes during the festival. And we had several premieres, like I said, all over Europe and Asia. It was really an incredible experience.

The Terminator trilogy made Arnold a household name. By the time he filmed Terminator 3, he was a lot older. Does the third Terminator surpass the second one, in your opinion?

Kristanna Loken: Oh, for sure. I think the Terminator franchise is huge and continues today. I mean, people love the Terminator franchise around the world. I mean, I constantly get fan mail from every corner of the world about Terminator. They have the kind of mystique and there's a real sense of the history and the complexity of the characters. And I think it will live on in people's memories for a long time to come. Well, of course, my opinion is a little biased. I was in Terminator 3. I think he got himself in incredible shape for this film. Obviously, when I worked with him we had a great cast. I really enjoyed working with Nick Stahl and Claire Danes - I've always been a fan of hers. I ironically ran into Nick on a plane. I hadn't seen him, I don't think, since we did the film and he was sitting right in front of me, which was ironic. I think Arnold has his muscle memory from all the years of bodybuilding and training. Of course, it's much easier for someone who's done all that work already to get into shape than a random person off the street. I thought he really looked amazing.

What was the most memorable moment?

Kristanna Loken: I think one of the things which stays with me is we had a huge premiere for the film in Tokyo in Japan. I just remember him complimenting me on the job well done, which was really nice to hear coming from him. He said I'd have a great career and this was the beginning of launching it in a very large global way. I think it was the biggest premiere we had. It was huge, they had it in a large stadium that was filled with capacity with people. I remember that they had a couple Special Olympics children there, who came up on the stage with us, because Arnold's a big advocate for the Special Olympics. The fans were crazy outside. I'll never forget that experience, it was like, you know, being a rock star onstage. It was huge.

DOLPH LUNDGREN

The Swedish-born actor Dolph Lundgren is perhaps best known for his breakout role in Rocky 4 in 1985. He also co-starred with Jean Claude Van Damme in Universal Soldier and became one of the top action stars. He also worked with Stallone in The Expendables.

Arnold made a cameo appearance in a movie which you co-starred in, The Expendables. When did your paths actually cross?

Dolph Lundgren: I met him actually on the set of the second Conan movie. I was a karate fighter, and I hadn't done movies yet. I was going out with Grace Jones, who was in the movie with Arnold. I met him on the set of that movie and we got on well. Basically, he just looked at me as an athlete, you know, a young Swedish kid who was this karate fighter. Then when I was doing the Rocky picture, I remember Grace had a party at my house that I was renting. I was in the guesthouse trying to get some sleep, because I had to get up and train with Sly in the morning. There was a knock on the door at midnight. I woke up and I said, "Who is it?" And I heard this voice outside, "It's your trainer. I'm here to check you out." It was Arnold. He's a funny guy and we got on well. I didn't do any scenes with him in The Expendables, but maybe in the sequel.

That's interesting, that you had met Arnold on the set of the second Conan movie. Do you think Arnold, the epitome of bodybuilding, was able to have an impact on Hollywood making the transition from a sportsman to the movie screen?

Dolph Lundgren: Yeah, huge impact! I think I moved here (California) before he got very famous. But yes, he did. I think it was Pumping Iron, the documentary that he was in which brought bodybuilding into the mainstream, and, of course, he was the figurehead of the whole movement. Bodybuilding in the '80s became a household name, and he was the figurehead of it. So, sure, he is, obviously, the most famous bodybuilder ever and probably will be forever. I think it will be hard to beat him. He was the first guy in the '80s who came from a sports background and made it in Hollywood. Then there's a bunch of guys. I mean, there's him, Van Damme, Seagal, myself, to some extent Chuck Norris. For some reason, in the '80s you had real athletes who became action stars and actors. And, of course, he's done extremely well in other walks of life; he became the governor so forth. He had a huge impact on bodybuilding. Of course, he's a truly charismatic bodybuilder. I guess the guy before him was Steve Reeves in the '50s, who did the same thing. Arnold is certainly one of the greats of both bodybuilding and cinema.

Anything interesting on the set of the second Conan movie, did you converse with him about training?

Dolph Lundgren: I was not doing a lot of lifting in those days; I was just fighting. I was actually thinking of becoming a professional fighter. A boxer actually, as well, so I was training boxing and also doing a lot of running, things of that nature. He was doing more weights. But, I mean, he was hanging out with his buddies, Sven Thorsen, who's a Danish powerlifter, and a couple of other guys. I think we just got along. Like I said, he looked at me as an athlete. But I remember watching him, and I was impressed with his physique and by his personality and charisma. I met Maria Shriver on the set, who was visiting, who became his wife, obviously, later. That was a good experience.

Did you both ever venture to work together or was this something which was never brought up?

Dolph Lundgren: I don't think we've been...I think for The Running Man I was up for a role. That was one of the films which he made. I think I was up for a role on that. Apart from that, no, we really haven't. He's kind of a step ahead of me all the time. Basically, by the time I appeared in big movies, he was already thinking about his political career. So, no, we haven't. But maybe, like I said, in the next Expendables perhaps.

Would I be right in saying you also were asked to pursue politics in your native country Sweden?

Dolph Lundgren: Yes. In Sweden they asked me to run for office for parliament for MP - the Green Party. It was a very flattering offer, but I couldn't do it because it would mean moving back to Sweden and I don't feel like doing that right now. But in the future I will do something like that, who knows.

Being in the Hollywood fraternity working with action stars, how would you define Arnold as an action hero? You came from the same generation - 1980s and 1990s. And you both came from Europe to find fame and fortune in America.

Dolph Lundgren: I think he's very charismatic, he's a very smart man, a businessman. He kind of was very, very clever in how he pursued his career. He does have a lot of charisma and charm as a person and he's done very, very well, better than most of the other people in the business. So I think he's certainly somebody that everyone could look up to as a role model when it comes to pursuing a career in this town.

Arnold had a cameo in The Expendables, will he be appearing in the sequel and how much of a part will he play in the sequel?
Dolph Lundgren: I think so. I haven't read the script yet. I haven't seen the script, so I don't know what his role is and how much he'll be in it. I assume he'll be in it quite a bit, and he's good friends with Sly now. So I'm sure they will both be fun to work with together.

The Expendables was the first time Arnold would be appearing on-screen with his friend and former competitor Sylvester Stallone, as well as former Planet Hollywood face Bruce Willis. Arnold and Willis appear for a very short time on-screen in their cameo roles. Stallone remarked, "Arnold was relentless, like this perfect machine. People asked if I could have played the Terminator. Are you kidding? Not a chance. I never could have played the Terminator." Stallone says he saw Arnold's eyes light up; it's one thing to run a state, but another thing to get back to what you're really known for, he added.

Arnold firmly believed he had the capacity to making good the laconic promise of "I'll be back" that he toned ominously in his custom-filled part in the past, which still resonates with fans and the public. He took a day off to film a scene for the film. The governor assured Stallone he'd do the role, making sure it wouldn't conflict with his duties as a governor. When the trio of iconic Hollywood stars arrived on the set, they all greeted each other with anticipation and excitement.

Did you extensively socialize with Arnold over the years, and did you get to know him well?
Dolph Lundgren: I'm close to Stallone I guess as a person. I spent more time with him than with Arnold. Arnold, we're just acquaintances, so we really didn't get into more personal conversations. He's a funny guy, basically. I remember at the opening of The Expendables, they pulled me out of my seat. We were flying out getting on a plane for Europe. Some guy pulled me through the Mann's Chinese Theater here in Hollywood, and I felt a big hand grab me. I looked up and there was the Governator with his wife, and he's going, "Congratulations, you look great." He takes everything with sense of humor, he doesn't take it all seriously, which I think is something you can learn from Arnold. He has this sense of humor about life and about business, which is important sometimes, you know.

PETER BART

A journalist and film producer, Peter Bart is widely known for his lengthy tenure as the editor of the entertainment-trade magazine Variety, for which he held the position for twenty years. He also worked at Paramount Pictures as an executive and Metro-Goldwyn-Mayer.

When did Arnold become prominent in the Hollywood community for the major media to take serious notice?

Peter Bart: It was quite some time ago, I don't have a list of the dates of his released pictures in front of me, but he has been a star a long time. Last Action Hero, which was done in the early '90s, was the beginning of not his downfall but it was his biggest flop. But he's been around for generations. He was also brilliant at self-promotion. I remember running into him in the '80s at the Cannes Film Festival, and he took me to the side and he was very boastful. He said, "I'm going to do fifty interviews." Some stars complain; they don't want to work as hard. He said, "I can just churn out the interviews. You watch, I'll do fifty." You know, he was just absolute frenzy of promotion and he loved doing it. I always felt that he was very much a very sharp marketing person. Now in Hollywood, everyone talks about brands. Long before everyone talked about brands, Arnold had an idea who his brand was and what it was. When you really think about it, he was a pioneer in managing his own brand.

His competitor was Sylvester Stallone in the 1980s and 1990s. Any intriguing stories when both stars went head-to-head to compete and churning out blockbusters?

Peter Bart: Yes. Stallone was amazing in that first he had the Rocky franchise, then the Rambo franchise. He was remarkable in being able to reinvent himself in different franchises, whilst Arnold was never quite that lucky or smart, he was always the "Arnold" franchise. And he had sort of, every picture he started from scratch, it wasn't, like, he had a series of sequels. I never discussed it with him, but I expect he was jealous of the fact he never could get into the sequels business.

You interviewed Arnold on numerous occasions. What was he like to interview?

Peter Bart: Yes, many times. The thing about Arnold is he was always very accessible, very good-natured. He was very anxious to sustain a good relationship with the press, and if you were fair and quoted him right then he was very good. I never like to do interviews on movie sets, because I always found that there's a lot of trouble getting there, and then you have to wait there a long time for the set ups. I always preferred to talk to people when they are not working. So I guess most of the interviews with Arnold were at the Cannes Festival, or when he was promoting a picture. We would be in a restaurant or something like that. I remember one time, he owned a restaurant in Los Angeles, Santa Monica. Sometimes I would go out to that restaurant, which I rather liked, actually, called Schatzi. It was very congenial, had German food which I happen to like, good beer which I happen to love, and it would be fun to go out there. So, you could talk to him and he could smoke his cigar.

What was one of the most intriguing interviews you did?
Peter Bart: Well, I think it was two or three years ago. I began to feel like talking to him about political events that I felt more and more he was caught in the middle of, because he really was a Republican. On the other hand, his position on many issues was not a conservative one. I mean, he understood the danger of global warming and he was very much in favor of healthcare. So in many ways, he was more liberal than he was conservative. And that's why I think he became isolated in California, because the Republican Party is so far to the right that he was just not conforming to their policies.

What are your sentiments pertaining to why Last Action Hero was a flop?
Peter Bart: I felt the basic concept of the movie was more like a comic book. It was before the era of the video games. But it was like a video game in a way, and I just didn't think.... I felt it was the wrong concept. I visited the set, not to interview him, but my friend Peter Gruber was the CEO of the company at that time, so I went and had lunch with Peter Gruber and then I walked over to the set. I just felt something that just struck me of simply being wrong. I mean, conceptually wrong. What happened was, the studio ended up nervous about the picture and decided to spend more money on marketing than less. They shouldn't have doubled it. It lost money. It was better overseas than in the US. The critics hated it, the audience just didn't buy it and it was really an embarrassing picture.

When you hired Arnold for a movie, as Columbia Pictures did for Last Action Hero, the industry's working assumption was that you couldn't miss $75 or $80 million at the box office, one Sony executive said.

Furthermore, the same amount would flow in from overseas receipts and similar scale from the video market at the time. For Mark Canton - one of the executives - who convinced Arnold to take on the self-spoofing role of Jack Slater, the movie became the costliest of blunders. In 1993, the Heidi Fleiss scandal had broken; some executives linked with the film were embroiled in one of the biggest controversies to hit Hollywood. This was another stigma which the company had to contend to.

When Arnold was in politics, he said, "Maria was always by my side, and always was participating in all decision-making, in my movie career, in my business and now also in politics. We are partners. That's why I got married, to have a great partner." Maria played an integral role in advising her husband pertaining to decision-making when it came to his movie career, often accompanying Arnold to meetings. She would often steer him toward what she felt was right, whether it was about taking certain roles or reading scripts, and giving her criticism. Often when they attended rough cuts of a movie, Maria would contentiously make notes and hand a long list of comments to the director. Last Action Hero seemingly alienated Schwarzenegger's action fans. With its violence softened to ensure a PG-13 rating, the film, said a source close to the production, "Landed between the cracks too old for kids and too young for adults." The best thing about Arnold was he was tough and mean, the source revealed. "The studio bent over backward to sanitize the movie, and they took out its primary appeal."

According to Arnold himself, Last Action Hero script was one of the best scripts he'd ever read. "It had a lot of comedy in it. It was bigger than life. It had two worlds in it: the world of reality and the world of an action hero inside the movie," says Arnold. The imperative thing for Arnold in Last Action Hero was to show the two worlds. It cost the studio around $120 million to make and market this disastrous film. For Columbia Pictures, reaching even the minimum threshold looked dicey. However, the studio was able to recoup the money coming close to breaking even. When it opened up, Steven Spielberg's Jurassic Park had also been released and was the big blockbuster which took over $500 million worldwide. And even Stallone's Cliffhanger overtook Last Action Hero.

Generally, Arnold's movies did really well overseas, particularly in Europe. That became an integral part of his success: the European marketplace.

Peter Bart: That's true. Just like Tom Cruise really worked very hard around the world to promote his pictures, so did Arnold. And it paid off. Arnold had such a good sense of humor, he made some good comedies in his later years and he enjoyed those. He was a very Austrian person, he does like to kid around. He loved making comedies to show he could do other things beside kill people. I'll give you an example of an actor who really grew as a person and became more thoughtful and much more sophisticated. There are some actors who shrink with celebrity and they isolate themselves. Arnold, I always respected him because he kept growing, read a lot and didn't become isolated, he was a very social person.

How was Arnold's relationship with his agents, who are the key people making decisions for their clients?
Peter Bart: I honestly do not know. I always had the feeling he had a strong say in what he was doing, and that he wasn't controlled by an agent. But I don't know. I wasn't that privy to his business life.

The decline at the box office came mid- and late 1990s with such movies End of Days and Collateral Damage. It's open to conjecture if a combination of age, fading novelty and diminishing prudence was the cause of this.
Peter Bart: Yes, exactly. That most definitely marked the decline. But he was also not lucky, he had a hot streak and he had a cold streak. I think he is a totally driven person. Very few people I've met are totally focused and ambitious like him, every career step was really life or death to him. I mean, he was not somebody who fooled around, and for that kind of ambition you have to respect and also can be intimidating.

Did you go to the premieres?
Peter Bart: You know, I hate to say but I don't like premieres. Because movies are supposed to start at eight o' clock, but you sit around and barely start at 9.15. I hate going to premieres. At parties he's always very jovial, always shaking hands, he doesn't hide in the corner like some stars; he's out there chatting. There's an extra version to him.

Can you tell me about your background in the movie business, were you an executive at Paramount?
Peter Bart: Yes, I was. I spent seventeen years as an executive at Paramount and MGM, and then more and more productions.

What made him succeed and become a major star when he wasn't really the best actor in the pure sense of the word?
Peter Bart: He could never lose his accent. I was talking to Mark Wahlberg one time, and he has a big Boston accent and he got trained to lose the accent. Arnold still has his Austrian accent. He never lost it.

ALEX BEN BLOCK

Alex Ben Block is the award-winning Hollywood entertainment industry veteran journalist, show business historian and author. A senior editor for The Hollywood Reporter, he has also been the associate editor of Forbes magazine and an editor at the Los Angeles Herald Examiner.

You're a veteran Hollywood journalist, who interviewed the icon Bruce Lee when he was at the brink of achieving global fame. Do you feel Bruce and Arnold, who both developed a physical persona, which countless men could resonate with, shared a commonality in a sense they had to overcome certain obstacles in achieving the American Dream?

Alex Ben Block: Well, Arnold Schwarzenegger, of course, took a different path to Bruce Lee; he was a bodybuilder and got great recognition in that area. When he came to the United States, he was already known in certain circles among the bodybuilders and his first movie roles and documentaries and movies related to his roles as a bodybuilder. He showed a great ability in business and building himself in business early on and started creating companies and selling products relating to his bodybuilding at first. So he got recognition that way. Then, of course, because of his huge physique he was cast in the early sandal flicks - the Conan movies so forth - that gave him a ticket to become known. And despite the accent and the unusual physique, he found unlikely stardom.

You have to remember, what happened to Bruce Lee was, he had lived in America and he was born in America, then he came back after his eighteenth birthday and lived many years here. He studied martial arts and went to the University of Washington. Then when he finally came to Los Angeles and wanted to be an actor, he found great prejudice. He was told he was too "Chinese" to play Chinese. There were no roles for Chinese, Asians and minorities in those days. So he had to go back to Hong Kong and make a couple of movies, which became successful. And after Enter the Dragon, he was accepted outside of China. And tragically, of course, he died before he could capitalize on that success. Whereas Arnold has lived a long life, and has been able to make very different kinds of movies, building his businesses and becoming very wealthy and then move into politics.

So they took very different roads. What I remember about the interview I did with Bruce Lee is that I was surprised he was so smart about philosophy, and how intelligent he was about what was going on in the world. How self-aware he was about what he had to do to have a career, and how charming he was. But most of all that he wasn't just about muscle, he wasn't just about money. He was about putting together philosophy and ideas along with culture in the muscle and all of that to create a very unique persona, and to become the first Asian American movie star to breakthrough on a global basis.

How much impact and contribution did Arnold's PR have in his meteoric rise to fame? Was it easy to have access to him through Charlotte Parker, who was his publicist? She ensured that the media coverage of her client was tightly controlled and was able to utilize the ever-intertwining tendrils of media conglomeration to her client's benefit.

Alex Ben Block: I know Charlotte very well and I actually first met Arnold through Charlotte. When he had something to promote, when he had a movie or product or he was in a business, he got attention. The bigger the movie, the more attention he got. So, the first problem was to get him interviews, then the problem was to not get interviews, because the job of the publicist becomes to control the gate more than it is to try get people to come in once you become a big star. Arnold is a very personable guy. He speaks very well, he's very boisterous in public. He's very animated, and he's got a way of being very charismatic in front of the crowd.

So, I think maybe very early on it was a problem to get publicity, even then he got publicity because of his relationship with the bodybuilding magazines; he got a lot of publicity in that area. So he wasn't an unknown quantity. Then once he became a hit in the movies, it wasn't just Charlotte Parker that was helping him, he had De Laurentiis' PR department and the studio PR department and other staff who worked on his behalf. When he started appearing with stars, he was part of the overall junket of the publicity machines of his movies. He did a lot of publicity. In the end, both the movies had to deliver and Arnold had to have the personality to be interesting enough so that they want to interview him - and he had both. So, it was quite natural for him to get more and more publicity.

Sylvester Stallone was a big box office, and there seemed to be an element of competitiveness going on. How did Hollywood perceive this?

Alex Ben Block: Well, Sylvester Stallone, again, took a very different path. In 1976, it was Rocky which became a big hit and an Academy Award nominee winner. He had a very different career and path. There is room in Hollywood and the world for more than one action star at a time. So, while they were competitors, each had plenty of their own things to do. Stallone's problem was very different. Stallone's problem became: how to manage his fame and how to choose the right vehicles, having to use his talent not just as an actor but as a producer, director and writer and an entrepreneur to further his career. He made some good choices and he made some not very good choices - that hurt him a lot more than any competitor ever hurt him. Stallone also played a lot of different kind of roles, he tried comedies, he tried dramas as well as action roles. He wasn't as successful in those as he became known for his Rambos, but he tried different things. I think maybe there was some professional jealousy, but that I'm not really aware of, but it really was more each of them had their own path. You can have two successful action movies in the same summer - there's room for everybody.

Arnold and Stallone, along with Bruce Willis, went on to pursue business ventures together and became the faces of Planet Hollywood, which was one of the most celebrated business venture of Arnold's career. Can you tell me more about the Planet Hollywood venture, please?
Alex Ben Block: Well, there was a man who was an entrepreneur who brought these stars in together to be investors. First, it looked like a very good idea. They could use the memorabilia and things to open the restaurant, and it worked. Most of the restaurants were opened in places where there were tourists. So in the beginning the restaurants were very successful, because of the association with famous people, and they were created to be a fun place. The restaurants failed not because of the celebrities, they failed because the food wasn't good and the service wasn't great. And after a while, it wasn't just enough to have just tourists; you also had to have repeat customers from the community. These restaurants offered greasy food with high prices. And if you've seen the memorabilia on the wall and gone a few times, the lure disappears very quickly. So, I think the celebrities were mostly just investors; they didn't play any big role beyond showing up and doing PR. It was a flawed concept. Eventually, the restaurant has to be a good restaurant, but they weren't very good restaurants.

Planet Hollywood was originated by Keith Barish, an entrepreneur and film producer (The Fugitive, The Running Man), and was the brainchild of Robert Earl, former president and CEO of Hard Rock Cafe and an entrepreneur, who also owns Everton Football Club. One of the global investors included Saudi Arabia's Prince Alwaleed Bin Talal. The first branch opened in New York in October 22, 1991. Arnold, along with fellow stars Sylvester Stallone, Bruce Willis and Demi Moore, were the public faces of Planet Hollywood. Stallone expressed, "Planet Hollywood's a success really because it's pure escapism. It's eating wonderful food around extraordinary surroundings, it's like being in a museum , but a light-hearted one, and I recommend it for everyone."

Arnold claimed he was involved in everything from finding sites, choosing what memorabilia would be displayed to picking the next town openings, and even the financial side of scale: how much money would be spent. According to Arnold, the stars were involved together in every business decision. But Jackie Stallone exclaimed "it was a lot of crap", as far as the stars claiming they had a much deeper role than being primarily responsible for showing up for publicity. She asserted, "They're getting paid for the use of their names, they're front-men. Maybe they put a dollar in."

When the London branch of Planet Hollywood opened in May 1993, in Piccadilly, Arnold, Stallone and Willis, as well as an array of celebrities, were present on the opening night. Arnold, always the ebullient star, said, "So many people out there, it was amazing. I mean, we have done a lot of openings before and we have seen a lot of people before when we go to the Academy Awards, or when we go to the movie premiere openings, or Planet Hollywood openings, but this was absolutely amazing. It was much bigger than ever before."

At the London opening, Arnold enthusiastically said, "Originally, when we started out with the Planet Hollywood concept, we didn't really know that we had such a great winning formula together - you never know when you start any business. And when we opened the Planet Hollywood in New York, we were hoping that we would have a thousand people through the restaurant eating and drinking and having a good time, buying, you know, memorabilia and t-shirts and hats, Planet Hollywood hats and jackets and all these things. But we ended up having now between two and four thousand people going through a day, so it's quite different than we thought. And it became a monster business, so we decided to open up in different places. And those places become successful. And now we are doing it overseas for the first time like London. I think that the future will be in Paris, in Tokyo, Moscow, Egypt somewhere. I mean, literally to open them up all over the world. Because I think that people are fascinated with Hollywood and love the idea of sitting around and seeing movie memorabilia and seeing stars coming in, if it's local stars or international Hollywood stars and so on."

The formidable restaurateur Peter Morton and Hard Rock Cafe investors in Chicago and Orange County filed lawsuits against Planet Hollywood alleging that it ripped off the rock "n" roll concept of Hard Rock and converted it into a movie theme. Despite success and backing from mega stars, who received stock in return for promotional work, and the ambience and glittering facade, the chain suffered from declining sales at many locations. Merchandize and t-shirt sales, which accounted for quarter of revenue, also fell.

In January 2000, merely four days after the troubled chain emerged from bankruptcy with new investors, Arnold broached he was terminating his five-year contract with Planet Hollywood. He said, "It was lots of fun and very challenging to come up with and develop the celebrity restaurant concept on an international level. Of course I'm disappointed that the company did not continue with the success I had expected and hoped for." He said he wished Planet Hollywood well and that now he was going to focus on new American and global business ventures as well as his movie career. The Orlando-based company, which at the time had almost eighty branches worldwide, had assets of $392.2 million and debts of $359.1 million.

Can you tell me about some of the Arnold movie premieres you attended?
Alex Ben Block: I attended premieres of his movies in the US and in Cannes. I attended Twins premiere, which starred him and Danny DeVito. In fact, by then they were already big stars and they had a big studio behind them. In that case, they had a big production team behind them as well. Like I said, Arnold is very good with crowds. I was once at a movie exhibitor's convention and he came and spoke to the group. He was very well received, because he told jokes and he related to what they were doing. He was actually very fun to watch up on the platform speaking to everybody. So, for the same reasons he became a successful politician. He's very people oriented, very charismatic, very magnetic when he's in a crowd. So it was a natural thing for him when he had a premiere or a public event, the media use his strong personality and his self-confidence. When he had something interesting, people would be interested to further his career, and he did this very well.

Let me say, I don't have any great friendship with Arnold Schwarzenegger. I met him on a professional capacity over the years, and I've observed him at a distance. I live in the state where he was the governor. I think he's successful, as a young man he had the hunger to become a bodybuilder, to be self-disciplined, then to become a movie star and then to marry into the Kennedy family and make a lot of money. He's obviously a very ambitious man, and he's succeeded in those ambitions.

When Arnold became a top star in Hollywood, did this place him in a despotic position, just how much power did he have as far as studio executives are concerned?

Alex Ben Block: When you become an A-list star, you have many, many choices. You also have a team of agents, managers, publicists and hangers-on and business people around you. He certainly had his. He also had a powerful wife. So within reason, he had a lot of choice. He could do what he wanted. He was able to use that power, not just limited to action roles, but also to do all these other things he wanted to try, from comedy to playing romantic roles and branch out into another area and do a lot of business deals. He's an entrepreneur with real estate, and he owned restaurants and all these other things. So, in his world in that era, he was a very powerful voice and he was able to make the choices he wanted to make, whether they were good choices or not, we can debate. He called his own shots.

In the beginning, do you feel he was cognizant of the fact he might be typecasted because of his accent and play a German role? Also what are your sentiments pertaining to his flops?
Alex Ben Block: I don't know if "typecasting" is the right word, I'd say "limited". In the beginning, it seemed like he was limited to certain roles because of the accent. But he was able to use it to his advantage by choosing roles and characters and developing scripts to challenge his capabilities and his accent. He became a big star despite his accent. He's a very talented performer. Some of the movies he was in were not successful, but it's rare you get anybody who had every movie successful. He reached a plateau of his career, it was more in his head than in his career. He got tired of doing the things he was doing. He continued to make movies, while some of them didn't work a lot of them did. His career didn't stop until he went into politics, because he was, let's say, Ronald Reagan's career was over by the time he went into politics. In this case, he took the opportunity and got involved in a special election in California to make a career and life decision to move in a different direction. And while he had some flops, he could've continued to be an A-list star for years to come.

Whenever you interviewed him, what significant element did you detect as far as the depth of his character?
Alex Ben Block: I did a couple of times over the years, and I certainly heard him interviewed. He's very self-confident. Whether he was talking about his movies, his business or his politics, he was very assertive. He had a strong point of view. What I remember about him most was the strength of the man - his character and his personality.

He no doubt developed a reputation within the circles for his voracious appetite for promoting. For example, someone had him logged for

290

twenty interviews, but he'd say he wanted to do forty.

Alex Ben Block: Well, the greatest movie stars, often they're able to use their magnetic personality for promotion. They can turn it on and off. And Arnold had that ability as a movie star. When he chose to, he was very charismatic. People wanted to talk to him, people wanted to be around him and he delivered. He told you stories and he had a personality. He was a lot of fun and he spoke his mind. So he was an easy person to be interested in. I saw him at conventions or a premiere. I remember seeing him at Cannes and covering him at Cannes. He'd sweep in with his bodyguards and his entourage, and at premieres do his thing. Once again, he was a great promoter and he had a great sense of awareness of what made him famous and he used it.

What was he like with the press?

Alex Ben Block: He could light up the room. He had a great personality and he loved to talk, smoke a cigar and hold court and people were fascinated.

Do you feel he still has goals to achieve?

Alex Ben Block: I waited and thought about what he'd do after he'd stop being the governor. I felt he had many opportunities from going back to the movie business, or he could go into private business, or he could go to Washington in public service.

Over the years, Arnold invested his bodybuilding and movie earnings in an array of stocks, bonds, privately controlled companies and real estate holdings. In 1977, when he already had started pursuing the movie business, Arnold set up the firm Oak Productions in Santa Monica. And it also became a vehicle through which Arnold got paid for his movie roles. Arnold's penchant for business is echoed in the following statement, "I come from a business background. I studied business in college, and I was always interested in the business side of everything. In all I've ever done - you know, bodybuilding, fitness, the movie business - I've always looked at it not only as the joy of doing the sport, or the joy of acting, but also: how do we make $1 into $10? How can we make a business out of it? Because everything has a business aspect."

In June 1997, he spent $38 million of his own money on a private Gulfstream jet. He also has a stake in Legend International Air, an aviation concern that, according to press reports, bought a jumbo jet from Singapore Airlines in 1996 worth $133 million. The former governor's portfolio included investments in General Electric Co.,

Coca-Cola, PepsiCo, Starbucks Coffee, Wal-Mart and Target stores, and Pfizer Inc., the pharmaceutical concern that sells Viagra, Dell, Microsoft and two media concerns, Gannett Co. and the Washington Post Co. Paul Watcher, a former Wall Street banker and a close friend of Arnold's, said Arnold's favorite investment was real estate. He invested millions of dollars in a shopping plaza in Santa Monica and a shopping mall in Ohio.

Watcher met the former governor in 1981when Watcher was working for Bobby Shriver, who would later become Arnold's brother-in-law. Later, when Watcher started his company called Main Street Advisors, in 1997, Arnold became his first client. Arnold once remarked, "Money doesn't make you happy. I now have $50 million, but I was just as happy when I had $48 million." He has also stated, "I've made many millions as a businessman many times over."

Do you feel Arnold had his fair share of critics during his movie career in the 1980s and 1990s?
Alex Ben Block: Of course. The critics like you or they don't like you. It's not based on who you are, but based on your work, and he always made the kind of movies the critics liked. There were times when the critics were bad, but that wasn't important, what was important was the public loved movies and they went to his movies. And if they were the right kind of movies, people turned out for him. Terminator 1 was kind of an accident. I mean, in Terminator 1 he played a villain. It's only from Terminator 2 that his character became heroic, and that became a huge worldwide success. They were very successful. With the movie, the merchandize and the markets, it was very successful.

Do you feel he was bigger than action movie stars such as Stallone, Van Damme, Seagal?
Alex Ben Block: I don't know if bigger, he was bigger than a lot of these stars. He was bigger than Bruce Willis. In his days, he was an A-list star, whereas Van Damme was never really an A-list star, he was always a B-list star. Arnold had a much more body of work and a much more powerful career.

What was one of the biggest news stories in Hollywood pertaining to Arnold?
Alex Ben Block: When he ran for the governor of California - that was a big story. It was a big surprise at the time. I think during his career, he became a phenomenon and he was an A-list star, he got a lot of publicity and a lot of attention. He was able to resonate with the

public, because he made very entertaining movies. He had a great magnetic presence on the screen and it was a lot of fun to watch great action movies, and that's why the public loved him. He became one of these unique characters and his image became iconic. He knew who he was and what he was all about and it was exciting. And if you're into movies, you want to know more about him. Not so many people have achieved that level.

Last words on Arnold.
Alex Ben Block: I want to tell you, I liked him much better as a movie star than I liked him as a governor. Hopefully, in the future he will stick to the movies and stay out of politics. It's not about the years, the question was: what is he going to do with them? If he is going back to the movies, he's going to have to pick his roles very carefully. He's not going to be the young action hero; It's not going to happen. I felt he'd find the right kind of vehicle just like Bruce Willis, it becomes harder and harder to find the kind of (action) roles as you get older.

Do you think he might have turned to directing and producing, when he left the political platform?
Alex Ben Block: He's certainly capable of it. He directed Christmas in Connecticut and he produced some movies. If he chooses to go in that direction, he's certainly capable. But I don't think he's going to; he's got business interests. He's been in politics now, and he's seen by the public in a different way. I'll be a little surprised if he wanted to go back to that, but we'll wait and see.

Speculation was mounting whether Arnold would be back in Hollywood after he left his political post. After he left the governor's office, he claimed he received fifteen offers from the film industry in Hollywood. In the future, he has to adapt to roles which reflect his age, just as Clint Eastwood did, he admitted. The former governor expressed that extreme fighting was not possible anymore. Another new project based on a comic book character was announced, which Arnold planned on promoting at the Cannes Film Festival, but he withdrew venturing there to take care of personal problems.

Hollywood was keen to embrace the star who had been out of the business for nearly eight years, preconceiving the potential box office success. Finally, he signed to star in Cry Macho for which he'd receive an advance of $10 million and also a portion of the movie's profits. Arnold was probably the first star in Hollywood who negotiated these type of deals when he made Twins in the late 1980's, for which he received a salary and portions of the profits. Soon other A-list stars were following in his footsteps. Other offers included remakes of Predator and The Running Man, and, of course, the new Terminator movie.

CHAPTER FOUR

POLITICAL FRATERNITY

IN PURSUIT OF POLITICS

Arnold Schwarzenegger was not the first Hollywood star to have political ambitions. One of the most prominent actor-turned-politicians was Ronald Reagan; a man Arnold adulated. To Arnold, President Reagan symbolized what America represented: hope, opportunity and freedom. Arnold said that he learned something special from Reagan: in America the greatest power is not derived from privilege, but it is derived from the people. He also believed Reagan represented a role model for those who have been granted the public trust as elected leaders.

Arnold has had political aspirations and interest in government since he was a young man in Austria. People he was growing up with were involved with politics and public affairs in Austria. After immigrating to America, the young man was intrigued by the political scene and conscientiously observed what was happening on the political front. Arnold explained why he became a Republican, "I came first of all from a socialistic country, which is Austria. And when I came over here in 1968, with the presidential elections coming up in November - I came over in October - I heard a lot of the press conferences from both of the candidates - Humphrey and Nixon. And Humphrey was talking about more government is the solution, protectionism, and everything he said about government involvement sounded to me more like Social Democratic Party of Austrian socialism."

It's clear that Arnold honed a keen sense of awareness when it came to politics, when he first arrived in America. "Then when I heard Nixon talk about it, he said open up the borders, the consumers should be represented there ultimately, and strengthen the military and get the government off our backs. I said to myself, what is this guy's party affiliation? I didn't know anything at that point. So I asked my friend, what is Nixon? He's a Republican. And I said I am a Republican. That's how I became a Republican."

In 1986, he married into a political family. His mother-in-law and father-in-law very much encouraged him in politics. The Kennedys - more accurately, the Shrivers - were hugely influential in pushing Arnold toward public service and politics. His mother-in-law Eunice Shriver had a great impact on his decision to run for governor. She encouraged him, prodded him and kept close to him throughout his governorship. In her first public campaign appearance in San Jose, the lifelong Democrat and sister of the late President John F. Kennedy broached to reporters, "I think he'd be a very good governor. He's been committed to people all his life. Since the day he first arrived here, he's been a success with people." She said that he'd make a very good governor, because he was interested in all kinds of subjects.

Arnold's wife Maria's greatest role was steering her husband to the right people - getting him the best political advisors who could take control of the chaos right after he announced about running for office in August 2003. She found Mike Murphy, who brought some stability to the Schwarzenegger campaign, and she helped make sure Arnold was getting good advice from the right advisers. Arnold's rolodex was vast, so he could really call anybody he wanted to. But it wasn't always the right person. Los Angeles Times political reporter Robert Salladay recalls, "It was by far the most intense and strangest elections I've covered. There were hundred and thirty-five candidates on the ballot, including Lt. Governor Cruz Bustamante and Arianna Huffington."

Others included Larry Flynt and the late Gary Coleman, star of the 1970s sitcom Diff'rent Strokes. The prerequisite for running for office was merely $3,500 and sixty-five signatures. But Arnold was the frontrunner based on name recognition alone. Arnold's improbable rise to political power played out before a rapt global audience. Campaigning as an outsider, borrowing a line from the movie Network to tell charged-up supporters that, "We're mad as hell and we're not going to take it anymore!"

The actor had honest strong views he wanted to get back. He was just intrigued by politics, he had a voracious appetite for achieving goal after goal. He liked politics and he immensely enjoyed new challenges. Arnold had met a lot of people in the profession he found to be pretty interesting. I think all of those things to some measure contributed in Arnold's quest to pursue politics. He was convinced that the state of California was in a bad way, and that he was someone independent enough have a better chance than most making the change. "I'm not sure things worked out turned out to be true, his time shows being independent and well-intentioned doesn't produce very much," says Joe Mathews, a prominent political reporter who covered the campaign.

California has a very difficult system, they have supermajority. It's almost impossible to get the Democrats and the Republicans together to agree and have consensus. This was one of Arnold's fundamental challenges. Arnold tried to solve it in many different ways, very pragmatic, but in the process he sort of proved that the California system doesn't work. Robert Salladay told me, "Arnold is in the communication business. He understands that it doesn't matter what policies you enact; you have to sell it to the public. There is no greater salesman in the political arena - he's a salesman." Arnold knew little about California public policy. So his team produced briefing books for him and Arnold studied them becoming cognizant. He apparently was a quick learner....

BRUCE E. CAIN

Bruce E. Cain is a professor of political science at UN Berkeley. He has served as a consultant to the Los Angeles Times and a polling consultant for state and Senate races. Professor Cain is also the executive director of the University of California, Washington Center.

Can you culminate on the magnitude of influence the Kennedy family had on Arnold, when he initially pursued politics, and the effect Eunice Shriver had on him?

Bruce Cain: I would say it helps in America to be tied to a political family, in particular an entertainer, because it gives you connections and networks. And it also kind of marks you as a serious person; this isn't just a random whim that you can get into politics. So, I think Schwarzenegger has had that effect that it made him part of a political family. It also helped him to signal that he was open to ties with the Democrats, so that when he put himself forward as a moderate Republican it was plausible. Because his wife was a Democrat and his family came from a very prominent Democratic family. He didn't really need the money that they were associated with, because he had his own personal wealth.

So, I would say that it was mainly that some level of credibility and a connection to the Democrats would soften his image as a Republican. I really don't know what effect Eunice Shriver had on Schwarzenegger, so that's something I'm not versed on. To be honest, I think that Arnold probably didn't need a lot of encouragement. I think he may well have been interested in and attracted to politics for quite a while. He may have got advice from her, but I don't think it was an idea that was put in his head by anybody. But, again, I don't know the relationship with Eunice, that's something that's been written about a lot in newspapers, maybe it is in some of the biographies on Schwarzenegger, but it's not something that's come up a lot in the last eight years.

Maria's greatest concern was that Arnold would be consumed by a political life. What role did Maria play when Arnold pursued a career in politics, and how did she support him?

Bruce Cain: Yeah. I think in particularly in the beginning, she put aside her own political career. She took on various causes in California, she's media savvy so she no doubt helped him think about that. In the end, I don't know how much influence she had over his ideas, because he fluctuated all over the map so much. There were years when he came across as a Bush Republican, and then there were years it looked like maybe he would head back to more moderate Republican direction. And I know at various times, he made comments to the effect that he had disastrous elections. For example, in 2005 in which he took a very conservative agenda to the electorate, and I remember that he very visibly said something after about how he should've listened to his wife, or she told him this was not going to work.

But interestingly enough, I think he took a woman named Susan Kennedy as an advisor and she made possible that Maria Shriver was not directly but indirectly the source of that, that he was getting advice from essentially from a moderate to conservative Democrat as opposed to a diehard Republican. When Susan Kennedy was put in there, it was a very controversial thing. If she had any connection to that, that's possible. But at any rate, Arnold felt comfortable from taking advice from a strong moderate Democratic woman, and it may well subconsciously have been a reason Susan Kennedy was chosen.

In the early years, Arnold had a problem being accepted by some of the Kennedys. Maria has said that everybody had a problem with Arnold; she didn't know a person who thought it was a good idea for them to get married. Do you think Arnold had a lot to prove for acceptance?
Bruce Cain: I'm sure that's true. Arnold Schwarzenegger is a very unconventional actor; he's an action hero type of a person. I think the Kennedys had the same reaction that everybody else would've had: is this person really serious? The kind of issues you need to be governor. But as a family, when you marry a Hollywood type, somebody who's had a bit of a reputation as a womanizer, as we recall that was a big issue in 2003 election, I'm sure there was a lot of skepticism. As you say, he proved people wrong. He became a dutiful husband, he seemed to have blended in the family pretty well. So, I think he's just not a person you can easily forget.

Arnold once said I wish I could experience the feeling President Kennedy had, speaking to fifty thousand people at one time and having them scream and be in agreement with him. Arnold seemed to have a penchant for leaders who were great speakers....
Bruce Cain: Yeah. I think that get's to work his concept of leadership, and I think that's right, he was probably very much attracted to the Kennedy family, because there's no figure in Europe who's more

revered, more admired than President Kennedy. Arnold is a good speaker, and many of his finest moments were prepared speeches that he gave. I think he did draw inspiration from that. I think saying the way he thought of being governor, which is that he could inspire with his rhetoric and salesmanship, people to follow him and agree with him.

I think probably one of the great disappointments with him, or maybe it was a surprise, that good rhetoric doesn't get you that far in terms of getting people to being inspired into following you, at least in the modern era it's a lot harder to do than when Kennedy was president. You have a much more partisan electorate, much more vehement meteorite on the other side than you had in the 1960s. It's all kinds of evidence which put science the matter of fact the temperatures are a just a lot warmer in contemporary politics than it was forty years ago. I think that was probably a dream he had, that he could also inspire people with speeches with his ability to persuade. And it worked for a certain moment, most of the time it didn't work, just like it doesn't work for Obama. People are going to look at the policies, or look at the budget and realize what the problems are and work who's going to lead them out of the rigid situation.

Arnold was elected in a controversial recall election in November 2003. What was so controversial about this?
Bruce Cain: First, we did not have much experience in California at state level with recalls; we had a lot of experience at local government level, City Council called out of office, but we did not have much experience in the state recall. And secondly, it was shall we say "freakish" kind of a show, because it was so easy to get on the ballot. We had dozens and dozens of candidates, some of them like Gary Coleman were actors, like Arnold, some of them were porn queens, some of them were just average deluded citizens who thought they could run. Some of them were celebrities like Arianna Huffington. It was just a mad zoo! And the procedures, we never did fix them. They made it very easy for anybody just to file and put their name to run for governor. So it was controversial for that reason. And it was controversial, thirdly, because the Democrats had one governorship under Gray Davis, and to many this looked like hijacking the process by the Republicans, initially when the recall started...then, of course, Arnold had his own money. There was a lot of confusion and anger on the Democrats side.

Out of all that, Arnold did win and it was probably the easiest way to win. I think he would have had a hard time in a regular election, getting nominated for the Republican Party as their candidate governor. Because the Republican nomination rule at the time was basically for semi-closed primaries, meaning only hardcore Republicans and state

Republican first round. And most experts believe that if Arnold tried to run outside the recall election, he had to go through this process where the most conservative Republicans had to choose, he wouldn't have gotten through the first round. So it was really a stroke of luck that opened up this much easier path for him and everything fell into place. It's not clear that if those things had happened, he would have been able to do this.

Democrat Dianne Feinstein bowed out of the race in early August, do you feel she was a primary threat to Arnold in some respects, which would have sent him in the depths of despair if she had ran for office?
Bruce Cain: Yeah, if she had run I think it would have been very hard for Arnold. It would have been much, much closer. Cruz Bustamante, who was the Lt. governor at the time, just doesn't have the same electorate. Dianne Feinstein is perhaps, in terms of public opinion, the most popular state official that California has. And that's been true for almost for all the time she's been in the office in the '90s. So it would've been a much tougher race. But fortunately for him, Dianne Feinstein flirts with the idea of running for governor, but often walks away from it. She's got a nice job as senator, and I think her husband's past would have been dragged out and scrutinized in the press. I think she didn't want to go through that again.

Can you shed some light on who was part of Arnold's integral campaign team? It included Mike Murphy and David Crane.
Bruce Cain: I think, as you say, Schutzman, basically I would characterize them as sort of the young turks, the younger Republican operatives. You had the older group of political operatives such as Wilson. So, you had Wilson, who I believe was involved in the campaign, you also had a lot of younger people that were like the next generation of political consultants. So, this was a real opening and opportunity, because many of them were looking at the fact that 2002 was very dismal for the Republicans, because they weren't winning anything. They lost the governorship, and it just looked like there wasn't going to be much business. So, for many of them, and this may seem a little harsh but it's true, having a celebrity who had already had recognition and had unlimited bank account was like a Christmas present. Because if you're consulting, you worry about whether you are going to get paid or not, particularly if somebody loses. If you're business people that nobody knows, you have to spend a lot of money introducing yourself or introducing this candidate. So to have a celebrity with a lot of money was a big deal for all of these guys.
    And, of course, once they had that success with Schwarzenegger,

that became their formula and they started to look for new millionaires that they could work for. That's, of course, what happened with Goodman. It's kind of, in my opinion, the lazy way out that the Republic consultants had taken. They wanted to make sure they got paid, and instead of looking for somebody who had paid their dues and worked their way up, they go out and find themselves a celebrity millionaire and latch onto that. And if they lose it's no big deal, because they'll get paid. Arnold was a success and a formula. I think what happened in the last election made him even surpass the whole formula.

Who were the most instrumental of his advisors when he stood for the first or second time, and were there any who were relinquished from their duties?
Bruce Cain: Most of that period I was in DC, I was not actually in Sacramento. So I didn't observe that sort of air and inner workings of his office. I think Susan Kennedy was a major figure, David Crane was a major figure. It seemed to me he dropped a lot of people, he had a bunch of people from the Wilson era that worked with him up until 2005. He had Tom Campbell in there and a bunch of other people. He got rid of the Wilson people for the most part and switched over to Susan Kennedy and David Crane and people like that.

Arnold bemoaned the failure of Gray Davis, expressing to talk show host Jay Leno, "The man that is failing the people more than anyone is Gray Davis." Can you please tell me about some of the obstacles Arnold had to overcome facing Davis in the first election?
Bruce Cain: Gray Davis had been in California government since the early '70s, he had served chief of staff to Jerry Brown in the '70s. He had been an Assembly man, he'd been the controller, Lt. governor. He had worked his way up. He was not and is not a charismatic guy, we had a whole bunch of non-charismatic governors. We had Pete Wilson who was non-charismatic, we had George Deukmejian who was non-charismatic. To many people, it looked as though California was destined to.... You need to have these solid non-charismatic people governors, because it just looked like if anybody had a strong personality they were going to get hit with lots of negative ads. Gray Davis was good at raising money. He was a Democrat. He won in '98 and he won in 2002. He knew a lot more about what was going on in the state.

So, on the face of it, here you had a rookie who knew very little about issues taking on a governor who was very experienced. Of course, he had the energy crisis he was dealing with and we were in the middle of a recession. Democrats were divided between liberals and moderates and were angry with Davis. So he was in a very weakened position when

Arnold ran against him in 2003. Voters were unhappy with the motor vehicle license fee which had been raised. And, of course, the way the formula...there were a lot of people who were angry at the governor and wanted to get rid of him. Arnold was on the top of the list.

Davis vacuously made a remark, "Someone who can't pronounce California should not be the governor." Did Arnold make any derogatory comments which may have offended Davis?
Bruce Cain: My memory was, Arnold didn't get involved in a lot of that. What I remember is that he was very focused on increasing the motor vehicle license fee, and Arnold was full of promises about reinventing government and making it more efficient and low in taxes. I don't recall there was, in Californian standards, a time that he took a very personal attack on Gray Davis. Again, that's partly because of the very unique of the recall election where you were basically asked whether or not you wanted to retain the governor. But everybody was unhappy with the governor and said no. Then all Arnold had to do was focus on the question of: would he be better than everybody else who was on the ticket on the second part of the ballot?

Arnold accused the Davis camp of playing dirty. What were some of the more controversial and scurrilous stories which came under close scrutiny, and to what extent did these influence the voters?
Bruce Cain: Well, in the end they didn't very much. But we didn't know that at the time, particularly there was some question about the LA Times investigation into sexual harassment claims and whether the Davis people had any role in it. In the end, I think if it had been a normal election, in which there was concern about the economy and the energy cost and the motor vehicle license fee, the issue of sexual harassment might have played more. But in the context of everything else, I don't think it did.

When Arnold was cogitating of seriously pursuing a career in politics by standing for governor in the 2002 election in California, Gary South, a political consultant, the eminence grise behind Arnold's opponent Gray Davis, faxed a Premiere magazine article to countless journalists containing derogatory allegations which would tar Arnold's reputation. Peter Jennings of ABC asked Arnold in an interview, "It cannot be easy to spend the last few days of this campaign having to deal constantly with being called a serial groper or a serial abuser of women and being compared in some way your admiration for Hitler. Is that tough?" Arnold replied, "I get upset about it. But I knew that before I got into this campaign, that this is going to be that kind of a situation where people will throw everything at me at the last minute and the last week, and it is going to become a dirty campaign, sleaze campaign. And, you know, down to the gutter. And I knew that. Because I was warned. People, political leaders from both parties said, 'You know, Arnold, I don't know if you want to do that. Because let me tell you, I've campaigned. I've run for office and all this, and the last week they throw things at you that is embarrassing many times. It's terrible for your family. You may want to think that over, because no matter what it is, they will find it.'"

Later, when the scandals broke about Arnold's behavior, his wife stood by him and supported him. In 2003, on the Oprah Winfrey Show Maria sought to put down reports that her husband was a womanizer. She exclaimed that he was a man who is the exact opposite. She added that she makes her opinion based on the man sitting in front of her and added, "I know the man that I'm married to."

In May 2011, Arnold and wife Maria separated. Mildred Baena, who was employed by the Schwarzeneggers for twenty years as a housekeeper, had given birth to a boy named Joseph. Arnold went public broaching he had fathered a child out of wedlock, born in 1997. In his statement, he said, "I understand and deserve the feelings of anger and disappointment among my friends and family. There are no excuses and I take full responsibility for the hurt I have caused. I have apologized to Maria, my children and my family. I am truly sorry. I ask that the media respect my wife and children through this extremely difficult time. While I deserve your attention and criticism, my family does not." The tabloid media frenzy continued.

Baena started to see the resemblance as her son grew. She says she knew Arnold was the father - she also said maybe her son also wondered as he got older. Joseph's grandmother sat him down a year before the scandal broke and told the young boy that Arnold was his father, to which he replied, "Cool!" Maria began to have her suspicions after she started hearing whispers pertaining to the pair's resemblance. One day Maria asked Baena point blank. Baena told Hello magazine, "She (Maria) was so strong. She cried with me and told me to get off my knees. We held each other and I told her it wasn't Arnie's fault, that it takes two."

Regardless of this scandal, Arnold is a human being and has made mistakes just like anyone else. But because him being in the public eye, the press seemingly took every opportunity to bringing him down. Had it been any other person off the street, who may have committed a serious crime, nobody would have taken much notice. Unfortunately, the media more often than not focuses on and culminates on the negative, deviating from projecting the celebrity's more palatable side when they can instead make sensational headlines. Someone's personal life is personal, and the media should respect the individual's and their family's privacy. But in the media frenzy world in which we live in, the more sensationalist material the more the public wants to know about it.

Arnold's popularity tumbled in America following revelations he had fathered a child out of wedlock. A new poll revealed his popularity had plummeted to its lowest level, which showed the disdainfulness from the public was reasonably rife. Even certain celebrities joined in. Sharon Osbourne told an entertainment source, "I was really, really disappointed at him for being so horribly disrespectful and deceitful to do that in your own home. He can do whatever he wants in hotels on the road, whatever, knock yourself out, but you don't disrespect your family by doing it in your own home. To me it's just unthinkable." She continued, "I would have chopped his (BLEEP) off. Arnie's (BLEEP) would have been down the disposal unit spinning around, that's where it'd be - and I'd make her (Baena) clean it up. That mop would have been wrapped around her head."

In June 2011, Prince William and Kate Middleton, according to sources, were to meet the former governor at the British Consulate-General's residence in Los Angeles, but the idea was nixed. However, a spokesman for the former governor insisted that no such meeting was ever scheduled in the first place.

Arnold's people seemed to have shielded him from the media journalists, in case he was put on the spot on intricate issues he lacked knowledge of, which may have been convoluted. What were Arnold's weak areas, at the time of running for the first time, and how was he able to elude these?
Bruce Cain: I think he just didn't know the issues as well as Gray Davis and Cruz Bustamante and the other people who were in California government. He had been involved in initiative campaign, so he wasn't ignorant. But you just couldn't compare the level of knowledge he had, and this is, of course, the way the Republicans deal with their novice candidate, if they try to shield them long enough so that these people can get up to speed and not get torn apart by the press. That's what they tried to do with Arnold.

In September 2003, Arnold did not participate in the debate where five of the other prime candidates, including Tom McClintock and Cruz Bustamante, would be confronting one another for the first time. Do you feel other candidates were much more cognizant of issues and policies which needed addressing in front of the California public?

Bruce Cain: Some of them were. Tom McClintock certainly was, Cruz Bustamante certainly was. Not all of them were. There were others who were on there but were not, who like Arnold did not know as much. In some circumstances that can be fatal, not knowing enough about government. But in this particular election, people were so angry that they were willing to try for an outsider who didn't know as much, because that person shared their anger basically. Tom McClintock had been the legislator for many years and was an articulate spokesperson, almost a libertarian, i.e., minimal government issues. So he was probably the most visible small government candidate in the race. He could be counted on to get a lot of support from the more conservative Republicans in the electorate. But in a sense, he made Arnold look like a moderate.

People could look at him and then look at Arnold, and if you were an independent or a Democrat you could say, "Yeah, I'd much prefer to have Arnold over McClintock." Cruz Bustamante was a conservative Democrat Latino from Central Valley. Soft-spoken, but I wouldn't say he's a dynamic guy; not the showman that Arnold was. As far as Latino goes, he was considered more conservative than most so he had some crossover appeal. He had been a speaker at the Assembly, and it's very hard to go from being a speaker in Assembly to having a state position. There's a few examples: Willie Brown became the mayor of San Francisco. But they don't generally go any further than that, because it's kind of an image of being an insider's politician as opposed to being the kind of salesman a politician like a governor can be.

When Arnold was whisked into office, just how big of a responsibility did he have on his hand?
Bruce Cain: He came in at a very hard time and there were a lot of issues pressing, most particularly what we call the "structural deficit". Meaning that the state had committed to programs like reducing classroom size, standard healthcare for children. We simply didn't have the revenues for when the stock market took a tank. So, I think Arnold recognized that, he recognized there had to be a way to bring the structural deficit. And he tried to do that by establishing a commission, which would look at the possibilities of efficiencies, closing down some of these commissions and boards that were very controversial.

But in the end, after a year of kind of study and serious recommendations, he backed off. He cut the vehicle motor license fee, which took money and revenue away from government and that made the structural deficit worse, because he didn't cut programs. So, I think Arnold found himself in a very difficult situation, but he was able to do some things that were very important such as signing the greenhouse gas bill. He managed to persuade the voters to pass some bond measures, it would finance projects that could no longer be funded under the general budget. But in the end, he was never really able to solve the structural deficit problem, and that's what Jerry Brown inherited in his third term now as governor.

Jesse Ventura, co-star of Arnold's action-packed movie Predator, former professional wrestling star and former governor of Minnesota, expressed in Time magazine, "Arnold, what the heck are you doing? You're getting out of Hollywood to go into politics? Well, then forget agents and studio bosses - now you're dealing with real predators." Ventura advised Arnold if he didn't know the answers to any questions then he should be upfront by saying he didn't know. Ventura himself had fed the people "pre-canned bullshit", as he put it himself. "Plenty of the old Republican gang will come around and want to be your new best friend," wrote Ventura in Time magazine. "That's fine, but let them know that you are in government to solve problems; not to help them hold on to their power."

Arnold ran for re-election against Phil Angelides in November 2006. Can you culminate on some of the prominent people involved in this, and how much support did Arnold receive?

Bruce Cain: I think by that time, he had got ridden of the Wilson people, he was pretty much using these younger Republican consultants and he was working with Susan Kennedy. He had had a very disastrous year in 2005, when he tried to pass a whole bunch of Republican measures. And the voters had rejected him in the special election. So he turned to the last so to speak and signed the global agreement, the greenhouse gas bill, with the Democrats. And for a period of time, the economy recovered from the dotcom bust and started to look again largely on the housing, the appreciation of housing. So, Arnold was flush with resources, and timing in politics is everything. Phil Angelides was looking at the structural deficit, saying we really have to adjust and increase the taxes. And that is something the voters didn't want to hear. Once Phil said that, basically Arnold just jumped over at that issue, all over it, and got himself re-elected. He also put himself in the box, meaning he couldn't find any permanent solution to the structural deficit, but it was enough to get him re-elected in 2006.

Can you tell me about the collaboration between Susan Kennedy and Arnold?

Bruce Cain: As far as we can tell, she really became his most important adviser. She had had a very important role with Gray Davis, advising him as cabinet secretary. She's very business oriented. She's a lesbian but, of course, that doesn't bother Arnold - he comes from the Hollywood world. I think they tried very hard to maintain a kind of a moderate agenda, not cutting social services and state by too much. But at the same time, Arnold was holding the line on taxes. So, on the one hand it took Arnold too far to the right, and on the other hand I think the fact he was trying to have it both ways to please the Democrats by not taking huge deficit programs but not please the Republicans by raising taxes. I think it was a middle-over-the-road strategy, which I'm sure Susan Kennedy had a lot to do with, which was what got him re-elected in 2006. But it didn't help solve the problems the state was confronted with.

When he stood for the second time, what promises did Arnold make this time to the people, not circumventing, and what were their thoughts in terms of whether these would materialize?
Bruce Cain: To be honest, I don't remember other than.... I can't recall he had a major theme; it was more that they jumped on top of Phil Angelides for his for tax increases. My impression is: he was largely running on his success, by that time he had become a sort of an environmental spokesman. He was going to implement the greenhouse gas law. So he was really running as a kind of a worldwide figure, a sort of Republican who cared about going green and carbon commissions. He was riding that image pretty heavily. But I don't recall that any of the other proposals were really important in that election. I'd have to go back and take a look.

Would I be right in saying that sometimes he was far from being a hyper-partisan politician. What were the hurdles and obstacles for Arnold to overcome in the 2006 re-election?
Bruce Cain: For the 2006 election, I don't think he had any. I think the problem was that Phil Angelides was going to raise his own money, because he had his own wealth. And at that point, it looked as though - the state is predominately Democratic - and many of the Republicans were very unhappy with Arnold. In fact, going into the 2006 elections his biggest challenge was that there were some Republicans that wanted to run a primary opponent against him, because they felt he was too moderate that he was almost a Democrat in drag if you like. So, his real problem on that side, in terms of the Democrats, he had a very good relationship with the speaker at the time when they cut the deal on the global warming bill and various other things. He basically was able to split the Democratic Party. So,

I think his major obstacle was the fact he didn't have the united backing of the Republicans, and they basically thought: well, it's better to have Arnold even though he's half Republican - not a real Republican - it's better to have him than a Democrat. He was able to prevail, even though there was a lot of discontent within his party.

Can you differentiate between the contrast between state politics and national politics in America - did Arnold influence national politics?
Bruce Cain: Well, I think that Arnold was able to do international politics by virtue of his climate change law, so he got to play an international role. I don't think he had much impact with the national side, because he was basically looking for the national government to give the state more money and they were not interested in helping bail out the state of California. So, even though he campaigned for Bush in 2004, in the end he really didn't have a good relationship with Bush. And in his travels to DC, aside from the fact that they were a bunch of political figures who wanted to have their picture taken with him, he was never really able to get anything out of the Republican Congress. So, he never really became a leading figure in a Republican Party. He was pretty much abandoned in 2006 as being way too liberal, and it was the best that California could produce. But it was clearly not going anywhere in the Republican Party.

So even if he had been a citizen of the USA, he would have had a hard time at a national level getting a presidential bid going. Because I don't think the Southern Republicans would have liked the fact his social views were so liberal and that his politics had been cooperative with the Democrats. So he would have had a hard time parlaying that into a presidential bid. But it definitely got the possibility that, if Arnold is healthy enough he might run for one of the Senates in a few years. I think it's fair to say that he has some big wins and some big loses. His big wins were in the area of green, carbon omissions and the environmental issues. I think his big loss will be in the area of the budget and his inability to really bring structural deficit in control. I think his legacy includes having some big achievements, like the global and greenhouse gases. I think this will be an enduring legacy.

Arnold had experienced the presence of Communism first hand. When he was growing up, the Soviets occupied part of Austria. "I saw their tanks in the streets. I saw Communism with my own eyes," Arnold remembers. "I remember the fear we had when we had to cross into the Soviet sector. Growing up we were told, don't look the soldiers in the eye; just look straight ahead. It was common belief that the Soviet

310

soldiers can take a man out of his own car and ship him back to the Soviet Union as slave labor. Now, my family didn't have a car, but one day we were in my uncle's car, it was dark as we came to the Soviet checkpoint. I was a little boy, I wasn't an action hero back then. But I remember how scared I was that the soldiers could pull my father and uncle out of the car and I would never see them again. My family and so many others lived in fear of the Soviet boot. Today, the world no longer fears the Soviet Union, and it is because of United States of America."

On the issues pertinent to international politics, Arnold didn't shy away from expressing his views. He openly supported the Iraq War, he expressed, "Bush didn't go into Iraq because the polls told him it was popular. But leadership isn't about polls. It's about making decisions you think are right and then standing behind them. That's why America is safer with Bush as president. He knows you don't reason with terrorists, you defeat them. He knows you can't reason with people blinded by hate. They hate the power of the individual. They hate the progress of women; the religious freedom of others. They hate the liberating breeze of democracy."

He echoed his admiration for Bush and the need for terminating terrorism. He had boundless admiration for Bush's steadfast leadership in the war against terrorism. He continued, "Our young men and women in uniform do not believe there are two Americas! We are one America - and Bush is defending it with all his heart and soul! That's what I admire most about Bush. He's a man of perseverance. He's a man of inner strength. He is a leader who doesn't flinch, doesn't waiver, does not back down. My fellow Americans, make no mistake about it, terrorism is more insidious than communism, because it yearns to destroy not just the individual but the entire international order."

In October 2010, the governor flew to the United Kingdom and joined David Cameron, the British prime minister, on a visit to Wellington Barracks near Buckingham Palace, where he met and spoke in front of three hundred troops. He addressed the troops, "I get hailed a lot of times when I travel around the world as being the action hero. But I know the difference between a movie action hero who is make-believe and the true action heroes. You all are the true action heroes because you are risking your life. You are risking your life every day when you go out to the front. So I say thank you, thank you, thank you for the great work that you are doing." The governor stated he's always interested to hang out with heroes.

He also managed to visit the barracks gym and witnessed the troops workout. He added in his speech, "First of all, I was amazed when I saw you guys pumping up in the gym with those deltoids and those biceps and the six-pack. Wow, you guys are really in great shape." He added that he was in contact with President Obama, "We are absolutely united in making sure we make Afghanistan safe from terror and that will make us safe from terror." The governor praised the troops for their outstanding work for keeping democracy. "It's because you, for hundreds of years, have fought for the freedom to keep these countries free and to keep these countries strong and to have the freedom of speech. Many countries in the world don't have that." Mr Cameron was able to strike up a relationship with Arnold when he visited the governor in California to discuss green policies back in 2007.

MIKE GENEST

Mike Genest served for four years as Governor Arnold Schwarzenegger's chief financial policy advisor. Prior to that, Genest was the director of the California Senate Republican Fiscal office. He worked closely with Arnold pertaining to the budget.

When Arnold became the governor, what were the core issues surrounding the budget which needed immediate attention with great prudence?

Mike Genest: The major issue was: the budget he inherited had a massive unfunded debt. They had simply spent more money than they could take in. And they had proposed to borrow $9 billion, and this is on a budget that was approximately seventy-six billion. So, that's a heck of a lot to borrow to finance a nine billion budget. There was no real good legal way to borrow. Probably the most urgent matter he faced upon taking office was how to finance the borrowing that had been assumed in the budget he had inherited, but that wasn't really a good thing to do. He did that.

The second biggest problem was that the trajectory of spending was to borrow more than any projections of our revenues could've supported it. So his second big task was to try to cut spending, not only in the year he took office, but more importantly the next year and the following years. He absolutely had to cut spending. Now, it's not clear exactly how much he had to cut, but it was quite a bit. Probably about at least 10 percent, or something like that, the budget needed to be cut in order to be more affordable. And then I guess the last big budget challenge beyond that was that the previous governor had raised the vehicle licensing fee dramatically, and Arnold Schwarzenegger felt that was both illegal and wrong. So, when he came in he reversed that action, and by restoring the vehicle licensing fee to a much lower previous levels. When he did that, he created even more need to cut money out of the budget. So in some sense, he made his budget problem worse by doing that. He felt it was a promise to the people and had to be done.

Some of the cuts and spending which were integral to the budget, what cuts was he proposing and was he being pragmatic?

Mike Genest: Initially, when he first issued his budget, which was about six weeks after he took office, he took a wide range of cuts. He proposed to cut nearly everything. He proposed to cut education substantially. He proposed to cut welfare and certain types of health services. He proposed a variety of cuts. One of the cuts he proposed was a program that provides a very rich mix treatment of care to children that are born with developmental disabilities. He proposed to cut that as well. That was startling to a lot of people, that he would be so hard-pressed as to have to cut that. But even before the legislator began threatening him for not doing what he was proposing, he relented on that particular cut. And he changed his mind and said I will not propose to make that cut. But he did stick with proposed cuts in a wider range of state services - nearly all of them.

Some things couldn't be cut; he couldn't cut the debt service on our outstanding bonds. That would have been a default. He couldn't do that. He could not cut union salaries that had already been negotiated by his predecessor, at least he couldn't do it without the help of the legislator, and there was no hope of getting that. There's a variety of things, retirement payments - he had no power to even propose the cut. Things that were legally feasible to cut, most of them he did propose to reduce substantially.

Arnold capitulated signing a bill to increase the state's minimum wage, a move once he opposed. Why did he pursue this?
Mike Genest: Well, I really don't know why he did that, it's not something I, as a budget person, had a direct immediate impact on the budget. It cost us a little money, because we had some people whose salary was paid by the state who were getting minimum wage. But that's a pretty small number of folks that are in that category, so it didn't really cost us a lot. So, I didn't really follow his logic on that.

Arnold laid out to the Democratic legislators his California Recovery Plan, what did this encompass?
Mike Genest: Yes. He pointed out that California infrastructure was designed and built, for the most part, in the '60s and '70s. And at the time, our population was something, like, twelve million - you'll have to look it up, I don't remember, but it was small. By the time he took office, the population was more than thirty million. And our infrastructure simply had not kept up. We had massive needs for more prisons because our prisons were overcrowded. We had a massive need to improve our highway system because they had been neglected. Our water delivery system was in severe trouble, especially during drought years. Even our parks needed some help. Our schools, we needed to build schools at

both at higher education university schools as well as other schools. So we had a lot of infrastructure needs that just had not kept up with the really substantial growth of our population.

So, he said, "Look, even though we're in a budget crisis, where we cannot afford to pay for services that we're required to provide by law, we can't ignore our infrastructure needs because that's our hope for the future. If we don't take care of our infrastructure, then our economic growth in the future will be severely impaired." He said we need to borrow a great deal of money to finance a significant expansion or improvement of our infrastructure throughout the state. Then he was successful in convincing them that it needed to be done. Even in the face of the difficult budget situation that the state struggled with.

Arnold had advisors advising him. Professor Edward Leamar advised him that he needed a three-year plan. Can you tell me about any meetings you were involved in with him and any assertions he complied with?
Mike Genest: I was involved in the initial Arnold Schwarzenegger team before he became governor. I had been working for the Senate with the Republicans at the time on the budget. I worked with a man named Professor John Cogan at the Hoover Institute at the Stamford University. It's a conservative...it includes the likes of George Shultz and other conservative economists and Cogan is one of those. Cogan and I worked out a good deal of the governor's proposed budget before he was even governor, and it was based on a situation that we had inherited. We knew there was just no way to cut enough spending to survive the debt that we had inherited, and the higher rate of spending that we had inherited. So we thought it would be wise to develop a workout plan as if it were a bankruptcy, where you have a bankruptcy you mark down your payments and take certain amount of time to work back into solvency. Well, we can't really declare bankruptcy as a state. In the United States, no state has the power to use the bankruptcy courts to solve its problems.

We had to come up with our own workout plans. And it was simply to borrow some money to pay off the debt, and to help survive for the first few years. Then he would freeze spending and substantially reduce the rate of growth in spending. So that over time, the revenue growth in the economy we expected to continue improving, would bring our revenues up to the point we could not only pay off the borrowing, but also get to a point where we wouldn't have to do any cutting. There was a plan that could've worked, but it wasn't fully implemented.

When Arnold became the governor, he proposed a comprehensive plan to deal with health insurance. What was he planning on doing, was this plausible and what was actually achieved?

Mike Genest: His health insurance plan was somewhat similar to the time recently adapted by the Congress, what we ultimately refer to as Obamacare. Meaning it's the President Obama's vision how to address healthcare in the United States. It's not the law of the land, but I guess there are two central features to it. One is, it's a requirement under law that every person in the United States must purchase health insurance - that was in the Governor Schwarzenegger's plan as well. And the other piece of that is, using government resources, tax money and variety of other mechanisms to provide insurance to people who can't afford it, or to subsidize insurance for people who can maybe afford a portion of it but not all of the costs of buying the mandatory healthcare. There were a lot more provisions than that, but I think those are the central features of his plan.

Arnold, himself an entrepreneur, was no doubt able to resonate with business owners in California. Can you tell me how businesses benefited, what did Arnold propose to help businesses in California?
Mike Genest: I think he did two really important things - at least in his first term. One important thing was that he took a massive and unprecedented reform of workers' compensation plan. This is the plan for workers who are hurt on the job. So, when you're hurt on the job there's a separate type of insurance that your employer in California, and most states in the United States, must by law purchase for you. The employer must have insurance to cover the eventualities of workers getting hurt whilst on the job. And that insurance covers time off work, it pays pain and suffering and it covers the necessary health costs. The governor reformed that insurance dramatically by things that would keep the costs of healthcare down by reducing the amount of pain and suffering damages that people could get, and by preventing fraud and abuse in the system.

By doing that one reform, the governor saved employers in the state of California billions and billions of dollars every year after the reform was active. It was probably the largest single benefit to businesses that's ever happened in the state from a reform of a government program. It was massive. The other thing that he did was he did not raise taxes. There was a great deal of pressure to raise taxes. Ultimately, in his second to the last year in office, recession forced him into a position where in addition to cutting things he had to raise taxes. But his initial years in office were very helpful to the business communities of our state, because he resisted to the call to raise taxes.

Do you think Arnold had the capacity to turn the budget around, or was it almost kind of an implausible task?

Mike Genest: Well, he tried very, very hard and he made some progress. But he didn't actually solve the state's budget problem. It turned out to be a bigger and a harder problem that even he could solve. And he solved some big things, he made some big differences but he didn't completely solve the problem. My personal opinion is that it was simply too difficult of a problem. When I say this, I don't mean to suggest the arithmetic was beyond him - not at all. He completely understood the arithmetic; he had no problem with figuring out how he would solve the budget problem. The problem was entirely political: how do you get politicians, especially more liberal politicians, to agree to solve a budget problem of that magnitude when they can instead find gimmicks and tricks and temporary measures to avoid having to do the tough things that are required that we have not yet been able to convince our legislator to do?

Now our new governor - Governor Brown - even though he is a Democrat from the liberal wing of the party, he is proposing massive cuts. Because I think we're finally getting to a point where the numbers are just so hard to address that the people are having to relapse logical boundaries somewhat. And because of that maybe now the problem can be solved, and maybe Governor Schwarzenegger gets a great deal of credit, should get a great deal of credit, for pushing on it for all these years. And between his efforts, and the fact that the situation has gotten progressively worst next to the recession, I think we may have some breakthroughs and actually start rolling possibly. But I think unfortunately we'll also have to raise taxes.

In 2009, to close the staggering $26.3 billion deficit, he demanded even deeper cuts that Democrats said will shred the social safety net.
Mike Genest: That claim was always made. By the way, there is a great deal of merit to that claim. The social safety net was simply more expensive than the state of California could afford to maintain, so the cuts that were necessary would have, in fact, dramatically altered the landscape of what our state provides its most vulnerable citizens. But I think we're going to end up doing it, anyway. And, in fact, the Democrats who made those statements are now completely in control of the budget here and they're acknowledging - including the new governor - that we're going to have to change what we provide our citizens, and we're not going to be able to maintain the safety net at the levels that we've always for many, many decades have come to expect.

An example is, we have a very rich program for taking care of older and disabled people in their own homes, so they don't have to go into an institution. But we have extended that program to appoint the people's relatives, their mothers, their daughters, their fathers and so forth can actually get paid to take care of them. So we're paying people to take care of their own relatives. Because it's gotten so big, and that is one of the reasons it's gotten so big. There have been many proposals to cut that program back dramatically. Arnold Schwarzenegger made some proposals that would have cut the number of hours of care that those people would have received. There were people who claim that by making that cut those people would be forced into a nursing home and an institution, or that they might even die. But he had no real choice but to propose those cuts. He got some of those cuts accepted, but not all. Some of the ones that he proposed that the Democrats objected to most vehemently, now the new governor, the Democrat, liberal governor, has come right back and proposed those very same cuts. I think that indicates Governor Schwarzenegger wasn't being mean-spirited when he proposed these cuts. As tough as they were, he was just trying to be realistic.

What was Arnold like in terms of taking advice from his advisors and to collaborate with?
Mike Genest: He was certainly a very polite and respectful man. He was fun to be around, a great sense of humor, very engaging and a really gracious boss on an interpersonal level. You could not say that about all bosses, but it is perfectly accurate to say this about Governor Schwarzenegger. I think, however, he took advise from far more people than bureaucrats like myself. He took advise from private people and people from outside of government. Sometimes some of us inside the government felt that he was not getting the best advice. I think he could've been more successful if he had played the budget game much harder and cut more things and unrelenting on more things. But perhaps it's easy to understand why it wasn't, because he's also a human being and cares about people. He listened to a lot of advisors, including Mrs. Schwarzenegger, who could not go along easily with the idea of such cuts in our budget. So often times, despite the physical numbers that he needed, he would either not make them or withdraw the cuts and I think that made it hard for him to balance the budget.

What was the most compelling conversation that you ever had with Arnold, whilst you were working with him on a professional or social level?
Mike Genest: As the director of finance you are in a very delicate situation, because the governor has to know that you will never reveal his private thoughts or illuminations. But I can tell you without getting specific that talking to him was a revelation, and listening to him talk about what was going on in the rest of the world. I often had the opportunity to fly on his private plane, and sometimes it was just he and

I. Whether it was his observations about fatherhood, he expressed a very good philosophy about being a father. And from everything I could tell, he was a great father. He cares greatly about his children. So, either listening to him talk about fatherhood or about some head of state he was going to meet so forth, or just guy talk sitting around waiting for the plane to land, he was always a fascinating person to be around. It was a great opportunity in my life to be able to speak with him privately and listen to some of his great stories about the movie industry or sports career. But I don't think it's appropriate for me to reveal any of the substance of that.

DANIEL WEINTRAUB

Veteran political reporter Daniel Weintraub followed Arnold Schwarzenegger's political career from the beginning to end. He began his career in journalism writing for the Los Angeles Times. Weintraub is a columnist for The Sacramento Bee and the author of Party of One.

When Arnold decided to run for office in 2003, in your opinion, what motivated him to pursue politics? He had already reached monumental heights in the sport of bodybuilding and the motion picture industry. He also said he would like to be the president one day, was this some unattainable dream or would this be possible?

Daniel Weintraub: I think it was some of the same impulses that drove him in his early years in his careers. He likes to be the center of attention. He likes to be the center of the action. Here's a chance for power and glory, and I think he enjoys a challenge. So, the idea that he could come in from the outside and as the person with no experience in government and try to fix these problems that the state has, I think this appealed to him. Sure, if he was allowed to run for president I'm sure he would have wanted to. I think he just loves to be in the center of attention. He likes power. He's got a big ego and he thinks he can do big things.

But, you see, the self-serving or serving the public in order to feed the ego, either way he likes to be in the center of the action. And either getting attention or exercising power to change the world, whether it's the world of bodybuilding, world of acting or the world of politics, he wants to tackle the biggest problems with the biggest challenges that people can throw at him. And he thinks he can find a solution. I think the biggest influence on him were the parents of his wife Maria Shriver. Eunice Kennedy, who was the sister of JFK, and her husband Sargent Shriver, who was involved with the Kennedy Administration, I think influenced Schwarzenegger when he was a young man. As I said before, he had this philosophy of which was kind of: every man for himself.

I think the Kennedy-Shriver family sort of took him around the world and showed him the way other people lived, and the way many people who are poor and have less going for them lived. They were born into that situation and find it very difficult to escape it without some outside help. I think their influence on him as a person really changed the way he viewed the world and society. I don't think any of the other Kennedys had a huge effect on him. Bobby Kennedy Jr., who is Robert F. Kennedy's son, is a very strong environmental activist. And at the time, Schwarzenegger was starting to explore formal omissions on environmental issues. I think Robert Kennedy Jr. did have some influence on him. Also, Ted Kennedy was more of a friendly rival. Ted Kennedy is a Democrat, but I think Schwarzenegger respectively rejected much of what Ted Kennedy had to say, even though they had a very friendly relationship on a personal level.

In 1999, when asked about whether he would run for public office, Arnold said he had contemplated many times. He said that the possibility was there because he had a feeling inside about it. He felt there were a lot of people standing still not doing enough, and that there was a vacuum. Reflecting on his move into politics, he said in the beginning he was selfish. It was all about: how do I build Arnold? How can I win the most Mr. Universe and Mr. Olympia contests? How can I get into the movies and get into business? "I was thinking about myself," Arnold admits. "As I grew up, got older, maybe wiser, I think your life is judged not by how much you have taken, but by how much you give back."

Before he stood for the race, what links did Arnold have to politicians? Obviously, he was a friend of the first President Bush and also admired Ronald Reagan. Can you elaborate on his links to politicians in the 1980s and 1990s?

Daniel Weintraub: He was definitely considered a much more conservative back in those days. He was almost a libertarian, an anti-government advocate. He was a friend of the first President Bush and admired Reagan. He was a big fan of the American economist Milton Friedman, who was also an advocate of a limited government and individual rights and responsibility. Arnold was a big supporter of a measure in California that changed the state's Constitution to limit the property taxes, which is always a controversial issue here. He was on the side of keeping that in place and keeping taxes low.

So he contributed a small amount of money to some politicians. But his role was more behind the scenes, and appearing occasionally at political fundraisers. He wasn't very much involved in state politics; he was more interested in national affairs and economic issues. His first real high-profile connection to state politics was in 2002, just before the recall election, when he advocated a measure that went on the ballet of California. We had direct democracy where the voters get to have the say in setting state policy by voting on measures of the ballot, and Schwarzenegger proposed and supported the measures to get more funding to after-school programs, which was one of the issues he had developed on his own with his own private foundation. So, he brought that to state political scene and successfully passed the measure to set some money on the side each year to expand after-school programs for the kids.

No one modeled their political career more on Ronald Reagan than Arnold Schwarzenegger. Arnold and Reagan both ventured into Hollywood before making that transition of pursuing politics. Both men possessed the qualities of charm and ebullience. Arnold expressed, "Reagan was a hero to me. I became a citizen of the United States when he was president, and he is the first president I voted for as an American citizen. He inspired me and made me even prouder to be a new American." Arnold developed a penchant for delivering one-liners with panache, just as his political hero had done in his prime. Reagan had a pragmatic streak that defies his acolytes among the current crop of Republicans.

Arnold remembers how Reagan used to talk about the letter he received from a man who said, "You can go and live in Turkey, but you can't become Turkish. You can go and live in Japan, but you can't become Japanese. You can go to live in Germany or France, but you can't become German or French." But the man said that anyone from any corner of the world could come to America and become an American. Arnold continues, "When I heard President Reagan tell that story, I said to myself, 'Arnold, you Austrian immigrant, he is talking to you. He is saying that you will fit in here. You will be a real American, able to follow your dreams.'" Another trait which Arnold seemingly "inherited" from his hero was, whenever Reagan didn't want to answer a question, he'd pretend he couldn't hear the question. It became apparent to observers the same strategy being implemented by Arnold, as he endeavored to delve into the political game.

As a political journalist, can you tell me what were some of the obstacles he had to overcome when he ran for the governor for the first time?
Daniel Weintraub: I think the biggest obstacle was just to being taken seriously. I don't think people at first believed that an action movie star and former bodybuilder could run a state government as large as California, or that he really knew anything about state politics or government. So, at first he had a lot of support just from movie fans and

bodybuilding fans who had heard of him. He was certainly one of the best-known people on the planet. So he had a significant base of support, but he really was not an immediate favorite to win the job. But he stayed in there and his people managed the campaign really well, because they sort of kept him under wraps and kept the expectations low. There was one debate among all the candidates in which he participated in, and he came into that well-prepared. He was able to do a good enough job that people who watched the debate and the journalists who watched commented that he seemed to have a grasp of the issues. Then when he was talking and once that debate happened, it really changed the tied of the campaign and people started taking him more seriously and saying that maybe he could do this job. From that point on, he went on to win the race.

For his first press conference as a politician, which took place outside the Burbank Studios of the Jay Leno Show, the world press was present. Was there anything significant in his speech which had substance which would resonate with the political journalists who were present?
Daniel Weintraub: Well, there was a point at the press conference when most of press reporters had moved on, because they were interested in the celebrity politics and the Hollywood connection. He started to talk about how he sort of had this middle ground economic philosophy, where he wanted to bolster the state's economy to create more jobs. Which would create more revenue for the state's government, which he then wanted to use to expand programs for people who needed them. So, he was espousing this sort of fusion, political message that started with a Republican idea, or a Conservative idea, of expanding the economy and creating jobs. And it ended with a liberal idea. In American politics we call it "liberal", but expanding government with more revenue. He really combined those two things into a single philosophy, which made him unique in Californian politics.

He made improving vocational education a big priority, can you elucidate on this and just how imperative was this issue for Arnold to address?
Daniel Weintraub: Yeah. He came from Europe, where vocational education is much more popular and sort of regimented and organized than it is in the United States where kids are pretty much on their own to do that sort of thing. I think he came into it with a respect and admiration for parts of that European system. He doesn't like the part of the European system as a German and Austrian system; his was sort of overly controlling of what individuals could do. But he did like the way they teach kids and young adults. So he committed to expanding that in California and did several initiatives to expand the state's offering of job

training and skill training, as appose to just try to teach every kid the academics they would need to go on to university. He knew from his own experience that many kids will either not go on to university, or if they do they'll eventually drop out. So he wanted to give more kids a chance and economic ability, by giving them a skill or trade that they could use if they didn't go on to college.

Can you highlight the issues on how he pursued healthcare?
Daniel Weintraub: Sure. Well, he didn't do much on healthcare in his first term. But in his second term in 2007, he proposed a comprehensive expansion and reordering of the healthcare system in California, which eventually more or less became the model for what President Obama did in 2010. It was a hybrid system of private and public care for people who could not afford private insurance and they were covered, almost all legal residents of California. He was not able to get that through. In part, because not a single member of his own party was supportive, because they didn't like the bigger role for government that he was proposing. Then the Democrats got into it, into party squabbles among the Democratic factions legislator and programs they normally would have embraced, and Democrats nationally embraced this year when President Obama was proposing it. The Democrats in California would not give Schwarzenegger the votes he needed to pass that in 2007. But he definitely helped blaze the trail for what came later on a national level.

Can you shed light on Arnold's take on environmental protection, which became epochal in his political career?
Daniel Weintraub: I mean, with the environment issue Schwarzenegger tried to find middle ground, although on the biggest issues he tended to actually lean with the opposing party - the Democrats. His most famous action was in supporting and signing legislation that put California in the lead in limiting greenhouse gases to fight global warming. That law is about to take full effect. It will require the state to limit the emission of greenhouse gases to the levels they were in 1990 by 2020.

So by the year 2020, California law will be omitting about 30 percent less greenhouse gases that otherwise would have been if things had been allowed to take their course. That's going to result in very stringent regulations of many different industries, the oil refineries, the power utilities, cement factories, standing out into the automobile manufacture even though California cannot directly regulate what automobile companies do across the country. California is such a big marker that regulations put in place eventually affect cars all across the country. So, that was a very controversial law. Because global warming by definition is a worldwide phenomenon. And I think what any single state can do is going to effect that very much. But California adapted what Schwarzenegger supported it as a way to lead the discussion and set an example that they hope eventually the world would follow, even if there was no direct environmental benefits to California. That probably is his most noteworthy environmental accomplishment. He also had been a big advocate of defending the oceans. His policy to control and regulate activity along the coast in order to preserve marine life. Those are probably two of his biggest environmental issues.

Arnold's stance on environmental issues was strong. He stated, "Global warming is one of those things, not like an earthquake where there's a big bang and you say, 'Oh, my God, this has really hit us.' It creeps up on you. Half a degree temperature difference from one year to the next, a little bit of rise of the ocean, a little bit of melting of the glaciers, and then all of a sudden it is too late to do something about it." He said we'd seen the photographs of the glaciers melting and the water rising, and that we are aware of the fact that we are polluting the world. All of this is a reality, he stated. "I'm an optimist. I don't look at this as if the world is coming to an end," the governor once declared. "I see it as a great opportunity to clean up our mess. We're grownups, we aren't children. And we can do it. That's why we like to be out front in California. That's power."

In June 2007, the governor visited Downing Street to meet Tony Blair, the British prime minister. The year before, both politicians had agreed a deal which stipulated commitment from California and the United Kingdom to cultivating low-carbon economies. Mr. Blair broached at a joint press conference, "There was no way this thing is going to work unless there is a deal with not just America and the developed world in it, but with China and India too." The governor applauded Mr. Blair for his policies reflecting an attempt to tackle global warming. He also admonished that it would cost hundreds of billions of dollars because of inaction. "So it is better to create the action, and Mr. Blair is the action hero," exclaimed the governor. The governor thanked the prime minister for his great friendship and leadership.

The media, gathered at Downing Street, asked the governor what job he would like to see Mr. Blair in after his exit from Downing Street. The governor said he would "feel good" if Mr. Blair did become the Mid-East envoy. Arnold was the prime minister's last official guest at 10 Downing Street as Mr. Blair headed for a lucrative new job pertaining to the Middle East. In 2011, in Redondo Beach, California, Arnold met up with the former prime minister to discuss and seek advice for his new role on the world stage after he exited the governor's office.

Arnold's visit to London in early 2011 included teaming up with Boris Johnson, the mayor of London, to discuss environmental issues. This included the Barclays Cycle Hire scheme, which allows cyclists to hire a bike for a fee at docking stations to get around the city. In 2007, Arnold had made a remark about the then Tory mayoral candidate, he was heard saying to aides, "This guy's fumbling all over the place," as he listened to his speech via video link. Johnson later responded by dismissing the governor as a "monosyllabic Austrian cyborg". Nonetheless, both men buried the hatchet as they discussed environmental issues. The mayor joined Arnold as he spoke to the press, "I made it clear to the mayor that we are very much aware in California for all the great work that has been going on in England, and in London specifically. If it has to do with the six thousand bicycles that are being made available to the public to ride around, which makes everyone get fit, and also it cuts down on greenhouse gases and pollution, the great work the mayor is doing here.... Also, making the buildings more energy efficient.... There's great work that's going on. This is, again, a point it has proven there's some national governments who are very important in the world when it comes to world environment."

The former governor said the scheme was a brilliant concept and it showed great leadership from the mayor. Furthermore, adding these were great ideas for the whole world, not just California. Arnold was invited to Mikhail Gorbachev's birthday celebrations at the Royal Albert Hall. Before the bash, he had met with Prime Minister David Cameron at the House of Commons to endorse the prime minister's leadership pertaining to the Libya situation.

What was he going to do to tackle the immigration issue, which is a sensitive issue, and what exactly did he pursue and accomplish? Furthermore, did this mollify the immigrants or have the opposite effect on them?

Daniel Weintraub: There's not a whole lot a state governor can do on immigration issues, because it's a national and federal matter. But Schwarzenegger talked about it. He also sent his National Guard, which is a state controlled reserve unit that's part of the US Army. But when they're on reserve duty, they're controlled by the governor of the state. He sent his National Guard reserves to the border to bolster patrols there. But mostly he talked about the issue and not always in the most effective terms. He had a kind of an additional view of it, being an immigrant himself and one that really embraced America and American culture that proceeded him.

He has a bias toward believing that immigrants should pretty much fold themselves into the existing American culture. And with our large Latin American population, there are large communities where that hasn't really been happening. They maintain the ways of the old country, and the language is in their own media and food and culture and everything else they do, which has been the pattern of immigration in America for couple of centuries now. The first generation immigrants tend to identify still with their own country, but as they have children, second generation starts to mix into the existing society. But Schwarzenegger spoke out a couple of times about the Latin American population, and his views that they were not moving quickly enough to sort of become Americanized got him into some hot water with Latin American and Mexican American advocates and actors in California.

Do you feel a lot of people were able to resonate with Arnold because of his celebrity status?
Daniel Weintraub: Yeah. I think he didn't have any political career (when he first stood for office). But I think people felt like they knew him, because they had seen him on the movie screen so many times. And he was a pretty visible public figure and, you know, he was on television and at public events a lot. So he really was someone that people felt familiar with and comfortable with, even though he had no record of politics. That definitely gave him a huge boost in office.

You have expressed that Arnold often used contradictory third-way politics, can you tell me exactly what you mean by this? Were there any oblique political maneuvers implemented?
Daniel Weintraub: United States and California, especially where we have a very polarized political system, we have a two-part system. And in that system, there's winners and losers and they tend to gravitate toward the extremes in each party. The Democrats are on the left, the Republicans are on the right, Conservatives and the parties tend to quit... forward for public office, candidates who are either very part of the right or very part of the left; there's just not much room in the middle. Most candidates who are moderate do not get in the office, because of the system we have. Schwarzenegger defied that and stood in the middle, not always, as a compromise between both sides. Sometimes he could be very conservative on some issues, such as economic and business issues. And he could be very liberal on other issues on environment and some social issues. So, at the time he did try to bridge the gap between the two. So he really stood off in our state political system alone, because there were just no other politicians that worked that way; they were either all in the part of the left or part of the right. That's where we got the title of my book Party of One. Officially, he was a Republican,

but he really was acting as an independent and he was out there by himself.

The budget was one of his biggest obstacles when he became the governor. Thus Arnold had been elected to office to resolve the budget crisis and return California's financial insolvency.

Daniel Weintraub: Definitely! It has been from the beginning to the end. As he wrapped up his time in office, there's no difference. Yeah, when he ran for office the state had a huge budget deficit, and he promised to erase it. I think he thought that was going to be a very simple exercise, but he later found out it was going to be a lot more complicated than he knew coming in. He really was never able to get control of it for a few years. In the middle of his term, he came close to balancing the budget as the economy improved and some of the measures he was able to take came into effect. But before he could ever achieve that goal, we had a great financial market catastrophe in 2008. California saw its tax revenue decline, income decline, and the budget deficit completely got out of control again. There's a projection of a twenty-five billion fall shortfall over two years, which is pretty much bad as what he inherited when he first took office.

At the election in 2006 - when he was re-elected - what did Arnold have to do to gain his trust to be voted in and did he exude altruistic qualities?

Daniel Weintraub: Well, it really started the year before, because in 2005 he took full measures to voters in a special election he called. There was no scheduled election that year, but he wanted to go around the legislature and get some things done. So he took full measures to voters, but they were all rejected by almost two-to-one or two-thirds margin. Sixty percent on average voters rejected his proposals. And in late 2005, just a year before he was going for the election, they had given him a huge vote of no confidence and well under the majority of voters said that they thought he deserved another term. So, that was the biggest obstacle. It was just winning back the voters' trust and confidence. He did that by really admitting that he had made a mistake in taking those measures to the voters without trying harder to get them through the legislator, and taking more time to prepare the groundwork for them.

I think he kind of escaped disaster by doing something most political officials almost never do. And that is: admit he was wrong and apologized to the voters for what he had done. Once he did that, he really turned around public opinion. And by the time the election came, he was back in command. He also worked that year with the Democrats on the global warming bill. And with both parties on a huge package of public bond to rebuild and expand the state infrastructure for flood control, education, highways, he built a pretty solid record of accomplishment in that year. So by the time he faced the voters at the end of 2006, they were admiring him again, the economy was booming again and he had a record of accomplishment in office that he could point to. So he easily won the re-election in the year as a Republican in a year that was a real big year for the Democrats. He definitely went against the tide.

Would I be right in saying he became arguably the nation's most successful Republican politician?
Daniel Weintraub: Certainly for a time he was at the height of his career as governor, from 2006 and 2007. At the time, the Democrats were ascending, which eventually lead to the election of President Obama. Schwarzenegger was one of the few Republicans in the country who continued to do well against that Democratic tied. So, yeah, that would be accurate.

There were a lot of controversial stories and headlines, which surfaced when he first pursued his political career which caused Arnold discomfiture. As a political journalist, do you feel some of them were to be dismissed as mere conjecture, and what stories do you feel had a profound impact on the voters if any?
Daniel Weintraub: I guess there were a lot of stories that came out of his career in Hollywood - very sensational. One of them was that his father was a Nazi in Germany, and Schwarzenegger had somehow had said something favorable toward Hitler, or his methods of governing, marshalling public opinion. So that was one issue that was used against him. And another was the more recent case about a story about him with a young woman - and on the movie sets - and that story appeared just days before the election. This could have damaged him pretty significantly, but he was able to successfully turn that into a story about the media being out to get him. So, he very joyfully turned that story around and survived it quite easily.

You interviewed Arnold on several occasions. From a personal perspective, how would you define Arnold?
Daniel Weintraub: He's amazingly well-grounded. I mean, here's a superstar athlete, superstar actor, finally superstar politician expecting to be kind of a prima donna and not in touch with kind of regular people, but he's actually grounded in a way that he has interests outside of politics. Most of the people who are elected the governor of the state of California, who have dedicated their entire lives to the political worlds,

they don't really have very many interests outside that. Schwarzenegger has lead such a varied life. His upbringing, which was in another country, was barely middleclass. It was even a little bit on the poor side. And so he had a lot of experiences that put him in touch with regular people all his life, and that really shows up when you talk to him. He's a good conversationalist. He listens and he doesn't always need to be the center of the conversation. He's himself. He talks. He's curious. He tries to ask questions and listen to what other people have to say. So, on a personal level, I'd say he's very charming.

What's the most intriguing speech or conversation you had with him which you found to be thought-provoking?
Daniel Weintraub: I'm not sure you can pick a single speech he's given that really would rise to that level. Certainly some of the things he said about the environment and trying to use environment protection to actually expand the economy and create jobs. But he's really not known for his speech-making. I guess just combining those two things. I think the most intriguing thing he said was when he was describing his transformation from a person who really believed in individual rights and personal freedom and was against any role for government into the more moderate person he has become. He talked about how he once believed that everybody like him could pull themselves up by their bootstraps. And later, he came to realize that not everyone has boots. So, it was just his way of describing how he modified his own ideology and political views from kind of an "everyman for himself" to the idea "the community did need to step up" and help some people.

You have said, "I have been disappointed often by Schwarzenegger's performance," in your summation of Arnold's political career, do you feel he could have done more in certain areas?
Daniel Weintraub: Yes, definitely. He really wasted the first couple of years he was in office. He came in with that celebrity power, and being elected in such an unusual election when the sitting governor was thrown out in the middle of his term. He really had a mandate to fundamentally change the state government structure and the way it worked and the political system. Instead he tried to master the existing system, rather than changing it, rather than overturning it. It was really what his mandate was. He just tried to become better at it than the people who had proceeded him. But as he later found out, it kind of was bigger than he was and the system ultimately defeated him, kind of chewed him up and spitted him out. So, it took him a few years to realize that before he could try to move out on his own and take a different

approach. But he never really advocated a fundamental overthrow of the system that he inherited. I think that was his biggest failure.

What legacy has Arnold Schwarzenegger left as far as American politics are concerned?
Daniel Weintraub: I think in the short term, people are going to remember him as pretty much a failure, because he was not able to fix the broken budget system and turn the state's economy around. But I think in the long term, he has undertaken several reforms that will change politics and government in California for many years now. A couple of them involved the way we elect our political leaders. He was able to change the way the political districts are drawn, taking that job away from the politicians and giving it to an independent commission. Most people believe that's going to lead to the election as more moderate legislators, because the old system was gained by the politicians who favor, again, the most extreme members of each party. The new system will avoid that.

Also, change the way your political primaries work. In California and the United States, historically each party choose its nominees and those nominees fight it out in the second round of the elections. And under the new system that Schwarzenegger supported, everyone who wants to run for office will be on the ballot together, and the top two finishers will move to the second round regardless of their party. That kind of allows members of other party to vote at any point in the process for the opposing party if they prefer that candidate, and allow independent voters to choose from either party if they want. Again, the effect of that is going to probably lead to more moderate politicians being elected. So, in the next five to ten years, you could see California change and more into a system that elects far more people who are like Schwarzenegger. People who have views that cross party lines and are willing to work with the opposing party to get something done. That's probably going to be his biggest legacy.

CARLA MARINUCCI

Award-winning journalist Carla Marinucci is a political reporter for the San Francisco Chronicle, specializing in California State gubernatorial politics and national politics. Marinucci covered Arnold's political career and broke numerous national news stories.

Carla, Arnold's critics argued that he had a historic opportunity to change the nature of California politics, can you shed some light on this, what is your conviction on this?

Carla Marinucci: Yeah. Well, Arnold Schwarzenegger was a politician, like, California and the United States had never seen before. A man who was, of course, the world's number-one action hero, who just a few years before was in movies and killing bad guys with a sword in Conan the Barbarian. Then when he ran for office, it was a shock and a surprise for everybody. In the face of ninety days, he went from an action hero to being the head of the world's eighth largest economy. And the recall campaign, which I covered from the beginning to the end, really showed how he had an enormous goodwill. He had the hopes of a lot of people and voters in California, they really believed that, you know, just like Conan could perform amazing feats, that Schwarzenegger could lift California out of an economic decline and a political decline.

Arnold had a tremendous charisma, and still does. He had the outsider's resume. Someone said he could clean up Sacramento, sweep it clean from special interests and bring a business outlook to California, which is the nation's most populous state. He charged into the governor's office and did things that we'd never seen before. He put up a smoking tent, he gave up the salary, he did things that no other politician had done in California. And a lot of people felt that he had the opportunity, because of that goodwill, because of the unusual nature of the recall in which he was elected, to use political capital and to get things done, to knock it together, as he did with Conan and The Terminator. But the Terminator wasn't able to terminate a political culture in Sacramento that is just extremely difficult to crack. And a lot of people thought, as an actor and entertainer you have to be liked, and Arnold wanted to be liked. In politics sometimes you have to do things that are very difficult and very unlikeable.

Many people thought that was his ultimate weakness, he didn't use the political capital that he had. It was enormous when he first came to office to do the tough things, to knock the heads together and let the opportunities go by which were really lost forever in terms of trying to turn around California's political culture. But that said, he did accomplish some things as well. Part of the issue was that the many promises he made coming into the office, he promised to blow up the boxes of state government, cutup the credit card, bring California to sanity. But the time he left office, California had $25 billion in deficit. He wasn't able to deliver on those huge promises. And the promises, it turned out, were even too huge for an action hero of his stature.

He broached he was going to be different to all the other politicians and was going to fix the mess in California. In what way did he endeavor to do things differently?

Carla Marinucci: You know, on style nobody could compete with Arnold Schwarzenegger. And they often had to say in terms of his sunny nepotism, the leadership, he still has a charisma I think that we haven't even seen in California governors. I mean, he was somebody who could attract huge crowds. I mean, as I said, he put up a smoking tent. He had his name in gold in the hallways. He rode his own Gulfstream jet to events. He set up his residence in a hotel penthouse across the street from the Capitol, you know. He was a governor who made headlines once by saving somebody's life who was drowning on a beach in Hawaii when on vacation. That doesn't often happen. I went with him on several occasions to the annual Arnold Classic in Columbus, which is a huge bodybuilding event you probably know about where you have a hundred thousand people who just worship him. And to walk through that event as the governor of California, to walk through that event with him it was kind of like being with The Beatles at the height of their fame. You just don't see that kind of turnout or adulation of any political figure anywhere. So, in that respect Arnold Schwarzenegger brought attention to the office of California, because of that he was able to get attention to some important issues such as trade and import.

I went with him to China and Mexico on trade missions, and there's no question that when Arnold Schwarzenegger was doing an event in China, talking about California products and how Chinese should buy more California strawberries, he would get dozens and dozens of TV cameras and herds and herds of autograph seekers and people who would turnout. This was the kind of turnout no governor could get. It's something only a head of state could get, that kind of attention in a foreign country. So, he got attention for California issues in Mexico, China and everywhere he traveled. He traveled around the world. Only a movie action hero could do that. So, in that respect Schwarzenegger was able to get attention for California issues on a world stage and get the kind of attention only a world leader could get.

He was very instrumental in passing climate change legislation here. The bill was called AB30. A landmark bill that to this day is considered sort of at the forefront climate change legislation around the world. That sort of will be his legacy, when it comes to his long-term accomplishments I think. On the other hand, he had some very big setbacks. He took issues before the voters, because he really believed he could sell anything to the California public. He was a great salesman coming into office, but he found himself really bruised and defeated some expensive campaigns and expensive unions came up against him. And he wasn't able to beat them. But in the big issue, I mean, some people say that the climate change regulations and issues like trade and imports in Southern California from abroad is what Schwarzenegger will be remembered for.

Because he did a lot of things for the infrastructure of the state. He put money into growth and in infrastructure issues, he got money passed for prison upgrading. He did a lot of projects when it came to growth and looking to the future of California. He worked with Mayor Bloomberg in New York on that. Infrastructure was a very big deal for him, as was the environment, and he supported the environment. So there are positive things that Schwarzenegger will be remembered for. And, of course, his wife Maria Shriver did huge work on women's issues and created an enormous body of work on those issues - the first lady of California. So, between them, Schwarzenegger and his wife went to an awful lot of effort. The California governor's office, that was a lot of muscle. That was only what a bodybuilder could do. He brought a lot of attention to issues like no sort of regular governor could've got. So there are some positives, absolutely.

Arnold broached, "We build more prisons or we release prisoners," because local jails and state prisons were overcrowded and criminals were being released early. What steps did Arnold take pertaining to crime prevention and the state's sprawling prison system?
Carla Marinucci: Well, this is a huge issue and an ongoing issue in California. The prison system is enormous. California Prison Guards is a powerful union. The cost of crime prevention is huge in California. California has the largest cost of any state in the nation when it comes to housing undocumented immigrants. Prison has always been an issue, and Schwarzenegger always tried to argue that California was not getting the fair share of money from the federal government for doing that for housing undocumented immigrants. He promised to be the collector and went back to Washington to get some of that money back.

He wasn't able to do that.

But the bottom line is: the prison population is growing here in part because of the three strikes law. That says that to increase the number of inmates, the number of prisons need to be built. It's a costly issue in California. Prisons are very overcrowded, the courts have stepped in and have said California must do something on that. But the state's in a huge financial crunch, and to this day Schwarzenegger was never able to solve. At some point, he said - and other legislators have said - we're going to have to let out the lower priority prisoners, some of those who have, for instance, have non-violent crimes that they're taking up space that California just does not have. So, California is the most populous state and it has the biggest problem on this. This is a problem that Schwarzenegger had and now the current government is wrestling with, and he was just not able to solve it.

In 2005, a federal judge in San Francisco took over the prison healthcare, declaring that the medical healthcare the state was providing did not meet the minimum standard required by the Constitution. How big of an issue was this?

Carla Marinucci: Well, yeah, the entire prison system in California and all the issues surrounding the healthcare have been massive. I mean, the federal judge basically said that Schwarzenegger was just moving too slow on giving prisoners adequate healthcare. The prison healthcare is enormously expensive, it's something that, as I said, California still struggles with today. Some critics have called it a "gold-plated healthcare system" - which means that the prisoners have been getting better healthcare than many average Californians. On the other hand, the federal judge, federal appeal court, said this system must be improved. There is a multibillion-dollar plan to rebuild the state prison healthcare system. But back then in 2005, US district judge rejected the state's attempt to regain control of the healthcare system. It's continual and an on-going issue. Schwarzenegger continued to wrestle with the prison system, its cost, its union and the high end of pay that they get, many different aspects of the prison system; they continued to be a huge problem and challenge in California government. He just was not able to get a handle on it.

In 2010, the family of Luis Santos filed a lawsuit. Arnold had the right to commute prison sentence of a political friend's son, but violated victim rights guaranteed under a water-approval measure. Can you elucidate on this, please?

Carla Marinucci: This was a controversy that became in the very last day, I believe, of his term in office. Schwarzenegger really kicked off a huge controversy, it was his final night before he left office. He commuted the prison sentence of the son of a very powerful former speaker of Assembly - Fabian Nunez. The young man had been sentenced to sixteen years in prison for a death stabbing; he didn't actually kill the victim, but he had a role in it. Schwarzenegger commuted the boy's sentence and reduced his sentence dramatically. The boy's father was a very powerful Democrat who was close to the governor. Fred Santos, who was the father of Luis Santos, was completely outraged. He's the victim of the man who was murdered. He was totally outraged.

He (Fabian Nunez) said to the governor to wait until the end of the last day to commute this - to do it undercover on the night. This was unjust and the family wasn't warned about it. The governor didn't have the courtesy to notify them. I believe he said by law the victim's family have to be notified, and they have challenged that in court. This is sort of a mark on Schwarzenegger. He waited till the last night when he would be leaving office to do that. He knew he was going to get a lot of political heat for it. And many people thought if he truly believed that this young man's sentence was fair and justice commuted, then he just should've done it and stood up and taken the heat for it and explained it to the people, instead he went in on the last minute. It is a mark I think on him and his final hours in office.

Hollywood actor Alec Baldwin expressed, I quote, "I am certainly not a supporter of Arnold Schwarzenegger. I think he was unqualified for his current job when he ran in the bogus recall election." Did Arnold have any particular supporters in the Hollywood community and what are your sentiments on this?

Carla Marinucci: He certainly got a lot of support from Hollywood while he was governor, because he supported Hollywood himself. He pushed for California to be...to make it easier for filmmakers to make films in California. He was a big supporter of the Hollywood community, and he often appeared at the major awards events - Academy Awards and the Golden Globe Awards. So he's remained close to the movie community throughout. But he was a Republican and the recall was.... Many of the Hollywood big stars are Democrats, or more liberal in their politics, and many of them did not support the recall election. The Democrat Gray Davis had the support, even for the fundraising section, from a lot of folks from Hollywood.

So the actual recall election was not very popular with the Hollywood community, the liberal community and the Democratic community, and is very liberal. I think many people in Hollywood probably did not like Schwarzenegger's politics, particularly his more conservative Republican politics. Although a lot of Republicans were angry at him for being too liberal. So, he was a moderate Republican moderating on social issues than more conservative on physical issues. So, when it came to the Hollywood community, they liked Arnold for what he did for movies and for Hollywood, for moviemaking in California, for supporting acting and the filmmaking industry. But many of them did not particularly like his politics.

Arnold felt film tax incentives were just one example of how to stimulate the economy. California was losing billions of dollars in revenues, he said. He exclaimed they should be filming six hundred and not two hundred films which were being churned out annually in Hollywood. After his meeting with the Democrat governor of New Mexico - Bill Richardson - Arnold later pronounced, "He was laughing at me, and he said, 'I know you guys are struggling in California, but just so you know, we in New Mexico, our economy is booming.'" Arnold continued, "What he was saying, really, is you guys are stupid. You guys are stupid for letting all of those Hollywood productions - Hollywood is known worldwide as the movie town and you're letting all this slip out to New Mexico and to Louisiana and to New York and to Vancouver and to all those other places, because you can't get your act together and offer a stimulus package to keep the productions there in Hollywood." Arnold persuaded the California Legislature to grant tax breaks to film and TV companies to lure productions into Hollywood. Most states were offering some kind of tax credit programs to attract productions. Los Angeles has seen a slew of films decamp to other states.

In 2004, a judge ruled Arnold had violated campaign laws and would have to pay $4.5 million from his own pockets. Can you elucidate on this, please?
Carla Marinucci: Schwarzenegger, his problem was when he came into power, he was saying he was going to sweep Sacramento clean, and the special interest in political gamesmanship. And he always said that he had enough money and that he would be owned by no special interest. But he did create sort of a special campaign organization. In this case the judge ruled that he violated campaign plans with a loan of $4.5 million. Schwarzenegger basically had, even though he said he was untouched by special interests, Schwarzenegger was a very, very good fundraiser as a governor. He raised millions of dollars from cooperative interest. In this case the judge said the governor violated campaign laws. The law that required disclosure to voters of all contributions in the excess of $100. There's no question, as much as he said he was completely apart from

special interests, it was clear he was raising money for both the ballot measures and his travel abroad and other things. So he did get a lot of backing from the cooperative interests in California. He wasn't as removed from that as he promised that he would be.

Arnold Schwarzenegger is a supporter of the Simon Wiesenthal Center, and has been for many years.

Carla Marinucci: Simon Wiesenthal Center is a renowned center that investigates Nazi activity, and Simon Wiesenthal is a renowned Nazi hunter. His center looks into similar issues, it funds the very famous Museum of Tolerance in Los Angeles. It's an extremely respected center that talks about educating people about the history of the Holocaust and the history of Nazi Germany. It's a hugely respected group, and Schwarzenegger had a great relationship with this group. He often visited them at the Museum of Tolerance. He appeared often with Rabbi Marvin Hier of the center. And that's also part of his support for the Holocaust education. He said he came from Austria where, obviously, the history of Holocaust is quite relevant.

When the Simon Wiesenthal Center further researched into Arnold's father's past, Rabbi Marvin Hier said whatever they find they will give it to Arnold, then to the public. "Whatever the record shows, so may it show. Should that record have any bearing on Arnold Schwarzenegger himself? In my opinion, absolutely not," exclaimed Hier.

Arnold had been unfamiliar with his father's Nazi membership until when he first started to become prominent in Hollywood. He had contacted Simon Wiesenthal Center around 1984 in pursuit of finding answers to questions pertaining to his father's Nazi connections, which he claimed he was unaware of. Whether he did this to pre-empt sensationalist media's curiosity or not, and the impact it would have on his career, it's debatable. However, I believe even if his father was found guilty to have taken part in any atrocities, it should in no way reflect on Arnold's character. Schwarzenegger campaign spokesman believed the actions of Arnold's father would not influence the voters in the election, he said, "We know what the SA and the Nazi Party stood for; Arnold knows this. And he's not proud of the fact that his father was a member of the Nazi Party and that his father was a member of the SA. This is a matter of deep embarrassment, but Arnold cannot be judged by his father."

It's no secret that when he was running for office, the media linked him to Nazi connections and pursued to probe into his past. Do you think there was an element of spuriousness that was blown out of proportion when it was claimed Arnold was an admirer of Hitler? As I understand, Arnold had a penchant for great leaders, but he did not admire what Hitler did.

Carla Marinucci: The whole issue of Schwarzenegger.... I mean, I don't know about it being blown out of proportion. Schwarzenegger sometimes made comments. It's from some outtake from Pumping Iron. Let me say it this way: when it comes to Pumping Iron and how that sort of related to his political career, Schwarzenegger, by the way, denied many times that he admired Hitler. But Pumping Iron had a lot of scenes in it that really sort of dramatized Arnold Schwarzenegger's crazy wild past. I mean, whether it's a scene of him taking marijuana, there's all kinds of statements he's making about women. It's the kind of activities which are not the norm for most politicians in political office. It really kind of shows how he cut a lot of flak by the public. They personally liked him and he was able to say that he was a changed man. But that didn't stop newspapers from looking into his past.

One of his biggest controversies was the groping incidents, and whether he was inappropriate with women as a bodybuilder and a movie star. But basically he did make many of the controversial comments, and many of his most controversial activities. He apologized publicly for many of those. He said that he never admired Hitler. And he denied that he ever admired Hitler. But just to recap, Pumping Iron contained many scenes and incidents that showed the wilder days of Schwarzenegger, and that was just one example of how he really was able to overcome a path that most politicians could not have overcome. Because many people thought of him as such a likeable character.

Arnold vehemently denied allegations such as his admiration for Hitler. He stated, "I have despised anything and everything that Hitler stands for. I have been from the time that I was a young kid fought against anyone that has protested for Nazis, or had any kind of Nazi sympathizing, or anything like this. And I campaigned against that. When I came over here I did the same thing. I always was against anything and despised anything that Hitler stood for and what the Nazis stood for. And I'm very sensitive about it, because I come from a country where we have a history of that. You know, people came up to me many times when I came over here with the hiel Hitler signs, and then say the boys from Brazil are coming and all those kind of derogatory, which I understood. But, I'm sensitive about that. So I've sued the tabloids when they've said anything about me being a Nazi, and I've won the lawsuits." When Arnold was growing up the family never brought up the subject of his father's past. So he didn't have any knowledge of his father's Nazi membership.

Jorg Haider, whose notoriety far exceeded his influence on national events, was an Austrian right-wing politician who made the headlines for the wrong reasons. His parents were active Nazis in the Second World War. In 2000, Arnold expressed his deep anger at his anti-immigration policies.

In a statement released by Arnold, he said, "As an immigrant myself, I am offended by anyone who makes anti-immigrant statements. And it is my opinion that someone who makes statements like Haider's has no place in government. I have never supported him in the past and do not now. I am hopeful that Austria will find a way through this. As an Austrian-born, I am so saddened that with all the progress we have made working for an open and tolerant society, one man's statements can taint world opinion of an entire country. I know that there are many tolerant people in Austria. It is my hope that their voices can and will be heard."

Haider praised the policies of Nazi Germany and the SS, which prompted widespread international concern. The far-right leader was killed in a car accident in 2008.

The year Arnold and Maria got married, Kurt Waldheim, the erudite diplomat, was running for president in Austria. Waldheim was a close friend of the Schwarzeneggers, who invited him to their wedding. It came to light this widely esteemed former secretary general of the United Nations had participated in Nazi atrocities in the Second World War. Waldheim was wanted for war crimes after the war. He had risen to the pinnacle of international diplomacy, but his Nazi past caught up with him when he was running for president. The US Justice Department put him on its watch list when Waldheim became the president. This may have left Arnold in a quandary. "My friends don't want me to mention Kurt's name, because of all the recent Nazi stuff and the U.N. controversy," Arnold made a statement at his wedding. "But I love him and Maria does too, and so thank you, Kurt." Waldheim did not make it to the wedding.

European historian Martin Lee told Amy Goodman in 2003, "For Schwarzenegger to have made (the wedding toast to Kurt Waldheim) at that time after these revelations surfaced is really quite shocking. It shows, at the very least, insensitivity to the victims of Nazism and anti-Semitism…One way or another the point is not that Schwarzenegger is a Nazi, the point is that it raises character issues that he's not qualified to be in public office."

Other than economic reform, no issue is more important to the future of California than a public education system. Can you elucidate on the path

Arnold pursued as far as teachers and education? He wanted merit pay for teachers.

Carla Marinucci: Yes, he did. He tried to push merit pay. He tried to push reforms on ten year. He tried to push sweeping education reforms to shape the school system. But he also got a lot of pushbacks from teachers union who said that he was unfairly putting in particularly inner-city schools at a huge disadvantage. He got a lot of praise, Arne Duncan, the US education secretary, praised him as being courageous and saying that some of his reforms could be national reforms.

He wanted things like some school districts to shut down, the lowest performing schools. He wanted to abolish the cap on charter schools. Some of these reforms have been fought and continue to be fought by the California Teachers Union - a very powerful and very large union. So, I think he gets credit for education, which was a very big issue for Schwarzenegger. But the funding for education was also a huge problem, where the tuitions for the University of California and the community colleges were not funded because of the deficit. At the same time, he did put out some ideas and proposal that are continuing to resonate today. He had very big ambitions for California education system and always put it on top of his agenda. But once again, he fell short of accomplishing them because of the political and financial realities of California.

Carla, regarding the immigration issue involving giving driving licenses to illegal immigrants, can you shed some light on this issue which happen to also make the headlines?

Carla Marinucci: The driver licenses for undocumented immigrants is a huge issue to the Latino community in California. Latinos are the fasting growing voting community in California. They're 50 percent of the voters here. Many of them support the idea of giving drivers licenses to undocumented individuals. Because they say it's just safer that people who have to pass a test and have an actual identification document are more likely to report crimes and are more likely to not be unafraid of coming forward as a witness to a crime, as well as public safety. The immigration issue is another big issue which Schwarzenegger had wrestled with, and on this one he did not have the support of the Latino community, because they were opposed to driver license for undocumented people. It's another issue which remains today in California.

When Arnold left the governor's office, he said he had a loss of earnings of $200 million. In other words, he could've made $200 million in the span of eight years making movies. What's your opinion, do you feel it was worth it for him to pursue a political career and become the governor?

Carla Marinucci: It's a question of whether he could've continued to earn $20 million a film after Terminator 3. But that said, there's no question that he took a financial hit, whether it was $200 million, it's debatable. But he did not take a salary; he did at his own expense travel up and down California and around the States and the world on his own Gulfstream jet. He did take a hit. But was it worth it for him? I think time will tell. I mean, being the head of the world's eighth largest economy is a position that no question is going to shape his future, and it has given him access to world leaders, the world's greatest innovators, the world's greatest capitalists, the kind of people that any savvy businessman could parlay into great earnings in the future. And if we know one thing about Arnold Schwarzenegger, it's that he's a very savvy business guy. He said he gave up $200 million, but he also had an opportunity and time and direct connection with people, and that's certainly going to help him also. I'm not sure how to calculate the cost. I don't think it's a losing position for him in the final, because Arnold Schwarzenegger's always been able to turn straw into gold in his life. I'm sure he's going to continue to do that.

When Arnold's time in office was terminated, he professed, "I have made it very clear with the Obama Administration in any way they need my help, if it's in environmental things or with other issues, and they feel I can utilize or they can utilize my talent, my personality, my star power and all of those things, I'm more than happy to help in any way possible. I don't have to be in the administration to do that. Remember my mother-in-law, who started Special Olympics, was never in any administration and she created Special Olympics in one hundred and one different countries, where they have now equality for people with mental disabilities or intellectually challenge people and so and so."

Arnold stated that he could help the Obama Administration in numerous ways without having to go to Washington and sitting there and being in charge of some kind of a department. "I still have the same interest in show business and movies, if it is as a producer, director or actor. As I have always said, I'm not going to go and look for my next job while I sit here...." Arnold also made it clear that he didn't have to worry about money. Money, it seems, was no longer necessarily the key motivation. "I've made enough money for the rest of my life," he claimed. "I never have to go out and look for a job or look for something. I only like to stay busy with the things that I love to do. I will be busy till the day I die."

EPILOG

Hollywood superstar Arnold Schwarzenegger has lived a rich and colorful life, reaching heights many can only dream of. Personally, the veneration I have for Arnold's drive is profound. I have long held the believe that if one is passionate enough, ambitious, cultivates a strong desire in whatever one pursues in life and pursues a dream, then the chances of prevailing are high. Most people relegate themselves to being mundane and languish in their progress, because they lack that drive which is all too important. I can resonate with Arnold's zeal and adamant philosophy which reflects the need to create a strong desire within.

Moreover, Arnold once said, "Most people are too close to what they're doing that they can't see themselves anymore. But I always step back and laugh at myself, because you can't take it seriously, the whole thing, you know, you can't. It's something I believe we have to do, certain things, in order to keep us going and motivated. And pick little goals and go after them and stuff like that." This is something which I have now been able to resonate with after having fallen in the trap of taking things too seriously sometimes.

As much as he cultivated an almost obsession-like aura, Arnold was cognizant that it was possible to get trapped into what you're doing that it would become a total obsession, which consequently can have adverse effects on you. Often, we tend to be critical of ourselves and take things too seriously. An artist, actor, writer or a musician who may at some point of his career produce a tenuous piece of work, which may cause him to be self-critical.

Indubitably the biggest star to ever come out from Hollywood, Arnold conveyed an image of invincibility. Since Arnold's departure from the Hollywood scene, the new breed of action man was perhaps typified by actors such as Matt Damon and Nicolas Cage. After a long hiatus, Arnold planned to return to Tinseltown, which has suffered from a lack of real brawny, laconic action heroes, which would inject a dose of the 1990s nostalgia. Arnold's political career only stoked his box office cred.

I hope the public won't be deterred by the drama amid the revelations which made the headlines after he left the governor's office, which often leads to bifurcation, and perceive him as a dubious character and feel a strong repugnance. This is something which may not be obliterated in some people's minds, but I'm impervious, and I'm sure so are many other people. Some people clearly fail to grasp the relevance such a thing should not have on the credibility of certain public figures. What Arnold did no doubt exacerbated the situation. However, this should have no bearing on his professional life, and even his personal life should be treated as personal.

Arnold became the biggest movie star in Hollywood and achieved global fame. He is a consummate professional. The sport of bodybuilding enjoys a platform on global stage in sports because of Arnold Schwarzenegger. He is likely to be remembered as the greatest the sport produced, if not in physique then in popularity. His ambition to run for president is unlikely to materialize. The credibility of his high-profile political advocacy was in question as the critics and general public's perception changed when his personal life was dragged into the open after he left the governor's office.

Nevertheless, the level of success the former governor achieved is unprecedented and should make him content. But he will always have a goal and abundance of passion to keep climbing the ladder and reaching further heights. The ambitious man once said, "My whole life I wanted to come to America. I came over here with empty pockets but with full of dreams, full of desire. I had this fire in my belly, and I knew that the United States was where I could really succeed. The possibilities here are endless. I wanted to live the American Dream." Arnold Schwarzenegger is the living embodiment of the American Dream, and you need to look no further if you have aspirations to succeed.

APPENDIX I:
BODYBUILDING TITLES

1965, Germany, Junior Mr. Europe

1966, Germany, Best Built Man of Europe

1966, Germany, Mr. Europe

1966, Germany, International Powerlifting Championship

1967, London, England, NABBA Mr. Universe, Amateur

1968, London, England, NABBA Mr. Universe, Professional

1968, Germany, German Powerlifting Championship

1968, Mexico, IFBB Mr. International

1969, New York, IFBB Mr. Universe, Amateur

1969, London, England, NABBA Mr. Universe, Professional

1970, London, England, NABBA Mr. Universe, Professional

1970, Ohio, Mr. World

1970, New York, IFBB Mr. Olympia

1971, Paris, France, IFBB Mr. Olympia

1972, Essen, Germany, IFBB Mr. Olympia

1973, New York, IFBB Mr. Olympia

1974, New York, IFBB Mr. Olympia

1975, Pretoria, South Africa, IFBB Mr. Olympia

1980, Sydney, Australia, IFBB Mr. Olympia

APPENDIX II:
FILMS

1970, Hercules in New York

1973, The Long Goodbye

1976, Stay Hungry

1977, Pumping Iron

1980, The Jayne Mansfield Story

1982, Conan the Barbarian

1984, Conan the Destroyer

1984, The Terminator

1985, Red Sonja

1985, Commando

1986, Raw Deal

1987, Predator

1987, The Running Man

1988, Red Heat

1988, Twins

1990, Total Recall

1990, Kindergarten Cop

1991, Terminator 2: Judgment Day

1993, Last Action Hero

1994, True Lies

1994, Junior

1996, Eraser

1996, Jingle All the Way

1997, Batman and Robin

1999, End of Days

2000, The 6th Day

2002, Collateral Damage

2003, Terminator 3: Rise of the Machines

2004, Around the World in 80 Days

2010, The Expendables

SOURCES

Watch, New York Daily, David Letterman, Making of Total Recall, Time, Entertainment Weekly, Howard Stern Show, Ask Jimmy Carter, Cigar Aficionado, Sister to Sister, Making of Batman and Robin, Marisa Mazzula interview, BBC, Carmen and Sally Cinema, People, New York Times, Paul Fischer, Variety, ET online, Starlog, Making of Terminator, Starburst, Conan, WABC Radio, Premiere, Metro, OUI, FLEX, Daily Telegraph, Making of Pumping Iron, True Myths by Nigel Andrews, The Governator by Ian Halperin, Arnold by Wendy Leigh, Time Out, USA Today, The Huffington Post, Republican Convention in Madison Square Garden in New York, MSNBC's Chris Matthews, ABC Peter Jennings interview, Slate, Talk, Guardian, Chuck Salter interview, Conan the Barbarian Behind the Scenes, Chicago Tribune, Prevue, NBC Chicago, Hello Magazine.

Author interviews with all the interviewed people in this publication, with additional author interviews with prominent political journalists Joe Mathews and Robert Salladay.

ABOUT THE AUTHOR

Fiaz Rafiq is a biographer of two of the most influential icons Bruce Lee and Muhammad Ali, as well as Hollywood superstar and former politician Arnold Schwarzenegger. He's authored the critically acclaimed biographies *Bruce Lee: Conversations*, *Muhammad Ali: Conversations* and *Arnold Schwarzenegger: Conversations*. He is one of only three people in the world to have authored biographies of both Lee and Ali, and the only person in the world to have authored Lee, Ali and Schwarzenegger biographies. He is also the author of *Ultimate Conversations*, which culminates on exclusive interviews with some of the top UFC fighters.

Rafiq is a sports and entertainment journalist and a major columnist for a bestselling combat sports magazine *M.A.I.* and a contributor to *Impact: The Global Action Movie Magazine*. He is also a contributor to *Men's Fitness* and *Muscle & Fitness*, and his work has appeared in numerous magazines in the USA, UK, Australia, France, Germany, Italy and

Dubai. He contributed to *The Sun*'s UFC coverage. He also contributed to *How Bruce Lee Changed the World* documentary film.

Rafiq is the founder and director of HNL Media Group/Publishing, a company dedicated to publishing entertainment and sports-related books for the international markets. He was also one of the co-executive producers of *Sensei*, a film directed by Bruce Lee's goddaughter Diana Lee Inosanto. Rafiq's diverse career has also seen him appear as a background artist in TV and movies. His qualification in Close Protection lead to work in security.

Author in Hollywood on Hollywood Boulevard

Having had a lifelong passion for the martial arts and being profoundly influenced by the late Bruce Lee since the mid-1980s, from 1996 onwards, he pursued his passion by making several trips to Los Angeles, California, to train with three of Bruce Lee's original students - also privately with UFC legend Royce Gracie. Acclaimed author, magazine columnist, journalist and publisher, Rafiq has interviewed a plethora of Hollywood actors, directors and producers, as well as many elite professional boxing champions, IFBB bodybuilding champions, UFC champions and stars and combat sports athletes in the world.

MUHAMMAD ALI
CONVERSATIONS

BRUCE LEE: CONVERSATIONS

BY FIAZ RAFIQ WITH A FOREWORD BY DIANA LEE INOSANTO

BRUCE LEE CONVERSATIONS

"An excellent alternative to the many threadbare Lee biographies available, and a fascinating read..."
- **FHM**

THE LIFE AND LEGACY OF A LEGEND

BY FIAZ RAFIQ

Foreword by Diana Lee Inosanto

EVERY WARRIOR MUST LEARN THE FINAL LESSON...

YOU HAVE A RIGHT TO DEFEND
YOURSELF AGAINST HATRED

THE SENSEI

WITHDRAWN